FIFTY CONTEMPORARY
CH

Fifty Contemporary Choreographe[...]
and work of today's most promine[...]
wide range of dance genres, from ba[...]
is discussed are Matthew Bourne, Wil[...]   [...]wyla Tharp.
The book locates each choreographer[...]   [...]xt of contemporary dance
theatre, and shows its influence upon m[...]   Each entry includes:

- a critical essay
- a short biography
- a list of choreographic works
- a detailed bibliography

An introduction by Deborah Jowitt of *The Village Voice* provides a superb overview of the world of modern dance, making this an invaluable reference source for all students and critics, dancers and general readers.

Martha Bremser is a freelance editor and writer, and edited the much praised *International Dictionary of Ballet* (St James Press, 1993).

Routledge Key Guides

Ancient History: Key Themes and Approaches
Neville Morley

Cinema Studies: The Key Concepts (Second Edition)
Susan Hayward

Eastern Philosophy: Key Readings
Oliver Leaman

Fifty Eastern Thinkers
Diané Collinson, Kathryn Plant and Robert Wilkinson

Fifty Contemporary Choreographers
Edited by Martha Bremser

Fifty Key Contemporary Thinkers
John Lechte

Fifty Key Jewish Thinkers
Dan Cohn-Sherbok

Fifty Key Thinkers on History
Marnie Hughes-Warrington

Fifty Key Thinkers in International Relations
Martin Griffiths

Fifty Major Philosophers
Diané Collinson

Key Concepts in Cultural Theory
Andrew Edgar and Peter Sedgwick

Key Concepts in Eastern Philosophy
Oliver Leaman

Key Concepts in Language and Linguistics
R. L. Trask

Key Concepts in the Philosophy of Education
John Gingell and Christopher Winch

Key Concepts in Popular Music
Roy Shuker

Post-Colonial Studies: The Key Concepts
Bill Ashcroft, Gareth Griffiths and Helen Tiffin

Social and Cultural Anthropology: The Key Concepts
Nigel Rapport and Joanna Overing

FIFTY CONTEMPORARY CHOREOGRAPHERS

Martha Bremser

With an Introduction by
Deborah Jowitt

Routledge
Taylor & Francis Group

LONDON AND NEW YORK

First published 1999 by Routledge
2 Park Square, Milton Park, Abingdon, Oxon, OX14 4RN

Simultaneously published in the USA and Canada
by Routledge
270 Madison Avenue, New York, NY 10016

Reprinted 2000, 2004, 2005

Routledge is an imprint of the Taylor & Francis Group

Typeset in Times by The Florence Group, Stoodleigh, Devon
Printed and bound in Great Britain by Biddles Ltd, King's Lynn, Norfolk

British Library Cataloguing in Publication Data
A catalogue record for this book is available from the British Library

Library of Congress Cataloguing in Publication Data
has been applied for

ISBN 0-415-10363-0 (hbk)
ISBN 0-415-10364-9 (pbk)

CONTENTS

CONTENTS

Contributors

Joan Acocella is the dance critic for *The New Yorker*. She is the author of *Mark Morris* (1993) and she has also edited *André Levinson on Dance: Writings from Paris in the Twenties* (with Lynn Garafola, 1991) and *The Diary of Vaslav Nijinsky* (1999).

Ann Cooper Albright is Associate Professor in the Theater and Dance Program of Oberlin College, Ohio. She has received several Ohio Arts Council awards in dance criticism, and is author of *Choreographing Difference: The Body and Identity in Contemporary Dance* (1997).

Judy Burns is based in New York and has taught at Brooklyn College. She has written for *Dance Research Journal*, *DCA News*, and *Women and Performance* (for which she has also been an editor).

Rachel Chamberlain Duerden is Senior Lecturer in Dance at Manchester Metropolitan University. She has written for several reference works on dance, including *The International Dictionary of Ballet* (1993).

Virginia Christian is a professional editor and freelance writer on dance who has contributed to *International Dictionary of Ballet* (1993) and other works.

Nicole Dekle Collins, based in New York, is a former associate editor of *Dance Magazine*, to which she also contributed many articles. She has also written for *Dance View*, *The Village Voice* and other publications.

Anita Donaldson is Dean of the Elder Conservatorium, School of Performing Arts, at the University of Adelaide, Australia. Her writings on dance include contributions to *Dance Australia* and *Brolga*.

George Dorris is a New York-based writer on dance and musical theatre. He has been co-editor of *Dance Chronicle* since 1977, contributed many 'New York Newsletters' to *Dancing Times* in London, and wrote the book *Paoli Rolli and the Italian Circle in London 1715–1744* (1967).

Sandra Genter is Professor of Dance at Barnard College (Columbia University), New York and also a choreographer. She has contributed articles to *Ballet Review* and *Dance Research Journal*.

Marianne Goldberg is a writer and choreographer based in New York. She has written a number of articles on choreography for *Contact Quarterly*, *Dance Research Journal*, *Dance Theatre Journal*, *The Drama Review*, and notably *Women & Performance*.

Nancy Goldner is a dance writer living in New York. She has been the dance critic for *The Nation*, *The Christian Science Monitor*, and *Dance News*, among other publications. Her books include *Choreography by George Balanchine: A Catalogue of Works* (edited, 1983), *Coppélia: New York City Ballet* (with Lincoln Kirstein, 1974), and *The Stravinsky Festival of the New York City Ballet* (1972).

Malve Gradinger is a dance critic based in Munich. Her many writings have appeared in *Ballett-Info*, *Ballett International*, *Tanz Affiche*, *Tanz International*, *Tanz Aktuell*, and various reference works.

Robert Greskovic is a dance critic and teacher living in New York. He is the author of *Ballet 101* (1998), consulting editor of *The Best Ever Book of Ballet* (1996), and author of the Afterword to *Balanchine Pointework* by Suki Schorer (1995). He also writes about dance for *The Wall Street Journal*.

Dale Harris was, until his death in 1996, a distinguished New York writer on music and dance, and professor of arts and humanities at Sarah Lawrence College, Bronxville, New York, and lastly at Cooper Union in New York City. He was dance critic for *The Wall Street Journal* and a music critic for *The Washington Post*. His other writings include contributions to *Ballet News*, *Ballet Review*, *Dancing Times*, *Opera*, *Opera Canada*, and a number of newspapers.

Joanna Harris is a writer on dance and dance therapy, based in Berkeley, California. Her articles have appeared in *American Journal of Dance Therapy*, and *Dance Research Journal*, and she has compiled several editions of the *Bibliography on Dance Therapy*.

Donald Hutera is a dance critic for London's *Time Out* and *The Times*, as well as a contributor to *Dance Europe*, *Dance Theatre Journal*, *Dance Now*, and various reference works on dance. He is co-author (with Allen Robertson) of *The Dance Handbook* (1988).

Stephanie Jordan is Professor of Dance Studies at Roehampton Institute London. She is author of *Moving Music* (due to be published in 1999) and *Striding Out: Aspects of Contemporary and New Dance in Britain* (1992). She has also written for a number of dance journals.

Deborah Jowitt teaches at New York University, and has been principal dance critic for New York's *Village Voice* since 1967. Her books include *Dance Beat: Selected Views and Reviews 1967–1976* (1977), *The Dance in Mind: Profiles and Reviews 1976–1983* (1985), *Time and the Dancing Image* (1988), and the anthology *Meredith Monk* (1997), which she edited. She has also contributed to a number of newspapers, magazines and journals.

Angela Kane is Principal Lecturer in Dance at Roehampton Institute London, and a freelance dance critic. She has written for *Dance Gazette*, *Dance Research*, *Dancing Times*, *Dance Theatre Journal*, and several reference works and essay collections.

Kathryn Kerby-Fulton is a freelance dance writer, as well as Professor of English at the University of Victoria, British Columbia, where she specializes in early English Literature.

Josephine Leask is a London-based dance critic and lecturer. She has been a regular contributor to *Ballett International* and *Dance Now*, as well as writing for *Dance Theatre Journal*, *Tanz Affiche*, and several newspapers.

Katy Matheson is a freelance dance critic and former Associate Editor of *Dance Magazine*, for which she has written regularly. Other publications include contributions to *Dance Theatre Journal*, articles for several reference books on dance, and a new chapter for the revised edition of Selma Jeanne Cohen's *Dance as a Theatre Art: Source Readings in Dance History from 1581 to the Present* (1992).

Giannandrea Poesio is Senior Lecturer in Dance at Roehampton Institute London and dance critic for the London *Spectator*. He is also a regular writer for *Dancing Times*, and has contributed to *Danza e Danza*, *Chorégraphie*, *Dance Research*, and a number of books, including *Rethinking the Sylph* (edited by Lynn Garafola, 1997).

Jennifer Predock-Linnell teaches in the Dance Program of the University of New Mexico, Albuquerque, and has contributed to the journal *Impulse* and other publications.

Stacey Prickett specializes in dance and cultural studies, and her writings have appeared in *Dance Research*, *Dance Theatre Journal*, *DCA News*, *Studies in Dance History*, and the collection *Dance in the City* (edited by Helen Thomas, 1997). She has lectured in dance at Sonoma State University, and she lives in Oakland, California.

Jane Pritchard is Archivist for the Rambert Dance Company and English National Ballet. She has compiled *Rambert: A Celebration* (1996) and the catalogue *Les Ballets 1933* (1987) for an exhibition of which she was also curator. She has also written for *Dance Chronicle*, *Dance Theatre Journal*, *Dancing Times*, and various reference works.

Lesley-Anne Sayers is a freelance dance critic. She has been a regular writer for *Dance Now* and *Dance Theatre Journal*, and has contributed to several collections and reference works on dance. She lives in Cheltenham, England.

Marcia B. Siegel is a dance critic, historian and teacher. She is author of *The Shapes of Change: Images of American Dance* (1979), *Days on Earth – The Dance of Doris Humphrey* (1987), and many of her reviews and articles have appeared in book form, in *At the Vanishing Point: A Critic Looks at Dance* (1972), *Watching the Dance Go By* (1977), and *The Tail of the Dragon: New Dance 1976–1982* (1991). She is also dance critic for *The Hudson Review* and *The Boston Phoenix*.

Bonnie Sue Stein is Artistic Director of GOH Productions, New York, and a freelance writer on various forms of Asian dance. She has contributed to *Dance Magazine*, *Attitude*, and other publications.

Ann Veronica Turnbull is a freelance dance writer based in Italy. She co-edited the encyclopedia *Danza e balletto* (with Mario Pasi, 1993), and has contributed to *Danza e Danza* and various reference works on dance and theatre.

Sarah Whatley is Head of Performing Arts at Coventry University and a graduate researcher in the Department of Dance, Roehampton Institute London.

EDITOR'S NOTE

This book was commissioned as a contribution to the 'Fifty Contemporary . . .' series intended to provide, in handbook form, introductory guides to fifty practitioners or thinkers in various fields.

In setting out to determine the scope of a book on choreographers, we decided that the notoriously fluid description 'contemporary' would, in this case, mean living choreographers whose work, spanning the decades from the late 1940s to the present, has often exemplified postwar trends in choreography. We therefore did not limit ourselves to a specific definition of the genre known as 'contemporary dance'. As Deborah Jowitt's Introduction suggests, the world of dance nowadays is witness to the blurring of boundaries, as choreographers once considered on the fringe of the dance world now undertake major commissions for established ballet companies, while the traditional balletic concentration on technique and music has increasingly worked its way into the practices of independent choreographers working with their own companies. As Deborah Jowitt summarizes it, 'the "contemporary" scene is as diverse as individual notions of contemporaneity.'

In terms of numbers we have bent the rules slightly, in that one of our fifty entrants is a duo – Eiko and Koma – and another is a collective – Pilobolus. But the choreographers included here are not intended to form a canonical or exclusive group. What we have tried to do in our selection – so far as is possible in a book about people and not dance forms – is to suggest the range (geographical and stylistic) of dance phenomena in these decades: the explosion of variegated activity in New York since the 1950s, the emergence of British New Dance since the 1970s, the French *nouvelle danse*, the psychological and dramatic concerns exemplified by Germany's Pina Bausch, the phenomenon of Japanese Butoh, the ballet experimentalists in Europe, and those areas where dance merges into other art forms, such as opera, drama, performance art, and the installation. The careers discussed here also highlight the internationalism of the life of the professional choreographer today.

A note on the entries

Each entry consist of four sections:

1 An essay on the choreographer's career by a commissioned contributor.
2 A biographical sketch, with essential details of birth, education and training, career, dance-company affiliations, and awards/honours.

3   A list of choreographic works, as comprehensive as possible, by year of premiere. Musical setting/composers and choreographic collaborators, where relevant (and known), appear in parentheses after titles. (Other important collaborators, such as scenic artists, are also often indicated by contributors in their essays.) Any significant later version of a work is usually noted alongside the original version: there are some exceptions here, usually involving a change of the work's title.

4   A list of Further reading, subdivided into interviews, articles, and books. Items are listed in chronological order. We have generally not included the normal review columns from newspapers and dance periodicals, though where a review has been substantial enough to become a feature article, then we have retained it. For the most part we have confined ourselves to English-language material, except in a few cases, where the most substantial writing existed in other widely spoken European languages. Where journals – usually quarterlies – designate issues by season (e.g. Winter 1988), we have preferred to list them thus; sometimes periodical series are inconsistent in this respect, and so some citations here include volume and issue numbers instead.

Acknowledgments

I would like to thank the following for their valuable help in providing information and answering factual queries at various stages of the project:

Joan Acocella; Richard Alston Dance Company; Karole Armitage and Maggiodanza; Adventures in Motion Pictures; Ballet Frankfurt; Peter Bassett and the Laban Centre Library staff; Laurie Booth; Matthew Bourne; Trisha Brown; Rosemary Butcher; Jonathan Burrows and Julia Carruthers; Lucinda Childs Dance Company; The Cholmondeleys; Compagnie Daniel Larrieu; Compagnie Maguy Marin; Siobhan Davies Dance Company; Downtown Art Company; Douglas Dunn and Dancers; Garth Fagan Dance; Feld Ballets NY; Nancy Goldner; David Gordon and Pick Up Company; Robert Greskovic; Dawn Hathaway; Deborah Heaney; Donald Hutera; Bill T. Jones/Arnie Zane Dance Company; Angela Kane; Pam King at Sydney Dance Company; Lar Lubovitch Dance Company; Bebe Miller Company; Meredith Monk and the House Foundation for the Arts; Mark Morris Dance Group; Julian Moss at Göteborg Ballet; Moving Earth Orient Sphere; National Ballet of Canada; Nikolais/Louis Foundation for Dance; Lloyd Newson and DV8; Larraine Nicholas; Steve Paxton; Mandy Payne; Stephen Petronio Company; Place Theatre Dance Services; Giannandrea Poesio; Jane Pritchard; Rosas; Ian Spink; Elizabeth Streb; Ivan Sygoda at Pentacle; Paul Taylor Dance Company; Ann Veronica Turnbull.

Finally, I should like to thank my husband, Mark Hawkins-Dady, whose modesty alone prevents him from being named co-editor of this project.

INTRODUCTION

In 1975, the erudite and cantankerous Lincoln Kirstein delivered the following broadside against the '*soi-disant* "*modern*"*-dance*': 'Essentially, the modern dance tradition is a meager school and is without audience, repertory, or issue; it never gained a mass public, a central system, nor a common repertory . . .'.[1] It was, in other words, no threat to opera-house ballet and, more particularly, no threat to the New York City Ballet, the company that Kirstein and George Balanchine founded in 1933.

Those critics judging modern dance (or 'contemporary dance', 'new dance', 'post-modern dance', etc.) by the rules and standards of the *danse d'école* inevitably find it wanting. In 1968, the London critic A.V. Coton referred to Paul Taylor's already highly developed and idiosyncratic aesthetic as 'this free-style mode of non-ballet dance'.[2] Modern dance choreographers have always had to defend themselves against charges that they lack identifiable 'technique' and indulge in careless public improvisation. This last, along with notions of 'self-expression', was (mistakenly) believed to be the legacy of Isadora Duncan, whose reputation was tainted by the flocks of young girls experiencing 'freedom' in Grecian tunics. In the early days of Twyla Tharp's choreographic career, it was often assumed that, because of the ver-nacular sputter of her movement style, her dancers were improvising. To counteract this, she created structures rigorous enough to guarantee planning and hours of stu-dio sweat. After all, if the three performers in her 1970 *The Fugue*, dancing only to the sound of their own boots on an amplified floor, end in perfect unison, not only is predetermined choreography a given, but a new kind of virtuosity is clearly abloom.

It is true, however, that modern dance has never scorned the amateur. In pre-World-War-II Germany, Rudolf von Laban and his disciples pieced together immense 'movement choirs' out of cadres of workers in various cities, creating idealistic proletarian spectacles unfortunately apt for being absorbed into the National Socialists' propaganda machine. In Britain, where Laban emigrated in 1938, children with no thought of becoming professionals learned to express them-selves through dance. Mary Wigman's Dresden studio offered both a professional training programme and *Tanzgymnastik* classes for the general public. Through organizations such as the New Dance Group in New York, fervently left-wing American dancers of the 1930s organized after-school and after-work classes to proclaim art as the birthright of the masses. In New York in the 1960s members of Judson Dance Theater and their followers used non-dancers in their works as a way of querying the primacy of the studio dancer.

Kirstein was right about several things, but not about the spin he put on them. Like contemporary concert-hall music, serious modern and postmodern dance rarely build huge audiences, perhaps because of choreographers' willingness – indeed, their frequent mission – to challenge the expectations and sensibilities of the public or to present unsettling images of contemporary life. To scholars and admirers of modern dance, its glory lies in its diversity. Although, as in modern painting, 'schools' may arise and imitators abound, at the core of each style is the single artist's way of moving and feeling, fuelled by his or her vision of what dance means in the world and how the world reveals itself in dance.

At this point, it must be stressed that one of the ironies of dance history is that the cross-pollinization of ballet and modern dance has not only produced hybrids, it has occasionally created balletmakers more 'contemporary' in outlook than some certifiably modern dance choreographers. And only in its early years could modern dance be considered to have anything at all in common with modernism as a movement in the arts. In 1959, as one of the New York City Ballet's occasional 'novelties', George Balanchine and Martha Graham each choreographed the two separate halves of *Episodes*, using for music the entire small *œuvre* of Anton Webern; Balanchine's ballet was cool, mysterious, and astringently contemporary, while Graham chose to set an historical biography (of Mary, Queen of Scots) in her by-then-traditional dramatic style. William Forsythe, trained in the classical lexicon and the director of the Frankfurt Ballet, is easily more 'contemporary' in style and outlook than some choreographers who have come up through modern dance and play its usual triple role of choreographer/company director/star.

It is instructive to look at J.E. Crawford Flitch's 1912 *Modern Dancing and Dancers* (by modern, Flitch meant not 'antique').[3] There, along with Russian ballerinas, and with Loie Fuller, Isadora Duncan and Ruth St Denis, the acknowledged foremothers of what came to be called 'modern dance', are the skirt dancers of the music halls and West End shows. Flitch's inclusion of these performers, who flourished in the late nineteenth and early twentieth centuries, was astute. Each woman was adept at creating a personal image on stage. Manipulating a skirt while performing movements drawn from ballet, step-dancing, and social dance, the performer could tease an audience with glimpses of stockinged thighs, adopting the persona of a shy maiden, a hussy, a dreamy romantic. She could also, however, enthrall the *ton* by designing more abstract images out of the swirling shapes of skirt, arms, and arching back, as did British music hall star Alice Lethbridge. George Bernard Shaw did not care for Lethbridge and could be savage about amateurish skirt dancers, but he waxed rhapsodic over Letty Lind in *Morocco Bound* in 1892.[4]

Fuller, Duncan, and St Denis all got their start as small-part actresses, musical comedy chorus girls, and variety show skirt dancers. But they took their theatrical savvy into new directions, dignifying dance by associating it with great art or music or philosophical ideas. Plying her yards of shimmering silk under innovative lighting that she designed herself, Fuller expanded skirt dancing into dazzling transformations – becoming fire, opening blossoms, butterflies, water. No wonder the symbolist poets fêted her. No wonder her Art Nouveau jewelbox theatre was a much-frequented site at the 1900 World's Fair in Paris.

At a time when dancing was 'show business' and dancers morally suspect, Duncan and St Denis insisted on the ability of dancing to deal with lofty ideas and emotions. This, along with the freedom of the body to be expressive in ways not prescribed by the academy, was their bequest to contemporary dance. Both were widely read; both nurtured themselves on the ideas of the French theoretician François Delsarte (1811–71), as systematized by such American disciples as Steele McKaye and Genevieve Stebbins. Delsarte's enthusiastically reasoned linking of the body's postures and gestures, the heart's emotions, and the mind's thoughts helped these dance soloists to dignify the body and make it a vehicle for complex expression. They transformed themselves from show-dancers into 'salon artists', performing in the homes of the wealthy, and finally into 'interpretative' dancers who could fill a concert hall and excite debate.

Duncan's plastic evocations of an idyllic Greece went beyond fashionable statue-posing. Dancing to Chopin, Bach, Wagner, Gluck, she translated current ideas about nature, freedom, individual will, evolution, and even electrical energy onto her womanly body. To a charmed European public, she stood, too, for the American vigour hymned by Walt Whitman, whose poetry she adored and on which she modelled some of her own public utterances. St Denis's goddesses, dancing girls, and harem women went beyond the popular orientalist fantasies to show the metamorphoses from the physical to the spiritual: the deity who dances out the temptations of the senses, only to renounce them all (*Radha*, 1906); the worshipper whose rippling arms become one with the smoke of her offering (*The Incense*, 1906); the geisha who casts off her robes, dance by alluring dance, to reveal herself as a goddess (*O-Mika*, 1912).

These vivid women, and others like Maud Allan (whose lascivious *Salomé* thrilled Edward VII), set a fashion for artful solo recitals. The first works of those American dancers, Martha Graham, Doris Humphrey, and Charles Weidman, who linked dance with modernism as a force in art and architecture, came out of Denishawn, the school and company founded in 1914 by St Denis and her husband Ted Shawn, a great proselytiser for virile male dancing. Humphrey's first solos were the hoop and scarf dances that could succeed either on the concert stage or, given their scanty costuming, on a vaudeville bill. Even as Humphrey and Weidman were presenting their first bravely modern works, Weidman offered such titles as *Rhythmic Patterns of Java* (1929), and many of Graham's first solos presented her as the same Chinese maidens and Arabic temptresses that she had played at Denishawn.

Contemporary dance, *pace* Kirstein, has not been without systems. These have usually arisen, however, out of the needs and ideals of individual creators, most of whom were also the stars and directors of their companies. In the early twentieth century, various systems of movement to promote an expressive and efficient body developed in the wake of Delsartism. In Switzerland, Emile Jaques-Dalcroze's exercises, aimed primarily at musicians, correlated motion with the rhythms, pitches, and phrase shapes of music. In Russia in the 1920s, the theatre director Vsevolod Meyerhold developed his biomechanical exercises, in part to train actors to negotiate the Constructivist sets that were a vital part of his enterprise. Nikolai Foregger's physical training system, *Tafiatrenage* (taffy-pulling), fed directly into the machine dances that he considered a vital expression of twentieth-century life. Laban built 'Eukinetics', analysing the expressiveness of the body's motion in relation to space and time. It became the custom for modern dance choreographers to design training systems based on their views of dance and the particular demands of their themes.

From the first compositions (around 1913) of Mary Wigman, the great pupil of Dalcroze and Laban, German *Ausdruckstanz* was allied not just with 'expression' (the name translates as 'Expression Dance') but with Expressionism. Wigman spoke of her creative process as a mystical communion with unknown forces:

> I shut myself in my golden room, leaned my head against the softly singing Siamese gong, and listened to myself deep within. I did so until a pose emerged out of the musing and resolved itself into the stylistically corresponding gesture.[5]

In her desire to find and project the gestural essence of an inner state, Wigman can be seen in relation to the Expressionist painters, several of whom were her friends. National Socialism, World War II, and the postwar politics of a divided Germany rubbed the radical sheen off Wigman's career and robbed *Ausdruckstanz* of much of its impetus. But in the first two decades of her career, Wigman trained and/or inspired a host of followers and gave modern dance two of its great early subjects: the human body and psyche as sites for conflicting forces, and the tension between the individual and the group.

Beginning in the late 1920s, American choreographers, too, were driven to express atavistic forces and committed to what Doris Humphrey termed 'moving from the inside out'.[6] By the 1930s and the socially conscious Depression years, they also felt a responsibility to articulate the spirit of the times and of their nation. Like many writers and painters, they gravitated towards native themes and images (breaking the habit of looking to Europe for inspiration became something of a moral imperative).

Graham in the 1930s turned her back on the exoticism of her Denishawn years and on the impressionistic studies of much 'interpretive dancing'. ('Why should an arm try to be corn; why should a hand try to be rain?', she wanted to know.[7]) Whether the choreographer was Graham, Humphrey, her colleague Weidman, the Wigman-trained Hanya Holm, Helen Tamiris, or their followers, the work tended to be as stripped down and powerful, as reduced to its essence, as modern architecture and design. Given that their medium was the human body and spirit, the choreographers could not achieve total abstraction, but they worked at distilling feeling into action. Believing that dance form and style sprang from emotional responses to life, Graham and Humphrey each created training techniques expressing potent dualities, Graham's based on contraction and release, Humphrey's on fall and recovery; both translated human struggle and aspiration into physical principals.

At least twice in the brief history of contemporary dance, renegade choreographers have rebelled against everything they have been taught, and pared dance back to a state of ardent simplicity. From this point, they gradually reintroduce, albeit in altered form, elements they had dispensed with. Critics like John Martin or Edwin Denby noted how the 'moderns' began to modulate their attack, broaden their vocabularies and subject-matter, and entertain the notion of role-playing. By the 1940s, Graham had entered the period of her great dance-dramas: *Letter to the World*, *Deaths and Entrances*, *Night Journey*. Cinematic in their play with time and space, mixing myth and psychology via Jungian insight, these dances generated immense theatrical power. A Humphrey-Weidman dancer, José Limón, who had been inspired to dance by a performance of the great German dancer-choreographer Harald Kreutzberg, created his brooding images of a tormented hero in such masterworks as *The Moor's Pavane* (1949).

Inevitably, as upstarts mature into established artists, they attract disciples and imitators. And ultimately others react against the prevailing styles. Among the next generation of choreographers were some mavericks who turned away from the increasingly dramatic and literary nature of modern dance, much as George Balanchine reacted against the story ballets he had been raised on. Coming to prominence early in the 1950s, Alwin Nikolais, a pupil of Hanya Holm, embedded nimble dancers in landscapes of light, altering their forms through ingenious costuming and movement, even as Loie Fuller and the Bauhaus artist Oskar Schlemmer had done before him. Erick Hawkins, Martha Graham's partner from 1938 until 1950, created poetic images of simplicity in gentle, harmonious nature rituals. And it was in the 1950s that Merce Cunningham, another former Graham dancer, began his controversial and thoroughly eye-opening reinvestigations of time, space and compositional procedures.

Redefining 'nature' has been a crucial mission in the development of contemporary dance. Cunningham's vision of nature was not the evocation of ancient, pastoral harmony that Isadora mounted in defiance of the Industrial Revolution, nor was it the urban landscape of grappling social forces that the early moderns explored. As Cunningham's colleague, the radical composer and theorist John Cage, wrote, 'Art changes because changes in science give the artist a different understanding of nature.'[8] Ideas from eastern philosophy and particle physics (some of them remarkably similar) shaped the aesthetic that Cunningham began to develop in the early 1950s. The apparent negation of causality in quantum mechanics, the fact that even our choices may be the result of chance or random selection – such theories found parallels in Cunningham's methods and in his vivid, disquieting stage pictures. His was a 'nature' so up-to-date that many could not recognize it as such.

Viewing space as an open field, Cunningham upset the convention of central focus, long a dominant feature of proscenium stage presentations. His compositional strategies included such chance procedures as tossing coins on charts to determine path, sequence, personnel, even movement. (Ever the vanguardist, he began, when just past seventy, to adapt these methods to a new way of inventing movement through a computer program called Life Forms.) His beautifully trained dancers have never played roles onstage or appeared to influence one another enduringly. In keeping with the Zen Buddhist principles he and Cage subscribed to, he allows each element of a dance to reveal its own nature with a minimum of manipulation: music, décor, lighting, costumes, and choreography exist as separate strands coming together only at the final rehearsal. The contemporary world mirrored in the process and formal practice of his dances is one of complexity and unpredictability. It still makes many people uncomfortable, but, even considering the spread of Graham technique or the explosion of *Tanztheater* in Europe in response to Pina Bausch's work in Wuppertal, Cunningham has possibly had more indirect impact on contemporary dancemaking in the latter half of the twentieth century than anyone else.

Certainly his ideas, and more particularly Cage's, sparked the influential revolution of the 1960s in New York, most of which occurred under the auspices of Judson Dance Theater, a group of smart and irreverent choreographers as iconoclastic and, in a way, as idealistic as the radicals of the 1920s and 1930s. They, too, wanted to understand the essence of dance, but, coming of age as artists in a vastly altered political and social climate, their questions and methods were different.

It is still debated whether the group, whose most prominent members included Yvonne Rainer, Trisha Brown, Steve Paxton, David Gordon, Lucinda Childs, Elaine Summers, Robert Rauschenberg, Alex Hay, and Deborah Hay, ought to be considered (along with Simone Forti) the first wave of 'postmodernists' in dance, as Sally Banes proposed in her important book *Terpsichore in Sneakers*. Yvonne Rainer originally used 'postmodern' to mean coming after modern dance, and certainly the Judson artists not only came after modern dance but felt it had had its shining hour, and were not about to repeat its effects or subscribe to its philosophies. In a preface to the second edition of her book, Banes distinguishes several strands, spanning three decades, of postmodernism in dance.[9] The term applies perhaps most neatly to choreographers of the 1980s and 1990s whose artistic strategies and interests are more in tune with postmodernism in art and architecture than were those of the Judson group and the independents who began to sprout around them (such as Meredith Monk, Kenneth King, and Twyla Tharp).

The radical dancers, composers, and painters of the 1960s have been compared to the Dadaists operating in Switzerland, Germany, and Paris around the time of World War I. True, some Judson performances echoed the witty and obstreperous playfulness of Dada performances where poets and painters read simultaneously, where nonsense syllables were gravely recited, where musicians banged on instruments, and where, according to Tristan Tzara, the act of demanding 'the right to piss in different colors', and following it up with demonstrations, counted as a performance activity.[10] However, neither the Judson dancers nor John Cage in his seminal composition courses at the New School for Social Research in New York were this nihilistic in their rowdiness. At a time when young people worldwide were questioning the political and social establishment, these artists were querying the separation of the arts, the hierarchical arrangement of compositional elements, the elitism and potential eradication of individuality inherent in much academic training. Further, if, according to Cage, any noise could be part of a musical composition, why couldn't any movement be considered dance?

Exploration of everyday movement, the use of untrained performers, dances structured like tasks or ingenious games, objects used literally, process as a possible element of performance, absence of narrative or emotion, avoidance of virtuosity and glamour to seduce an audience – these gave many dances of the 1960s a resolute purity similar in intent, if not in style, to the dances of the 1930s. And the iconoclasm of the 1960s, like that of the 1930s, initiated another cycle of invention, development, imitation, and potential stagnation.

American contemporary dance emerged from the 1960s with a new look. The various individual styles developed by such choreographers as Brown, Gordon, Tharp, Paxton, and Childs were seeded in part from ordinary behaviour, rough-and-tumble athletics, Asian martial arts forms, and the casual dislocations of rock and roll; they little resembled the dominant 'modern' dance. The loose, fumbly duets of Paxton's contact improvisation, Gordon's complicated wordplay, Childs's exacting rhythmic patterns of travelling steps, the liquid-bodies dancing and brainy structures Brown built, Tharp's equally rigorous experiments with a style that, increasingly, drew on black vernacular dancing for its casual wit and complexity – however difficult these styles were to execute, they bred dancers more focused on the business of doing than of showing, dancers who aimed to look more spontaneous and more relaxed than, say, the Graham-trained dancer. Analysing her processes in 1976, Brown remarked, 'If I am beginning to sound like a bricklayer with a sense of humor, you are beginning to understand my work.'[11]

Following Cunningham's example, and perhaps Balanchine's too, many American choreographers of the 1970s tended to focus on movement and form, believing that these were in themselves expressive. However, radical choreographers elsewhere were not fighting to free dance of literary-dramatic trappings; they had other vital agendas. Butoh – a style and an artistic movement – developed in Japan during the 1960s as part of a reaction in all the arts against the rapid Westernization of the postwar years. The impulse of the two men acknowledged as founders of Butoh, Tatsumi Hijikata and Kazuo Ohno (the latter performing into his eighties) was, like that of the Americans in Judson Dance Theater, transgressive and anti-conventional in expertise, but it took a different, darkly dramatic form. Like the work of radical contemporary Japanese writers, painters, and theatre directors, Butoh emphasized poverty of means, bad taste, and extreme physical and spiritual states. It moved with excruciating slowness. Although the new style might refer to traditional Japanese theatre and folk forms as well as to firmly transplanted German *Ausdruckstanz*, it shattered all conventions, presenting the body with its imperfections magnified; toed in, club-footed, twitching, grimacing, knotted with tension, the dancer creeps into the skin of the foetus, the cripple, the spastic. Images of violence, eroticism, and androgyny permeate the work, offset by irony and absurdity. A main goal of Butoh has always been getting in touch with the inner self; for Hijikata (who died in 1986), it was also a search for the Japanese body in relation to the landscape and customs that spawned it. These goals link him with the expressionism of early modern dance, with Wigman's sense of the German soul and the Americans' quest for 'American' forms and spirit:

> The body is fundamentally chaotic; the Japanese body particularly, which in comparison with the coherent body of the Occidental (both religiously and culturally), is unsure in its stance. Occidentals have their feet planted firmly on the ground, forming a pyramid, whereas the Japanese seem to be performing acrobatic feats on oil paper. Therefore, they have to find their balance on twisted legs.[12]

The influence of Butoh has extended not only to such Japanese artists as Eiko and Koma (now resident in the United States), but to non-Asian choreographers in Canada, the United States, and Europe.

The term *Tanztheatre* is applied to the work of choreographers beside Pina Bausch, but it is she who made it world-famous. This renascence of bold contemporary dance in the Germany of the 1970s shared with *Ausdruckstanz* its essentially dark nature and view of life as a struggle of adversarial forces. In Bausch's work, these forces are no longer located within the body as much as they are outside it; in her hours-long theatrical spectacles, performers persist in impossible or humiliating tasks, or battle one another. Involving singing, speech, and motion (less and less 'dance' as the years go by), her pieces are collages of small intense scenes, which acquire a ritualistic fervour through the use of almost numbing repetition. With immense theatricality, they present life as a no-win battle of the sexes in an inertly bourgeois world. Compared to the abstract images of society in struggle that the early modern dancers created, Bausch's society is without visible ideals or heroes.

Looking back over the past two decades as the millennium approaches, one can note the remarkably accelerated growth of innovative contemporary forms in countries such as Great Britain, France, Spain, Belgium, the Netherlands, and Canada, which either had scant history of modern dance performance, or came late to it. Martha Graham's formidable technique was already over 30 years old when Robin Howard fell in love with it and founded the London School of Contemporary Dance (1966) and London Contemporary Dance Theatre (1967). Less than five years later, a choreographer like Richard Alston, groomed in the Graham tradition, was already attracted to a less emotion-laden aesthetic inspired by

Cunningham. Mary Fulkerson and her fostering of release work and contact improvisation soon after its 'invention' by Steve Paxton also influenced Alston's company Strider, and the historian Stephanie Jordan sees the explosion of British 'fringe' dance beginning in the late 1970s as being triggered in part by the arrival on the scene of the first graduating class trained by Fulkerson at Dartington College of Arts in Devon.[13] In effect, England was getting its first look at new trends abroad at the same time that choreographers like those associated with the X6 Collective (Fergus Early, Maedé Duprès, Jacky Lansley, Emilyn Claid, and Mary Prestidge) and those who presented work under X6's auspices (Laurie Booth, Rosemary Butcher, and others), were creating Britain's 'New Dance'.

Another intriguing aspect of the scene in the 1990s has been the way that contemporary choreographers who built on the radical experimental work of the 1960s have gradually reintroduced in new guises much of what was discarded. Virtuosity, once told to stay in the ballet world were it belonged, now often works in ironic companionship with the unassuming, everyday look cultivated by dancers during the 1960s. Someone slouches or saunters onto the stage, perhaps wearing street clothes, then offhandedly flings a leg towards the roof. For some choreographers, such as Belgium's Wim Vandekeybus, Britain's Lloyd Newson, Canada's Edouard Locke, or the United States's Elizabeth Streb (four highly dissimilar artists), virtuosity has been reconstrued as ordeal or as risk. Putting the dancers in what looks like danger or working them to a point of visible exhaustion induces in spectators sensitized by the fitness craze a kinaesthetic response, different in quality but similar in effect to that caused by a ballet dancer's phenomenal leap.

Improvisation, for some time unfashionable in modern dance because of its aforementioned connotations of 'free expression', gained credibility in the 1960s in connection with task or game structures that depended on individual interpretation of rules in performance. In some contemporary work, it can be thought of as a manifestation of the new virtuosity. Improvisation as Bill T. Jones has used it in solos may involve spontaneously generated monologue and accompanying movement springing from a predetermined subject. For Kenneth King's dancers, improvisation means being free in performance to choose from among various composed phrases and movements. Dana Reitz, who once likened her composition-improvisation strategies to those of jazz musicians ringing changes on a known melody,[14] creates solos so elegant and formally coherent that people are often unaware of the role that improvisation plays.

Contact improvisation, as Steve Paxton formulated it, was an 'art sport', a totally improvised duet form that featured exchanges of weight, with partners clambering over each other or levering one another off the floor. Because hands are so rarely used to initiate moves, the action, although it can look erotic or competitive, never seems manipulative. Contact improvisation opened up new possibilities for a generation of choreographers and is still practised in its 'pure' form.

One notable trend of the 1980s was a rekindled interest in emotion and narrative among choreographers who had been nurtured on the Cunningham aesthetic. Economic pressures, feelings of political helplessness, and the spread of AIDS may have had some influence in spawning themes of dependency, helplessness, anger. And, in response, a gritty physicality perhaps derived from contact improvisation has become, in the works of choreographers from countries as diverse as Canada, Croatia, and Venezuela, a metaphor for flawed human relationships. The lifts and supports are neither effortless nor attractive; they may be about a person who can hardly stand up trying to help another, about the terrible weight of a human body, about embraces that never quite work, about diving through the air and daring someone to catch you.

These contacts are not always tender. Postmodern dance and European dance-theatre alike often feature a violence that is more unabashed and far less glamorous than its equivalent in modern dance or contemporary ballet. Thinking over the contemporary scene of the last decade, one garners images of fierce, unstopping energy (as in the work of Stephen Petronio), but also more obvious ones of boots stomping, of people hauling one another around in painful or humiliating ways. In Jean-Claude Gallotta's *Docteur Labus* (1988), created for his Grenoble-based Groupe Emile Dubois, a man raised a woman by sticking his fingers in her ears; another pulled his partner around by a hand jammed into her mouth.

Many of the elements that characterize postmodernism in art and architecture also figure in contemporary dance forms. The emphasis is not, as it once was, on discovering personal vocabularies and training others in idiosyncratic techniques. Eclectisism is no longer a pejorative term. Just as interior decorators mate Queen Anne with the Bauhaus, choreographers feel free to borrow from, say, ballet and street dancing in the same work. Choreographers such as Karole Armitage and Michael Clark have mixed ballet-born vocabularies with pop imagery. The American Doug Elkins has all but created a personal style by melding break-dance moves with other steps.

Critics of postmodernism have deplored its addiction to making references to the past as purposeless nostalgia and pastiche. I would contest that, in dance, such references often do point out ironic structural parallels, or disassemble the traditional so that new meanings may be squeezed out. One example is Pina Bausch's disconcertingly desolate and poignant update of Bluebeard (*Blaubart*, 1977). In *Last Supper at Uncle Tom's Cabin/The Promised Land* (1990), Bill T. Jones used fragments of text and action drawn from Harriet Beecher Stowe's anti-slavery novel (with a performer representing Stowe as reader and commentator), poses from Leonardo da Vinci's masterpiece, and a number of other 'texts' to inquire into religious faith and the often subtle nature of prejudice against blacks, women and homosexuals. Equally political, Matthew Bourne's all-male *Swan Lake* (1995) not only wreaked gender havoc on a nineteenth-century classic, but aimed darts at monarchy's power plays in general and Britain's royal family in particular. Jane Comfort's *Cliff Notes – Macbeth* (1988) offered Shakespeare's plot and some of his lines, which, interspersed with commentary from classics-made-easy guidebooks and Comfort's own sly additions, created an ironic contemporary gloss on the play.

The widespread fascination with history and text even crosses the line between ballet and modern dance: William Forsythe, a ballet choreographer working within the framework of a state-subsidized theatre, made *Impressing the Czar* (1988), a thoroughly postmodern deconstruction of *fin-de-siècle* Russian art and social politics, while postmodern dancemaker Timothy Buckley built his 1993 *A Letter to Diaghilev* (both a tragic-comic solo and a group work) around elements from the life and diary of a great ballet dancer, Vaslav Nijinsky.

Postmodernism even embraces an artist like Mark Morris, who in some ways might be considered a throwback to Balanchine because of his emphasis on music and musicality, and to Paul Taylor's modern dance world of sunny innocence and midnight depravity. Such practices as blending exalted feeling with down-to-earth manners, embracing culture via its music and social conventions, and downplaying or reversing traditional gender roles define Morris as undeniably contemporary. So do his references to past styles. But the evocations of Balkan dance, early German modern dance, Greek friezes, scarf dancers, or down-and-dirty dancing are not simply quotations, but transformations. As a contemporary classicist and something of a utopian, Morris can be considered in relation to such Arcadian painters as Milet Andrejevic, Thomas Cornell, and Lennart Anderson, whose works show people in contemporary clothing, posed in fields or city parks like mild Dionysian revellers, nymphs, or gods on the brink of mythic encounter.

Because of dance's ephemerality, styles of the past are continually being recycled in a more literal way too. Ballet choreographers recreate late nineteenth-century Russia; Asian choreographers pay homage to Martha Graham. Great choreographers, like Paul Taylor, who had developed his style by the early 1960s, flourish untouched by current fashions in choreography. In a larger sense, the 'contemporary' scene is as diverse as individual notions of contemporaneity.

However, much of the presumed cutting-edge dance of the past two decades can be characterized by its frequent social, political, and historical concerns, its voracious strain of eclecticism, its interest in text and narrative. These interests may broaden and deepen dancing itself or, as some fear, weaken movement invention. When choreographers (Lloyd Newson and Susan Marshall for example) turn to writing plays, does this mean that dance no longer serves their expressive needs? Which artists who consider themselves 'contemporary' are responding directly to contemporary life and which are simply shaping their ideas in accord with current trends is a question that can probably not be answered until the passage of time gives us perspective. We should, however, be grateful that modern dance did not become a powerful monolithic entity like ballet, that choreographers can remain utterly susceptible to the world around them, able to design the present, even sometimes the future, on moving bodies.

Deborah Jowitt

Notes

1 Klosty, James (ed.), *Merce Cunningham* (1975), 2nd edition with a new foreword, New York: Limelight Editions, 1986, p. 89.
2 Coton, A.V., *Writings on Dance, 1938–68*, London: Dance Books, 1975, p. 152.

3 Flitch, J.E. Crawford, *Modern Dancing and Dancers*, London: Grant Richards and Philadelphia: J.B. Lippincott Co., 1912.

4 Shaw, George Bernard, (22 November 1892), collected in *Music in London, 1890–4*, London: Constable, 1931, p. 102.

5 Wigman, Mary, *The Language of Dance*, trans. Walter Sorell, Middletown, Conn.: Wesleyan University Press, 1966, p. 33.

6 Humphrey, Doris, letter to her parents, 8 August 1927, Doris Humphrey Letters (New York Public Library).

7 Armitage, Merle (ed.), *Martha Graham: The Early Years* (1937), New York: Da Capo Press, 1978, p. 67.

8 Cage, John, *Silence: Lectures and Writings*, Middletown, Conn.: Wesleyan University Press, 1973, p. 194.

9 Banes, Sally, *Terpsichore in Sneakers* (1980), 2nd edition with a new preface, Middlebury, Conn.: Wesleyan University Press, 1987.

10 Goldberg, RoseLee, *Performance: Live Art 1909 to the Present*, New York: Harry N. Abrams, 1979, p. 41.

11 Livet, Ann (ed.), *Contemporary Dance*, New York: Abbeville Press (in association with the Fort Worth Art Museum, Texas), 1978, p. 54.

12 Viala, Jean and Nourit Masson-Sekine, *Butoh: Shades of Darkness*, Tokyo: Shufunotomo, 1988, p. 188.

13 Jordan, Stephanie, *Striding Out: Aspects of Contemporary and New Dance in Britain*, London: Dance Books, 1992, p. 61.

14 Jowitt, Deborah, 'Dana Reitz', *The Drama Review*, 24(4) (T88), December 1980, p. 36.

RICHARD ALSTON

Richard Alston combines the innovative and temporal expectations we have of a 'contemporary' choreographer. Moreover, his career epitomizes the changing aesthetics and politics that have shaped British dance since the 1960s. As a student at the London School of Contemporary Dance (LSCD) (1967–1970), he was one of the first in Britain to benefit from a systematic training in modern dance. The school aimed to develop essentially Graham-style performers, but its syllabus also included regular classes in classical ballet, historical dance, and choreography. Significantly, it was this breadth of training that appealed most to Alston and, as opposed to many of his contemporaries, choreography (often created for dancers other than himself) was his main interest. He experimented with a range of techniques and structures – so much so that, even before modern dance became established as a mainstream form in Britain, Alston was regarded as its first rebel.

Initially, his decision to eschew the current 'contemporary dance' form was most marked in theme rather than content. Whereas the evolving Graham-influenced genre sought out expressionistic subject-matter, Alston chose to create works about dancing itself. In 1971, his choice of title for *END which is never more than this instant, than you on this instant, figuring it out and acting so. If there is any absolute, it is never more than this one, you, this instant, in action, which ought to get us on* was an intended criticism of the narrative works that increasingly typified the repertories of London Contemporary Dance Theatre and Ballet Rambert.

Alston, however, was no *enfant terrible*. His emphasis on movement – on motion, not emotion – links his choreography to the work of George Balanchine, Merce Cunningham, and Frederick Ashton in his plotless ballets. All four choreographers find expression in formal elements. There is a close correlation between subject and structure, and as Alston became more experienced in developing the dance elements themselves as themes, his structures became more complex. In *Nowhere Slowly* (1970), *Windhover* (1972), and *Blue Schubert Fragments* (1974), for example, the main choreography was organized as solos and duets. These occurred predominantly *sur place*, with simple walking and running sequences moving the dancers from one place to the next. A decade later, his organization of movement around 'nuclei' (Alston's own term) had evolved into large-scale, multi-layered structures in which transitional phrases were as complex as the nuclei themselves. Two works that best illustrate this are *Dangerous Liaisons* (1985) and *Strong Language* (1987). The subject of both is the realization of their sound accompaniments in dance terms. In the former, Alston analysed the ticks, clangs, and chimes of Simon Waters's electronic tape in order to find its rhythmic progression. The accompaniment is linear in structure: there are five major sections, which are repeated (with the fourth and fifth reversed), and the tape ends with a new sound section and coda. Similarly, the dance follows these larger sections and, within each, there is an aural-visual correspondence between the timbres and tensions of Waters's tape and Alston's movement phrases. Also, through their various groupings, the six dancers (four women and two men) echo the varying intensities of sound.

The challenge for Alston in *Strong Language* was to make 'dance sense' of the myriad rhythms in John-Marc Gowans's collage tape. The contrasts between and within the various sound sections can be detected in Alston's naming of four of them: 'String of sounds', 'Strumming', 'Swing and sway', and 'Funk'. Rhythmic phrases are juxtaposed with one another to highlight differences in sound quality and cadence, but whereas the larger, linear structure of

Dangerous Liaisons was Alston's *raison d'être*, his organizing principle in *Strong Language* derives from the shorter, over-lapping rhythms of Gowan's multi-track tape. Thus, the progression in *Strong Language* is episodic, and Alston uses repetition as his main structuring device. It is most evident in 'Strumming', a complicated five-minute dance of continually repeated material. Through a succession of entrances and exits, dancers join in this undulating adagio section, either singly or in pairs. Sometimes, they create larger unison groups; elsewhere, their accumulations occur as overlapping, canonic layers of movement. The fact that the same choreography is common to all is not always obvious but, in seeing it repeated and re-echoed by different dancers, from different areas of the stage, the full shape and patterning of the material is revealed.

Repetition is a recurring structural device in Alston's work. As his choreography has become more complex, he has attempted to aid perception and continuity by repeating key material. The title of one of his dances, *Doublework* (1978), alludes to this: although the principal aim was to create a dance essentially about duets, a secondary goal was the re-stating of material at various points in the dance. Repetition also reinforces certain movement preferences: the high, bent elbow in the lunges of *Connecting Passages* (1977) and *Soda Lake* (1981), and in the parallel *retirés* and leaps of *Rainbow Bandit/Rainbow Ripples* (1974, 1980); the springing, turning *sissonnes* in *Soda Lake*, *Dutiful Ducks* (1982, rev. 1986), and *Pulcinella* (1987); and the sudden shifts of weight onto and out of *fondu-retiré* which propel the dancers in many Alston works – these elicit much about his particular movement concerns.

His most favoured motifs illuminate two very telling prerequisites of the Alston style: co-ordination and the ability to move easily, either at great speed or extremely slowly. Impulse and ongoing momentum originate from deep within the torso, with small shifts in the hip or back providing the impetus for larger movement. Emanating from the spine is a sense of centre line – a lateral extension of the torso – which often produces *épaulement* and *éffacé* positions.

What characterizes Alston's style most is its openness, physically and philosophically. Much of this stems from the many types of dance training and performance that he encountered during his formative years. At LSCD it was his interest in such 'alternative' styles as Tai Chi and Cunningham that set him apart from other young choreographers there. With his first company, Strider (1972–75), he attempted to fuse the tilts and twists of the Cunningham technique with the fluid, tension-free concepts of release work. Then, while studying in New York with Cunningham and the former Ballets Russes de Monte Carlo teacher, Alfredo Corvino, he spent much of his free time seeing a wide spectrum of work – from the virtuosities of Balanchine's choreography (New York City Ballet) to the pedestrian non-performances of the American postmodernists.

After Alston's return from New York in 1977, other Cunningham traits were observable in his choreography, particularly the clarity of *contrapposto* torso positions and precision at speed. These were consolidated during his twelve-year association with Ballet Rambert, first as resident choreographer (1980–86) and, to a lesser degree, when he was artistic director (1986–92), during which time the company was renamed the Rambert Dance Company. Alston's arrival at Rambert initiated his longest consecutive commitment to one company. More importantly, it marked the beginning of his choreographic maturity. In interview, he revealed that one of the reasons why he decided to join the company was his interest in seeing how a work evolves with repeated performance. As a repertory company, Rambert provided opportunities for him to revise his choreography, either during the early performances of a work or when re-casting it, sometimes years later. (Examples of the latter are the revivals of *Rainbow Ripples* in 1985, *Wildlife* in 1992, and two different versions of *Mythologies* in 1985 and 1989.)

Ballet Rambert also facilitated Alston's first three-way collaboration. Previously, for Strider, he had commissioned scores from contemporary composers (such as Anna Lockwood and Stephen Montague). His interest in the visual arts had begun even earlier. (Before attending the LSCD, Alston had studied theatre design at Croydon Art College.) However, the opportunity to work in larger theatres, with greater technical (and financial) resources, only arose once Alston joined Rambert. The most immediate effect of this was his incorporation of commissioned designs, from the photographer David Buckland (*Rainbow Ripples*), painter Howard Hodgkin (*Night Music* (1981) and later, *Pulcinella*), and from lighting supremo Peter Mumford. (Mumford designed the lighting for almost all Alston's work for Rambert and he created the sets for several works, too.) But it was in *Wildlife* (1984) that Alston realized his long-time ambition for a dance–music–design collaboration.

Wildlife was a landmark for Alston, not least because it confirmed his ability to work as part of a collaborative team. Importantly, this ability relates also to the reciprocal relationship that he developed with his dancers during the rehearsal process – one which became crucial when, two years later, he assumed the role of artistic director. Though the concept of *Wildlife* developed out of lengthy discussions with the composer, Nigel Osborne, and designer Richard Smith, Alston created the choreography at break-neck speed. Not only did the six dancers learn quickly, they were also instrumental in forging *Wildlife*'s taut, angular style. The zig-zag contours of Smith's kites and the explosive bursts of energy in Osborne's music meant that, in *Wildlife*, Alston addressed extremes of movement – both physically and dynamically – for the first time. (It was also the first time that he

worked with a commissioned score in a truly *musical* way.) Such extreme possibilities of movement demanded that the dancers be receptive to the rapid changes of body position and flow in *Wildlife*'s faster sections and also to the contrasting *adagio* control which the work equally required (especially in the central male–female duet).

The qualities introduced in *Wildlife* were developed further in *Dangerous Liaisons* the following year and in *Zansa* (1986), the latter of which Alston has described as '*Wildlife* Mark II'. Though *Zansa* features the same angularities and urgent rhythms (and a second commissioned score by Osborne), it is far more sophisticated, spatially, than any other Alston work. This is particularly evident in his manipulation of groups. The multiple crossings of the blue-clad ensemble and the double duets for two couples dressed in yellow, both connected at crucial points – sequentially and thematically – by the interweavings of the female protagonist, together resulted in Alston's finest and most densely textured choreography.

Zansa was created in the same year that Alston became artistic director. As resident choreographer, Alston had continued to work in a freelance capacity. This had enabled him to choreograph for soloists such as Michael Clark (in 1981 and again in 1982); for the Royal Ballet (1983) and Extemporary Dance Theatre (1985); and in 1982, to co-found Second Stride (with Siobhan Davies and Ian Spink). These different working associations invigorated Alston choreographically and, in the longer term, there were advantageous for the Rambert company, too. (Several works created for these other groups were revived, often in a revised form, for Rambert.) However, once Alston became artistic director, this dual allegiance ceased and, despite making important contributions to Rambert's repertory (most notably with *Pulcinella*, *Strong Language*, and *Hymnos* (1988)), he found that much of his time was taken up with programme-planning and policy decisions.

The years of Alston's directorship were the least distinguished choreographically. Sadly, they were also the years during which recession-hit dance companies were being forced to compromise artistic vision for the sake of box office sales. As director, Alston resisted such pressures, even though audiences – and Rambert's own board – believed the repertory he built to be too austere in its focus on formalist works. (Trisha Brown, Lucinda Childs, Merce Cunningham, and David Gordon all worked with the company during Alston's directorship.)

In the autumn of 1992, Alston decided to take a short sabbatical in order to work with the French dance company Regine Chopinot/Ballet Atlantique. The outcome of this sortie was the creation of *Le Marteau sans maître* (and a revival of *Rainbow Bandit*). It was the most exciting statement by Alston in over six years and, at the time of *Le Marteau sans maître*'s premiere in December 1992, there was talk of the work being restaged for Rambert the following year. Ironically, on Alston's return to London, only days after the premiere, he was dismissed by the Rambert board. Dance politics thus proved to be more powerful than the pursuit of an individual aesthetic.

What followed for Alston was a two-year period of enforced freelance activity (and ongoing press speculation as to his future in British dance). He had once described his work with Strider as a 'sorting-out period', during which he was able to work through a range of ideas choreographically and also to take stock of his career. Twenty years on, Alston appeared to have come full circle. Between 1992 and 1994, he accepted a diversity of commissions, with Shobana Jeyasingh, London Contemporary Dance Theatre (LCDT), and student groups at LSCD and the Laban Centre. It was an enforced but necessary phase in which he could reassess his position as one of Britain's foremost choreographers.

Fortunately for Alston, he was soon to embark on another full-time commitment.

From September 1994, he began to direct his own company. Changes of policy and personnel at The Place (the home of LCDT and LSCD since 1969) led to considerable reorganization, and, as artistic director of the Contemporary Dance Trust, Alston assumed responsibility for spearheading developments, both at The Place Theatre and at LSCD. With only nine dancers to begin with, the new company took the name of the Richard Alston Dance Company, with its focus (almost exclusively in the first season) on Alston's own choreography. With this venture Alston aimed to re-establish himself, yet again, as an artist at the cutting edge of contemporary choreography. His recent choreography has seen him engage with the work of leading international contemporary composers, such as Harrison Birtwhistle, (*Secret Theatre*, *Orpheus Singing and Dreaming*, and *Bach Measures*, all in 1996) and Iannis Xenakis (*Okho*, 1996).

Angela Kane

Biographical details

Born in Stoughton, Sussex, England, 30 October 1948. **Studied** at Croydon College of Art, 1965–67; London School of Contemporary Dance, from 1967; with Merce Cunningham in New York, 1975–77 also studied with Alfred Corvino and Valda Setterfield. **Career** Worked as a choreographer for London Contemporary Dance Theatre, 1970–72, and for own company Strider (founded with Gulbenkian Award), 1972–75; also choreographed while studying with Cunningham, presenting programme at the Cunningham Studio, New York, 1976; resident choreographer, Ballet Rambert (London), 1980–86; guest choreographer, Second Stride, 1982–83; artistic director, Ballet Rambert (Rambert Dance Company from 1987), 1986–92; founder, Richard Alston Dance Company, in residence at The Place Theatre, London, 1994. Has also choreographed for Royal Danish Ballet, Scottish Ballet, Extemporary Dance Theatre, Royal Ballet, English National Opera, Compagnie Chopinot, and Shobana Jeyasingh Company. **Awards and honours** include honorary doctorate, Surrey University, 1992; Chevalier de l'Ordre des Arts et des Lettres (France), 1995.

Works

Transit (mus. Ronald Lopresti, 1968), *Matrix* (mus. Bahutu chanting, 1968), *Something to Do* (text Gertrude Stein, 1969), *Still Moving Still* (mus. Shakuhachi, 1969), *Cycladic Figure* (mus. John Cage, 1969), *Winter Music* (mus. John Cage, 1970), *Fall* (revised version of *Cycladic Figure*; mus. John Cage, 1970), *Departing in Yellow* (mus. Michael Finnissy, 1970), *Pace* (mus. Handel, 1970), *Broadwhite* (revised version of *Departing in Yellow*; mus. Michael Finnissy, 1970), *Nowhere Slowly* (mus. Stockhausen, 1970; later versions set to Terry Riley), *Goldrush* (mus. Neil Young, 1970), *END, which is never more than this instant, than you on this instant, figuring it out and acting so. If there is any absolute, it is never more than this one, you, this instant, in action, which ought to get us on* (mus. Michael Finnissy, 1971), *Shiftwork* (mus. Rossini, 1971), *Cold* (mus. John Adam, 1971), *After Follows Before* (mus. Wagner, 1971), *Who is Twyla Tharp?* (text Peter and Alison Smithson, 1971), *Combines* (mus. various, 1972), *Balkan Sobranie* (mus. Jean Françaix, Stravinsky, Fukushimo, 1972), *Routine Couple* (taped conversation of George Burns and Gracie Allen, 1972), *Thunder* (mus. Harold Arlen, 1972), *Tiger Balm* (mus. Anna Lockwood, 1972), *Windhover* (mus. Anna Lockwood, 1972), *Headlong* (originally *Trailer*, a work-in-progress; mus. Anna Lockwood, 1973), *Interior* (with others; mus. Scott Joplin, folk, 1973), *The Average Leap Forward* (mus. Majorca Orchestra, 1973), *Lay-Out* (mus. Anna Lockwood, 1973), *Rainbow Bandit* (mus. Charles Amirkhanian, 1974), *Blue Schubert Fragments* (mus. Schubert, 1974), *Soft Verges/Hard Shoulder* (later known as *Soft Verges*; mus. Anna Lockwood, Stephen Montague, 1974), *Split* (with D. Greenwood; mus. Corner after Chopin, 1974), *Slow Field* (mus. Stephen Montague, 1974), *Souvenir* (mus. Satie, 1975), *Zero Through Nine* (mus. Stephen Montague, 1975), *Two Saints in Three Acts* (1975), *Standard Steps* (mus. Satie, voice of Marcel Duchamp, 1975), *Compass* (1975), *Slight Adventure* (film, 1975), *Solo Soft Verges* (1976), *Edge* (1976), *UnAmerican Activities* (1976), *Connecting Passages* (1977), *Blueprint* (1977–78; mus. Ruggles, 1978), *Home Ground* (mus. Purcell, 1978), *Breaking Ground* (mus. Purcell, 1978), *Doublework* (1978; revised version, mus. James Fulkerson, 1982), *The Seven Deadly Sins* (mus. Weill, text Bertolt Brecht, 1978), *Distant Rebound* (mus. Gordon Mumma, 1978), *Unknown Banker Buys Atlantic* (mus. Cole Porter, 1978), *Behind the Piano* (mus. Satie, 1979), *Elegiac Blues* (mus. Constant Lambert, 1979), *Dumka* (mus. Dvořák, 1979), *Bell High* (mus. Peter Maxwell Davies, 1980), *Schubert Dances* (mus. Schubert, 1980), *The Field of Mustard* (mus. Vaughan Williams, 1980), *Landscape* (mus. Vaughan Williams, 1980), *Rainbow Ripples* (mus. Charles Armirkhanian, 1980), *Sugar* (mus. Fats Waller, 1981), *The Rite of Spring* (mus. Stravinsky, 1981), *Soda Lake* (1981), *Swedish Dances* (mus. Swedish folk, 1981), *Berceuse* (mus. Chopin, 1981), *Night Music* (mus. Mozart, 1981), *Bellezza Flash* (mus. Monteverdi, 1982), *The Kingdom of the Pagodas* (mus. Britten, 1982), *Dutiful Ducks* (mus. Charles Amirkhanian, 1982; revised version, 1986), *Crown Diamonds* (mus. D. Auber, 1982), *Apollo Distraught* (mus. Nigel Osborne, 1982), *Fantasie* (mus. Mozart, 1982), *Chicago Brass* (mus. Hindemith, 1983), *Facing Out* (mus. Lindsay Cooper, 1983), *Java* (mus. The Inkspots, 1983; revised version, 1985), *The Brilliant and the Dark* (mus. Britten, 1983), *Midsummer* (mus. Tippett, 1983), *Voices and Light Footsteps* (mus. Monteverdi, 1984), *Wildlife* (mus. Nigel Osborne, 1984), *Coursing* (mus. Oliver Knussen, 1984), *Mythologies* (mus. Nigel Osborne, 1985), *Dangerous Liaisons* (mus. Simon Waters, 1985), *Cutter* (mus. John-Marc Gowans, 1985), *Zansa* (mus. Nigel Osborne, 1986), *Pulcinella* (mus. Stravinsky, 1987), *Strong Language* (incorporating material from *Cutter*; mus. John-Marc Gowans, 1987; video version, 1988), *Rhapsody in Blue* (mus. Gershwin, 1988), *Hymnos* (mus. Peter Maxwell Davies, 1988), *Cinema* (mus. Satie, 1989), *Pulau Dewata* (mus. Claude Vivier, 1989), *Mythologies* (new version; mus. Nigel Osborne, 1989), *Dealing with Shadows* (mus. Mozart, 1990), *Roughcut* (mus. Steve Reich, 1990), *Cat's Eye* (mus. David Sawyer, 1992), *Le Marteau sans maître* (mus. Pierre Boulez, 1992), *The Perilous Night* (mus. John Cage, 1993), *Delicious Arbour* (mus. Purcell, 1993), *Rumours, Visions* (mus. Britten, 1993), *Romance, with Footnotes* (mus. Purcell, 1993), *Shadow Realm* (mus. Simon Holt, 1994), *Sad Eyes* (includes *Lachrymae*; mus. Britten, 1994), *Something in the City* (mus. Man Jumping, 1994), *Three Movements from Petrushka* (mus. Stravinsky, 1994), *Weep No More* (mus. Billie Holliday, Cavalli, 1994), *Sometimes I Wonder* (mus. Hoagy Carmichael, 1995), *Secret Theatre* (mus. Harrison Birtwhistle, 1996), *Orpheus Singing and Dreaming* (mus. Harrison Birtwhistle, 1996), *Bach Measures* (mus. J.S. Bach, Harrison Birtwhistle, 1996; revised version, as *Beyond Measure*, later the same year), *Okho* (mus. Iannis Xenakis, 1996), *Brisk Singing* (mus. Rameau, 1997), *Light Flooding into Darkened Rooms* (mus. various guitar pieces, 1997).

Further reading

Interviews with Sarah Rubidge in 'The Rambert Reaches Sixty', *Dance Theatre Journal*, Summer 1986; with Barbara Newman in 'Richard Alston',

17

RICHARD ALSTON

Dancing Times, January 1987; with Sophie Constanti in 'Richard Alston: The Humanistic Approach', *Dance Theatre Journal*, Autumn 1989; with Angela Kane, in 'Shared Enthusiasms', *Dance and Dancers*, October 1991; with Stephanie Jordan, in 'Interviews with Richard Alston and Nigel Osborne', *Choreography and Dance*, 1(4), 1995; with Allen Robertson, in 'Full Circle', *Dance Now*, Spring 1995.

Articles Sophie Constanti, 'Passion in Parts', *Dance Theatre Journal*, Spring 1985; Alastair Macaulay, 'The Rambertians', *Dancing Times*, May 1985; Angela Kane, 'Alston's Doublework on Video', *Dance Theatre Journal*, Spring–1986; Alastair Macaulay, 'Second Striders Past and Present', *Dance Theatre Journal*, Summer 1986; Barbara Newman, 'Richard Alston', *Dancing Times*, January 1987; Special Rambert Issue of *Dance Theatre Journal*, Summer 1987, includes: Judith Mackrell's 'Rambert 1987', Stephanie Jordan's 'Alston's Rambert', Alastair Macaulay's 'Rambert's Alston', and 'Choreography by Richard Alston'; John Percival, 'Rambert under Alston', *Dance and Dancers*, June 1989; Angela Kane, 'Richard Alston: Twenty-one Years of Choreography', *Dance Research*, Autumn 1989; Sophie Constanti, 'Richard Alston: The Humanistic Approach', *Dance Theatre Journal*, Autumn 1989; Stephanie Jordan, 'British Modern Dance: Early Radicalism', *Dance Research*, Autumn 1989; Angela Kane, 'Cunningham – Alston: Rambert's Double Indemnity', *Dancing Times*, April 1990; Peter Brinson, 'To Be Ahead', *Dance and Dancers*, June 1990; Judith Mackrell, 'Post-modern Dance in Britain', *Dance Research*, Spring 1991; Alastair Macaulay, 'Richard Alston: Back at The Place', *Dancing Times*, January 1995; Richard Alston, 'Passing Through Time (*An Orpheus Singing*)', *Dance Theatre Journal*, Summer 1996; Judith Mackrell, 'Secret Theatres', *Dance Now*, Summer 1996; Alastair Macaulay, 'Real Dancing, and/or Richard Alston', *Dancing Times*, January 1998.

Books Joan W. White (ed.), *Twentieth-Century Dance in Britain: A History of Major Dance Companies in Britain*, London, 1985; Stephanie Jordan, *Striding Out: Aspects of Contemporary and New Dance in Britain*, London, 1992.

LEA ANDERSON

One of the brightest discoveries of contemporary British dance in the mid-1980s was the Cholmondeleys (pronounced 'chumleez'), a hilariously, startlingly original trio named after an Elizabethan painting hanging in the Tate Gallery. Choreographer-dancer Lea Anderson, like her company co-founders Teresa Barker and Gaynor Coward, was a graduate of London's Laban Centre for Movement and Dance. A dropout from St Martin's School of Art, she had fronted rock bands prior to emerging from the Laban chrysalis. This background may help to explain her visual flair, and her early habit of constructing dances with the impact of a 45 rpm record; even some of her later, full-length work possesses the deliberate consecutiveness of an album or music gig. Another reason for the brevity, and scaled-down detail, of the first Cholmondeleys pieces was the size and nature of the venues they played: cramped clubs, rough pubs, even a space in a tunnel beneath the Thames, or on board a small riverboat-cum-art-gallery. This was fringe/chamber/cabaret dance. Perhaps Anderson, with her eye for offbeat, code-like gestures and telling physical quirks, was simply a born miniaturist.

In any case, she and her collaborators shared a view of human behaviour expressed in movement quite unlike anyone else's. The dances had a certain 'pop' quality, but were refreshingly free of predictability or cliché. Anderson's kinetic vocabulary sprouted from her observations of everyday body language mixed in with images, or moments, seized from cinema, magazine graphics, and the plastic arts. Her inventive use of Celtic jigs, Spanish dance, sports moves, and the like is a further demonstration of her satirical magpie mentality. And her rhythmic sense, evident in her unison work and tight patterning, was either acute or, as some critics have said, obsessively tidy, even rigid.

The dancers themselves flouted convention. None had the body of a classical ballet's fairy-tale princess, nor the showgirl willowiness common in mainstream contemporary dance. These young women were supple but sturdy, with a hidden reserve of hip, working-class character. When they eventually courted the glamorous, donning designer Sandy Powell's black rubber ballgowns or candy-coloured, feather-trimmed party frocks, it was never without an ironic awareness that these were costumes, whether funny, beautiful, or both. (Powell is one of Anderson's regular collaborators, along with Steve Blake, composer of peculiarly perky, brassy, powerfully percussive music, and Drostan Madden, a master of mix-and-match pre-recorded sound manipulation. That Anderson's creative cohorts, onstage and off, are her friends lends the work a trusting, generous tone that usually avoids insularity.)

In their early pieces the Cholmondeleys were deliciously dry-humoured comediennes, eager to scratch the itch out of formal dance rules; yet they also had no qualms about tickling the funnybone before delivering, with a flourish, a fast fist to the chest. Got up like white-faced, full-frocked ballerinas in their titular début dance *The Cholmondeley Sisters* in 1984, Anderson and Barker subtly thumbed their noses at classical stereotypes by concentrating on distractions (sweets, lipstick, hairpins) rather than proper poses. The ritualistic *Dragon* in 1985 started as a driven solo and ended as a trio, each new dancer repeating the same fierce, weighted moves executed by the first. *Baby, Baby, Baby* (1986), one of their most popular dances, was perfectly timed to a Nina Simone recording and marked by the kind of knowing, low-key, flutter-fingered idiosyncrasy of which Anderson is so fond. There was more gravity in *Marina* (1986), where vaguely aquatic moves were emotionally highlighted with shards of Bizet, Verdi, and Rossini, and *No Joy* (1987), in which sign language and facial manipulation were used to make distressing suggestions about levels of power and limits of communication.

As the Cholmondeleys expanded to include new members like the late Rossana Sen, Emma Gladstone (an erstwhile member of Matthew Bourne's Adventures in Motion Pictures), and Alexandra Reynolds (formerly half of the Sisters Bon Bon), so did Anderson's interest in choreographing for men as well as women. For the record, men had made a token appearance as backups in *Baby, Baby, Baby*. But in 1988, officially, the all-male Featherstonehaughs (pronounced 'fan-shaws') were born. In *Clump* (1987), one of their first dances and a tense, cunning, examination of masculine group mechanisms, Anderson had six men stomping, slouching, and strutting their way in and out of Tweedledum-Tweedledee conformity.

Working with both sexes may have enabled Anderson to test herself on a more ambitious scale. Since the unexpectedly epic *Flag* (1988), in which the two companies explored together the clichés and patterns of nationalism, she has taken risks with full-length, collage-like shows often built around a theme. In these she combines or separates the Chums and the Fans, as they're affectionately known, as she sees fit. Both troupes participated in *Birthday* in 1992, a sparkling blend of the funny, the wistful, and the anarchic, and in 1993's *Precious*, a piece predicated on aspects of alchemy and featuring some of Anderson's biggest, most free-flowing choreography to date.

Flesh and Blood (1989, revised version 1997) sent the Cholmondeleys alone into a more introspective state, in a piece that dwelt on obsession and fanaticism à la Joan of Arc. (It has the distinction of being the first postmodern dance to be set for A-level students.) The springboard for *Cold Sweat* (1990) was a diversity of climates and how that affected movement and mood. *Walky Talky* (1992), set in and around a huge bed, employed spoken text and a gentle sensuality to help bring the Chums' sisterly intimacy to the foreground. Anderson turned to road movies as inspiration for *Metacholica* (1994), as seven biker women teamed up in search of escape. In *Car* (1995), the company freed itself from the confinement of theatres and took to the road, touring to public spaces throughout Britain with three 15-minute shows set in, on, and around one sleek Saab 9000. Examining the role of the automobile as icon, the Cholmondeleys appeared consecutively as cool chicks in cat-suits, identically dressed Jackie Kennedys circa 22 November 1963, and Dadaists decked out in back-to-front period clothes.

The Featherstonehaughs have developed a collective identity quite distinct from their distaff siblings. Both *The Show* (1990) and *Big Feature* (1991), as well as *The Featherstonehaughs Go Las Vegas* (1995) consisted of short, sharp pieces strung together for an engaging gang of guys free of narcissistic macho attitude. Perhaps even more than the Chums, the Fans have come in all shapes and sizes, with backgrounds in such occupations as medicine, hairdressing, and tree surgery (further proof that Anderson rates a performer's personality above technical training). They mine something substantial out of a frisky, witty, deceptively casual style. Their performances are a seemingly loosely packaged collection of sophisticated, dance-based games whose starting-points range from cowboy and gangster movies and religious tableaux to boxing, show-biz superficiality, and Sinatra. They also hit emotive notes of anxiety, anger, passion, and tenderness without ever being ponderous. Working with men has elicited some of what is best in Anderson's dancemaking: her ability to take pop culture and kitsch and then to pinch, twist, and subvert them to her own ends; her application of cinematic editing techniques to dance, in order to change stage focus; and her penchant for cocking a snook at social role models.

With flair and imagination, Anderson has shown herself capable of breaking the Fans out of the formulas she created for them. Inspired in part by the films *Das Boot* and *Performance*, *The Bends* (1994–95) was originally staged as part of an all-night extravaganza in a London club. *Immaculate Conception* (1992) took place out of doors, as Anderson tried to fuse the effects of *film*

noir and Renaissance frescoes. For 1998's *The Featherstonehaughs Draw on the Sketch Books of Egon Schiele*, she has hooked her fastidious and beguiling aesthetic to that of the mannered, morbid Viennese painter Schiele, with striking results.

Anderson has choreographed for theatre and film, and television has afforded her the space to deploy her skills as a film-maker. Apart from creating new pieces and adapting previously staged ones for the small screen, she has written and presented two seasons of *Tights, Camera, Action!*, a television series based on her pick of short dance films from the archives of the British Channel 4 station. She has also received commissions from several dance and theatre companies, and taken up innovative, large-scale projects. In 1989 the French government invited her to Paris to choreograph the British section of a parade commemorating the bicentennial celebrations of the French Revolution; two years later she staged *Opéra sportif*, an open-air athletics theatre event involving over a hundred performers in Leicester.

Anderson has underwhelmed some British critics, especially those who adhere to a more traditional credo. They say she has not developed much beyond the small, jokey talent she had when she started out, that she can do little more than concoct absurdist vignettes, getting stuck in choreographic grooves and surrounding herself with dancers as incapable of virtuosity as she is. It is true that at times some of her work has seemed habitually clever rather than inspired, and she has occasionally lapsed into the choreographic doldrums bred by over-familiarity. Yet Anderson is far from burned out (she has remarked that she hopes to be making dances for middle-aged Chums and Fans), and the inventive fun she and her dancers have, and give, onstage goes beyond the frivolous. Together Anderson's two companies seem likely to remain a vital force in British dance beyond the millennium.

Donald Hutera

Biographical details

Born in London, 13 June 1959. **Studied** at
Middlesex College, 1977; studied art at St Martin's
School of Art, London, 1978–79; studied dance at
the Laban Centre, London, 1981–84. **Career** Co-
founder and choreographer of the female dancing
trio, the Cholmondeley Sisters (later renamed
the Cholmondeleys), 1986: company became a
quartet in 1988; also co-founder and choreographer of a male sextet, the Featherstonehaughs, in
1988. Presented series, *Tights, Camera, Action!*,
for British television, 1992. **Awards** between 1988
and 1997 include Bonnie Bird Award, three *Time
Out* Awards, two Digital Dance Awards, two
London Dance and Performance Awards, and a
Bagnolet Festival Award; in 1997 was made a
Laban Centre Honorary Fellow.

Works

The Cholmondeley Sisters (mus. Drostan Madden,
1984), *Pole Dance* (mus. Dead Can Dance, 1984),
Health and Efficiency (mus. Drostan Madden,
1984), *Dragon* (mus. Drostan Madden, 1985),
Signals (mus. Goat, 1985), *Kolo* (1985), *Cutty Sark*
(ambient sound, 1985), *The Clichés and the
Holidays* (mus. traditional Catalan, 1985), *Baby,
Baby, Baby* (mus. Donaldson, Kahn, sung by Nina
Simone, 1986), *La Paloma* (mus. Mexican, 1986),
The Fly and the Crow (mus. Drostan Madden,
1986), *Heel in the Earth* (mus. Cocteau Twins,
1986), *Renoir, mon tricot* (no music, 1986), *Marina*
(mus. Bizet, Rossini, Verdi, 1986), *But We Don't
Know What . . .* (mus. Drostan Madden, 1987), *No
Joy* (mus. Drostan Madden, 1987), *Fish Wreck*
(mus. Drostan Madden, 1987), *Carriage of Arms*
(mus. traditional Bulgarian, 1987), *Clump* (mus.
Steve Blake, 1987), *Wear 2 Next* (mus. Steve
Blake, 1988), *Big Dance Number* (mus. Drostan
Madden, Steve Blake, 1988), *Pastorale* (mus. Steve
Blake, 1988), *Venus in the Mourning* (mus.
Drostan Madden, 1988), *Parfum de la nuit* (mus.
Bellini, sung by Maria Callas, 1988), *The Futurists*
(mus. Drostan Madden, 1988), *Flag* (mus. Drostan
Madden, Steve Blake, 1988), *Slump* (mus. Steve
Blake, 1988), *Flesh and Blood* (mus. Steve Blake,
1989; revised version, mus. Steve Blake, Victims
of Death, 1997), *Factor 6* (mus. Steve Blake, 1990),
The Show (mus. various, 1990), *Marseillaise*
(1990), *Cold Sweat* (mus. Drostan Madden, Steve
Blake, 1990), *Le Jeu interior de tennis* (mus.
Drostan Madden, C. Khader, 1990), *Sardinas*
(mus. Steve Blake, 1990), *Big Feature* (mus. various, 1991), *Opéra sportif* (mus. Steve Blake, 1991),
Birthday (mus. Steve Blake, 1992), *Walky Talky*
(with Anne Rabbitt, mus. Drostan Madden, 1992),
Immaculate Conception (mus. Steve Blake, 1992),

Cross Channel (mus. Steve Blake, 1992), *Perfect
Moment* (mus. Steve Blake, 1992), *Jesus Baby
Heater* (mus. Steve Blake, 1992), *Precious* (mus.
Steve Blake, 1993), *Dirt* (mus. Perry Mackintosh,
The Fall, 1993), *Metalcholica* (mus. Drostan
Madden, 1994), *Waiting* (mus. Steve Blake, 1994),
Spectre de la rose (mus. Drostan Madden, 1994;
video version, 1995), *Joan* (solo for television,
mus. Drostan Madden, 1994), *Cabaret* (musical by
John Kander and Fred Ebb, 1994), *Khovanschina*
(opera by Mussorgsky, 1994), *24-Hour Feather-
stonehaughs* (mus. Drostan Madden, 1994; touring version, as *The Bends*, 1995), *The Featherstonehaughs Go Las Vegas* (mus. Steve Blake
and Drostan Madden, 1995), *Car* (mus. Drostan
Madden, 1995; film version, 1997), *Reverse Effect*
(mus. Steve Blake, Victims of Death 1996), *Les
Six Belles* (piece for dance students, 1997).

Further reading

Interviews with Barbara Newman, in 'Lea
Anderson of the Cholmondeleys', *Dancing Times*,
November 1987; with Valerie Briginshaw, *Dance
Matters*, Summer 1995; with Sophie Constanti, *The
Independent*, 15 July 1995.

Articles Judith Mackrell, 'Cholmondeleyism',
Dance Theatre Journal, Summer 1986; Sophie
Constanti, 'Easing the Load', *Dance Theatre
Journal*, Summer 1987; Sarah Rubidge, 'Political
Dance', *Dance Theatre Journal*, Autumn 1989;
Sophie Constanti, 'First and Last', *Dancing Times*,
January 1990; David Hughes, 'Cholmondeleys',
Dance Theatre Journal, Summer 1990; Allen
Robertson, 'Letter from Europe', *Dance Ink*,
December 1990; Jann Parry, 'Opéra sportif',
Dance Theatre Journal, Summer 1991; Klaus
Witzeling, 'Lea Anderson at Kampnagel', *Ballett
International*, July 1994; Sherril Dodds, 'Lea
Anderson and the Age of Spectacle', *Dance
Theatre Journal*, Winter 1995/96; Valerie
Briginshaw, 'Getting the Glamour on Our Own
Terms', *Dance Theatre Journal*, Winter 1995/96.

Books Allen Robertson and Donald Hutera, *The
Dance Handbook*, Harlow, Essex, 1988; Judith
Mackrell, *Out of Line: The Story of British New
Dance*, London, 1992.

KAROLE ARMITAGE

If, during her professional beginnings with
the ballet company of the Grand Théâtre de

Genève, the young American Karole Armitage made any kind of splash dancing corps de ballet roles, our dance literature doesn't prominently record it. By 1977, however, after a year in the Merce Cunningham Dance Company, the wiry young woman from Kansas had come to some notice. The newcomer was paired with the choreographer himself in a duet from his new *Squaregame*. Furthermore, Armitage's rangy reach and delicate control of Cunninghamian complexity told of personal distinction quite apart from that of being chosen to work directly alongside the maestro himself. With her almost pixie-like face, enigmatically impassive and framed by a precisely fringed haircut, Armitage gently drew her viewers into her expert way with Cunningham's art. In Arlene Croce's essay on the Cunningham season that offered the premiere of *Squaregame* and the local debut of Armitage, the critic singled out the 'duet in which [Cunningham] supports the most talented of his new dancers, Karole Armitage'.

More roles and more notice followed at an increasing pace. Soon, the notable dancer put on her own show. Her choreographic debut work, *Ne* (1978), took place in a high school gymnasium. It featured Armitage and two other dancers, some neon light tubes, and a rock band called The The. Croce found the event impressive. She called Armitage's vision 'new' and 'right', suggesting that *Ne* would be remembered because of 'its audacity for bringing concert dance together with punk-rock music'.

By 1981, Armitage had left Cunningham. In the process she had punked her smooth hairdo into feathery spikes and she gained further notice the same year with perhaps her most ambitious work to date: a hurricane-wild and thunderously loud creation for six dancers, including Armitage, as well as five musicians, including Rhys Chatham, the composer. Called *Drastic Classicism*, the two-part work had dark-toned, chic costuming by Charles Atlas (stiff tutus over

skinny trousers, for example). The high-decibel sound level of the score prompted the management of the small-space theatre, New York City's Dance Theater Workshop, to provide earplugs for the faint of eardrum. In impact, Armitage's dance inventions had the air of Cunninghamian and ballet-schooled moves put in a blender set at higher and higher speed.

Following somewhat in the footsteps of Loie Fuller and Isadora Duncan, Armitage decided to pursue her choreographic career in Europe, partly in England, largely in France. Ironically, Britain's Michael Clark, the ballet dancer turned new-wave choreographer whom Armitage profoundly inspired and influenced, first worked with her in New York, during one of her returns to home turf. What might be called the Atlas phase of Armitage's career was played out during the first half of the 1980s. Atlas not only provided Armitage with original and eye-catching design elements for her works, but also collaborated closely with her on film and video projects of his own direction.

This period culminated in 1985 with a suite of duets, $-p = dH/dq$, later re-titled *The Watteau Duets*. In this series of unconventional *pas de deux*, Armitage, partnered by the former Cunningham dancer Joseph Lennon, variously put herself on pointe. The space-age-ballerina look to these moments no doubt recalled the pointework choreography Armitage explored in *GV–10*, a 1984 commission from the Paris Opéra Ballet's director Rudolf Nureyev for his troupe's experimental wing. (One of the dancers Armitage cast in this work was Sylvie Guillem, soon to be an internationally acclaimed ballerina, who was then finishing her school years.)

The latter half of the 1980s marks the Salle period of Armitage's work, identifying her collaboration with the American post-modernist/neo-expressionist painter David Salle. This phase began with a grand concoction for American Ballet Theatre, called *The Mollino Room* (1985) and starring Mikhail

Baryshnikov. First unveiled on the opera house stage of Washington, D.C.'s Kennedy Center and subsequently given on the even vaster stage of New York's Metropolitan Opera House, Armitage's work for male dancer, solo couple, and subsidiary ensemble couples tickled the fancy of some in the know and aroused the ire of other critics. (*The New York Post*'s Clive Barnes characterized the affair with phrases like 'pretentious monstrosity' and 'a cultural con job'.) Set to some astringent music by Paul Hindemith and an acidly funny routine by the comedy team Nichols and May, *The Mollino Room* was withdrawn from repertory before it could really hit its stride. Salle's decor and costumes were wilfully disconnected and uncommonly handsome; Armitage's casting and choreography were largely witty and confidently discursive.

Some of Armitage's most lavish creations occurred in collaboration with Salle. In 1986, when the choreographer founded her own company, Armitage Ballet, she choreographed *The Elizabethan Phrasing of the Late Albert Ayler*, a three-act work that built on the scheme of *The Mollino Room*. Sometimes Armitage would dance, on and off pointe, in the pieces of this period. Other times she presented work made on the often notably talented, unknown ballet dancers she had hired. Salle's high-profile art world fellows also came to collaborate with Armitage, notably the controversial and fun-loving Jeff Koons. Throughout these and later creations, Armitage was an inspired director. Though her design elements came from a range of hands – Salle, Koons, Christian Lacroix – her stage pictures regularly achieved final results of indelible and spectacular dance theatre that can only be called Armitagean.

Though Armitage's artistic connection to Salle continued intermittently as her career moved into the late 1990s, her consistent collaboration with him more or less ended at the same time as their personal relationship about 1990. Around this time,

the choreographer, who had become more favoured in the art world than in the dance quarter, lost some of her dancemaking career's momentum. For a period she abandoned dance and studied filmmaking. She also freelanced as a choreographer for music videos and touring rock shows, including work with the Dyvinals, Milli Vanilli, Madonna, and Michael Jackson.

With her own troupe disbanded, Armitage once more turned to the world of stage choreography, working mostly with ballet troupes on a European circuit. These works have consistently intermingled her interests in *danse d'école* methods with the visions of bold costuming and stage decoration. The 'company' credit for *The Dog is Us* (1994) lists Deutsche Oper Ballett, Berlin, and six poodles. The last named 'performers' are also part of Salle's set, which shows six clear-coloured niches framing as many standard French poodles, each seemingly dressed in human-scale evening gowns and gesticulating evening-gloved arms.

After writing and directing her own 1992 film, *Hall of Mirrors*, Armitage went on to appear in Salle's first film project, *Search and Destroy* (1994). The title, derived from a military maneuvre inspiring the name of the play that gave the film its script, resonates with Armitagean philosophy. In promotional work and artistic deed, Karole Armitage has zeroed in on the state of her dance culture and, with relish, the postmodern ballerina-turned-dancemaker looks for the nearest sitting duck and zaps it.

After freelancing with a variety of German, Swiss and French companies, Armitage was appointed in 1996 as Artistic Director of the MaggioDanza, in Florence. Here she continued her ambitious theatrical mixtures of music, dance, and spectacle – and her fondness for working with noted designers. In 1997 she choreographed Handel's *Apollo e Dafne*, transforming the allegorical symbols of the original into modern-day imagery, the choreography underpinned by a full orchestra of contemporary instruments and with set and costume designs by the period-film director/designer James Ivory. At the time of writing, her plans for 1998 included a version of *Pinocchio* with costumes by the fashion iconoclast Jean-Paul Gaultier.

Robert Greskovic

Biographical details

Born in Madison, Wisconsin, United States, 3 March 1954. **Studied** at the North Carolina School of the Arts, and with Bill Evans, University of Utah, 1971–72; also a scholarship student at the School of American Ballet and the Harkness School of Dance. **Career** Danced with Geneva Opéra Ballet (under Patricia Neary), Switzerland, 1972–75, and with the Merce Cunningham Dance Company, 1976–80; began choreographing for own group from 1978, becoming artistic director of the Armitage Dance Company, based in New York, 1980–86, sometimes appearing as Armitage Gone! Dance (from c.1983), and becoming the Armitage Ballet from 1986; appointed artistic director, MaggioDanza, Florence, 1996. Has also choreographed for American Ballet Theatre, Ballet de Monte Carlo, Bavarian State Opera Ballet (Munich), Charleroi Danse, Extemporary Dance Theatre, Deutsch Oper Ballett (Berlin), Lyon Opéra Ballet, Les Nomades (Lausanne), Oregon Ballet Theater, Paris Opéra Ballet, Tasmanian Dance Company, and for the singers Madonna and Michael Jackson. **Awards** include Guggenheim Fellowship, 1986.

Works

Ne (mus. The The, 1978), *Do We Could* (silent, 1979), *Objectstacle* (1980), *Vertige* (mus. Rhys Chatham, 1980), *Drastic Classicism* (mus. Rhys Chatham, 1981), *It Happened at Club Bombay Cinema* (mus. various, 1982), *Slaughter on McDougal Street* (mus. Rhys Chatham, 1982), *Paradise* (1982; revised version, mus. Jeffrey Lohn, 1983), *The Nutcracker* (with Rosella Hightower; mus. Tchaikovsky, 1982), *The Last Gone Dance* (mus. David Linton, 1983), *A Real Gone Dance* (mus. Jeffrey Lohn, 1983), *Parafango* (television dance, 1983), *Contact* (1984), *Tasmanian Devil* (also called *G-Vehicle*; mus. Sara Hopkins, 1984), *GV-10* (mus. Stockhausen, 1984), *Ex-Romance* (mus. Jeffrey Lohn, 1984), *The Watteau Duets* (originally entitled *–p = dH/dq*; mus. David Linton, 1985), *The Mollino Room*

(mus. Hindemith, 1985), *The Elizabethan Phrasing of the Late Albert Ayler* (mus. various, 1986), *Les Anges ternis* (The Tarnished Angels) (mus. Charles Mingus, 1987), *Les Stances à Sophie* (mus. Art Ensemble of Chicago, 1987), *Duck Dances* (mus. Jeffrey Lohn, 1988), *Kammerdisco* (mus. Jeffrey Lohn, 1988), *GoGo Ballerina* (mus. Jimi Hendrix, 1988), *Contempt* (mus. various, text Bret Easton Ellis, 1989), *Without You I'm Nothing* (film, dir. Boskovich, 1989), *Forty Guns* (mus. traditional American, 1990), *Dancing Zappa* (mus. Frank Zappa, 1990), *Jack and Betty* (mus. John Zorn, 1990), *The Marmot Quickstep* (mus. David Shea, 1991), *Renegade Dance Wave* (mus. Renegade Sound Wave, 808 State, 1991), *Overboard* (mus. David Shea, 1991), *Vogue* (video clip for Madonna, 1991), *Chain of Desire* (film, dir. Lopez, 1991), *Segunda Piel* (mus. David Shea, 1992), *Happy Birthday Rossini* (mus. Rossini, David Shea, 1992), *In the Closet* (video clip for Michael Jackson, 1992), *Hall of Mirrors* (film, dir. Armitage, 1992), *Hucksters of the Soul* (David Shea, 1993), *I Had a Dream* (mus. various baroque, 1993), *Hovering at the Edge of Chaos* (mus. various, 1994), *Tattoo and Tutu* (mus. Shocklee Brothers, 1994), *The Dog is Us* (mus. Carl Stalling, David Shea, Shocklee Brothers, 1994), *Search and Destroy* (film, dir. Salle, 1994), *Il viaggio di Scherazade* (mus. David Shea, Rimsky-Korsakov, Roy Nathanson, 1995), *The Predators' Ball* (expanded version of *Hucksters of the Soul*; mus. Phillip Johnson, Public Enemy; script John Gould Rubin, 1996), *Apollo e Dafne* (mus. Handel, 1997), *Weather of Reality* (mus. Seanski, 1997).

Further reading

Interviews with Otis Stuart, in 'Madonna of the Rock', *Ballett International*, January 1985; with John Mueller, in 'Making Musical Dance', *Ballet Review*, Winter 1986.

Articles Marcelle Michel and others, 'Danser au soleil', *Pour la Danse*, October 1980; Jochen Schmidt, 'What Moves Them and How', *Ballett International*, June/July 1982; Jann Parry, 'Of a Feather, Flock', *Dance and Dancers*, November 1982; Christine Rhodes, 'Karole Armitage à la pointe de l'aiguille', *Pour la Danse*, October 1982; Alastair Macaulay, 'Not Actually Extemporising', *Dance Theatre Journal*, May 1983; Odon-Jérôme Lemaître, 'Paradise de Karole Armitage', *Pour la Danse*, January 1984; Otis Stuart, 'Karole Armitage', *Pour la Danse*, February 1985; Robert Greskovic, 'Armitagean Physics, or the Shoes of a Ballerina', *Ballet Review*, Summer 1985; Jean Claude Diénis, 'Karole Armitage, danseuse de haut volt', *Danser*, September 1985; John Mueller, 'Making Musical Dance', *Ballet Review*, Winter 1986; Elizabeth Zimmer, 'Out There with Karole Armitage', *Dance Magazine*, May 1986; Judith Mackrell, 'Kitsch and Courtship at the Umbrella', *Dance Theatre Journal*, Spring 1986; J. Johnston, 'The Punk Princess and the Postmodern Prince', *Art in America* (Marion, Ohio), October 1986; Anita Finkel, 'New York: Thème de Karole', *Ballett International*, April 1987; Stuart Otis, 'The Neoclassical Phrasing of the Now Karole Armitage', *Ballet Review*, Winter 1988; Tiziana Mantovani, 'La principessa della danza contemporanea', *Danza e danza*, November 1989; special Armitage issue of *Les Saisons de la Danse*, October 1993; Francesca Pedroni, 'Armitage in Florence', *Ballett International*, December 1995.

Books Arlene Croce, *Going to the Dance*, New York, 1982; Deborah Jowitt, *The Dance in Mind*, Boston, 1985; Arlene Croce, *Sight Lines*, New York, 1987; Allen Robertson and Donald Hutera, *The Dance Handbook*, Harlow, Essex, 1988; Peter Schjeldahl, *Karole Armitage and David Salle: 3 Years of the Ballet Stage*, Kyoto, Japan, 1989; Sally Banes, *Writing Dancing in the Age of Postmodernism*, Hanover (New Hampshire) and London, 1994.

PINA BAUSCH

Pina Bausch is one of the outstanding personalities of dance in the second half of the twentieth century. From the start, her dance-theatre was a revolt against classical ballet which was then, as she saw it, stuck in provincialism and beauty as an end in itself. Her theatrical montage of scenes always has the same subject: human relationships, especially the relationship between men and women. Her approach became a model and a credo for a whole generation of choreographers, directors, and filmmakers. By rejecting harmonious and aesthetic dance she has focused on the expressionism of movement.

Pina Bausch began her dancing career in 1955, at the age of fourteen, at the Folkwang School in Essen, where she trained under Kurt Jooss, himself a pupil of Rudolf von Laban, the theoretician of movement and initiator of German expressionist dancing. Jooss, a choreographer devoted to the theatre, pointed the young Bausch in the direction of the theatre. In the late 1950s she studied in New York under Antony Tudor, José Limón, Alfredo Corvino, La Méri, and Louis Horst. She danced at the Metropolitan Opera in the companies of Paul Sanasardo and Donya Feuer, and she worked with the Graham soloist Paul Taylor. Here she must have experienced the American pluralism of styles and the beginning of the postmodernist movement.

In 1962 Pina Bausch became a soloist with Kurt Jooss's newly founded Folkwang Ballet in Essen; in 1969 she took over its direction. Her first creative period in the late 1960s and early 1970s was contemporary with the time of angry young filmmakers, who radically changed the classics and used unusual techniques, such as rock and pop music, and projections or works of art instead of illustrative settings. This antibourgeois and partly anarchistic theatre looked for a new language and for the immediacy of a lost sensuality. It also questioned its own medium. What is theatre, what can it do, what does it want? Theatre and modern dance turned to new methods. Especially in the United States, stage and film actors trained in the sense-memory approach according to the Strasberg method, incorporating their own experiences, and thus improvisation was increasingly used by both actors and dancers.

Improvisation and the memory of her own experiences also characterize Pina Bausch's work. On the one hand she provides movements with which the dancers can improvise further. On the other hand she asks questions – about parents, childhood, feelings in specific situations, the use of objects, dislikes, injuries, aspirations. From the answers develop gestures, sentences, dialogues, little scenes. When a dancer hops around and around in a circle singing 'I am tired, I am tired' (*Tanzabend I*), the moment recalls a childhood ritual seeking consolation from loneliness and tiredness. Other scenes are more complicated and can only be explained in connection with other thematically related scenes. For each production Pina Bausch collects scraps of memory and ideas for movements. She once said: 'Es ist ja alles erst einmal nichts ... Es beginnt ganz klein und wird dann größer' [In the beginning there is nothing. It starts very small and then becomes bigger]. Before starting rehearsal she has a concept, but she changes it all the time (even after the dress-rehearsal or the first night), rearranging the scenes and finally linking them together. In this process the dancers provide the biographical material, but Pina Bausch is the stimulating and continuously reorganizing authority.

The result is a series of scenes including speech and direct contact with the audience, with loud, revue-type formations and long, still, almost photographic picture settings, always interrupted by short dancing sequences: these include an ironically suggested classic combination of steps, a short modern solo, a typical 'Bausch-Reigen' in which the whole ensemble moves one after the other across the stage performing identical movements. All these choreographical novelties were iconoclastic in the 1970s and early 1980s, but have now become common dance methods and strategies.

Bausch developed her open dance-theatre in stages. In *Im Wind der Seit* (1968), her breakthrough piece, she still worked with traditional composition techniques and the vocabulary of modern dance which she had learned at the Folkwang School in Essen and in New York. In *Nachnull* of 1970 the vocabulary began to break up. In *Aktionen für Tänzer* (1971) she further developed the broken-up style and included theatrical elements.

This development was briefly halted when she became director in Wuppertal. Under the influence of the manager, Arno Wüstenhöfer, she choreographed Wagner's *Tannhäuser* in 1972 and the Gluck operas

Iphigenie auf Tauris and *Orpheus und Eurydike* in 1974 and 1975. Her last fully choreographed piece was Stravinsky's *Frühlingsopfer* in 1975. After that followed a series of dance-theatre plays commencing with *Komm, tanz mit mir* (1977), a form which she had already introduced in 1974 in *Fritz* and the half-hour-long *Ich Bring dich um die Ecke*. Thus Bausch has stooped to work with libretti and classic musical compositions on occasions, but these occasions have been few. And when she did, it was only to break them up, and alter them, as the title of her 1977 work declares: *Blaubart – beim Anhören einer Tonbandaufnahme von Béla Bartóks Oper 'Herzog Blaubarts Burg'* [Bluebeard – While listening to a recording of Béla Bartók's opera 'Herzog Blaubarts Burg']. In this work, Bausch has Bluebeard listening to the opera on a tape recorder on wheels; he often interrupts to rewind and replay sequences. Thus the symbolic story of Bluebeard is shattered and transposed into a contemporary reality.

Some of Pina Bausch's work reflects the patterns of masculine behaviour. There are scenes in which several men continuously stroke the same woman, touch her and pose in front of her. Women are seen to defend themselves physically in her works. Bausch clearly expresses her feminist position, turning against the old patriarchal clichés without, however, denouncing men. Characteristically, men often wear women's clothes, signalling that Bausch considers them to be as sensitive as women. In all her scenes, whether sarcastic, shrill, humorous, or quiet, one feeling above all is expressed: the longing to be loved.

Bausch has broken with traditions and conventions wherever she can. Thus she has not used conventional décor. Usually the whole stage is empty and the brick walls are visible. But then the empty space is crammed with tables and chairs, as in *Café Müller* (1978), with armchairs and realistic crocodiles, as in *Keuschheitslegende* (1979), or with a fairground booth, a piano, a water-sprinkler in other productions. With this sort of furniture Bausch's most important stage-designers, her partner Rolf Borzig (up to his death in 1980), Peter Pabst, Ulrich Bergfelder, and Gralf-Edzart Habben created stylized, everyday places – living rooms, cafés, public spaces – the limitations these imposed on the dances being intentional. At other times the stage has been turned into a natural environment with the help of old leaves, layers of peat, puddles of water, grass, bushes, large cacti, fields of carnations, sand-dunes, and so forth. These wonderful stage-landscapes could be created because Bausch allowed her designers to develop their own artistic ideas and creative powers. Her intention was not to present dance as necessarily pretty, but to test the expressive possibilities of dance.

Bausch also rejected customary approaches to costuming. Men wear suits and women high-heeled shoes, dresses, and evening gowns in the 1950s style; later costumes became more timeless and were made from richer and more luxurious materials and colours. This typical Bausch look was quickly copied. It emphasizes its opposition to classical ballet and strongly evokes social reality.

After *Blaubart* the music to Bausch's works became collages. With very few exceptions Bausch's new dramatization of loosely connected scenes almost necessitated spliced-in, prerecorded music. She used clips from classical works, arias, folk songs, marches, tangos and above all popular songs from the 1920s to 1950s. This approach enabled her to evoke a different atmosphere quickly, or to make musical, contextual comments. The songs are used partly to make ironic comments or to suggest the insincerity of the texts or one's own wishful notions.

These play situations and picture metaphors, developed from autobiographical contributions and improvisation, are meant to encourage the audience to sympathize. At first they confused and irritated the audience; the new fragmentary character of the works was found to be provocative. As a reflection of a battered world it was unconsciously felt to be threatening; its closeness to the private sphere seemed shocking. Indeed, although the private moments and personal settings were artistically handled and stylistically transformed, there remained an intimacy that was unsettling. But the consternation and confusion an audience might feel is intended. Her theatrical forms are a means to an end; she wants to send a message to the audience and force them out of a mood of passive reception. Bausch's style has, however, changed over the years; the provocation has become quieter. The later work has emphasized poetic quality.

Finally, Bausch was the choreographer who rediscovered body language. By rejecting the aesthetic beauty of codified classical dance, she returned to the natural beauty of movement and focused on the smallest gestures – the movement of a leg, a hip, a shoulder. Bausch can make every part of the body dance. Such small, isolated movements can be happy, cheeky explorations of the body; but Bausch also shows us the other side of the coin, the whole repertoire of everyday gestures, unconsciously learned, in which dangerous clichés manifest themselves. By highlighting these patterns of behaviour and mannerisms she makes us aware of the danger of manipulation. As she has asked, 'Was Spiele ich, täusche ich vor und wer bin ich wirklich?' [Which role am I acting, what do I pretend and who am I really?], Bausch questions the nature of identity. In the deeply distressing image that dominated one piece, the body of a dancer, Dominique Mercy, collapsed and was moved and manipulated by other dancers. Mercy becomes a helpless nonbeing. Only someone who continues to question herself, like Bausch, is able to create such deeply touching physical images. They have existed for a long time, but it took Bausch to force us to re-examine them. There have been many imitators, but none has been able, like Bausch, to create such an atmosphere with an empty room, a song, a little, apparently meaningless gesture.

Malve Gradinger

Biographical details

Born Philippine Bausch in Solingen, Germany, 27 July 1940. **Studied** with Kurt Jooss at the Folkwang School, Essen, 1955–59, and later with Antony Tudor and José Limón at the Juilliard School of Music, New York, 1960–61. **Career** Danced in the United States with the New American Ballet and Metropolitan Opera Ballet (under Tudor), New York, 1961–62, and with the Paul Taylor Company, 1962; soloist, Folkwang Ballet, Essen, 1962–68, choreographing her first work for the company (*Fragmente*) in 1968; made director of the Folkwang Ballet's Dance Studio, 1969; freelance soloist and choreographer in Europe and the United States, 1970–73; founder and artistic director, Wuppertal Tanztheater, Wuppertal, 1973; director, dance section of the Conservatoire Folkwang, 1983–89, and head of its dance studio since 1983. Elected to East Berlin Academy of Arts, 1991. **Awards** include Cologne Choreography Competition First Prize, 1969; German Dance Prize, 1995; Joana Maria Gorvin Dance Prize, 1995.

Works

Fragmente [Fragments] (mus. Bartók, 1968), *Im Wind der Zeit* [In the Winds of Time] (mus. Mirko Dorner, 1968), *The Fairie Queen* (opera by Purcell, 1969), *Nachnull* [After-zero] (mus. Ivo Malec, 1970), *Aktionen für Tänzer* [Actions for Dancers] (mus. Günter Becker, 1971), *Tannhäuser-Bacchanale* (mus. Wagner, 1972), *Wiegenlied* [Lullaby] (mus. song 'Maikäfer flieg', 1972), *Fritz* (mus. Mahler, Gustav Hufschmidt, 1974), *Iphigenie auf Tauris* [Iphigenia in Tauris] (opera by Gluck, 1974), *Zwei Kravatten* [Two Ties] (mus. Detlef Schoenberg, Günter Christmann, 1974), *Ich bring dich um die Ecke . . .* [I murder you] (mus. various pop songs, 1974), *Orpheus und Eurydike* (opera; mus. Gluck, 1975), *Frühlingsopfer* [The Rite of Spring] (consisting of *Wind from the West, The Second Spring*, and *Le Sacre du Printemps*; mus. Stravinsky, 1975), *Die sieben Todsünden* [The Seven Deadly Sins] (consisting of *The Seven Deadly Sins of the Bourgeoisie* and *Don't Be Afraid*; mus. Weill, 1976), *Blaubart – beim Anhören einer Tonbandaufnahme von Béla Bartóks Oper 'Herzog Blaubarts Burg'* [Bluebeard – While Listening to a Tape Recording of Béla Bartók's Opera 'Duke Bluebeard's Castle'] (mus. Bartók, 1977), *Komm, tanz mit mir* [Come, Dance with Me] (mus. folk songs, 1977), *Renate Wandert Aus* [Renate Emigrates] (mus. various, 1977), *Er nimmt sie an der Hand und führt sie in das Schloss, die anderen folgen* [He Takes Her by the Hand and Leads Her into the Castle – The Others Follow] (1978), *Café Müller* (mus. Purcell, 1978), *Kontakthof* (mus. various, 1978), *Arien* [Arias] (mus. various, 1979), *Keuschheitslegende* [Legend of Chastity] (mus. and texts various, 1979), *1980 – Ein Stück von Pina Bausch* [1980 – A Piece by Pina Bausch] (mus. various, 1980), *Bandoneon* (mus. tangos, 1980) *Walzer* [Waltzes] (mus. waltzes and traditional, 1982), *Tanzabend 1* [Dance Evening 1] (mus. collage, 1982), *Nelken* [Carnations] (mus. various, 1982; revised version, 1983), *Auf dem Gebirge hat Man ein Geschrie Gehört* [On the Mountain a Cry Was Heard] (mus. various, 1984), *Two Cigarettes in the Dark* (mus. Ravel, 1985), *Viktor* (mus. collage, 1986), *Ahnen* [Foreshadowers] (mus. collage, 1987), *Palermo, Palermo* (mus. collage, 1990), *Tanzabend 2* [Dance Evening 2] (world music, arr. Matthias Burkart, 1991), *Das Schiff* [The Ship] (mus. various ethnic, 1993), *Ein Trauerspiel* [A Tragedy] (mus. collage, 1994), *Über allen Gipfel ist Ruh* [Peace Reigns over the Mountain Tops] (1995), *Danzon* (mus. various, 1995), *Nur Du* [Only You] (mus. various pop, 1996), *Das Fensterputzer* [The Window Washer] (mus. various, 1997).

Further reading

Interview with Nadine Meisner, in 'Come Dance with Me', *Dance and Dancers*, November 1992.

Articles Horst Koegler, 'Exponent of the Avant-garde: Pina Bausch', *Dance Magazine*, February 1979; Raimund Hoghe, 'The Theatre of Pina Bausch', *Drama Review*, March 1980; Norbert Servos, 'Emancipation of Dance: Pina Bausch and the Wuppertal Dance Theatre', *Modern Drama*, January 1981; Helmut Scheier, 'The Woman from Wuppertal: The Career of Pina Bausch and Her Wuppertal Dance Theatre', *Dance and Dancers*, September 1982; F. Quadri (trans. M. Shore), 'The Auto-representation of Pina Bausch', *Art Forum*, February 1984; Allen Robertson, 'Close Encounters', *Ballet News*, June 1984; R. Langer (trans. R. Sikes), 'A Commentary of the Place of Pina Bausch in Contemporary Dance' and 'Compulsion and Restraint, Love and Angst: The Postwar Expressionism of Pina Bausch', *Dance Magazine*, June 1984; Philippa Wehle, 'Pina

Bausch's Tanztheater: A Place of Difficult Encounter', *Women and Performance*, Winter 1984; 'Pina Bausch' entry in *Current Biography Yearbook 1986*; Marcia Siegel, 'Carabosse in a Cocktail Dress', *Hudson Review*, Spring 1986; Ann Daly, 'Tanztheater: The Thrill of the Lynch Mob or the Rage of a Woman?', *Drama Review*, Summer 1986; 'What the Critics Say about Tanztheater', *Drama Review*, Summer 1986; Larry Kaplan, 'Pina Bausch: Dancing Around the Issue', *Ballet Review*, Spring 1987; Marianne Goldberg, 'Artifice and Authenticity: Gender Scenarios in Pina Bausch's Dance Theatre', *Women and Performance*, 4(2), 1989; Jochen Schmidt, 'The Wuppertal Choreographer Pina Bausch: The Mother Courage of Modern Dance', *Ballett International*, June/July 1990; D.W. Price, 'The Politics of the Body: Pina Bausch's Tanztheater', *Theatre Journal*, October 1990; Chris de Marigny, 'Theatre of Despair and Survival', *Dance Theatre Journal*, Autumn 1991; Ann Nugent, '*The Green Table* and *Café Müller*', *Dance Now*, Autumn 1992; Susan Kozel, 'Bausch and Phenomenology', *Dance Now*, Winter 1993/94; Kay Kirchman, 'The Totality of the Body: An Essay on Pina Bausch's Aesthetic', *Ballett International*, May 1994; Josephine Leask, 'Pictures from Childhood', *Dance Now*, Autumn 1995; Norbert Servos, 'Why Do People Fall in Love' (on *Nur Du*), *Ballett International*, 7, 1996.

Books Raimund Hoghe, *Bandoneon: Für wass kann Tango alles gut sein?*, Darmstadt, 1981; Leonetta Bentivoglio (ed.), *Tanztheater: dalla espressionista a Pina Bausch*, Rome, 1982; Norbert Servos, *Pina Bausch Wuppertal Dance Theatre, or the Art of Training a Goldfish*, translated by Patricia Stadié, Cologne, 1984; Guy Delahaye (photographs), with Raphael de Gubernatis and Leonetta Bentivoglio (texts), *Pina Bausch*, Malakoff, France, 1986; Raimund Hoghe, *Pina Bausch: Tanztheatergeschichten*, Frankfurt, 1986 (in French, as *Pina Bausch: Histoires de théâtre dansé*, Paris, 1987); Arlene Croce, *Sight Lines*, New York, 1987; Leonore Mau (photos) and Ronald Kay (text), *Ensemble: Pina Bausch, Das Tanztheater Wuppertal: Portraits*, St Gallen, 1988; Johannes Birringer, 'Pina Bausch: Dancing Across Borders', in his *Theatre, Theory, Postmodernism*, Bloomington, Indiana, 1991; Ana Sanchez-Colberg, '"You put your left foot in, then you shake it all about . . .": Excursions and Incursions into Feminism and Bausch's Tanztheater', in *Dance, Gender and Culture*, edited by Helen Thomas, New York, 1993; Detlef Erler, *Pina Bausch* (photos), Zurich, 1994; Elise Vaccarino, *Pina Bausch: Parlez-moi d'amour*, Paris, 1995 (translated from 1993 Italian edition).

LAURIE BOOTH

We live in such a stupid culture, cut off from our roots and removed from our appetites. So anything creating a moment when people can face up to the body itself, fully aware of its situation, is powerfully psychic.

(Laurie Booth, 1994)[1]

The centrality of the body moving in space, responding to the minute-by-minute challenges of improvisation and change, is the key to all of Booth's work. A strong performer himself, with a remarkable fluidity and quality of sustained control even in clear risk-taking situations, Laurie Booth has continually explored the possibilities of improvisation in the making and performing of work, both as a soloist and in collaboration with other practitioners and dance companies. In preparation for performance Booth has explained that he might make nine or ten phrases of movement (as he did for *ACT/ual f/ACT/ual* in 1997) to form the basis of a piece, and that these could be broken apart and reassembled in different ways in response to the structured visual, spatial and aural environment.

Notable characteristics of movement style in works by Booth are grace, flow, control, a low centre of gravity, the use of off-balance, and an inward focus to much of the movement. These features reflect his background, training, and interests as well as a wider historical context. In many ways it is a very idiosyncratic combination of elements, and in this respect Booth (encouraged by his Dartington training) is like modern dance pioneers whose physiques and movement characteristics themselves shaped their work so definitively.

Judith Mackrell has written of Booth that 'he mixes release and contact improvisation with acrobatics and the Brazilian martial art Capoeira – as Mary Fulkerson once said, he "has virtually invented his own technique".'[2] Booth himself has written about Capoeira, and his descriptions are enlightening in relation to his own work and areas of interest in movement and dance.

The Capoeirista is one who feels comfortable in unstable, chaotic and unusual situations. Even upside down the Capoeirista is in a good position for fighting. To be balanced when off-balance, to be moving with subtlety and cunning, to be free and unpredictable and finally to handle the flow of circumstances with style and magic. That is Capoeira.[3]

Of improvisation Booth has said, 'it is neither predictable nor does it make any particular effort to be accessible to an imagined audience of lowest common demonimators'.[4] This reveals both his commitment to the importance of continual development and renewal through the exploratory processes of improvisation, and a disinclination to compromise.

In interview with Stephanie Jordan,[5] Booth remarked that he was, at the time of developing ideas for *Crazy Daisy and the Northern Lights* (1987), interested in what he termed 'sloppy' movement – unfinished, almost 'marked' movement, as frequently manipulated by Steve Paxton in his own work. Talking to himself while working also led Booth to ideas ('lazy–daisy–crazy daisy'), and his own sketches developed the idea of a marionette strapped to the body of a person. Through all these techniques he began to link sketches and movement ideas, and to discuss possibilities with his collaborators. The doll's features, he said, were important; they seemed to reflect what he described as a fantasy image of Japanese theatre – not based on knowledge but on imagination. Details of her person and clothing became very important aspects for discussion as the doll was created. Movement ideas came not only from within his own body and experience (he maintained) but also from what he referred to as 'information', and he linked this to the notion of the doll's story being told through

him, or *vice versa* – how the doll would move him, rather than the other way round. These remarks go some way towards illuminating Booth's reliance on, and development of, ideas which may come from disparate sources in the initial stages of making work.

Booth is also a practitioner who likes to work in collaboration with other artists, and to explore the possibilities for improvisational techniques in this context. These artists have been performers, such as Steve Paxton, Dana Reitz, and Russell Maliphant; composers, such as Philip Jeck and Gavin Bryars; and sculptors, such as Anish Kapoor and Richard Long. In *Suspect Terrain* (1989), for example, Booth collaborated with Steve Paxton, Dana Reitz, Polly Motley, and Hans-Peter Kuhn. He has worked in the medium of television on a number of occasions: *Crazy Daisy and the Northern Lights* was re-worked for television, and he made *Close to the Ground* (1991), a solo for television, in response to Richard Long's installation at the Tate Gallery the same year, *Walking in Circles*. He has also made work for BBC Television's 'Dance House' series.

According to Booth himself (specifically in relation to *Crazy Daisy and the Northern Lights*, but equally applicable to other works), the major movement features of his work are gravity, the use of the floor, and a sense of the body's own centre. Aikido, tai chi, and contact improvisation are major sources. Booth perceives everything – the planes of the body, even the floor – as curved, tracing the inner surface of a sphere. The pronounced internal focus of all his movement – introverted, inward-turning, self-indulgent even – bears this out very clearly.

The influence of tai chi is evident in the smooth transitions between movements, but also in the unexpected, unpredictable nature of Booth's risk-taking, allowing things to take their course. While improvisation is an integral factor in the making of work, Mackrell has suggested that this element provides excitement but also potentially disappointment as ideas may remain unarticulated. She sees *Mercurial States* (1987), for example, as more successful than some other pieces, showing 'unusually clear, entertaining and economical' work, because of its tight thematic structure, which forced Booth to channel his ideas very carefully.[6] *Mercurial States* was based on a short story by G.K. Chesterton, and allowed for the development of characterization through movement, focused within a clearly defined scenario.

The aural dimension of Booth's work sometimes operates with other components in a relationship of 'peaceful co-existence', in the sense that the sounds or music may contribute to an overall, understated atmosphere. At other times, as with the relentless telephone bell or sometimes distant jazz music in *Crazy Daisy*, this element may suggest related ideas (communication, or non-communication – an idea particularly evident in *ACT/ual f/ACT/ual*) or affect the movement, by seeming to galvanize an increase of speed and more specifically articulated rhythms for a time. In *Close to the Ground*, the sound in the first section consisted of faint, distorted voices – hinting at ideas, of something beyond the dancer and the road and separate from them. In the second section, the sound of water contrasted with the visual images, which suggested, if anything, an arid, dry landscape. Again, there is the sense of something beyond, out of reach of the dancer and the installation – another, parallel, unattainable world.

In *Fixed Memory Fix* (1988) Booth collaborated with the performer Dana Reitz; critic Sophie Constanti noticed that two very individual artists may not easily manage to create a cohesive style together in collaborative ventures. In view of Booth's own very distinctive movement and choreography style, which may not blend readily with another style – or, indeed, be readily assimilated by other dancers – this is not, perhaps, too surprising. However, in addition to the many works made in collaboration with other performers and his own group, Booth made *Completely Birdland* for the Rambert Dance Company in 1991, and has collaborated with the Dutch National Ballet.

Fixed Memory Fix drew upon live music by composer Philip Jeck and film, reflecting Booth's interest in the incorporation of other theatrical media in his works. Sophie Constanti writes:

> it was ironic that *Fixed Memory Fix* revealed its performers' extraordinary capacities as independent artists rather than any ability to form a cohesive unit. This was highlighted by the overall smartness of the production's filmwork, live sound and lighting which, unlike the dancers, seemed to work in absolute accordance with each other. In performance, Booth, more than Reitz, found difficulty in surrendering his autonomy for the possible rewards of partnership. While this means that his talents were not diluted or shamelessly adapted to fit the circumstances, it also showed the disadvantage of possessing a movement vocabulary which is so self-evolved and idiosyncratic that nobody else can respond to it or enter its zones.[7]

Mackrell, writing in 1992 of *A Bone to Pick* (1988), in which Booth collaborated with Harry de Wit, suggests that this work seemed to have a political intention in the 'angry and disruptive gestures'. Political issues have sometimes been the focus of Booth's work, as in *Animal Parts* (1984), although they do not often take centre stage. Mackrell also writes that 'it is possible that what Booth is most anxious to disrupt is his audience's pleasure in watching him dance' – the point being that he only does this for 'short bursts' and does not seem to enjoy it.

Mackrell also makes comparison with *Mercurial States*, which had text and plot character, and seemed to encourage and produce a much more focused choreography. 'Booth no longer seemed like a wonderful dancer, awkwardly wedded to a half-baked concept, but a performer freed from his own self-consciousness by the discipline of working inside someone else's vision'. This highlights the tensions inherent in a situation where individual performers' styles are particularly distinctive.

However, while in some works the relationship of component parts may consist in independent 'peaceful co-existence', in others they come together in a more integrated way, as John Percival noted of *Wonderlawn* (1994): 'During the first half, body patterns like the profilings of ancient Egyptian painting are noticeable; during the second, moving with (or, more precisely, opposite) another dancer becomes more prominent, with the whole group converging at the end.' Percival concluded, 'Finally, *Wonderlawn* provides more than just the sum of its parts: music, dance and design come together into a theatrical totality, mysterious but fascinating'.[8]

In 1995, Booth made *New Tango* (part of *Tango Variations*), of which the choreographer himself said:

> Composer Hans Peter Kuhn is creating a large sound environment within which will be live tango music from the highly acclaimed Juan Cedron Quarteto. But it won't be folkloric reconstruction. It's more concerned with the duet and a clear statement of two people. It will have the sense of etiquette and passion with the interior heart of the world inside this form.
> (quoted in Whitehead, 1994: see note 1)

There is a clear intention stated here of developing thematic ideas, especially the relationship between two people, but also a concern with an inner world of experience, as in many of Booth's works. Booth explained that, in *Tango Variations*, he was interested in deconstructing the tango and taking apart the duet form in order to attempt to rework and reassemble the material from a solo, postmodern point of view. He has commented that he felt that the piece

was not as successful artistically as it could have been – because of constraints of time and money, chiefly, which hindered the in-depth research into the tango form – but that the ideas generated continued to provide material for further work, teaching, and workshops. This is, perhaps, indicative of his approach to choreography overall, in that there is a sense in which the whole of his creative career could be seen as the development of a form of research into improvisational techniques in different contexts.

Also typical in *Tango Variations* was the importance of collaboration in the making of work. Here Hans-Peter Kuhn created the sound environment, and Michael Hill the visual environment within which the structured improvisational choreography developed. In the following year, *Stormgarden* and *ACT/ual f/ACT/ual* also showed this kind of collaboration in practice. *Stormgarden* was a Brighton Festival commission, which Booth created with Russell Maliphant, and himself described as a 'strange and beautiful piece', blood-red, dark and contemplative, but very challenging physically. *ACT/ual f/ACT/ual* (a trio for Booth, Shelley Baker and Gary Lambert) displays in its title Booth's sense of postmodern playfulness. He described his interest in making this piece as deriving from the striking contrast between technological sophistication in the late twentieth century and the banality of most mobile-phone conversations. Sound was produced through the sampling of live telephone conversations during performance, and the visual environment created through a set of columns of twisted videotape, weighted to make them spin like tornadoes.

Booth's latest work at the time of writing, in preparation for 1998, is a solo in which Booth is collaborating with Darrell Viner, who makes robotic sculptures which are interactive and semi-autonomous. And so the development of shifting environment continues, as do the levels of collaboration and structured improvisation. Booth's costume for this solo includes an infra-red device which enables him to alter the rhythmic patterns created by the robotic sculptures.

Booth's performance and choreographic styles are closely linked, and this is a characteristic shared with perhaps many dancer-choreographers, although some find it easier than others to transcend their own preferences when making work on other dancers. Booth clearly likes to work collaboratively with other artists, and to explore the relationship between different elements in a composition, but in many cases the dance element gives to the piece as a whole little beyond its own, self-contained nature. The aural dimension of Booth's works often operates in the background, contributing to general, non-specific mood or ambience – sometimes including more direct references to things outside which may either hint at layers of possible meanings, or alternatively may suggest a sense of distance, detachment, or alienation, even. The movement style's inward focus tends towards an introverted appearance. Its fluidity and weight give it a sensual quality which, combined with the inward focus, may tend to a reading of either self-indulgence or self-sufficiency. Effort is altogether disguised, so that even as the audience may marvel at the strength, control, and daring of the performer in a Booth work, so the opportunities for identification with the performer may be denied.

Rachel Chamberlain Duerden

Notes

1 Whitehead, Janet, 'Booth and His Body', *The Stage*, 6 October 1994.
2 Mackrell, Judith, *Out of Line: The Story of British New Dance*, London: Dance Books, 1992.
3 Booth, Laurie, 'The Hottest Game in Town', *Dance Theatre Journal*, Summer 1984.
4 Ibid.
5 'Crazy Daisy and the Northern Lights' (video), London Video Arts, 1987.
6 Mackrell, Judith, 'Umbrella Dance and Dancers', *Dance Theatre Journal*, Spring 1988.
7 Constanti, Sophie, 'International Dance Season: The Place Theatre, April 1988', *Dance Theatre Journal*, 6(2) 1988.
8 Percival, John, 'Daring Bud of May', *The Times*, 10 May 1994.

Biographical details

Born in London, 22 December 1954. **Studied** at the Dartington School of the Arts, Devon, 1976–79. **Career** Began working with experimental theatre groups, including Triple Action and Cardiff Laboratory Theatre, from 1979; then freelance choreographer and performer; co-founded Transitional Identity, 1981; founder of own group, Laurie Booth & Company, 1991. Has also created works for television and gallery installations, and for Extemporary Dance Theatre, Dutch National Ballet, Rambert Dance Company, and Shobana Jeyasingh Company. **Awards** *Time Out* Dance Award, 1990 and 1991; Digital Dance Award, 1991.

Works

Manipulatin' Motion (Pictures) (1981), *Animal Parts* (1984), *Yip Yip Mix and the 20th C* (mus. Philip Jeck, 1984), *An Axe to Grind* (mus. Harry de Wit, 1985), *Elbow Room Game* (mus. Philip Jeck, 1986), *Euroshima* (mus. Philip Jeck, 1986), *Crazy Daisy and the Northern Lights* (mus. Philip Jeck, 1987), *Mercurial States* (mus. Philip Jeck, 1987), *Fixed Memory Fix* (with Dana Reitz; mus. Philip Jeck, 1988), *A Bone to Pick* (mus. Harry de Wit, 1988), *Suspect Terrain* (with Dana Reitz, Steve Paxton, and Polly Motley; mus. Hans-Peter Kuhn, 1989), *Terminus Terminux* (mus. Philip Jeck, 1989), *Well Known Worlds* (solo; mus. Hans-Peter Kuhn, 1990), *Spatial Decay* (mus. Hans-Peter Kuhn, 1990), *TV Dante* (for television, dir. Peter Greenaway, 1990), *Completely Birdland* (mus. Hans-Peter Kuhn, 1991), *New Text/New Kingdom* (mus. Hans-Peter Kuhn, 1991), *Close to the Ground* (installation, with artist Richard Long; mus. Hans-Peter Kuhn, 1991; also televised), *Dance House* (for BBC television, 1991), *Requiair* (mus. Hans-Peter Kuhn, 1992), *River Run* (mus. Hans-Peter Kuhn, 1993), *Deepfield Line* (mus. Hans-Peter Kuhn, 1993), *Brilliant Bird* (mus. Alexander Balenescu, 1993), *Wonderlawn* (mus. Gavin Bryars, 1994), *A Little Light Possession* (mus. Alexander Balenescu, 1994), *Tango Variations* (includes *New Tango*; mus. Juan Cedron, Hans-Peter Kuhn, 1995),

Stormgarden (mus. Hans-Peter Kuhn, 1996),
Sinking Dreams (mus. Hans-Peter Kuhn, 1996),
ACT/ual f/ACT/ual (mus D.J. Scanner, 1997),
Astral Shadows ('sound-space installation', mus.
Rolf Gehlar, 1997).

Further reading

Interviews with Stephanie Jordan, 'Crazy Daisy
and the Northern Lights' (video), London Video
Arts, 1987; with Judith Mackrell, in 'Off the Top
of Your Head', *The Independent*, 17 October 1990.

Articles Kathy Elgin, 'Laurie Booth', *Dance and
Dancers*, February 1983 and June 1983; Ramsay
Burt, 'Avant-garde Tendencies', *New Dance*,
Winter 1983; Claire Hayes, 'Dance Umbrella',
New Dance, Winter/Spring 1983/84; Alastair
Macaulay, 'Umbrelladom', *Dancing Times*,
January 1984; Laurie Booth, 'The Hottest Game
in Town', *Dance Theatre Journal*, Summer 1984;
Judith Mackrell, 'Laurie Booth in *Animal Parts*',
Dance Theatre Journal, Winter 1984; Sophie
Constanti, 'Passion in Parts', *Dance Theatre
Journal*, Spring 1985; Sophie Constanti, 'Dance
Umbrella: Dreams and a Diary', *Dance Theatre
Journal*, Spring 1986; Sophie Constanti, 'Laurie
Booth's Soap Opera', *Dance Theatre Journal*,
Autumn 1986; Merry Dufton, 'Laurie Booth and
the Cargo Cult in Euroshima', *New Dance*,
Autumn 1986; Judith Mackrell, 'Umbrella Dance
and Dancers', *Dance Theatre Journal*, Spring 1988;
Sophie Constanti, 'International Dance Season:
The Place Theatre, April 1988', *Dance Theatre
Journal*, Summer 1988; Sophie Constanti, 'First
and Last', *Dancing Times*, January 1990; Louise
Levene, 'From Corsets to Cassocks', *Dance and
Dancers*, December 1990; Marilyn Hunt, '... and
Quiet Flows the Thames', *Dance Theatre Journal*,
Spring 1991; David Hughes, 'Momentary
Perfection: A Look at Laurie Booth and
Improvisation', *Dance Theatre Journal*, Spring
1992; John Percival, 'Daring Bud of May', *The
Times*, 10 May 1994; Janet Whitehead, 'Booth and
His Body', *The Stage*, 6 October 1994.

Books Valerie Briginshaw, 'Approaches to
New Dance: An Analysis of Two Works' [on
Manipulatin' Motion (Pictures)], in *Dance
Analysis: Theory and Practice*, edited by Janet
Adshead, London, 1988; Judith Mackrell, *Out of
Line: The Story of British New Dance*, London,
1992; Laurie Booth, 'The Making of *River Run*',
in *Parallel Structures: Art, Dance, Music*, edited
by Clare Farrow, London, 1993.

MATTHEW BOURNE

Considered in relation to the various trends
that characterize British modern and postmodern dance, Matthew Bourne's is a
unique and isolated case. Bourne is not
interested in abstract compositions or in
experimenting with new means of expression. His principal aim is to create dances in
which the theatrical element is particularly
evident, for he believes strongly in what can
be called pure 'theatre magic' – whether it
be the refined scenario of a ballet classic or
the spectacular panache of a Busby Berkeley
musical. In every work, from *Overlap Lovers*
(1987), the first he created for his group,
Adventures in Motion Pictures, Bourne's
personal adaptation of theatre magic is
instantly recognizable.

Without seeking the assistance of the
latest technology, Bourne can create impressive imagery and situations, merely by drawing from the language of dance. An example
is his version of the familiar ballet, *The
Nutcracker* (1992). The first act of Bourne's
version ends with a skating tableau: female
dancers stand on one leg and hold their skirts
as if they were floating in a winter breeze.
By nothing more than a simple visual trick,
an effective stage illusion is immediately
created.

The inspiration for these images comes
mainly from Bourne's own multifaceted
cultural background. Prior to embracing
dance as a profession, Bourne was an enthusiastic fan of almost every form of performing art. As he has confirmed in interviews, he used to attend the theatre more
than twice a week on a regular basis. Old
films of musicals held a particular fascination for him. It is not merely incidental,
therefore, that many of the images absorbed
during those years provide the backbone to
his works. *The Percys of Fitzrovia* (1992) is
derived from the works of Noël Coward;
Deadly Serious (1992) draws on the films of
Alfred Hitchcock; and both the skating

scene and the Kingdom of the Sweets scenario in his *Nutcracker* refer, respectively, to the choreographies of Frederick Ashton and Busby Berkeley.

The fact that theatre is fundamental to Bourne's choreography also dictates that narrative is a constant in his creations. Although some of his early works do not have a defined plot as such, narrative elements are always present in his works. This undoubtedly contributes to the accessibility and, therefore, the popularity of Bourne's choreography. Another important factor is the choreographer's innate sense of comedy, which can find expression in sharp satire, subtle irony, or dark humour.

Bourne's movement vocabulary is characterized by the constant adaptation of the dance idiom to a dramatic context. Although one can speak of the 'Bourne style', it would be difficult actually to define its technical elements. As a student at the Laban Centre in London, Bourne received a heterogeneous training which included some of the major dance techniques, ranging from Graham technique to ballet. His own vocabulary originally grew from this combination of styles and techniques, but it developed through the years, taking in other forms of movement and expression and eventually acquiring its own individuality. A significant trait is his use of music. This is especially evident in such creations as *The Nutcracker*, *Highland Fling* (1994), and *Swan Lake* (1995), where the dance action is set to familiar, pre-existing scores rather than to scores composed for the occasion. Bourne manages to capture the essence of the original music, giving a new and personal, distinctive choreographic reading of it. A notable example of his willingness to reinterpret a score is the disco sequence in *Highland Fling*, set to the Scottish dance of Løvenskjold's 1836 score, *La Sylphide*.

In 1992, the director of Britain's Opera North commissioned a new version of *The Nutcracker* from Bourne, as part of the celebrations to mark the centenary of Tchaikovsky's death. Although Bourne and his company were already a familiar presence on the British dance scene, this was the work through which the young choreographer acquired his first taste of wider popularity. Bourne's *Nutcracker* retains part of the original scenario, although the context and action differ considerably from their nineteenth-century antecedent. A gloomy Victorian workhouse, within which orphans try to enjoy themselves, is humorously juxtaposed with the plush surroundings of the traditional *Nutcracker* Christmas party. The Kingdom of the Sweets, too, is subjected to some radical alterations: it becomes a caricature of contemporary society wherein people, being apparently literally 'sweet', lick one another. Several tongue-in-cheek references to illustrious choreographic examples from the past – such as Ashton's *Les Patineurs* – punctuate the work. The dance vocabulary is an amalgam of techniques and styles, ranging from ballet (although *pointe* shoes are never used) to disco-dancing.

Highland Fling is structured according to a similar formula. As with *The Nutcracker*, *Highland Fling* – subtitled *'A Romantic "Wee" Ballet'* – is a contemporary adaptation of a familiar nineteenth-century ballet, this time August Bournonville's *La Sylphide*. The original story-line is retained almost in its entirety, while the time and the context of the action are updated to today. The Sylph becomes the product of James's drug-induced hallucinations, and the second act, focusing on James's vain struggle to join the sylphs, becomes an allegory of man's struggle and realization of his limitations. Cultural references to other nineteenth-century ballets occur throughout the ballet, mainly in the form of choreographic parody. Once again, the dance vocabulary is a combination of different styles, although ballet is the predominant one.

In Bourne's *Swan Lake*, these techniques of parody and cultural reference are used again to equal effect. With *Swan Lake*, the choreographer took perhaps his greatest risk be reinterpreting one of the most familiar and best-loved of nineteenth-century ballet scores, Tchaikovsky's 1877 masterpiece. Bourne's prince is a tortured soul who longs for freedom within the constrictive world of court society, and identifies this freedom with a male swan who has haunted his dreams since childhood. In an effective reinterpretation of the famous 'white act' of the ballet, the unhappy prince finds himself in a moonlit park where he encounters the swan and his group of swan-companions – but rather than ballerinas in tutus, these are male, bare-chested, and barefooted swans. As in the original libretto, the lead swan has a doppelgänger: Bourne's equivalent of the evil Black Swan is a leather-clad youth who crashes the royal ball and seduces the queen, driving the prince mad with despair. Isolated and rejected by society, the prince is finally rounded upon by the corps of swans, who peck both him and the intervening chief swan to death. Once again the cultural references are strong, from the butterfly ballet-within-a-ballet that recalls Jerome Robbins's *The Concert* (1956) to the ballroom dancing sequences which bring to mind the imagery of Hollywood musicals. But the strongest scenes are undoubtedly the 'white' or swan scenes, which reveal Bourne's true choreographic genius.

Some critics regard the reinterpreted classics as significant landmarks in Bourne's career, as if the revising and updating of ballets from the past indicated an artistic change of direction for him. Others consider such works as an alarming signal of the choreographer's lack of inventiveness – and indeed, his 1997 version of *Cinderella* did not explore to the full the many symbolic and metaphorical possibilities offered by the story or the music. Still, it is difficult to give credit to either point of view. When analysed in detail, these works do not reveal a drastic departure from Bourne's artistic canon. Rather, they are at the same time a compendium of Bourne's choreographic

formulae and an exploration of new possibilities, often along the lines of North European contemporary dance (although a parallel between Bourne and, say, Mats Ek, would be hazardous). As Bourne himself has confirmed, his reinterpretations of the classics represent a constructive exploration of new possibilities rather than a retreat or change of direction. To be continually open to new and different types of artistic experience is a guiding principle of Matthew Bourne's work and of his company, Adventures in Motion Pictures.

Giannadrea Poesio

Biographical details

Born in London, 13 January 1960. **Studied** at the Laban Centre, London, 1982–85, receiving BA in Dance and Theatre. **Career** Danced with Laban Centre's Transitions Dance Company, 1985–86, Adventures in Motion Pictures (founder member), London, from 1987, and Lea Anderson's The Featherstonehaughs (founder member), London, 1988; began choreographing for Adventures in Motion Pictures, 1987, becoming its artistic director in 1987. Has also staged works for the Royal Shakespeare Company, Aix-en-Provence Festival, Malmö Stadsteater (Sweden), and National Youth Theatre (London). **Awards** The Place Portfolio, 1989; Bonnie Bird Choreography Award, 1989; Barclays New Stages Award, 1991; *Time Out* Award, 1995; Olivier Award for Best New Dance Production (*Swan Lake*), 1996; Laban Centre Honorary Fellowship, 1997.

Works

Overlap Lovers (mus. Stravinsky, 1987), *Spitfire* (mus. Glazunov, Minkus, 1988), *Buck + Wing* (mus. Steve Blake, 1988), *The Infernal Galop* (mus. various, 1989), *As You Like It* (play by Shakespeare, 1989), *Singer* (play by Peter Barnes, 1989), *Children of Eden* (musical by Stephen Schwartz, 1990), *Leonce and Lena* (play by Lyndsay Posner, 1990), *The Terra Firma* (opera by Steve Martland), *Town and Country* (mus. various, 1991), *A Midsummer Night's Dream* (opera by Britten, 1991), *Showboat* (musical by Oscar Hammerstein, 1991), *The Nutcracker* (mus. Tchaikovsky, 1992), *Deadly Serious* (mus. various, 1992), *The Percys of Fitzrovia* (mus various, 1992), *The Tempest* (play by Shakespeare, 1993),

Late-Flowering Lust (for television, text John Betjeman poems, 1993), *Drip – A Love Story* (for television, 1993), *Highland Fling: A Romantic 'Wee' Ballet* (mus. Løvenskjold, 1994), *Oliver!* (musical by Lionel Bart, 1994), *Peer Gynt* (play by Ibsen, 1994), *Swan Lake* (mus. Tchaikovsky, 1995; also televised), *Little Red Riding Hood* (for television, based on Roald Dahl story, 1995), *Watch Your Step!* (gala; mus. Irving Berlin, 1995); *Cinderella* (mus. Prokofiev, 1997).

Further reading

Interview with Allen Robertson in 'High Voltage', *Dance Now*, Autumn 1995; with Mark Wilder in *Gay Times*, November 1995; with Christopher Bowen in *The Scotsman*, 2 April 1996.

Articles Sophie Constanti, 'Dance Umbrella 1988', *Dancing Times*, December 1988; Jann Parry, 'Adventures in Motion Pictures: Company at a Crossroads', *Dance Theatre Journal*, Summer 1990; James Belsey, 'Dance Scene: Adventures in Motion Pictures', *Dancing Times*, May 1991; Judith Mackrell, 'Gingering up the Dolly Mixture', *The Independent*, 14 August 1992; Fiona Burnside, 'Matthew Bourne and Kim Brandstrup: Telling Other Men's Tales', *Dance Theatre Journal*, Spring/Summer 1994; Giannandrea Poesio, 'Spotlight on Matthew Bourne', *Dancing Times*, January 1994; Jann Parry, 'AMP's *Swan Lake*', *Dance Now*, Winter 1995; Christopher Benson, 'Matthew Bourne: Giving the Classics a Shot of Irony', *Dance Magazine*, May 1997; Louise Levene, 'Cinderella Makes Progress', *Dance Theatre Journal*, 14(1), 1998.

Books Judith Mackrell, *Out of Line: The Story of British New Dance*, London, 1992.

TRISHA BROWN

Trisha Brown's dances are shaped by dreams of levitation, by geometry, enigma, physics, by memory, mathematics and geography, by language. Her gestural imagery challenges perception of the moving body, making the impossible appear possible. Imagining that dancers can fall not only down but up or sideways, Brown makes the rules of life seem arbitrary, offering an exhilarating transcendence of physical limits. Since 1962 her choreography has explored the interplay of intellect and instinct, paradoxes of logic and non sequitur, interpenetrations of present and past, coincidences of abstract form and mythic action, and the edges between visibility and invisibility.

Brown was born in rural Aberdeen, Washington, where she immersed herself in her wilderness environment, in dance, and in athletics. While attending Mills College in California she studied modern dance technique and composition derived from the teachings of Martha Graham and Louis Horst. At a workshop with the dance innovator Anna Halprin, she explored experiential anatomy, task-based improvisation, breath and vocalization, and sensory awareness of the environment. This led to further investigations of experimental structures in the early 1960s in New York City – improvisational 'rulegames' with Simone Forti, indeterminate dances and spoken text with Yvonne Rainer, 'happenings' with Robert Whitman, Fluxus events with poets and composers, and performance pieces with Robert Rauschenberg.

At the Merce Cunningham studio, Brown was introduced to chance organization of movement and stage space. The aesthetic philosophy of the composer John Cage also became a source of ideas through his performed lectures and through Robert Dunn's Cage-sponsored composition course. Dunn emphasized conceptual strategies for composing dances, influenced by chance scores, Bauhaus approaches to materials and structure, Eastern philosophy, and existentialism. Brown presented her earliest works with Judson Church Dance Theater, the home of a revolutionary movement in dance composition that evolved from Dunn's classes. *Trillium* (1962), *Lightfall* (1963), and *Rulegame 5* (1964) were highly physical responses to improvisational scores. In *Trillium* she took simple instructions to sit, stand, or lie down to illogical conclusions and ended up 'lying' flat out in the air, suspended.

During the late 1960s, Brown initiated a series of autobiographical pieces exploring self-transformation and gesture: *Homemade* (1966), *Inside* (1966), *Skunk Cabbage, Salt Grass, and Waders* (1967), *Ballet* (1968), and *Dance with a Duck's Head* (1968). Full of physical and emotional risk, these were personally created rituals in which Brown posed the self as a dilemma, making identity vulnerable to disassembly. More performance-art pieces than dances, their predecessors were 'happenings'. Brown conflated private and public spaces by using a barely converted industrial loft as both home and studio, putting domestic gestures into her dances like found objects. She overlaid personal history with live improvisation, exorcizing, for example, the violence of hunting experiences as a teenager with her father. She pursued sudden disorientations in off-balance moves, hurling herself, plummeting, and rebounding. With filmic projections she took metaphoric flight from the constraints of femininity, using props like tutus and tightropes to fulfil fantastical images.

From 1968 to 1975 Brown created a series of suspension works, constructing specialized surfaces and devising equipment that enabled dancers to traverse them. In *Planes* (1968), *Man Walking Down the Side of a Building* (1970), *The Floor of the Forest* (1970), *Leaning Duets* (1970), *Walking on the Wall* (1971), *Roof Piece* (1971), and *Spiral* (1974), she suspended dancers in unusual relationships to gravity. She celebrated downtown Manhattan's architecture, its raw interior lofts and expansive outside spaces. She estranged pedestrian activities by shifting around the ways that floors, walls, or ceilings frame them: three women navigated a huge pegboard wall, using holes as hand and footholds; a man keeled forward atop a seven-storey building and ambulated downwards perpendicular to it; performers climbed in and out of clothing strung horizontally across a huge pipe grid rigged at eye level in an empty room. Dancers walked on the walls of the Whitney Museum, viewed

by spectators as if from a tall building looking down, or they cantilevered out from pillars in a loft space, spiralling their way around horizontally until they reached the ground. Elevated above the city, performers stationed on rooftops relayed gestures across a mile-long span of skyline.

Overlapping these works, from 1971 to 1975, Brown invented eight dances in a new 'accumulation' genre, including *Accumulation* (1971), *Group Primary Accumulation* (1973), *Accumulation With Talking* (1973), and *Group Primary Accumulation: Raft Version* (1974). She pared movement down to sparse gestures played out serially, following mathematical dictates. Standing or prone, in solo or unison group forms, in museums, parks, or floating on rafts on a lagoon, in silence or while talking, she and her dancers articulated one move, then another, then returned to the first, moved on to the second, added a third, and so on until they had accumulated a list of basic flexions and rotations of the joints, negating any rationale for moving other than being attentively present.

Structured Pieces (1973–76) – including *Sticks, Discs, Mistitled (5 Clacker), Spanish Dance, Solo Olos,* and *Figure 8* – and *Pamplona Stones* (1974) were composed of activities with objects and were formal considerations of geometric line or metric time. Presented in lofts, galleries, and museums, these works reflected a sensitivity to architecture and space similar to sculptural installations in the visual arts. Dancers performed tongue-in-cheek tricks with long white poles, 'sat' in chairs turned on their sides, or ran as cardboard discs were thrown under their feet. The objects as nonhuman partners gave the pieces a material, external quality and facilitated communication about balance, weight state, or line. There was both risk and absurdity in these tasks, and the possibility of success or error was approached in a matter-of-fact way.

Indoors or outdoors, spectators of the *Accumulations* or *Structured Pieces* moved from site to site to encounter the dancer-objects, who became part of architectural features or of the ambient motion of the surroundings – for example, that of bicyclists, pedestrians, rainstorms – evoking a palpable connection between person and place. In *Locus* (1975), Brown created a virtual room for the human body: an imaginary cube, its faces subdivided into 26 points that corresponded to letters of the alphabet. Gesturing to each point with mechanical motions of the joints such as hinging, rotating, or leaning, Brown intended no emotional or narrative content. As anatomical structure fulfilled line and volume, the body became an insistently formal entity, the skeletal system articulating angles of 45, 90, and 180 degrees. The dance, freed from connotation, became animated by a structural language of grids, angles, and semaphore-like moves.

While in the early 1970s Brown was interested in the sheer presence of the performer in the moment of performing, from 1976 to 1983 she memorized spontaneous moments. *Locus* gave her tools to graph complex movement three-dimensionally. In *Line Up* (1976), she asked dancers to remember improvised phrases based on permutations of lines. In her 1978 breakthrough solo, *Watermotor*, Brown tapped memory by choreographing moments from her personal history, placing them amidst fluid, multi-directional moves. In *Accumulation with Talking Plus Watermotor*, she developed this approach by splicing gestures from *Watermotor* into a standing *Accumulation*, and layering this with extemporaneous speaking. She cut between two stories and two dances at once, pushing order-making capacity to the limit, overcoming possible disintegration or memory loss.

Brown set improvised forms with her company in *Glacial Decoy* (1979), *Opal Loop* (1980), *Son of Gone Fishin'* (1981), and *Set and Reset* (1983). These pieces range from the interior and the cryptic to outgoing and geometrical. In high-flying ensemble moves from improvisation and

recall, responding to instructions like 'act on instinct', dancers met, interlocked for an instant, and passed on, guided by intricate cueing systems. Timing was malleable, gauged to the effects of gravity on the off-kilter moving body. The space between bodies was charged with comings and goings, near or actual collisions, and split-second unisons. Anatomical functions became choreographic principles as the group extended, folded, or rotated. Any part of the body was free to combine with any other in an overall democratic vision of the relation between limbs and torso, centerstage and periphery, individual and group.

From *Trillium* to *Set and Reset*, Brown honed the fit between formal structure, or the dance score, and raw material, or the movement. Engaging the score kinaesthetically, dancers physically manifested its idea. Linked to mathematical and geometric progression in minimal art, Brown's structures have subverted subjective compositional choice, so central to expressionist modern dance. Hewn from principles greater than the choreographer's personal imagination, Brown has called her scores 'dance machines' – objective mechanisms that collaborate with the choreographer to determine the where, when, and how of the dance.

In *Accumulation* and *Locus*, Brown built structures in front of the audience, so that the excitement of discerning them became a pleasure of viewing. In later multi-layered works, the formal structure became a nearly invisible undergirding, subliminally suggesting priority of thought as a foil to the instinctive dancing. The 'machine' in *Primary Accumulation* was mathematical serial progression, in *Man Walking Down the Side of a Building* spatial progression from top to bottom, in *Locus* numerical-linguistic-spatial co-ordination of gestures, in *Line-up* the forming and dissolution of lines, in *Set and Reset* a rectangular progression that traced the stage edges.

Each of Brown's formal structures elicited from the dancers an integral clarity in terms of anatomical and spatial intention. Feeding into this developing physical knowledge were Brown's studies, from the early 1970s onwards, in alternative approaches to dance training – Kinetic Awareness with Elaine Summers, the Alexander Technique, and, since 1985, Susan Klein Technique. Brown relearned to articulate each body part separately or in co-ordination, expanding range and diversity of motion. Her signature sequential style evolved from fluid joints, responsive without obstruction. Release techniques encourage ergonomic efficiency, and Brown began to divest her designs of ornament, using limbs as levers or shifting weight like a hydraulic press. Physical dynamism found an analogy in technological power. Her 'dance machine' works intertwined America's dual love of technology and wilderness, the raw material of unrestricted movement civilized by the mechanized score.

By 1985, as the kinaesthetic sources of her dancing became integrated with her formal concerns, Brown no longer utilized scores as organizing principles, and focused more on movement ideas that evolved from the physical state of the body. In *Lateral Pass* (1985), *Newark* (1987), and *Astral Convertible* (1989), dancers loped by with large-bodied, muscled momentum, shifting from floorbound to upright, to airborne positions. Rather than use partnering for presentational display, they assisted one another to realize movement more fully. The entire group became a mechanism to heave individuals airborne, so that partnering became a sort of acrobatic cantilevering as bodies hurled, thrusted, swung, and rebounded, building and dispersing architectural forms, constantly changing plane, direction, and dimension.

A high degree of virtuosity gives these works a striking theatricality. Contributing to this, beginning in 1979, Brown collaborated with composers and visual artists on large-scale productions for the proscenium theatre. She commissioned musical scores by Robert Ashley, Laurie Anderson, Peter Zummo, Richard Landry, John Cage, and Alvin Curran. Visual presentations by Robert Rauschenberg, Fujiko Nakaja, Donald Judd, Nancy Graves, and Roland Aeschlimann established environments inside the theatre, obscuring dancers in fog or dissecting space into quadrants with richly coloured drops that spanned the proscenium horizon. Neon-coloured sculptures flew in and out as dancers careened around them. Larger than life-size photographs travelled silently across the back wall, or car-light-studded towers blinked like an airport terminal at night.

Brown designed many of her formal structures to challenge the traditional relationship of dance to the theatrical frame, and she carried her sensitivity to environmental space into the proscenium theatre. She composed movement explicitly for the stage edge, so that entrances and exits, visible through sheer wings, questioned conventional boundaries of vision. For example, she arranged a quartet to slide in and out of view, laterally: as one dancer slipped offstage, another replaced her way across on the other side, creating an illusion that the one just out of view continued on invisibly, the proscenium unable to frame or contain her.

In 1990, following her large-scale geometric works, Brown turned to softer chamber forms that explored processes of perception, whether in the performer's or the spectator's mind. In *Foray Forêt* (1990), *For MG: The Movie* (1991), and *Another Story as in falling* (1993), she began to build character out of abstract form. In 1986, Brown's choreography for Lina Wertmuller's opera production of *Carmen* had pressed abstraction into confrontation with high drama and character; in *For MG*, with an object-like performing presence that still carried Judson influences, dancers fulfilled purely physical acts that suggested isolated moments of a story. Mythic, archetypal figures emerged – a woman running, a man standing still. When they did so long enough their exertions became metaphorical acts of endurance.

In these works, moves, placed like objects in time and space, suddenly become loaded with story or metaphor, but feeling dissolves back into geometrics. The dancers stand for nothing other than what they are, yet in their play with front, back, nearness, or distance, emotional meanings emerge as unexpected insights. The works are studded with empty spaces that evoke contemplation. Sometimes in the breaks between moves, the body gestures reflexively, turbulently, inscrutably, or incoherently or abruptly enters into prolonged stillness. Movement ideas become so clear that the thinker disappears and only the articulation of form is visible.

Marianne Goldberg

Biographical details

Born Patricia Brown in Aberdeen, Washington, United States, 25 November 1936. **Studied** at Mills College, Oakland, California, obtaining a BA degree in Dance, 1958; studied with Anna Halprin in Marin County, California, 1959, with José Limón, Merce Cunningham, and Louis Horst at Connecticut College, summers 1955, 1959, and 1960, and with Robert Dunn, New York, 1960. **Career** Taught dance at Reed College, Portland, Oregon, 1958–59; moved to New York, after having met Yvonne Rainer and Simone Forti, 1960, becoming one of the founder members of Judson Dance Theater, 1962–68, and of Grand Union, 1970–76; founded Trisha Brown Company, 1970, remaining choreographer and director ever since. Appointed to US National Council on the Arts, 1994. **Awards** Fellowships in Choreography from Guggenheim Foundation, 1975, 1984, and National Endowment for the Arts, 1977, 1981, 1982, 1983, 1984; Creative Arts Medal in Dance from Brandeis University, 1982; Honorary Doctorate in Fine Arts from Oberlin College, 1983; New York Dance and Performance Award ('Bessie'), 1984, 1986; *Dance Magazine* Award, 1987; Olivier Award, 1987; Chevalier de l'Ordre des Arts et des Lettres (France), 1988; MacArthur Foundation Fellowship Award, 1991; Samuel H. Scripps American Dance Festival Award, 1993.

Works

Trillium (mus. Philip Corner, J.S. Bach, 1962), *Lightfall* (mus. Simone Morris, 1963), *2 Improvisations on the Nuclei for Simone by Jackson Maclow* (1963), *Improvisation on a Chicken Coop Roof* (1963), *Falling Solo with Singing* (mus. Honegger, 1963), *Chanteuse Eccentrique Américaine* (1963), *Rulegame 5* (1964), *Target* (1964), *Motor* (1965), *Homemade* (1965), *A String* (consisting of *Motor*, *Homemade*, and *Inside*, 1966), *Skunk Cabbage, Salt Grass and Waders* (1967), *Medicine Dance* (1967), *Planes* (mus. Simone Forti, 1968), *Snapshots* (mus. Simone Forti, 1968), *Falling Duet* (1968), *Ballet* (1968), *Dance with a Duck's Head* (1968), *Yellow Belly* (1969), *Skymap* (1969), *Man Walking Down the Side of the Building* (1970), *Clothes Pipe, The Floor of the Forest, and Other Miracles, etc.* (1970), *Leaning Duets* (1970), *The Stream* (1970), *Walking on the Wall* (1971), *Leaning Duets II* (1971), *Falling Duet II* (1971), *Accumulation* (1971), *Rummage Sale and the Floor of the Forest* (1971), *Roof Piece* (1971), *Accumulation 55'* (1972), *Primary Accumulation* (mus. The Grateful Dead, 1972), *Theme and Variations* (1972), *Woman Walking Down a Ladder* (1973), *Accumulation Pieces* (1973), *Group Accumulation I* (1973), *Group Primary Accumulation* (1973), *Group Accumulation II* (1973), *Structured Pieces I* (1973), *Group Primary Accumulation: Raft Version* (1974), *Figure 8* (1974), *Split Solo* (1974), *Drift* (1974), *Spiral* (1974), *Pamplona Stones* (1974), *Structured Pieces II* (1974), *Locus* (1975), *Pyramid* (1975), *Structured Pieces III* (1975), *Solo Olos* (1976), *Duetude* (1976), *Line Up* (mus. various, 1976), *Structured Pieces IV* (1976), *Line Up 1977* (mus. Bob Dylan, 1977), *Watermotor* (solo; 1978), *Splang* (1978), *Accumulation with Talking Plus Watermotor* (versions of the three earlier pieces, 1979), *Glacial Decoy* (visual presentation Robert Rauschenberg, 1979), *Opal Loop* (visual presentation Fujiko Nakaya, 1980), *Son of Gone Fishin'* (visual presentation Donald Judd, mus. Robert Ashley, 1981), *Set and Reset* (includes *Decoy* and *Opal Loop*; visual presentation Rauschenberg, mus. Laurie Anderson, 1983), *Lateral Pass* (visual presentation Nancy Graves, mus. Peter Zummo, 1985), *Carmen* (opera by Bizet, 1986), *Newark* (visual presentation and sound Donald Judd, orchestration Peter Zummo, 1987), *Astral Convertible* (visual presentation Rauschenberg, sound Richard Landry, 1989), *Foray Forêt* (visual presentation Rauschenberg, mus. Marching Band, 1990), *Astral Converted (50")* (visual presentation Rauschenberg, mus. John Cage, 1991), *For MG: The Movie* (mus. Alvin Curran, 1991), *One Story as in falling* (visual presentation Roland Aeschlimann, mus. Alvin Curran, 1992), *Another Story as in falling* (visual presentation Aeschlimann, mus. Alvin Curran, 1993), *If you couldn't see me* (solo; mus. Robert Rauschenberg, 1994; duet version with Mikhail Baryshnikov, *You can see us*, 1995), *Long and Dream* (with Steve Paxton; mus. 'Blue' Gene Tyranny, 1994), *M.O.* (mus. J.S. Bach, 1995), *Twelve Ton Rose* (mus. Webern, 1996), *Canto/Pianto* (mus. Monteverdi, 1997).

Further reading

Interviews with Sally Sommer, in 'Trisha Brown Making Dances', *Dance Scope*, Spring 1977; in 'Dialog on Dance', in *The Vision of Modern Dance* edited by Jean Morrison Brown, Princeton, New Jersey, 1979; in *Contemporary Dance* edited by Anne Livet, New York, 1978; with David Sears, in 'Forever New', *Dance News*, October 1981; with Marianne Goldberg, in 'Trisha Brown', *Drama Review*, Spring 1986; with Christy Adair, in 'Trisha Brown Dance Company at Sadler's Wells', *New Dance*, January 1988; with Marianne Goldberg, in 'Trisha Brown's Accumulations', *Dance Theatre Journal*, Autumn 1991; with Yvonne Rainer, in 'Trisha Brown', *Bomb Magazine*, October 1993; with Carol Pratl, in 'Trisha Brown', *Dance Europe*, June/July 1997.

Articles Sally Sommer, 'Equipment Dances: Trisha Brown', *Drama Review*, September 1972; Sally Sommer, 'Trisha Brown Making Dances', *Dance Scope*, Spring/Summer 1977; Sally Banes, 'Gravity and Levity: Up and Down with Trisha Brown', *Dance Magazine*, March 1978; Mona Sulzman, 'Choice/Form in Trisha Brown's Locus: A View from Inside the Cube', *Dance Chronicle*, 2(2), 1978; David Sears, 'A Trisha Brown/ Robert Rauschenberg Collage', *Ballet Review*, Fall 1982; Camille Hardy, 'Trisha Brown: Pushing Postmodern Art into Orbit', *Dance Magazine*, March 1985; Michael Huxley, 'Lines of Least Resistance: Trisha Brown Company', *New Dance*, Spring 1986; Allen Robertson, 'Gravity's Rainbow', *Ballet News*, September 1985; Marianne Goldberg, 'Trisha Brown: All of the Person's Person Arriving', *Drama Review*, Spring 1986; K. Kertsee, 'Dancing with Carmen', *Art in America*, April 1987; Deborah Jowitt, 'Trisha and France: A Love Story', *Dance Magazine*, September 1990; Elizabeth Kendall, 'Trisha Brown Comes Down to Earth', *Dance Ink*, April 1991; Sally Sommer, 'The Sound of Movement', *Dance Ink*, Spring 1993; Rosalyn Sulcas, 'Trisha Brown: Choreography That Spans Continents and Oceans', *Dance Magazine*, April 1995; Trisha

Brown and Bill T. Jones, 'Body Politics, Postmodernism and Political Correctness', in *Ballett International*, August 1995; Rita Felciano, 'Trisha Brown', *Dance Now*, Spring 1996; Wendy Perron, 'Trisha Brown on Tour', *Dancing Times*, May 1996.

Books Don McDonagh, *The Complete Guide to Modern Dance*, New York, 1976; Anne Livet (ed.), *Contemporary Dance*, New York, 1978; Peter Wynne (ed.), *Judson Dance: An Annotated Bibliography of the Judson Dance Theater and of Five Major Choreographers*, Englewood Cliffs, New Jersey, 1978; Sally Banes, *Terpsichore in Sneakers: Post-modern Dance*, Boston, 1980; Sally Banes, *Democracy's Body: Judson Dance Theater 1962–1964*, Ann Arbor, Michigan, 1983 (reprinted, Durham, North Carolina, 1993); Deborah Jowitt, *The Dance in Mind*, Boston, 1985; Lise Brunel, *Trisha Brown* (in French and English), Paris, 1987; 'Trisha Brown: An Informal Performance', in *Breakthroughs: Avant-garde Artists in Europe and America, 1950–1990*, New York, 1991.

CHRISTOPHER BRUCE

Christopher Bruce maintains that his ballets are not essentially about movement but about ideas. They may not have an obvious story-line and may be episodic in structure, but they generally include dramatic or emotive elements that make an immediate impact on the audience. While the works portray recognizable experiences, they are also open to a variety of interpretations, and Bruce prefers his audience to watch them unencumbered by pre-conceived notions. For this reason he usually avoids programme notes, and many of the titles of his works (such as *Land* (1985), *Waiting* (1993), *Crossing* (1994), and *Meeting Point* (1995)) leave their subject without narrative boundaries. Although the ideas are central to the productions, Bruce's concern is to create a dance, not a statement.

Bruce was encouraged to dance by his father, and his training from the age of eleven was in ballet, tap, and acrobatics. After two years he was accepted into the

Rambert School. The 1960s were Bruce's formative years. Working with Walter Gore's London Ballet and Ballet Rambert, while that company still focused on classical ballet, exposed him to narrative works and to the use of demi-caractère dancing, as well as to the understated, yet universal drama of Antony Tudor. He learned to appreciate the importance of theatrical presentation and he recognized the high standards Marie Rambert instilled into all her choreographers. The 1960s were a period of change in British dance, and after Ballet Rambert's 1966 reconstitution, which returned the company once again into a more creative ensemble, Graham technique, as transplanted into Britain, became part of his experience.

At this time Bruce attracted attention as a dancer for his superb interpretation of the title role in Glen Tetley's *Pierrot Lunaire*. For two decades he was recognized as 'one of the most potent and sharply focused dancers in Britain', and he was compared with the great French dancer Jean Babilée, with whom he shared a remarkable stage presence and the ability to act through dance. Appearing in a wide repertory of ballets, from the title roles in Nijinsky's *L'Après-midi d'un faune* in 1967 and Fokine's *Petrouchka* in 1988, to created roles such as Prospero in Tetley's *The Tempest* (1979), provided Bruce with a rich background for his own choreography. In his own productions the creation of the central role of the Poet in *Cruel Garden* (1977), happily recorded for posterity, remains a particularly potent memory.

Tetley's impact on Rambert was considerable, particularly given his ability to marry classical and contemporary choreography. Like Bruce, Tetley's background included working with classical, contemporary, and popular dance forms. Tetley encouraged Bruce in his first choreographic experiments, and Bruce's starting-point for his third creation, *Wings* (1970), was movement developed from a section of Tetley's *Ziggurat*. Bruce was also encouraged by

Rambert's associate director, Norman Morrice. (Morrice had enabled him to create his first dance role in *Realms of Choice* and then gave him opportunities to choreograph.) Morrice's own ballets at this period moved away from specific dramas to more universal themes, and he invited a variety of American contemporary choreographers to work with Rambert. Among them was Anna Sokolow, whose works ranged from pop-ballets (*Opus 65*) to socially aware dramas (*Deserts*).

If the work of these choreographers provided the context for Bruce's own choreography, it must be stressed that he did not imitate them but found encouragement from their creative range. Bruce's first ballet, *George Frideric* (1969), to music by Handel, reflected a trend for setting light, lyric dance to baroque music (as seen in Paul Taylor's *Aureole*). It was a competent first work and did not reveal to the audience the agony of its slow creation. It remains one of Bruce's few dances that simply reflect its music. Indeed, with many of his early works Bruce tried to avoid expressing, or responding to, music, claiming in an interview that he did not want his dances to be reliant on another art form. For some productions, including *Duets* (1973), *Weekend* (1974), and *There Was a Time* (1973, inspired by the Trojan Wars), the electronic scores were added after the choreography was more or less complete. From the mid-1970s Bruce began to feel more confident in choosing scores, responding particularly to the compositions of George Crumb and also commissioning material from Philip Chambon, whom he met in 1984, for *Swansong* (1987), *Nature Dances* (1992), and *Stream* (1996). With some scores, such as the folk songs used for *Ghost Dances* (1981), Janáček's *Intimate Pages* quartet (1984), and Stravinsky's *Symphony in Three Movements* (1989), Bruce waited a number of years to find the right opportunity to create dances. Since the 1980s he has responded to pop songs (mostly from the 1960s) by Billie Holliday,

Joan Baez, Bob Dylan, John Lennon, and the Rolling Stones.

Bruce's second work, *Living Space* (1969), was more dramatic. Danced to poems by Robert Cockburn, Bruce's choreography sometimes took its literal cue from the spoken words; and this continues to be seen in his productions to song cycles, such as *Sergeant Early's Dream* (1984) and *Rooster* (1991), which use select phrases mimetically. Bruce has also been stimulated in his work by literature – fact and fiction, poetry, prose, and journalism. He never puts an epic work on stage, preferring to select themes that can be successfully conveyed in dance. *Swansong* was, in part, inspired by a description of a political prisoner's torture in Oriana Fallaci's novel *A Man*. Although *Sergeant Early's Dream* was primarily an excuse for some lively dances to Irish and American folk songs, it also drew on John Preble's description of highland clearance and migration in the nineteenth century. *Dancing Day* (1981), *Cantata* (1981), and *Ceremonies* (1986) derived from a fascination with the mixing of the sacred and secular in mediaeval society, as conveyed in the life of alchemist Dr John Dee and in such novels as Umberto Eco's *The Name of the Rose*.

Although Bruce has achieved some of the most striking translations of literature into dance, knowledge of a source-work is never essential for the appreciation of the choreography. This is as true of the use of the poems of Federico García Lorca as it is of the use of sections of novels. A work such as his stunning *Cruel Garden* draws on Lorca's musical compositions and sketches as well as his poems, plays, and filmscripts, to create from his life and experience a multi-layered collage. It was a collaborative creation with Lindsay Kemp, who shared Bruce's fascination with Lorca. Undoubtedly some of the richness of the ideas came from Kemp, who claimed 'I think of myself as Cocteau to Christopher's Massine' – but the humanity of the work, with its inclusion of

Lorca's concern for oppressed minorities, derives from Bruce's personal convictions.

The subject matter of Bruce's work has attracted attention because it reflects his sensitive awareness of the larger social, political, and ecological issues of our time. Bruce has said, 'I don't do my ballets to get social messages across; these things just come naturally out of me'. Nevertheless, on occasions the choice of subject-matter is intentional. *Ghost Dances*, which draws on pre-Hispanic death culture, is dedicated to 'the innocent people of South America who . . . have been continuously devastated by political oppression'. *Waiting*, set to music celebrating Nelson Mandela's release from prison, was based on images of life in a South African township. *Berlin Requiem* (1982), developing themes from Kurt Weill music and Bertold Brecht's words, portrayed the decadence and fall of the Weimar Republic. *Berlin Requiem* was choreographed to a planned scenario, but the shape of many of Bruce's ballets emerges when working with his dancers in the studio.

Observations on the brutality and futility of war have recurred in such works as *Land* and *for these who die as cattle* (1982) (created under the working title of *The Warriors* until Bruce read Wilfred Owen's war poem, which conveyed precisely the situation he had already choreographed). Taking their cue from the title of Arne Nordheim's music, *Warsaw*, critics initially discussed *Land* as referring back to the rape of Poland, but more recent revivals have made them aware of its more immediate relevance to the contemporary situation in Bosnia. In both '*cattle*' and *Land*, as well as other less harrowing but nevertheless intense works such as *Intimate Pages*, the women, or one central strong woman, provides the work's emotional focus.

Bruce's knowledge of the international dance repertory also colours his work. *Meeting Point*, created for the UNited We Dance Festival (to mark the fiftieth anniversary of the signing of the United Nations Charter) deliberately evoked the opening and closing sections of Kurt Jooss's *The Green Table*; and *Land*, with its sense of loss, has choreographic resonances of Tudor's *Dark Elegies*.

Bruce's creative stimulus is, on occasion, strongly autobiographical. *Weekend* reflected the stress of touring on his family, *Swansong* the struggle to come to terms with the end of his performing career. His love of children was seen clearly in *Ancient Voices of Children* (1975) and *Preludes and Songs* (1980), created when his own children were growing up. In other works the autobiographical element is retrospective. Discussing *The Dream is Over* (1986) in the television programme on John Lennon in which it was first shown, he said, 'I thought it would be nice to do something about my contemporaries, and the times we went through, and Lennon's lyrics seemed to speak for us and what we felt about life.'

Settings for Bruce's productions are uncluttered but apt, allowing space for movement. Initially he regularly turned to Nadine Baylis and John B. Read, whose combined talents gave the new Rambert its visual signature. For more elaborate productions he has worked with Pamela Marre and Ralph Koltai. Marre provided the neon-lit bar which disappeared to become a barren landscape for *Berlin Requiem* and Koltai the blood-spattered bull-ring of *Cruel Garden* (originally presented at the Roundhouse in London). Walter Nobbe, responsible for painterly and evocative landscapes enhanced by lighting, has been a regular collaborator, and Bruce has worked effectively with his wife Marian Bruce. He has also designed some of his own productions, contributing the costumes for *Swansong* and the Andean landscape for *Ghost Dances* (Belinda Scarlett designed the half-tattered costumes symbolizing the characters' transition from life to death).

As a creator of dances Bruce cannot be pigeonholed. His choreography combines elements of the varied styles he has worked with, usually based on classical and contemporary dance. His range is further extended by incorporating popular and folk dance. He finds this useful, as popular and folk dance, like pop songs and folk music, give his work both universality and a sense of particular community. His dancers thus appear as real people with recognizable emotions. His own 'esperanto folk dance', incorporating circles and lines, often with arms linked in a 'Zorba chain', has become a signature motif. The folk element has been present from his first work – for *George Frideric* included heel–toe steps. The feet are often parallel, without concern for turnout, and Bruce's works often feature small, quick steps which contrast with bold circular gestures – full-skirted swirls and scooping movements, twisting the torso. Bruce exploits a low centre of gravity seen in lunges and deep *pliés* characteristic of contemporary dance.

Bruce has choreographed more than fifty ballets in addition to musicals, plays, operas, and works for television. Much of his working life has been based at Rambert – as student, dancer, and choreographer – although for a decade he worked as a freelance choreographer. Even then, he held long-term contracts, first with English National Ballet and then with the Houston Ballet. He prefers to work with groups of dancers he knows, supervising new productions of his own works and new casts in revivals. In this way he has regularly returned to specific companies, most notably Nederlands Dans Theater, Cullberg Ballet in Sweden, the Gulbenkian Ballet of Lisbon, Ballet du Grand Théâtre Geneva, and Houston Ballet. As artistic director of Rambert Dance Company, a position he took up in 1994, he has benefited from working internationally, having built up relationships with a range of like-minded choreographers whom he has invited to work with his dancers. He has also drawn on his experience of seeing his own ballets programmed in different situations. As a director, just as when he choreographs, his concern is to make lively contact with his audience. Productions may have a serious message or be comic, but Bruce never loses his awareness of the fact that he is working in the theatre.

Jane Pritchard

Biographical details

Born in Leicester, England, 3 October 1945. **Studied** at Benson Stage Academy, Scarborough, and at the Ballet Rambert School, London. **Career** Dancing debut with Walter Gore's London Ballet, 1963; Joined Ballet Rambert in 1963, becoming leading dancer in modern roles, from 1966; choreographer for Ballet Rambert (which became Rambert Dance Company in 1987), from 1969, becoming associate choreographer, 1975–87, and associate director, 1975–79; associate choreographer for London Festival Ballet (becoming English National Ballet in 1989), 1986–91; resident choreographer, Houston Ballet, 1989–98; artistic director, replacing Richard Alston, Rambert Dance Company, from April 1994. Has also staged works for Royal Ballet, Scottish Ballet, Israel's Batsheva Dance Company, Munich Opera Ballet, Gulbenkian Ballet Company, Australian Dance Theatre, Royal Danish Ballet, Royal Swedish Ballet, Tanz-Forum (Cologne), Nederlands Dans Theater, Geneva Ballet, Cincinnati Ballet, and Dutch National Ballet; has worked as choreographer/producer of operas, musicals, and television programmes. **Awards** include *Evening Standard* Award, 1974 and 1997; Prix Italia (for television production of *Cruel Garden*), 1982; International Theatre Institute Award, 1993.

Works

George Frideric (mus. Handel, 1969), *Living Space* (poetry by Robert Cockburn, 1969), *Wings* (mus. Bob Downes, 1970), *for these who die as cattle* (silent, 1972), *Joseph and the Amazing Technicolour Dreamcoat* (musical by Andrew Lloyd-Webber, 1972), *There Was a Time* (mus. Brian Hodgson, 1973), *Duets* (mus. Brian Hodgson, 1973), *Weekend* (mus. Brian Hodgson, 1974), *Unfamiliar Playground* (mus. Brian Hodgson, Antony Hymas, 1974), *Jeeves* (musical by Andrew Lloyd-Webber, 1975), *Ancient Voices of Children* (mus. George Crumb, 1975), *Voices* (mus. Kodály, 1976), *Black Angels* (mus. George Crumb, 1976), *Girl with Straw Hat* (mus. Brahms, 1976), *Promenade* (mus. J.S. Bach, 1976), *Echoes of a Night Sky* (mus. George Crumb, 1976), *Cruel Garden* (with Lindsey Kemp; mus. Carlos Miranda, 1977), *Responses* (silent, 1977),

Labyrinth (mus. Morton Subotnick, 1979), *Night with Waning Moon* (mus. George Crumb, 1979), *Sidewalk* (mus. Constant Lambert, 1979), *Interactions* (mus. Gary Carpenter, 1980), *Il ballo del Ingrate* (opera by Monteverdi, 1980), *Venus and Adonis* (mus. John Blow, 1980), *Preludes and Songs* (mus. Antony Hymas, 1980), *Dancing Day* (mus. Holst, 1981), *Cantata* (mus. Stravinsky, 1981), *Combattimento di Tancredi e Clorinda* (opera by Monteverdi, 1981), *Ghost Dances* (mus. Latin American folk, 1981), *Holiday Sketches* (mus. Billie Holliday, 1981), *Village Songs* (mus. Bartók, 1981), *Agrippina* (opera by Handel, 1982), *Berlin Requiem* (mus. Weill, 1982), *In Alium* (mus. John Taverner, 1982), *Concertino* (mus. Janáček, 1983), *Curses and Blessings* (with Jiří Kylián; mus. Petr Eben, 1983), *Silence is the End of Our Song* (set to Chilean poetry, 1983), *Intimate Pages* (mus. Janáček, 1984), *Sergeant Early's Dream* (mus. folk music of British Isles and America, 1984), *Remembered Dances* (mus. Janáček, 1985), *Mutiny* (musical by David Essex, 1985), *Land* (mus. Arne Nordheim, 1985), *Ceremonies* (mus. Edward Shipley, 1986), *The World Again* (mus. Geoffrey Burgon, 1986), *The Dream is Over* (mus. John Lennon, 1986), *The Winter's Tale* (play by Shakespeare, 1987), *Swansong* (mus. Philip Chambon, 1987), *The Changeling* (play by Thomas Middleton, 1988), *Song* (mus. George Crumb, 1988), *Gautama Buddha* (mus. Naresh Sohal, 1989), *Les Noces* (mus. Stravinsky, 1989), *Symphony in Three Movements* (mus. Stravinsky, 1989), *Journey* (mus. Palle Mikkelborg, 1990), *Rooster* (mus. The Rolling Stones, 1991), *Nature Dances* (mus. Philip Chambon, 1992), *Kingdom* (mus. Barry Guy, 1993), *Moonshine* (mus. Bob Dylan, 1993), *Waiting* (mus. Errolyn Wallen, 1993), *Crossing* (mus. Górecki, 1994), *Meeting Point* (mus. Michael Nyman, 1995), *Quicksilver* (mus. Michael Nyman 1996), *Stream* (mus. Philip Chambon, 1996), *Four Scenes* (mus. Dave Heath, 1998).

Further reading

Interviews in 'Curtain Up', *Dance and Dancers*, June 1986; with Ann Nugent, in 'Waiting with Certainty', *Dance Now*, Autumn 1993; in Jo Butterworth and Gill Clarke (eds.), *Dancemakers' Portfolio: Conversations with Choreographers*, Bretton Hall, 1998.

Articles Charles Gow, 'Christopher Bruce', *Dancing Times*, March 1973; Noël Goodwin, 'Elegiac Images', *Dance and Dancers*, September 1975; David Dougill, 'Where Bruce Gets His Ideas From', *Classical Music*, 2 October 1976; Noël Goodwin, 'Shadows and Substances', *Dance and Dancers*, September 1981; Nadine Meisner,

'A Dream by the Ocean', *Dance and Dancers*, December 1984; Sophie Constanti, 'Ballet Rambert', *Dance Theatre Journal*, Summer 1985; Sophie Constanti, 'London Festival Ballet and Christopher Bruce', *Dancing Times*, July 1988; Kathrine Sorley Walker, 'Violence and Poetry', *Dance and Dancers*, August 1988; Angela Kane, 'Christopher Bruce's Choreography: Inroads or Re-Tracing Old Steps?', *Dancing Times*, October 1991; Christopher Bruce, 'There's Always an Idea', *Dance and Dancers*, January 1993; Ann Nugent, 'Waiting with Certainty', *Dance Now*, Autumn 1993; Christopher Bruce, 'The Christopher Bruce Manifesto', *Dancing Times*, November 1994; Judith Mackrell, 'Mission – Impossible?', *Dance Now*, Autumn 1995; Kathrine Sorley Walker, 'Christopher Bruce and Rambert Dance Company', *Dancing Times*, July 1996; Josephine Leask, 'Diversity in Unity: Rambert Dance Company Celebrates Its 70th Birthday', *Ballett International*, 7, 1996.

Books Richard Austin, *The Birth of a Ballet*, London, 1976; Clement Crisp, Anya Sainsbury, and Peter Williams, *Ballet Rambert: 50 Years and On*, London, 1981; John Percival, *Modern Ballet*, London, 1981; Peter Brinson and Clement Crisp, *The Pan Book of Ballet and Dance*, London, 1981; Allen Robertson and Donald Hutera, *The Dance Handbook*, Harlow, Essex, 1988; Jane Pritchard, *Rambert: A Celebration*, London, 1996; Jane Pritchard, *Swansong Study Notes*, London, 1998.

JONATHAN BURROWS

Jonathan Burrows has developed a movement language with little emphasis given to theatrical components, its focus being directed instead towards the detail of movement itself. His works are characterized by a range of movement material that is apparently very far from the classical ballet training of the choreographer, and therefore also very different from the work of his contemporary at the Royal Ballet School, Michael Clark. Hallmarks include energy and attack, even – perhaps especially – in the context of small details, dramatic variations in rhythms and speed, and the use of stillness, developed furthest in *The Stop Quartet* (1996). Structurally, Burrow's

choreography shows a clarity of overall shape, which is made interesting and even surprising by small deviations and shifts of focus. Focus, indeed, is one of his central concerns: the focus of one dancer on another, in particular, is key in many works, especially duets, which show how the issue of communication between people – or lack of it – can be a powerful theme for dance.

Burrows's background is in classical ballet, and, at the Junior School of the Royal Ballet School, where he was trained, Morris dancing was also taught. This latter form is one occasionally referred to by critics, and indeed by Burrows himself, as a possible influence on his style, although it is less apparent in more recent works. As a choreographer, he made some early works for Sadler's Wells Royal Ballet and the Royal Ballet Choreographic Group before striking out on his own with a few dancers to form the Jonathan Burrows Group. He danced for a while with Rosemary Butcher, and she has spoken of Burrows's inherent ability to attend to detail and precision – to work, as it were, in a small way. The influence of Butcher is evident occasionally in *The Stop Quartet*, with its relaxed quality of 'flung' gestures and low centre of gravity.

While making experimental work at the Riverside Studios, Hammersmith, early in his career, Burrows was exposed to various manifestations of New Dance, and he has since acknowledged the influence of Steve Paxton, among others. He has also expressed admiration for Bronislava Nijinska (specifically *Les Noces*), David Gordon, and Lucinda Childs. It is interesting to consider possible reflections of these practitioners' styles in Burrows's choreography: the pared-down, minimal approach of Childs, for example, might find parallel in Burrows's abstraction of movement ideas or in the importance he gives to clear rhythmic manipulation, albeit in a very different way. In both we see the potential of tiny detail to become germane to the development of a dance idea. David Gordon's quirky sense of humour and interest in the foibles of the individual human being find echoes in the strange, evocative, sometimes very witty gestures, poses, and movements that are sprinkled throughout Burrows's work. The influences of Steve Paxton and contact improvisation – the partner work, taking weight, taking risks, trusting and having to trust people – are also apparent as contributing features. At the same time, however, it is also clear that Burrows possesses a distinctive choreographic 'voice': in his assimilation and transformation of such influences and ideas, he is able to manipulate those ideas in an original way for each different work.

The critic Judith Mackrell has described aspects of Burrows' style as emanating from the influences of folk-dance, classicism, and, more weighted, 'postmodern' movement. Burrows himself, in speaking about the process of choreography, mentions the use of so-called 'images' in dancemaking, relating the process and effectiveness to homeopathy and thereby illustrating his commitment to a concept of abstraction:

> You start with a 100 per cent solution which would be say 100 per cent image ... Then, as in homeopathy, you dilute it by one hundred times – the actual solution gets weaker but the potency gets stronger. So once the images were found, the idea was to dilute it by concentrating more and more on the physical sense of it and letting go more and more of the emotional sense of it. Thereby producing something which was less confrontational, less demanding and therefore more powerful.[1]

Various points Burrows makes, and the ideas he seems to be dealing with, suggest the need for a different approach to each work, according to its demands, and point to his notion of refining and paring down images and movements so that the emotional impulse can be totally removed and the movement freed to speak for itself. What is interesting is Burrows's absorption with the materials of dance itself, and his belief in dance's ability to be relevant to and expressive of the human condition without the trappings of theatre, lighting (although this aspect has become increasingly important in his work), costume, thematic development, or 'issues'. Instead, he puts all those elements on one side in order to focus on what might be described as the unique distinguishing features of dance *per se*. Burrows's classical background is evident in the versatility, strength, and physical understanding of movement for its own sake that underpins his work, perhaps even when it is least 'classical' – as in *Very* (1992), for example, which is non-balletic and often pedestrian in appearance. Ballet is evident also in the tight structural clarity of Burrows's work.

Edward Thorp, however, writes:

> Burrows' wide-ranging choreographic conceptions have nothing in them that is recognisably classical, except that the dancers' balletic training has given them the agility, suppleness, balance, control and stamina that his works demand. He uses many everyday, naturalistic movements, poses and gestures that are recognisable as common body-language, supercharged with a strange assortment of sudden stampings, falls, twists, flurries and angled limbs together with deliberately awkward lifts – humping sacks comes to mind – and moments of stasis, very often in a prone position, to create an elaborate dance structure that is continually fascinating to watch even without trying to impose narrative ideas upon it.[2]

In Burrows's work, then, it is possible to perceive invention and skill in the construction of original dance movements and phrases into a coherent dance work, one that has a dynamic excitement and imaginative delineation of movement, and a richness that can sustain the interest without the need for the spectator to read specific or even hinted-at 'meanings'. This links in turn with Burrows's own comments on the homeopathic parallel, and the idea that something may be most effective when most abstracted. (See, for example, the use of stillness in *The Stop Quartet*, and Burrows's reference to 'holes' in the music through which the dance can be seen, and *vice versa*,[3] also the deliberately restricted perspective of the film work, for example *blue yellow* (1995) made for Sylvie Guillem, and the film version of *Very* (1993). The audience must create the imaginative space for the dance to exist within.)

John Percival has written of *Hymns* (originally a duet, then extended to include a trio for three other men) that the duet shows two men who 'undertake proudly minimal, pious parades' and that the three other men 'engage in schoolboy ... gestures where attitudes are hinted through tiny confrontations'.[4] Those 'tiny confrontations' indicate a very economical approach to movement; such containment and understatement can be very telling about a choreographer's approach, and Burrows has continued to explore them through his later work.

Stoics (1991) is a work which, unlike *Hymns*, could be seen as violent, dangerous, and even nasty at times, as Burrows himself has suggested. Highlighted in this work is the potential of the movement itself, rather than any facial expression, to be expressive of emotion or passion. The choice of some of Mendelssohn's *Songs Without Words* for solo piano is especially interesting, particularly in view of the fact that the dance seems to be dealing with an inability to communicate, with people speaking different languages or not understanding each other. *Stoics*, as Burrows has explained, is so called because of the idea of the 'stiff upper lip' that characterizes a certain type of social behaviour, maintained none the less at the same time as a sense of humour throughout life's difficult events.

Audiences have perceived *Stoics* as funny rather than menacing, however, and it is easy to see why, because the dynamic shaping of the movement, whether it be aggressive, violent, or threatening, is somehow channelled differently so that it is never focused one person on the other – though dancers may stop to watch or contemplate each other from time to time. There is the sense of being an outsider, of looking at foreign customs, social interaction, war-dances (and this is equally true of *Very*) – but not quite, because the fact of each dancer stopping to watch the other 'breaks the frame' and highlights instead the human capacity for mutual misunderstanding. The hint of potential violence is made much more explicit, however, in small moments in *The Stop Quartet*; but these are not developed thematically, and so again the sense of possible danger is dispelled.

Burrows's movement style is frequently characterized by a powerful impetus from the exact centre – not from the centre of the body, but rather from deep at the point of attachment, for example in the shoulder or hip joint – which very quickly dissipates, with a 'flung' quality so that directions do not seem to be important, or focused (although it should be said that in some works the focus is very clearly articulated, as in *Very* and several sections of *The Stop Quartet*). It is the constant awareness of a centre from which movements emanate, however violently, which contributes much to the clear focus of the structure, or the way in which the movements are structured. There is a contrasting moment of repose in *Stoics*, for example, during some close partner work, when Burrows crouches down and allows the woman to climb on to his back and then to be carried around by him. Her carriage is characteristically upright, and hands are joined again, but this time one hand is placed gently on top of the other. This relaxing of the tension in the moment diffuses the tension of the whole for a brief span, albeit to a limited extent, because of her ramrod posture and direct gaze; it is not a weakening, but a softening.

Clement Crisp has written (in the *Financial Times* in 1994) of the early works that 'Burrows saw lives that were a stifled cry of pain and his movement, wild, autistic, sometimes very funny, provided an exact parallel without descending into mimicry'. He also noted that *Very* was 'too cussed and uncommunicative' (suggesting the misfiring of communication in *Stoics* taken to extremes), but that in *Our* (1994), 'movement is fluid, structure more relaxed in outline and broader in dynamic range'. Both *Our* and *Very* recall *Stoics* in different ways. In *Our* it is the intensity of focus one dancer directs towards another at various times, although with perhaps less sense of the ridiculous and more of the hopeless. In *Very* there is a similar sense of struggling to achieve something or find something, for example in the forced *attitude* with arched back, and the purposeful, clearly articulated gestural movements of hands brushing across the body, front and back.

In the programme note for *Our*, Burrows included a quotation by Baudelaire: 'To express at once the attitude and the gesture of living beings whether solemn or grotesque, and their luminous explosion in space'. He explained that the reason for using this text was 'to gently give those people [whose intuitive response might be blocked by working too hard] a framework in which to see [*Our*]'. This suggests a perceptive view of audiences as well as the conviction that dance can communicate something of life. Perhaps it indicates an awareness of the need for work to be 'accessible' – that is, that dance should make some attempt to reach its audience, while challenging them at the same time.

Sophie Constanti, writing in the *Guardian* of *Our*, felt that 'here, Burrows seems as concerned with stillness as with action and has discarded many of the more homespun eccentricities of his works in favour of a more noble exploration of the soul of contemporary human kind'. Constanti seems to suggest that 'homespun eccentricities' are an aberration. It might be argued, however, that they represent, or manifest in some way, an existentialist approach to dance and art, and that the detail of human eccentricity, the mundane, the everyday, are the stuff of life rather more than 'a more noble exploration of the soul of contemporary human kind'.

Chris de Marigny likened Burrows's work to Trisha Brown's in its 'rhythmic complexity'. This comparison, taken in conjunction with the choreographer's acknowledged debt to Childs, Nijinska, and Morris dancing, points to the importance of rhythm, which is given a privileged place in Burrows's structuring of both movement phrases and whole works. While the rhythmic structures that Burrows uses are perhaps less obviously highlighted than in these other choreographers and styles, certainly in later works they are key to the dynamic clarity and effectiveness of the pieces. There is nothing arbitrary about the play of speed, stillness, and rhythm, and this is further underlined when looking at works with music. Sometimes the music has its own clear rhythmic shaping, and Burrows counterpoints that with movement phrases of sometimes quite complex rhythmic change, as in, for example, both *Hymns* and *Stoics*. At other times the relationship is more fluid and more to do with atmospheric layering and the possibility of glimpsing each component through 'holes' in the others, as the audience glimpses Sylvie Guillem through the doorway in *blue yellow*: a spatial exploration of the same idea, which encourages imaginative engagement on the part of the audience to create a space – literal, aural, or conceptual – for the dance to inhabit.

Rachel Chamberlain Duerden

Notes

1 de Marigny, Chris, 'Burrows: Our Thoughts', *Dance Theatre Journal*, 11(2), 1994.

2 Thorpe, Edward, 'Talking to an Engima', *Dance and Dancers*, June/July 1991.

3 See Burrows' comments in Nadine Meisner's 'Closing in on Ballet', *Dance Theatre Journal*, 13(2), 1996.

4 Percival, John, 'Home Reviews: Victoria Marks, Jonathan Burrows. The Place', *Dance and Dancers*, November/December 1988.

Biographical details

Born in Bishop Auckland, County Durham, England, 1960. **Studied** at the Royal Ballet School, London, 1970–79, under Richard Glasstone: winner of an Ursula Morton award for student piece of choreography, *3 Solos*. **Career** Danced with the Royal Ballet, London, 1979–91, and with the Rosemary Butcher Dance Company; early pieces choreographed for Extemporary Dance Theatre, Spiral Dance Company, Sadler's Wells Royal Ballet, and the Royal Ballet Choreographic Group; founded Jonathan Burrows Group in 1988, which became a resident company at The Place Theatre, London, 1992–94, and entered into several co-productions with theatres in Ghent (Belgium), Angers (France), and Utrecht (Netherlands), 1995–96. Has also choreographed for Frankfurt Ballet. **Awards** Frederick Ashton Choreographic Award, 1990; Digital Dance Award, 1992; *Time Out* Award, 1994; Prudential Award, 1995.

Works

Catch (mus. Douglas Gould, 1980), *Listen* (1980), *Cloister* (mus. Edward Lambert, 1982), *The Winter Play* (mus. Dudley Simpson, 1983), *Hymns, Parts 1–3* (1985), *Squash* (mus. Nicholas Wilson, 1985), *Hymns* (1986), *A Tremulous Heart Requires* (mus. Nicholas Wilson, 1986), *Hymns: Complete Version* (1988), *dull morning, cloudy mild* (mus. Matteo Fargion, 1989), *Stoics* (mus. Matteo Fargion, Mendelssohn, 1991), *Very* (mus. Matteo Fargion, 1992), *Very* (film, dir. Adam Roberts, 1993), *Our* (mus. Matteo Fargion, 1994; film version, dir. Adam Roberts, same year), *Hands* (film; dir. Adam Roberts, mus. Matteo Fargion, 1995), *blue yellow* (film solo; dir. Adam Roberts, mus. Kevin Volans, 1995), *The Stop Quartet* (mus. Kevin Volans, Matteo Fargion, 1996; film version, dir. Adam Roberts, same year), *Walking/music* (mus. Kevin Volans, 1997), *Quintet* (mus. and text Tom Johnson, 1997).

Further reading

Interviews with Edward Thorpe, in 'Talking to an Enigma', *Dance and Dancers*, June/July, 1991;

Chris de Marigny, in 'Burrows: Our Thoughts', *Dance Theatre Journal*, Spring/Summer 1994; with Myriam Van Imschoot, in 'Lost in the Singing of Oneself', in *De Morgan* (Belgium), 3 May 1996; with Ismene Brown, in 'One Step Beyond', *Daily Telegraph*, 22 October 1996; with Kevin Volans, in dance issue of *The Full Score*, Autumn/Winter 1996; with Edith Boxberger, in 'Liberating the Imagination', *Ballett International*, December 1996; in Jo Butterworth and Gill Clarke (eds), *Dancemakers' Portfolio*: Conversations with Choreographers, Bretton Hall, 1998.

Articles John Percival, 'Home Reviews: Victoria Marks, Jonathan Burrows. The Place', *Dance and Dancers*, November/December 1988; David Dougill, 'Cultural Fusion on a Natural High', *Sunday Times*, 1 October 1989; 'Young Classical Choreographers', Dance Study Supplement 4, *Dancing Times*, January 1990; Angela Kane, 'Dance Scene: The Jonathan Burrows Group', *Dancing Times*, June 1991; Jann Parry, 'Living on Spare Time and Borrowed Dancers', *Observer*, 27 October 1991; Carol Brown, Eleanor Brickhill, Ann Nugent, 'Three by Three', *Dance Now*, Spring 1993; Marilyn Hunt, 'Jonathan Burrows: The Laughter of Recognition', *Dance Magazine*, October 1993; 'Leading Lights', *Dance Now*, Spring 1994; Ann Nugent, 'Dream Ticket', *Dance Now*, Summer 1994; Sophie Constanti, 'Jonathan Burrows' New Work for Sylvie Guillem' (on *Blue Yellow*), *Dance Theatre Journal*, Winter 1995/96; Sophie Constanti, 'Jonathan Burrows Group', *Dancing Times*, July 1996; Nadine Meisner, 'Closing in on Ballet?', *Dance Theatre Journal*, 13(2), 1996.

ROSEMARY BUTCHER

Rosemary Butcher trained at Dartington College during the mid- to late 1960s, taking extra classes in Graham technique at the then new London School of Contemporary Dance alongside Richard Alston and Siobhan Davies. She went on to further studies in North America, studying the techniques of Doris Humphrey and Merce Cunningham. The artists to have the greatest influence on her, however, were those at the vanguard of American postmodern dance, such as Yvonne Rainer, Trisha Brown, Steve Paxton, Anna Halprin, Elaine Summers, and Lucinda Childs. Butcher returned to England at a significant time in the development of British dance, and although she is renowned for her idiosyncracity, she became, through both her teaching and her choreography, an influence on a new generation of British artists who were making radical departures from established norms under the umbrella title of 'New Dance'.

Looking retrospectively at Butcher's work is particularly rewarding; the phases of her artistic development become clear with an underlying continuity of theme and concern. Yet, as far as critical recognition is concerned, she has had a chequered career. An early work, *Landings* (1976), met with some acclaim, as did *Anchor Relay* (1978). The originality of the work, in terms of its cool, relaxed contrast to the dramatic style of Graham technique, in itself commanded attention. The use of pedestrian movement, repetition, and improvisation was as yet still dynamically varied and physical. The influence of Doris Humphrey could be seen in Butcher's emphasis on fall and recovery and athleticism contrasted with soft, sensual communication between dancers.

The increasing minimalism of Butcher's work in the late 1970s and early 1980s, however, lost her a great deal of support. The preoccupation with the pull of gravity and the transfer of weight within the body and between dancers, along with the deliberate banality of performance, came across to many as turgid and boring. Certainly Butcher did not think like a theatrical choreographer. She used movement like a visual artist and her concern was to explore process as part of work, which needed to be seen as an ongoing development. While it could be said that many dance critics, struggling as they were with a variety of choreographers who demanded a completely new set of criteria, did not understand what Butcher was doing, they undoubtedly represented the general dance-going public in their bafflement.

The period, characterized by austere works with a very limited dynamic range and performed most often in silence, may have lost her fans, but it was no doubt an important phase in Butcher's choreographic development. Her work is appreciative of simple 'natural' forms rather than speculative with a highly developed language. While her increasing minimalism can certainly be looked at in terms of her own development as a choreographer, it also had something in itself to offer to those members of the dance audience who were able to go along with her experiment and share in her explorations. In drawing on aspects of release work and contact improvisation, the physical sensuality of Butcher's work has always been one way into an appreciation of it. In even her most minimalist works there was a sense of poetic space, of resonant silence and the qualities of stillness. In her later works Butcher was to allow these aspects a more expressive presence.

With Butcher's style there is often a depressing sense of isolation and hopelessness. In *Spaces 4* (1981), for example, dancers hold and support one another with Butcher's usual contemplative sensuality, but their actions can easily suggest consolation rather than nurturing or enabling. There is a sense of resignation, and of inertia, which can sometimes threaten completely to overcome the spirit of human vitality and creative resistance that is so central to the notion of dance. During the 1980s, however, the calmly meditative qualities of Butcher's work, and her tendency to explore only within a limited dynamic, were gradually taking on new expressive potential; and this in itself gave rise to a more energizing sense of artistic control. The sense of the choreographer having loosely structured what was essentially an exploration for the dancers was fading. But far from detracting from the qualities that her minimalism had enabled audiences to rediscover in simple movement, Butcher's more expressive collaborations now helped audiences to appreciate her more abstract concerns.

By *The Site* in 1983, for example, Butcher was allowing her dancers to work with imagery rather than the abstract instructions of earlier works. This work was one of Butcher's many successful collaborations with the sculptor Heinz-Dieter Pietsch and with the use of sound scapes, created in this instance by Malcolm Clark. Although the movement was limited in range and dynamic, the work achieved a powerfully dramatic sense of threat, of community and isolation, and of urban wasteland. In *The Site*, and *Imprints* (also 1983), the formal qualities which had hitherto been of a primarily abstract interest now took on an expressive resonance.

With *Flying Lines* of 1985, Butcher met with a new upsurge of critical acclaim. Here her preoccupation with weight and gravity allowed also its opposite in light, soaring movements. The mesmeric qualities of her use of repetition were particularly successful in this work – partly, perhaps, because Michael Nyman's accessible use of musical repetition helped audiences to understand better what Butcher was doing, and gave them a means of allowing it to affect and involve them. Rather than experiencing repetition as monotonous, the audience experienced an overpowering sense of liberation and heightened awareness of the smallest development.

In 1987, again in collaboration with Michael Nyman and with Heinz-Dieter Pietsch, Butcher produced one of her most successful works, *Touch the Earth*, in which many of her developing interests and concerns appeared to come to fruition. Originally performed at the Whitechapel Art Gallery, it went on to be performed in a very different space at the Queen Elizabeth Hall, also in London, and was later televised. The broad theme, as in many of her works, was territory. Sources included ideas about the loss of the American Indian's way of life described in T.C. McLuhan's book *Touch the Earth*. Although the work, as always with Butcher, was purely qualita-

tive and suggestive, rather than narrative or overtly didactic, the programme note invited the audience to draw parallels with the (then) very recent Chernobyl nuclear disaster. Nyman's music looked to the rhythms and tempo of processions and to the singing gondoliers of Venice, while Pietsch's set was inspired by the materials used by ancient farmers.

Throughout her career, Butcher has sited her dancers in a wide range of performance environments; her work relates closely and sensitively to its particular environment, be it studio stage space, a gallery, a church, or a warehouse. But there is a deeper sense in which Butcher's work is concerned with the environment of the human being; it is as if dance can be a way of claiming back lost spatial relations, as if the aim of the movement is to reclaim physical memories, and to put us back in touch with the earth and its sensual rhythms. Butcher has always been thought of as the apolitical exception to the rule within the politicized arena of New Dance. But there is perhaps a politics within the work which is not so far removed from the tendency towards various kinds of essentialism that defines the New Dance movement as a whole. Butcher has never concerned herself with sexual politics in the overt way that many of her contemporaries have done, but her basic affiliation with ecological and environmentalist attitudes is an important aspect of her work, whether or not this has been her conscious intention.

Even in her period of greatest minimalism, Butcher's casual movement could look dreamy, its deliberation indolent, its simple physicality sensual, and its use of space impressionistic. It is perhaps easier to be abstract in dance when the dancers are doing more rather than less; when the convoluted complexities of a highly technical movement vocabulary distance the audience from the dancers. In retrospect the quality of their neutrality has always made Butcher's dancers to some extent politically and dramatically resonant.

Despite fluctuating financial support, Butcher has shown herself capable of constant renewal, and her work has steadily developed in a number of interesting and sometimes surprising directions. In the late 1980s and early 1990s she produced a number of particularly grand conceptions, such as a collaboration with architects Zaha Hadid and John Lyall on a three-part work, *d1*, *d2*, and *3d* (1989–90) for a variety of different sites. She has also shown a strong interest in the adaptation of her work for film; in *Of Shadows and Walls* (1991), she worked with filmmaker Nicola Baldwin on an installation which involved the use of twelve video monitors. Siting her work as part of an installation and embracing new technology point both to Butcher's consistency of interest and to her openness to new possibilities. Her work invites comparisons and parallels, particularly with artists working in the visual arts, but Butcher remains a unique presence in British dance. She has also been an important influence on a wide range of British artists including Sue Maclennan, Miranda Tuffnel, Gaby Agis, Ashley Page, and Jonathan Burrows. However, given that her work has contributed more generally to the expansion of our ways of seeing and siting dance, Rosemary Butcher's influence goes much further.

Lesley-Anne Sayers

Biographical details

Born in Bristol, England, 4 February 1947. **Studied** at Dartington College of Arts, Devon, 1965–69, under Ruth Foster and Flora Cushman; studied in the United States, 1968–69, including with Dorothy Madden at University of Maryland and at the Merce Cunningham Studio in New York; also attended workshops by Anna Halprin and Doris Humphrey. **Career** Danced with Elaine Summers' Intermedia Dance Foundation while in the United States, 1970–72; first choreography, for Scottish Ballet's Moveable Workshop, 1974; founded Rosemary Butcher Dance Company in 1975; appeared regularly at Dance Umbrella and at Dartington festivals, 1978–86, subsequently staging works independently; teaching posts and choreographic residencies include Dunfermline College, 1973–74, Dartington College, 1980–81, the Riverside Studios, London, and the Laban Centre for Movement and Dance; appointed to the staff of Surrey University, Guildford, 1994, and is a visiting fellow for the Royal College of Art. In the mid-1990s began a retrospective aimed at producing all the works of her thirty-year career. **Awards** Royal Society of Arts Scholarship, 1978.

Works

Musical accompaniment where indicated.

Uneven Time (1974), *Multiple Event* (1974), *Pause and Loss* (mus. Alan Lamb, 1976), *Landings* (mus. Alan Lamb, 1976), *Ground Line* (1976), *Passage North East* (1976), *Multiple Event* (1976), *Space Between* (1977), *White Field* (mus. Colin Wood, 1977; later performances silent), *Empty Signals* (mus. Colin Wood, 1977; later performances silent, then with music by J.S. Bach), *First Step* (duet from *Pause and Loss*; mus. Alan Lamb, Schubert), *Anchor Relay* (1978; revised as *Anchor Relay 2* [duet], 1979), *Theme* (1978), *Suggestion and Action* (1978), *Uneven Time* (solo; 1978), *Touch and Go* (1978), *Catch 5, Catch 6* (1978), *Dances for Different Spaces* (mus. Jane Wells, 1979), *Untitled* (1979), *Landscape* (mus. George Crumb, 1979), *Catch 3, Catch 4* (revised version of *Catch 5, Catch 6*; 1979), *Five-Sided Figure* (mus. Mark Turner, Jane Wells, Peter Wiegold, 1980), *Six Tracks* (1980), *Solo Dance for Different Spaces* (1980), *Solo from Instructions* (1980), *Shell: Force Fields and Spaces* (mus. Jim Fulkerson, 1981), *Solo/Duo* (revised version of *Untitled*, 1981), *Spaces 4* (1981), *Traces* (mus. Tom Dolby, 1982), *Field Beyond the Maps* (mus. Jim Fulkerson, 1982), *The Site* (mus. Malcolm Clarke, 1983), *Imprints* (mus. Malcolm Clarke, 1983), *Night Mooring Stones* (mus. Max Easterly, 1984), *Flying Lines* (mus. Michael Nyman, 1985), *Touch the Earth* (mus. Michael Nyman, 1987), *After the Crying and the Shouting* (mus. Wim Mertens, 1989), *d1* (mus. Jim Fulkerson, 1989), *d2* (mus. Jim Fulkerson, 1990), *3-d* (mus. Jim Fulkerson, 1990), *Of Shadows and Walls* (installation, 1991), *The Body as Site* (includes *Tracer*, *The Wasp*, *Tension/Compression*, *Recover*; 1993), *Unbroken View* (1995), *After the Last Sky* (includes film footage, 1996), *Fractured Landscape, Fragmented Narratives* (mus. Johnny Clark, 1997).

Further reading

Articles Dee Conway, 'Rosemary Butcher', *New Dance*, Winter 1983; Alastair Macaulay, 'One at a Time', *Dance Theatre Journal*, Spring 1983;

Sarah Rubidge, 'Traces', *Dance and Dancers*, February 1983; Sally Watts, 'New British Dance', *Dancing Times*, May 1984; Lesley-Anne Davis, 'Collaborations', *Dance Theatre Journal*, Spring 1985; Stephanie Jordan, 'Rosemary Butcher', *Dance Theatre Journal*, Summer 1986; Christopher Crickmay, 'Dialogues with Rosemary Butcher: A Decade of Her Work', *New Dance*, Spring 1986; Judith Mackrell, 'Kitsch and Courtship at the Umbrella', *Dance Theatre Journal*, Spring 1986; Nadine Meisner, 'An English Pioneer', *Dance and Dancers*, February 1987; John Percival, 'What's New?', *Dance and Dancers*, July 1987; Stephanie Jordan, 'London', *Ballet Review*, Winter 1988; Judith Mackrell, 'Post-modern Dance in Britain', *Dance Research*, Spring 1991; Judith Butcher, 'What is Dance?', *Dance Now*, Summer 1992; Nadine Meisner, 'Body as Site – Image as Event', *Dance and Dancers*, May 1993; Andrea Phillips, 'Rosemary Butcher and *The Body as Site*', *Dance Theatre Journal*, Spring/Summer 1993, Sherril Dodds, 'The Momentum Continues', *Dance Theatre Journal*, Spring 1997; Nadine Meisner, 'Rosemary Butcher', *Dance Now*, Summer 1997.

Books Allen Robertson and Donald Hutera, *The Dance Handbook*, Harlow, Essex, 1988; Stephanie Jordon, *Striding Out: Aspects of Contemporary and New Dance in Britain*, London, 1992; Judith Mackrell, *Out of Line: The Story of British New Dance*, London, 1992.

CAROLYN CARLSON

In a 1986 article entitled 'The Metamorphoses of a Beautiful Witch', the critic Marcelle Michel called Carolyn Carlson 'a sort of distant cousin of Isadora Duncan ... [who] quite purely and simply expressed her life in terms of dance, and it is precisely in this manner that her inspiration finds constant renewal.'[1] The importance of Carolyn Carlson on the European dance scene is probably revealed more by the numerous groups and dancers that her teaching has influenced than by her own career, which has often received mixed reviews from the critics. While only occasionally belying her qualities as a dancer of rare technical ability and unique poetic inter-

pretation, her choreographic works have often come in for some negative criticism.

It would be difficult, if not impossible and perhaps unnecessary, to quantify the impact made by Carlson. However, it can be said that the European artistic environment was shaken by her presence above all during the 1970s and 1980s, when her influence as a mentor and teacher for a whole generation of young dancers and choreographers was most strongly felt in France and Italy.

The *nouvelle danse française*, as well as a number of postmodern dance groups in Italy, owe much to Carlson. In France, Dominique Bagouet (who died prematurely in 1993), Dominique Petite, and Caroline Maracade began in her company, while the group which was founded in Venice under her guidance at Teatro la Fenice stayed together after her departure and became known as Sosta Palmizi.

For her part, Carlson remains faithful to her own image and continues her research into a mystical, almost 'naive' world on stage. It is a world composed of sensations, dreams, traces of memory, containing images from everyday life interwoven with a simple, unpolluted, uncontaminated nature. The 'innocence' and 'purity' which form part of her image are what make her seem a sort of late twentieth-century Isadora Duncan. Although she uses repetition as a choreographic device, this never reaches the same level of anguish as that in Pina Bausch's works or in Susanne Linke and the German neo-expressionist school, but is limited to a sort of mirroring of the mechanical elements of modern life.

Carlson has distanced herself artistically from the formalism of her first great teacher, Alwin Nikolais. However, in the creative methods she uses with her dancers (improvisation as a way towards self-understanding and expression in movement), and in her innate expressionism, she is clearly linked by a thread which reaches back through Nikolais and Hanya Holm to the mid-European school of Mary Wigman.

Born in California of Finnish ancestry, Carlson still has close ties with the city of Helsinki, as demonstrated by an RAI (Radio Audiovisione Italiana) video. She started her early dance training with Clarie-Lauche Porter of the San Francisco Ballet and at the University of Utah. Certainly her formative years coincided with a period of great social upheaval and unrest among American youth, and the social and cultural climate to which Carlson was exposed made her very much part of what was later to be called 'the sixties generation'. As Allen Robertson has written, 'Carlson often seems to be a flower child who grew up managing to preserve the ideals of her generation ... Both her work and her personality stem from the Woodstock generation.'[2] A characteristic that runs through much of Carlson's works is a sense of roots both American (*Underwood*, with music by René Aubry, 1982) and, more remotely, Finnish (the RAI video). At the same time, as Robertson suggests, her artistic philosophy can be traced to a certain time and life style, which also include Zen as a way of approaching her work. In 1978, Carlson showed the extent of her interest in Zen when she choreographed *The Year of the Horse*. This philosophy still guides her principles to the extent that she always considers the *now* to be the most important aspect of her life and work, for, as she has said, 'Zen is for me simply a philosophy of art and life – not as a source of psycho-analysis but as a source of inspiration.'[3]

Carlson's acceptance of Zen philosophy also means that she dislikes the idea of a repertoire and her works have rarely been revived. She has said on many occasions that the works are born and die in a certain time and that it is useless to try to preserve them when the people, the mood, the sensations which gave them life, change. She is quoted: 'I don't like to keep a repertoire. My pieces live and die with the time they were made and the people who perform them.'[4] Giorgio Rossi, one of the original

dancers with Carlson at the Teatro la Fenice in Venice, has said, 'She changes continually. She is constantly working on a piece ... the piece never dies because it is always changing and is kept alive by all these changes.' A work for Carlson is never 'fixed': something – a movement, a gesture, the music – which seemed to work the day before is now no longer acceptable and is replaced. Carlson has always referred to her pieces as 'works-in-progress'. They must be adaptable, responsive to shifts in mood and circumstances. An extreme example of this is *L'Orso e la luna* (1983), which not only changed in length from over two hours to one hour and twenty minutes but changed title as well to *Chalk Work*. The problems this creates for the dance researcher are easily imagined. Carlson herself needs constant renewal and new input, so that often the dancers alternate, first used for one piece and later recalled for another. Carlson says, 'In most cases my choices occur by instinct. I feel a certain person functions or will function and usually I am never wrong.'[5]

In discussing Carlson's creative methods, Giorgio Rossi says that she uses improvisation above all in the early stages of a work's development, largely as a form of training for her dancers. She uses it, explains Rossi, as a way of getting to know the body and controlling it along the concepts of time, space, form rhythm, and motion of the German Expressionist tradition. However for Carlson, the person – the individual – is the most important element to be developed. The dancer is a dancer/actor who must transform him/herself into fire, wind, water, good, bad, grotesque, and so on. To this end Carlson also uses her own sketches and poems as a source of inspiration, and when she comes to rehearsals, 'she comes with sensations', as Giorgio Rossi explained in 1989.[6] As Rossi points out, the shift in emphasis with Carlson is away from the purely formal, impersonal geometry of her teacher Nikolais to a personal, individual interpretation which still creates geometrical forms between the dancers.

While Carlson has refuted the ideas of a Carlson *technique*, she acknowledges a Carlson *style*, what she calls 'my personal interpretation of the relationship between space and time, between motion and energy'. As far as her relationship to music is concerned, she has referred to it as 'a subsequent problem'. She likes to work closely with a composer for a continuous exchange of ideas, but feels unable to choreograph on ready-made music and likes the music to adapt to the dance.[7]

From her earliest performances Carlson has always been respected as a great dancer. Throughout her career, references can be found to the long elegant lines of her arabesques, the supple lyricism and dream-like quality of her movement, the highly individual use of her long arms which can sweep gracefully around her head but finish in a cutting movement across her waist as she executes a deep contraction. However, in a review of an early work, a solo entitled *Densité 21.5* (first performed at the Paris Opéra in May 1973), John Percival mentions 'the tiny flickering movements largely on one spot'.[8] There is only an apparent contradiction in terms of individual movement to what has been mentioned above, as over a period of time Carlson has developed a personal style which comprises both of these extremes of movement, and which she applies to the choreographic effect she wishes to obtain.

Commenting on *Commedia* (1993), Carlson's work inspired by Dante's *La Divina Commedia*, Gérard Mannoni summarizes the overall qualities of Carlson's long choreographic output and the difficulties of writing about it. He writes about the images which her work provokes, the purity and beauty of line, the originality and expressiveness of the dancing, and the rigour of form which is underlined by the quality of lighting, reminding the viewer of Robert Wilson's works. He writes of a movement language that is constantly evolving, changing, and creating wonder with each new piece, and of a group of dancers of exceptional talent. But above all he writes of Carlson herself, saying, 'Nobody can imitate the way she dances the Universe, her presence is always simply stunning.'[9]

Ann Veronica Turnbull

Notes

1 Michel, Marcelle, 'The Metamorphosis of a Beautiful Witch' *Ballett International*, 9(7/8), July/August 1986, pp. 84–5.
2 Robertson, Allen, 'In the Now', *Ballet News*, 5(5), November 1983, pp. 30–2.
3 Bentivoglio, Leonetta, 'Carolyn Carlson: Pure Dance is Purely Poetic', *Ballett International*, 5(2), February 1982, pp. 34–5.
4 Robertson, op. cit., p. 31.
5 Bentivoglio, op. cit. p. 35.
6 Interview with Ann Turnbull published in *Society of Dance History Scholars Proceedings*, 1992.
7 Bentivoglio, op. cit. pp. 34–5.
8 Percival, John, 'Homage to Varèse', *Dance and Dancers*, 24(8), August 1973, pp. 24–7.
9 Mannoni, quoted in *Teatro Mese*, 4(5), 1993.

Biographical details

Born in Oakland, California, United States, 7 March 1943. Studied with Claire-Lauche Porter, at San Francisco Ballet School; attended University of Utah; also trained with Alwin Nikolais. **Career** Danced with Alwin Nikolais Company, 1965–71; subsequent career primarily in Europe; danced with Compagnie Anne Béranger, 1971–72; invited to stage work for Paris Opéra Ballet in 1973, thereafter becoming *danseuse étoile chorégraphique* there, 1973–80, where she founded the Groupe de Recherches Théâtrales de l'Opéra; choreographer, directing own group for Teatro la Fenice in Venice, 1980–84; returned to Paris to stage pieces at Théâtre de la Ville; in the late 1980s and early 1990s choreographed for Folkwang Tanzstudio in Essen, Germany, and acted as guest choreographer for Nederlands Dans Theater, Helsinki City Theatre Ballet, and the Finnish National Ballet; succeeded Mats Ek as artistic director, Cullberg Ballet, Sweden, 1994–95; subsequently freelance choreographer.

Works*

Rituel pour un rêve mort (mus. B Galuppi, Morton Feldman, Pierre Henry, 1972), *Densité 21.5* (mus. Varèse, 1973), *Enivrez-vous* (mus. Pierre Henry, 1973), *Onirocri* (mus. Barre Phillips, 1973), *Verfangen* (mus. Pierre Henry, 1973), *L'Or des fous* (mus. Girolamo Arrigo, 1974), *Les Fous d'or* (mus. Igor Wakhevitch, 1974), *Sablier prison* (mus. various, 1974), *Il y'a juste un instant* (mus. Barre Phillips, 1974), *X Land* (mus. Barre Phillips, John Surman, 1975), *Spar* (solo for Paolo Bortoluzzi; mus. Ragnar Grappe, 1974), *Quinine* (mus. Stu Martin, 1975), *Wind, Water, Sand* (mus. John Surman, Barre Phillips, 1976), *Theta* (mus. John Surman, 1976), *Untitled* (silent, 1976), *Cipher* (mus. Igor Wakhevitch, 1976), *Haiku* (Matti Pirigo Bergstrom, 1976), *This, That* (mus. John Surman, Barre Phillips, 1977), *The Other* (mus. Igor Wakhevitch, 1977), *The Beginning ... and the End* (mus. Igor Wakhevitch, 1977), *The Year of the Horse* (mus. Jean Schwarz, 1978), *Cipher II* (mus. John Surman, 1978), *Writings in the Wall* (mus. John Surman, 1979), *Amble & Running on the Sounds of a Thousand Stones* (mus. René Aubry, 1979), *Trio* (mus. John Surman, Barre Phillips, Hervé Bourde, 1979), *Slow, Heavy and Blue* (mus. René Aubry, 1980), *The Architects* (mus. J.S. Bach, 1980), *Undici Onde* (mus. René Aubry, Jean Schwarz, 1981), *Underwood* (mus. René Aubry, 1982), *Solo* (mus. René Aubry, 1983), *L'Orso e la luna* (later retitled *Chalk Work*; mus. Igor Wakhevitch, H.J. Rodelius, John Surman, 1983), *Blue Lady* (revised version of *Solo*, 1985), *Still Waters (Wood, Light and Stones)* (mus. René Aubry, Jean Schwarz, 1986), *A Time Exposure* (mus. Joachim Kuhn, 1987), *Shamrock* (mus. Gabriel Yard, 1987), *Dark* (mus. Joachim Kuhn, 1988), *Danza, un personaggio una città* (for Italian RAI television, 1988), *Cosmopolitan Greetings* (jazz opera by Robert Wilson, Rolf Liebermann, Allen Ginsberg, Georges Gruntz; 1988), *Improvisations* (mus. Michel Portal, John Surman, Miguel-Angel Estrella, Ivry Gitlis, 1989), *Steppe* (mus. René Aubry, 1990), *Breath of Life* (mus. René Aubry, 1990), *Going Home* (mus. René Aubry, 1991), *Cornerstone* (mus. John Surman, 1991), *Elokuu* (mus. Mikko Mikkola, David W. Yoken, 1992), *Maa – Crossing the Great Waters* (1992), *Settembre* (mus. Mikko Mikkola, 1992), *Commedia* (mus. Michel Portal, 1993), *Them* (mus. Terry Riley, 1993), *Don't Look Back* (1993), *Vu d'ici* (mus. Gabriel Yared, 1995), *Sub Rosa* (mus. various, texts T.S. Eliot, Fernando Pessoa, 1995), *Syyskuu* (1995), *Signes* (mus. René Aubry, 1997), *Improvisata* (duet; 1997).

*List based on material supplied by Ann Turnbull.

Further reading

Interviews with Rolf Garske and Rick Takvorian, in 'Beyond Abstraction', *Ballett International*, April 1986; with Aline Apostolska, in 'Carolyn Carlson: La danse cosmique', *Les Saisons de la Danse*, May 1993; with Charlotte Lipinska, in 'Vue d'elle', *Les Saisons de la Danse*, July 1995; with Carol Pratl, in 'Carolyn Carlson Talks to Carol Pratl', *Dance Europe*, June/July 1996.

Articles Jean-Claude Diénis, 'Carlson à l'Opéra', *Les Saisons de la Danse*, June 1977; Lucile Rossel, 'Carlson: Le Cycle achevé', *Les Sasions de la Danse*, November 1977; Jean-Claude Dienis, 'Carolyn Carlson', *Les Saisons de la Danse*, March 1980; Gaston Moutet, 'D'Oakland à Venise, la longue marche de Carolyn', *Pour la Danse*, March 1980; Leonetta Bentivoglio, 'Carolyn Carlson', *Ballett International*, February 1982; Allen Robertson, 'In the Now', *Ballet News*, November 1983; Marcelle Michel, 'The Metamorphoses of a Beautiful Witch', *Ballett International*, July/August 1986; Eva Van Schait, 'Dream or Nightmare?', *Ballett International*, January 1988; Jean-Marc Adolphe, 'Carolyn Carlson', *Pour la Danse*, February 1989; Ann Veronica Turnbull, 'Carolyn Carlson's Years at Il Teatro la Fenice, Venice, Italy, 1980–1984', *Society of Dance History Scholars Proceedings*, 1992; Mårten Spangberg, 'Myths of Time' (on *Sub Rosa*), *Ballett International*, March 1995.

Books Leonetta Bentivoglio, *La danza contemporanea*, Milan, 1985; Alain Macaire and Michel Marcelle, *Carolyn Carlson*, Paris, 1986; Guy Delahaye, *Carolyn Carlson* (photographs), Grenoble, 1988; Allen Robertson and Donald Hutera, *The Dance Handbook*, Harlow, Essex, 1988.

LUCINDA CHILDS

To American dance audiences, the name Lucinda Childs conjures up a cool, upright, elegantly severe presence, as well as the choreographic epitome of minimalism: a stripped-down vocabulary performed along geometric floor plans, in rigorous structures that repeat or mutate minutely and precisely over time.

In certain ways, Childs's work seems the perfect embodiment of the analytic postmodernism that Sally Barnes has identified as an outgrowth of the Judson Church dance experiments.[1] Rejecting the overt, intentional expression of classic modern dance, with its carefully honed technique and measured phrasing, its significant lighting and music – let alone the codified, virtuosic vocabulary and spectacular presentation of ballet[2] – this new approach tended to objectify movement, both in the sense of doing away with subjective, emotive rationales for dance, and in the sense of making movement itself a detached object of scrutiny.[3] Yet, Childs's choreographic sensibility is rather different from other Judson choreographers, and she has pushed certain of the concerns of American postmodern dance further, and for a longer period of time, moving in directions that may be surprising, but which conform to the logic of her own concerns.

Unlike many Judson-era choreographers' work in the 1960s and 1970s, Childs's minimalism has not been a democratic statement, a paean to pedestrianism. Her own body looks – and is – ballet- and Cunningham-trained: pulled up, aligned to maximum function and clarity, even if the arms have often been used in a relaxed manner. Her post-Judson dancers have almost all been technically sophisticated, exhibiting the uncluttered, open-body characteristic of ballet and Cunningham. This classic body, somewhat paradoxically, is one form that Childs's commitment to the Judson's task-like (rather than dramatic or emotive) movement has taken, and is matched by the demeanour of her own performance persona, as well as that of her dancers: not just neutral, but deeply cool, impersonal or, as Susan Sontag has said, 'transpersonal'.[4] In Childs's case, this has often been read as severity, but perhaps its ideal manifestation lies in the pristine transparency of a dancer like Meg Harper, whose presence seems inseparable from the execution of the movement itself. Similarly, Childs's habit of choreographing for unison ensemble or contrapuntal units thereof is not about

community; rather it is another way in which her dances shun expressivity by focusing the power of the choreography within a structure that is larger than individuals or pairs. Until recently, her dances have avoided anything that might suggest dramatic interaction, such as partnering; now that she allows herself that 'luxury', such interactions still exist to support or elaborate spatial patterns rather than to advance a story.

Like many choreographers in the 1960s and 1970s, Childs worked with a radically simplified vocabulary – in her case, walking, turning, small skips, and later, leaps. This restriction does not seem to have been about exploring the mechanics of movement or rediscovering the meaning of everyday gesture. It has not even been about creating a new dance vocabulary in quite the same way as for most other Judson choreographers, whose rejection of the conventional dance techniques afforded an opportunity for postmodern dance to luxuriate in the plethora of motions formerly excluded from 'dance' and, ultimately, to enlarge vastly the possibilities for dance movement in new hybrid vocabularies. Over the years, Childs's choreographic vocabulary has very gradually expanded to include quite a few ballet-derived steps, always in the service of geometric structure and visual clarity. What has grown and developed since the early 1970s has been the way in which the steps are assembled, accumulated, varied through re-viewing from different points of view, and intensified through repetition or doubling – in short, the style of her choreography.

As the vocabulary has enlarged, and the works have become more complex, what has remained remarkably constant – and faithful to her Judson roots and her Cunningham training – is the dynamic with which her choreography is performed. Her dancers are always either completely still, or in motion; there are no marked transitions between 'steps', no traditional preparations, only the physical adjustments the body *must* make from movement to movement. Neither is there an ebb and flow of energy intensity that signals, 'this movement is more important than that one'. Rather there is a matter-of-fact evenness of effort that reminds one of Yvonne Rainer's *Trio A*, but transferred to everything from *adagio* to leaps. The visual effect of such performance is distinctly different from conventional ballet, and is undoubtedly physically challenging for dancers since it requires both a more continuous effort and a damping of extreme steps such as leaps. In performance, this dynamic not only short-circuits the dramatic, but also focuses attention on ensemble interaction in an impersonal way, so that bodies become agents of time and space. On the other hand, neither would Childs's work be confused with Merce Cunningham's, even though her vocabulary and dynamic resemble his, because of the very different structuring and spatial vision of her dances, which tend to emphasize symmetry and balance.

Unlike the game or chance structures used by many of her Judson-era contemporaries, her work has not tended to incorporate improvisation or the everyday, in the sense of the 'happenstance' or the 'messy'; rather, it has been disciplined and controlled to an extreme. This is most apparent, perhaps, in her precise, deceptively simple choreographic structures. In one of her early Judson pieces, *Museum Piece* (1965), Childs placed coloured circles from an enlargement of a section of Seurat's painting *Le Cirque* on the floor, and then stepped backwards from dot to dot, looking through a mirror, enacting what was to become her ongoing concern with point of view.[5] Her evocation of Seurat, in this case, also seems like a particularly appropriate way to begin considering dance as energy visually conceived in space and time,[6] since in pointillism precisely-spaced dots of colour interact with one another to bring a flat canvas to a pulsating three-dimensionality. Childs's dances of the late 1960s and early 1970s were organized, spatially, along clear geometric floor paths and, temporally, through elementary units of simple movement that repeated or changed slightly. Throughout these dances, Childs explored, with a sort of scientific exactness, a central theme of her work: the importance – and the great difficulty – of seeing movement clearly.[7] Some of her dances of this period seemed, in fact, to push the limits of how 'simple' a dance could be and still elude the viewer's complete perception. Many of the dances suggested the shimmering visual ambiguity of Op Art.

Childs's work with Robert Wilson in *Einstein on the Beach* (1976) opened up new structural principles for her, spatially, in the expanded architecture and precisely focused geometries of a proscenium stage. Childs has noted that 'Wilson is able to transform that space because of the way he plays into the classical lines and, in some surrealistic way, also plays against those existing architectural values.'[8] Like Wilson, Childs both exploits and 'transforms' the proscenium in ways I have already suggested: her use of ensemble; spare, angular vocabulary; rigorous attention to spatial placement and scale; repetition and shifts in point of view; and, most importantly, her emphasis on the diagonal.[9] All point to the pure geometry of the stage space on a scale that is larger than individual human beings. Sensitively designed sets have played their part in this effort as well, such as Sol LeWitt's oversize projections of the dancers in *Dance* (1979) and Frank Geary's two-layer set for *Available Light* (1983).

Childs's involvement in *Einstein* also suggested a new form of temporal structure in the form of music. Her dances of the early 1970s were performed in silence and organized by elaborate counts.[10] Inspired by Wilson's collaboration with Philip Glass, Childs tended during the later 1970s and 1980s to structure her dances around and against the duration, tempi, and rhythms of minimalist compositions whose precise, repetitive, gradually shifting structures paralleled her own choreographic concerns. Childs's use of music and sets in these dances, and in her subsequent work, has not at all been like Merce Cunningham's collaborations in which each element is independent of the others and comes together only in performance. In keeping with Childs's tight control of the choreographic process, music, design, and dance all evolve in a completely unified project.[11] Very much like Seurat's pointillism, Childs played movement and music against one another – for example, a series of skimming leaps along geometrically significant pathways and intersections, over a pulse that is two or four times the speed of the leap phrase, to energize the entire stage space. The result was frequently an excess of carefully calibrated specifics, a perceptual overload that was ecstatic in the extreme.

In keeping with the twin themes of *Einstein*, Childs's eloquence with the transpersonal raw elements of dance and physics reached a peak in the late 1970s and early 1980s, which only a few choreographers have matched – one thinks specifically of Cunningham and Elizabeth Streb. In the later 1980s and the 1990s, Childs choreographed for a number of ballet companies, many of them European. Her work from this period became less explicitly analytic and closer to traditional concepts of choreography, although it continued to build, for aesthetic ends, on the insights of the earlier analysis. Whereas in her earlier dances, she might elaborate the point of view by turning the dancers, or elevating them, or incorporating giant film projections, these more recent dances have used quite complex vocabularies to map elegantly clear spatial patterns. For example, in *Four Elements* (1990), which Childs choreographed for the Rambert Dance Company, the diagonal was enacted not only as a pathway, as in so many Childs dances, but from numerous vertical perspectives. It appeared in versions of arabesques and lifts; it was also subtly distorted into an arc by a tilted head in an off-centre turn, or the angle of an over-the-back lift, or was momentarily brought into

focus in the stress of two dancers pulling against one another. Music has remained a primary structuring element, and Childs's use of music has become more complex and subtle, drawing on rhythm, energy, dynamics, and timbre. The music itself has become more varied, as well, in contemporary works with romantic or baroque overtones by composers such as Gavin Bryars, György Ligeti, Iannis Xenakis, and Henryk Górecki. While remaining non-descriptive or illustrative, her choreography has become more closely entwined with what one might almost call musical mood.

In this recent period of her career, visual clarity has been an abiding concern, not so much in response to its difficulty, more for the sake of its beauty. Formalism has become – relatively – less a polemic and more an aesthetic. Some American viewers have undoubtedly mourned this 'mellowing' of her stance. Nevertheless, Childs's work remains exhilarating and intriguing, at the cutting edge of the intersection of postmodern dance and classicism.

Judy Burns

Notes

1 Sally Banes, *Terpsichore in Sneakers*, reprinted edition, Middletown, Conn.: Wesleyan University Press, 1987, pp. xx–xi.
2 See Yvonne Rainer, 'A Quasi Survey of Some "Minimalist" Tendencies in the Quantitatively Minimal Dance Activity Midst the Plethora; or an Analysis of *Trio A*', *Work 1961–73*, Halifax, Nova Scotia: Press of The Nova Scotia College of Art and Design and New York: New York University Press, 1974, pp. 63–9.
3 Banes, pp. xxi–xxii.
4 Susan Sontag, 'For "Available Light": A Brief Lexicon', *Art in America*, December 1983, p. 105. Sontag uses this word to make a distinction between Yvonne Rainer's 'neutral doer' and a more elevated impersonality in which grace is without inwardness, which Sontag located in Kleist's essay on puppetry and in George Balanchine's choreography.
5 Banes, p. 135.
6 A number of writers, notably Sally Banes, have accurately identified and discussed Childs's visual emphasis, but that visualness can be

further defined. Much of the power of Childs's choreography – the 'shimmering' quality of these early dances, for example – lies in the structurally focused tension between kinetic energies and precise spatial placements or pathways; this effect is enhanced in the late 1970s and the 1980s when Childs incorporated airborne movements and musical pulse. See also Susan Sontag's discussion of repetition (p. 109).

7 See Childs, quoted in Banes, p. 139.
8 Sophie Constanti, 'Swimming against the Tide', *Dance Theatre Journal*, Spring 1991, p. 8.
9 Ann Daly's observations concerning Robert Wilson's use of the diagonal to offset the horizontal and vertical in the proscenium, as well as her paraphrase of Wilson's comment, 'counterpoint clarifies', are suggestive in regard to Childs's own practices. See Ann Daly, 'The Closet Classicist', *Danceview*, Winter 1993–94, pp. 3, 6.
10 Sontag, p. 105. Sontag implies a connection between Seurat's belief that beauty has an 'objective, measurable basis' and Childs's own aesthetic, and asserts that time and space come together through counting.
11 For some descriptions of the connection between specific music and Childs's dances in the early 1980s, see Nancy Goldner, 'The Festival May Be New Wave, But the Dancing Celebrated the Tried and True', *Christian Science Monitor*, 8 November 1983, p. 26, and Allen Robertson, 'Be Am Is Are Was Were Been', *Soho News*, 25 March 1981, p. 59.

Biographical details

Born in New York, 26 June 1940. **Studied** at Sarah Lawrence College, Bronxville, New York (earning BA degree in Dance, 1962), the American Ballet Center, and with Merce Cunningham. **Career** Danced with Judson Dance Theater, working as choreographer (mostly of own solos), c.1962–66; founding dancer, choreographer, and director, Lucinda Childs Dance Company, New York, 1973 to the present. Has also choreographed for other companies, including Bavarian State Opera Ballet, Rambert Dance Company, Lyon Opéra Ballet, Ohio Ballet, and Paris Opéra Ballet. **Awards** include Obie Award, 1976; Guggenheim Fellowship, 1979.

Works

Pastime (1963), *Three Pieces* (mus. M. Goldstein, 1963), *Minus Auditorium Equipment and Furnishings* (1963), *Egg Deal* (1963), *Cancellation Sample* (1964), *Carnation* (1964), *Street Dance* (1964), *Model* (soundtrack of taped dialogue, 1964), *Geranium* (1965), *Scarf* (1965), *Museum Piece* (1965), *Screen* (1965), *Agriculture* (1965), *Vehicle* (in *Nine Evenings of Theater and Engineering*; 1966), *Untitled Trio* (1968; revised version, 1973), *Particular Reel* (1973), *Checkered Drift* (1973), *Calico Mingling* (1973), *Duplicate Suite* (1975), *Reclining Rondo* (1975), *Congeries on Edges for 20 Obliques* (1975), *Radial Courses* (1976), *Mix Detail* (1976), *Transverse Exchanges* (1976), *Solo: Character on Three Diagonals* (from opera *Einstein on the Beach* by Philip Glass, 1976), *Cross Words* (1976), *Figure Eights* (1976), *Plaza* (1977), *Melody Excerpt* (1977), *Interior Drama* (1977), *Katema* (1978), *Dance* (mus. Philip Glass, 1979), *Mad Rush* (mus. Philip Glass, 1981), *Relative Calm* (mus. Jon Gibson, 1981), *Formal Abandon, Part I* (solo; mus. Michael Riesman, 1982), *Formal Abandon, Part II* (quartet; mus. Michael Riesman, 1982), *Available Light* (mus. John Adams, 1983, revised later the same year), *Formal Abandon, Part III* (mus. Michael Riesman, 1983), *Cascade* (mus. Steve Reich, 1984), *Outline* (mus. Gavin Bryars, 1984), *Première Orage* (mus. Shostakovich, 1984), *Field Dances* (dances in opera *Einstein on the Beach* by Philip Glass, 1984), *Portraits in Reflection* (mus. Michael Galasso, Michael Nyman, Allen Shawn, Elizabeth Swados, 1986), *Clarion* (mus. Paul Chihara, 1986), *Hungarian Rock* (mus. György Ligeti, 1986), *Calyx* (mus. Harry de Wit, 1987), *Lichtknall* (opera; Erhard Grosskopf, 1987), *Mayday* (in collaboration with Sol LeWitt; mus. Christian Wolff, 1989), *Perfect Stranger* (mus. Frank Zappa, 1990), *Four Elements* (mus. Gavin Bryars, 1990), *Rhythm Plus* (mus. György Ligeti, Luc Ferrari, 1991), *Oophaa Naama* (mus. Iannis Xenakis, 1992), *Concerto* (mus. Górecki, 1993), *One and One* (mus. Iannis Xenakis, 1993), *Impromptu* (mus. Andrzej Kurylewicz, 1993), *Chamber Symphony* (mus. John Adams, 1994), *Trilogies* (mus. Paul Schwartz, 1994), *Commencement* (mus. Zygmunt Krauze, 1995), *Solstice* (mus. François-Bernard Mâche, 1995), *Kengir* (mus. François-Bernard Mâche, 1995), *From the White Edge of Phrygia* (mus. Stephen Montague, 1995), *Hammerklavier* (mus. Moritz Eggert, 1996).

Further reading

Interviews with Daryl Chin, in 'Talking with Lucinda Childs', *Dance Scope*, Winter/Spring 1979/80; with Connie Kreemer, in her *Further Steps: Fifteen Choreographers on Modern Dance*, New York, 1987; with Bernadette Bonis, in 'Lucinda Childs: La danse post-moderne a cassé l'idée d'objet d'art', *Danser*, September 1990; with Sophie Constanti, in 'Swimming Against the Tide',

Dance Theatre Journal, Spring 1991; with Jörn Rohwer, in 'Timeless Everyday', *Ballett International*, October 1995.

Articles Jill Johnston, 'Judson 1964: End of an Era', *Ballet Review*, 1(6), 1967; Lucinda Childs, 'Notes: '64-'74', *Drama Review*, 1975; John Percival, 'Paris International Dance Festival: American Emphasis', *Dance and Dancers*, December 1979; Barry Laine, 'Dance Forecast, 1980–81', *Ballet News*, September 1980; Barry Laine, 'In Search of Judson', *Dance Magazine*, September 1982; 'Lucinda Childs', *Current Biography Yearbook 1984*; Deborah Rawson, 'Child's Play', *Ballet News*, December 1984; Iris Fanger, 'The New Lucinda Childs', *Dance Magazine*, October 1989; Ann Daly, 'The Closet Classicist', *Danceview*, Winter 1993–94; Maria Shevstova, 'La Maladie de la mort', *Dance Theatre Journal*, 14(1), 1998.

Books Don McDonagh, *The Complete Guide to Modern Dance*, New York, 1976; Peter Wynne (ed.), *Judson Dance: An Annotated Bibliography of the Judson Dance Theater and of Five Major Choreographers*, Englewood Cliffs, New Jersey, 1978; Anne Livet, *Contemporary Dance*, New York, 1978; Sally Banes, *Terpsichore in Sneakers: Post-modern Dance*, Boston, 1980; Arlene Croce, *Going to the Dance*, New York, 1982; Sally Banes, *Democracy's Body: Judson Dance Theater 1962–1964*, Ann Arbor, Michigan, 1983 (reprinted, Durham, North Carolina, 1993).

MICHAEL CLARK

Michael Clark has attracted considerable attention since the early 1980s, and for a number of reasons. Most obviously, his anarchic blend of technically proficient dance performance with incongruous, often subversive use of costumes, props, music, and thematic material has provoked responses of delight and disapproval in varying measure. His popularity (and notoriety) over a period of years has given him a status in the dance world and beyond that has allowed him to pursue, develop, and refine his interests in a number of contexts.

As well as inspiring a widely diverse critical response, Clark's work has attracted a new audience for dance. Characteristic features of his style include clear references to, and manipulation of, classical ballet technique (and ballet's tradition) juxtaposed with rock music, exaggerated and often deliberately shocking costumes, the use of non-dancers, such as personal friends and family, and postmodern references to contemporary issues – frequently made in a childlike or playful way. His interest in classicism is apparent throughout his work, although the extent to which Clark may be seen to be redefining classicism, or developing a new strand within it, is hard to assess. In reference to ballet, he has spoken of Balanchine's *Apollo* as:

> an amazing piece of work, but I hate the idea that you can't create anything new, that everything is just a pastiche of what has gone before. If ballet is going to survive then it will be because dancers and choreographers challenge it. You have to re-define classicism – I couldn't do a piece that was just made up of classical vocabulary. You have to add new words to the language or it dies out.[1]

After early studies in Scottish dancing, Clark trained in ballet at the Royal Ballet School, where one of his contemporaries was the dancer and choreographer Jonathan Burrows. Scottish dancing itself makes an appearance in some of Clark's works. The classical foundation of his training, however, extends throughout his work, underpinning all his choreography and, latterly especially, his chosen themes.

Clark's own performance style demonstrated considerable accomplishment; his fluid, clear line, highly arched feet, strong extensions, speed, and precision are all facets of classical technique to which dancers aspire. These qualities drew attention when he was a very young dancer, and the choreographer Richard Alston exploited some of the potential of Clark's ability in, for example, *Soda Lake* (1981). It is easy enough to trace links back to this in Clark's own choreographies – for example in the use of precision in rhythm and weight changes, and in the clarity of shape, movement and phrasing. Also apparent is the influence of Cunningham (as in Alston's work) in the manipulation of fast, technical, clear work of limbs and torso placement, for example in Clark's solo in *No Fire Escape in Hell* (1986).

Clark frequently foregrounds the more obvious facets of classical ballet – the outward rotation of the legs from the hip socket, the opening of the whole body in confident, outward-focused movement, the strong extension of legs and feet, the use of strength and control both in sustained movement and in fast footwork and jumps. Like Cunningham, and like Tharp in her very different way, Clark combines apparently 'straight' ballet with incongruous tilts and twists of the body, and off-balance shifts of weight and changes of direction. Unlike them, though, he sometimes makes ballet movements look distorted or dream-like because of the odd, unexpected juxtaposition of direct quotations (such as *cabrioles*, *pirouettes*, and so on being couched in peculiar phrases), but also, of course – and this aspect is driven home sometimes before all the rest – because of the very idiosyncratic, imaginative, and sometimes perverse (or subversive) choice of costume, set, props, and music.

Although Clark's own dance style is classically beautiful in its clarity, balance, harmony, and supreme control, he does use his dancers differently – that is, by exploiting their own technical accomplishments and their individuality. Dancers do not need to become 'Clark clones' necessarily (except occasionally – as seemed to be the intention at times in *O* (1994)), and the use of non-dancers – his friends and his mother – shows further diversification. Recently, Clark said that he was 'more interested in stretching other people, but they've got to be better than me to start with'.[2]

Richard Glasstone has written of the important influence of ballet and specifically the Cecchetti *ports de bras* and directions of the body in Clark's work, not only in his own performance style, but quite specifically in his choice of movement ideas from which to develop choreography.[3] Glasstone likens Clark to Frederick Ashton in this respect. Clark told Alastair Macaulay in 1984 of his perception of the central importance of ballet in his work, the physical understanding it provides, as well as the speed, total control of weight, sense of movement and line, and so on.[4] He referred to this more recently in relation to *O* (see below).

Certainly one can see this in much of Clark's work, sandwiched, with more or less prominence, among the punk postmodern. Glasstone asks whether, in fact, the distortions introduced by Clark might not eventually be refined and made more safe, as *pointe* work was. Jann Parry also comments on the 'pelvic shift' evident in *Mmm ...* (1992) and *O* in these terms, suggesting links to Balanchine's manipulation and extension of the canon of classical ballet. The context of postmodernism is so different, however, and dance is much more multifaceted than it was (as are almost all art forms and the position of art in society), that the nature of Clark's work leads to problems of response and of definition. Parry, writing of *Mmm ...* , in 1992, said:

> 'Post modernism' has become so devalued a term in dance that I am using it in the way it is often applied to architecture: an acknowledgement of a classical past, combined with an eclectic anthology of interests and influences, sprinkled with a knowing sense of irony.[5]

Burnside, also considering the problems of characterizing and responding to Clark's work, writes that

> he may ransack the past for ideas or images but only to illustrate some aspect of the present ... The dislocated values of the fragmented twentieth century society are present in all his works and

not less so in this one [*O*] merely because the more extravagant trappings of his anarchism are less evident.[6]

Burnside suggests that Clark has an ability as a creator and manipulator of movement that has sometimes been obscured by fashionable trappings. Certainly, the theatrical and shocking aspects of his work may distract the audience's attention too much from a paucity of invention or, when invention is there, from the value of it. This does beg some questions about the nature and 'purpose' of postmodern dance, concerning the appropriateness of response to, and critical engagement with, the work. Is it appropriate, for example, to attempt to separate out the movement material from the overall context of fragmented and subversive images and structures? Critics have clearly been hard pressed at times to find the right approach to writing about the work (see David Hughes below), partly because the theatrical colour and diversity and the gleefully subversive imagery present compelling spectacle which demands its own response regardless of the extent to which the material itself may be inventive and skilfully structured.

Mmm ... and *O* both link themselves to the Diaghilev period and, beyond that, to classicism and notions of the binary opposites Apollo and Dionysos. Clark himself said:

Stravinsky was more or less disowning *The Rite* when he came to write *Apollo*, and though the music is more purified and less violent, the works are two sides of the same coin. It's that thing of opposites confirming one another. *The Rite* is the music of Dionysos, of drunkenness and ecstasy and abandon and submission to inevitable change. After all, the ritual in *The Rite* was the one that changed winter into spring. I wanted a quality there of the phrase doing a dancer, rather than the dancer doing a phrase. In contrast, Apollo is the Sun God. He's in control, he divides

day from night, a god of clarity. Apollo moves to make the only possible choice from one reason to the next, and you could say that my difficulty with all this is that we work in a society that doesn't consider dance as something we *need*, and it is so hard to relay these matters to audiences nowadays.[7]

In much, or even all, of Clark's work, there is evidence of postmodern references to and reframing of the past, specifically through the medium of ballet, and this provides an underlying current throughout.

In *Because We Must* (1987) there is again extensive use of classical vocabulary – both specifically and in inflection – and many references to ballet, such as barre-work, as well as more obvious 'steps' and alignment of the body, control, and attack. The appearance of the nude guitarists, and of Clark standing in a barefoot fifth position, suggest the possibility that the parallel, or turned-in, or otherwise different aspects of movement vocabulary simply act in a 'chromatic' way. To push the musical parallel further, the chromaticism may escalate but tonality never completely dissolves.

Clark could be seen, perhaps, as working more in the tradition of Balanchine in terms of the expansion of the classical vocabulary into realms often perceived as ugly, distorted, going counter to the prevailing ethos. Ballet's deep-rooted tradition and discipline, and its proven ability to develop and change through changing cultural climates, have shown its resilience and provided a rich resource for future choreographers. As Clark has noted in relation to *O*:

I realise now that I'm looking for rigour ... I've begun to understand more recently about the precision and definition of ballet dancing, and how I require that in my work ... I like the fearlessness that goes with youth, but I love what experience brings. I used to be drawn to the individuality of performers – like Leigh Bowery or old lovers – who were untrained, but now I'm more interested in stretching other people, but they've got to be better than me to start with.[8]

Meisner (1984) maintains that Clark

knows his sources intimately. He respects the music's narrative sub-text. He evokes Balanchine, occasionally even quoting him directly, as in touching of fingers between Apollo and Terpsichore, which Balanchine took from Michelangelo's image of God giving life to Adam.

This may well be true, and be convincingly argued. However, this view could suggest Meisner's own intimate knowledge of sources, and her reading of their use in *O*. Perhaps Clark plays games with his critics by hinting in this way, making references and knowing or anticipating that they will respond with just such erudite speculation. There is no doubt, though, of Clark's deep respect for and valuing of the classical tradition, since his work is so very clearly rooted in it, despite all the trappings of post-punk anarchy in some works. This respect may well extend to the repertoire of ballet, too, and the possibility offered for cross-referencing almost to vanishing point.

Parry also notes the visual links to *Apollo*, and the link between *Rite* and *Apollo* in ballet's history, via the Sun King – Louis XIV, who gave ballet its 'academic foundation' – and the sacrifice to the god of the sun in *Rite* to ensure the return of spring. As she notes, 'Clark's Apollonian fifth positions were a recall to order in the midst of his irreverent experiments with movement and music'.[9] This could be seen in earlier work, too. In *Because We Must*, for example, Clark could be seen as 'professing his faith' (reminiscent of Nureyev's 'sign of the cross' every day) through the demonstration of the fifth position. In this instance, as noted above, it was a barefoot rendition, which itself carried a number of resonances – vulnerability, technique as a skill acquired or superimposed on the body.

David Hughes, in a review of *Mmm . . .*, demonstrates how dance critics have felt the need to find different ways of responding to Clark's work and articulating the significance of that response. Hughes chose to locate Clark's work firmly in the poststructural world of 'Masochism, mirrors, mother, Michael, myths: *posting the modern*':

Clark is a product of a moment of history, the punk aesthetic, the post-modern, the parodic, pop art, performance art, dance itself. A product not of a moment of history, but of histories, then, conflated in a moment. This is the condition of the work itself, a compacting of references and a series of images which run into each other through their connecting elements.[10]

Perhaps it is the case that Clark seems to have drawn together some central or recurrent premises of postmodernism. The question remains whether Clark has contributed something beyond superficial originality, or successfully controlled the disparate elements of his work, and, indeed, whether these are appropriate criteria of excellence in relation to his work at all.

Shortly after the appearance of *O*, Michael Clark's career seemed to flounder: a commission from the Royal Ballet was ultimately dropped, and the dancer-choreographer sustained a serious knee injury, which necessitated the cancellation of a ten-year retrospective in 1995. In early 1997, however, Clark was able to return to the studio, and was awarded a Wingate scholarship to take a film course in New York. His long-term interest and involvement in video and filmmaking (evidenced in his collaboration with Charles Atlas) made this a logical next step for his further development as a creative artist. By late 1997, Clark was planning a new full-length work to be toured during 1998.

Rachel Chamberlain Duerden

Notes

1 See Clark's comments in K. Watson's 'Time for the Tutus to Come Off', *Guardian* (Arts section), 3 May 1994.
2 Clark interviewed by D. Witts, 'An Impure Queer in a Dickhead World', *City Life*, April 1994.
3 Glasstone, Richard, 'Michael Clark's Use of Ballet Technique', *Dance Now*, Winter 1994.
4 Macaulay, Alastair, 'Michael Clark Talks!', *Dance Theatre Journal*, Autumn 1984.
5 Parry, Jann, '*Mmm* ... Michael Clark', *Dance Now*, Summer 1992.
6 Burnside, Fiona, 'Michael Clark's *O*', *Dance Theatre Journal*, Autumn 1994.
7 Clark, quoted by Witts, op. cit.
8 Ibid.
9 Parry, op. cit.
10 Hughes, David, 'Michael Clark's *Mmm* ... ', *Dance Theatre Journal*, Spring 1992.

Biographical details

Born in Aberdeen, Scotland, 2 July 1962. **Studied** Scottish dance as a child; studied with Richard Glasstone at the Royal Ballet School, London, 1975–79; also attended a Merce Cunningham summer school. **Career** Dancer with Ballet Rambert, London, 1979–81; dancer and choreographer with Karole Armitage Company, from 1981; choreographer-in-residence, Riverside Studios, London, 1983; began collaborating with Ellen van Schuylenburch in 1984, leading to the founding of Michael Clark and Dancers, 1984. Has also choreographed for Paris Opéra Ballet, Groupe de Recherche Chorégraphique de l'Opéra de Paris (GRCOP), Extemporary Dance Theatre, Scottish Ballet, and London Festival Ballet, and has collaborated on several projects with film-maker Charles Atlas; also danced the role of Caliban in Peter Greenaway's film *Prospero's Books* (1991), a version of Shakespeare's *The Tempest*. Following a Royal Ballet commission that did not reach completion, his career was interrupted in 1995 by injury. **Awards** include Wingate Scholarship, 1997.

Works

Surface Values (1980), *Of a Feather, Flock* (sound Eric Clermontet, 1981; revised version, 1982), *A Wish Sandwich* (1982), *Rush* (1982), *Parts I-IV* (various, 1983), *12XU* (1983), *1st Orange Segment* (1983), *Morag's Wedding* (1984), *Flippin' Eck/O Thweet Myth-tery of Life* (1984), *New Puritans* (mus. The Fall, 1984), *Do You Me? I Did* (mus. Bruce Gilbert, 1984), *Le French Revolting* (mus.

The Fall, 1984), *HAIL the Classical* (mus. various, 1985; filmed version by Charles Atlas, as *Hail the New Puritans*, 1986), *Angel Food* (mus. Bruce Gilbert, 1985), *Not H.air* (1985), *our caca phoney H, our caca phoney H* (mus. The Fall, Jeffrey Hinton, 1985), *Drop Your Pearls and Hog it, Girl* (1986), *Swamp* (revised version of *Do You Me? I Did*, mus. Bruce Gilbert, 1986; film version by Charles Atlas), *No Fire Escape in Hell* (mus. various, 1986; video version, 1986), *Because We Must* (film, 1987), *Pure Pre-Scenes* (1987), *I am Curious, Orange* (mus. The Fall, 1988; film version by Charles Atlas), *Heterospective* (1989), *Rights* (1990), *Mmm...* (mus. various, 1992; film version by Charles Atlas), *Modern Masterpiece* (mus. Stravinsky, 1992), *O* (mus. Stravinsky, 1994).

Further reading

Interviews with Alastair Macaulay, in 'Michael Clark Talks!', *Dance Theatre Journal*, Autumn 1984; with Chris de Marigny (also interviewing Charles Atlas), in 'Hail, the Video Dance Maker', *Dance Theatre Journal*, Summer 1986; with D. Witts, 'An Impure Queer in a Dickhead World', *City Life*, April 1994; with Lynn Barber, in 'Good Boy Now', *Independent on Sunday*, 7 June 1997.

Articles Alastair Macaulay, 'One at a Time', *Dance Theatre Journal*, Spring 1983; Alastair Macaulay, 'Down at the Riverside', *Dancing Times*, October 1983; Chris Savage-King, 'Maverick Makes Good', *Dance Theatre Journal*, Winter 1984; Sally Watts, 'New British Dance', *Dancing Times*, May 1984; Nadine Meisner, 'Michael Clark and Company', *Dance and Dancers*, September 1984; Chris Savage-King, 'Back to the Sixties with Michael Clark', *Dance Theatre Journal*, Winter 1985; Judith Cruikshank, 'Michael Clark, Riverside Studios', *Dance and Dancers*, November 1985; Maureen Cleave, 'Leading Them a Dance', *Observer Magazine*, 18 May 1986; Alastair Macaulay, 'Michael Clark: The Angry Young Man with the Disposable Hair', *Dance Magazine*, October 1986; Alastair Macaulay, 'Clarksville', *Dancing Times*, November 1986; Catherine Debray, 'Michel ange et démon', *Danser*, February 1987; Alastair Macaulay, 'The Addict of Camp: Michael Clark, *Because We Must*', *Dancing Times*, February 1988; Judith Mackrell, 'Post-modern Dance in Britain', *Dance Research*, Spring 1991; Anita Finkel, 'Trying the *Tempest*', *New Dance Review*, October/November 1991; Jann Parry, '*Mmm* ... Michael Clark', *Dance Now*, Summer 1992; David Hughes, 'Michael Clark's *Mmm* ... ', *Dance Theatre Journal*, Autumn 1992; Ann Nugent, 'Dream Ticket', *Dance Now*, Summer 1994; Clifford Bishop, 'Michael Clark', *Opera House*,

MICHAEL CLARK

3 August 1994; Fiona Burnside, 'Michael Clark's *O*', *Dance Theatre Journal*, Autumn 1994; Richard Glasstone, 'Michael Clark's Use of Ballet Technique', *Dance Now*, Winter 1994; Jann Parry, 'Rites and Wrongs of an Outrageous Dancer', *Observer Review*, 15 May 1994.

Books Allen Robertson and Donald Hutera, *The Dance Handbook*, Harlow, Essex, 1988; Judith Mackrell, *Out of Line: The Story of British New Dance*, London, 1992; Sally Banes, *Writing Dancing in the Age of Postmodernism*, Hanover (New Hampshire) and London, 1994.

ROBERT COHAN

The documentary film *A Dancer's World* (1957) not only demonstrates the extent to which Martha Graham had codified her technique by the mid-1950s. It also serves as a record of the individual and collective talents of her company at that time. Of the men featured in the film, Robert Cohan is clearly the most lithe, both in terms of physique and in the way that he executes the various classroom exercises. A decade later, when he became responsible for the development of the Graham technique at the London School of Contemporary Dance (LSCD) and London Contemporary Dance Theatre (LCDT), these physical traits became particularly important. Although it was perhaps inevitable that the technique would change when transplanted into a new context, the distinct strain that Cohan developed – one in which the Graham contraction was less percussive and less overtly emotive, and movements in general appeared less anchored to the floor – was shaped as much through his classes and choreography as from the fact that it was forged on different bodies and temperaments.

The making of *A Dancer's World* was Cohan's last involvement with the Graham company for five years. However, he continued his link with the company indirectly, first through teaching at the Graham school and, in 1959, by drawing on his Graham colleagues to set up the Robert Cohan Dance Company. The main reason for forming his own company was the increased opportunities it provided him for choreography. Cohan had created his first work during the Graham company's residency at the 1955 American Dance Festival at Connecticut College, but, significantly, it was the dances he choreographed from 1959 onwards that were to survive beyond their initial performances – and two works created in 1959, *Eclipse* and *Hunter of Angels*, were the earliest of his choreography to be staged in Britain.

The experience gained in directing his own company was to prove an invaluable prerequisite for Cohan's appointment as artistic director of the Contemporary Dance Trust.[1] By 1967, several of Graham's dancers were familiar to British students and audiences, mostly through Robin Howard's efforts to establish regular classes in Graham technique in London and, further afield, through the lecture-demonstrations presented by the touring unit, Ballet for All. Additionally, *A Dancer's World* had been televised by the BBC in 1959 and most of the dancers appearing in the film were also part of the Graham company's highly successful seasons in Edinburgh and London in 1963. That Howard sought Cohan to set up a company for graduates of LSCD is a measure of the latter's all-round ability. Cohan became the Contemporary Dance Group/LCDT's director, a position he held for over two decades. He was chief choreographer and teacher for many years; and, along with other Graham stars who appeared as guest artists, he was one of the group's leading dancers during the early years. Also, using the pseudonym Charter, he was the lighting designer of many works. (He lit the majority of his own works and those of several other choreographers associated with the group.)

Initially, Cohan combined his pioneering work in London with continued performance as a member of the Martha Graham Dance

Company. (He had rejoined the company in 1962, and, four years later, became one of Graham's co-directors.) After two years of transatlantic travelling between the two companies, however, he opted for a full-time commitment to Howard's London-based Contemporary Dance Trust. Howard had acquired premises opposite Euston Station – thereafter known as The Place – and this soon became the epicentre of Britain's modern dance movement. Although Cohan's greatest contribution was as artistic director, it is significant that one of his best works, *Cell*, was created for the first season of performances at The Place, in September 1969.

The season marked the official opening of The Place Theatre and the launch of the London Contemporary Dance Group.[2] As well as *Cell*, Cohan created *Side Scene* and *Shanta Quintet*, and just as Graham had worked successfully with the sculptor Isamu Noguchi, the season established Norberto Chiesa (for *Cell* and *Side Scene*) as Cohan's long-term collaborator. The partnership produced many theatrical works in which the architectural – and often allegorical – structures designed by Chiesa were as integral to the progression of Cohan's dance ideas as the movement itself.

Though Cohan modified Graham's technique, he continued many of her choreographic concerns. Myth, dreams, love, and jealousy have been recurring themes. Many of his works have incorporated striking, three-dimensional sets and, true to the Denishawn–Graham tradition, some of these have involved the manipulation of reams of material. Furthermore, even though Cohan evolved a less accentuated physicality, his choreography remained essentially expressionistic in its intent. Two evening-length works, *Stages* (1971) and *Dances of Love and Death* (1981), were his most ambitious attempts at developing complex narratives and emotional states through the medium of dance. And just as Graham explored broad religious and moralistic themes, so too did Cohan in several biblically inspired

works. Of these, *Stabat Mater* (1975) is the simplest yet most empathetic. It is also his most lyrical work. Ironically, Cohan created *Stabat Mater* as much because of his directorial responsibilities as because of his interest in developing the subject matter of Vivaldi's music through an all-female group of dancers. (It was created to complement the male casting of Robert North's *Troy Game*.)

As artistic director, Cohan was responsible for spearheading other important decisions. In 1976, he initiated a series of LCDT residencies in the north of England. His aim was to increase access and audiences; and, in addition to the company's offering classes, lecture-demonstrations, and performances, Cohan attempted to demystify modern dance choreography by creating a work in public. The result was *Khamsin* (1976), which, Cohan suggests, was structured as several mini-climaxes owing to rotating groups of people attending his rehearsals. The following year, when choreographing in similar circumstances, he chose not to create climaxes to order. This would influence *Forest* (1977), the work that emerged from LCDT's next series of residencies (after Cohan had abandoned his original idea of incorporating the material he had created during the residencies into the four-choreographer 1977 collaboration, *Nightwatch*). Where previously his works had been mainly episodic – the clearest examples being *Cell* and *Waterless Method of Swimming Instruction* (1974) – *Forest* introduced a more linear progression. Sections connected or overlapped in one continuous, onward flow, and although Cohan continued to juxtapose contrasting action (both dramatic and physical) in subsequent works, any devices he employed to indicate shifts in time and/or place – as, for example, in *Songs, Lamentations and Praises* (1979), and *Dances of Love and Death* – were woven into the choreography with greater continuity.

Another policy he pursued during his directorship of LCDT concerned in-house choreographers. Until the mid-1980s, Cohan's work was the mainstay of the repertory (and the model for several of his dancers), but his encouragement of new talent from within the company helped to produce two generations of contemporary choreographers. Cohan provided Richard Alston with his first professional opportunities and, in 1974, he appointed two LCDT dancers (Robert North and Siobhan Davies) as his associate choreographers. More recently, he has advised many young artists, both at LCDT and at choreographer/composer courses directed by him in England and Canada.

Cohan choreographed his last works for LCDT in 1989, the year he retired from the Contemporary Dance Trust. At that time, it was assumed that Cohan would re-direct his energies to tending his farmhouse and garden in southern France; however, following two short-lived directorships of LCDT (by Dan Wagoner and Nancy Duncan), Cohan returned as artistic adviser in 1992. The experience of being embroiled once again in the pressures and politics of a dance company was a positive one for Cohan.

In 1993, a commission from Scottish Ballet persuaded him to delay his retirement and to venture into what was for him new territory. *A Midsummer Night's Dream* (1993) was his first choreography for a classically trained company. (From the outset, the LSCD included classical ballet classes in its curriculum and some founder members of LCDT had a strong grounding in the technique, but this was the first time that Cohan included pointework and the classical *pas de deux* form in his choreography.) He created the main dances for Titania and Hippolyta (which he cast as two separate roles) and for some of the fairies *en pointe*, and he devised tap routines for the mechanicals so as to differentiate their 'Pyramus–Thisbe play' from the rest of the ballet. More predictably, *A Midsummer Night's Dream* was a collabora-tion between Cohan and Chiesa, the latter demonstrating yet again how his familiar white sets can be constructed and lit in innumerable ways. The production also involved the composer Barrington Pheloung (another LCDT associate) who, in order to extend Mendelsshon's incidental music into a ninety-minute accompaniment, interpolated newly composed variations into the original score.

Cohan has referred to this recent collaboration as a 'challenge'. It was the challenge of starting something from nothing that brought him to Britain in 1967. Now, in the 1990s, after achieving so much, he has remained excited by the possibility of new discoveries.

Angela Kane

Notes

1 Initially, in order to obtain the support of a predominantly ballet-orientated public, Howard had titled his organization the Contemporary Ballet Trust. Significantly, the substitution of 'Dance' in the title came relatively early, that is, in 1971. The Trust was the umbrella organization of the London School of Contemporary Dance, London Contemporary Dance Theatre and, from 1969, The Place Theatre.
2 The company continued to be known as the London Contemporary Dance Group for this first season.

Biographical details

Born in New York City, 27 March 1925. **Studied** at the Martha Graham School, New York. **Career** Danced with Martha Graham Company, 1946–57 (becoming Graham's partner in 1950); presented first choreography in 1955; danced in musicals after 1957; worked as a teacher and freelance choreographer, founding his own school in Boston, 1959–62; also directed his own group, performing as Robert Cohan Dance Company, 1962; returned to Graham, 1962, becoming co-director of her company, 1966; was invited to become founding artistic director of London School of Contemporary Dance and director of the associated London Contemporary Dance Trust, 1967; artistic director and chief choreographer, London Contemporary Dance Theatre,

1969–87, acting as director, 1987–88; artistic adviser, Batsheva Dance Company, Israel, 1980; became British citizen, 1989; retired from Contemporary Dance Trust in 1989, returning as artistic adviser in 1992, while maintaining career as freelance choreographer and teacher. Has also acted as director to York University Toronto Choreographic Summer School, 1977, Gulbenkian Choreographic Summer School, University of Surrey, 1978, 1979, and 1982, Banff School of Fine Arts Choreographic Seminar, Canada, 1980, New Zealand Choreographic Seminar, 1982, Simon Frazer University Choreographic Seminar, Vancouver, 1985, and International Dance Course for Professional Choreographers and Composers, Surrey University, 1985, 1989. **Awards and honours** *Evening Standard* Award, 1975; Society of West End Theatres Award, 1978; Honorary Fellow, York University, Toronto, 1977; Companion of the British Empire (CBE), 1988; honorary degrees from the University of Exeter, 1993, and University of Middlesex, 1994.

Works

Perchance to Dream (mus. Debussy, 1955), *Streams* (mus. Hovhaness, 1958; revised version, 1970), *Seabourne* (mus. Eugene Lester, 1959), *The Pass* (1959; revised version, 1960), *Eclipse* (mus. Eugene Lester, 1959; revised version, 1967), *Ceremony for Serpents* (mus. Eugene Lester, 1959), *Hunter of Angels* (mus. Bruno Maderna, 1959), *Veiled Women* (1960), *Vestige* (mus. Eugene Lester, 1960), *Praises* (mus. Hovhaness, 1960), *The Tomb* (mus. Eugene Lester, 1960), *Luna Park* (mus. Eugene Lester, 1964), *Celebrants* (mus. Carlos Surinach, 1964), *Hall of Mirrors* (mus. Naom Shariff, 1965), *Tzaikerk* (mus. Hovhaness, 1967), *Sky* (mus. Eugene Lester, 1967), *Shanta Quintet* (mus. John Mayer, 1969), *Side Scene* (mus. early and Baroque, 1969), *Cell* (mus. Ronald Lloyd, 1969), *X* (mus. Mauricio Kagel, 1970), *Consolation of the Rising Moon* (mus. arr. John Williams, 1971), *Stages* (mus. Arne Nordheim, Bob Downes, 1971), *People Alone* (mus. Bob Downes, 1972), *People Together* (mus. Bob Downes, 1973), *Mass* (mus. Vladimir Rodzianko, Judith Weir, 1973), *Waterless Method of Swimming Instruction* (mus. Bob Downes, 1974), *No Man's Land* (mus. Barry Guy, 1974), *Class* (mus. John Keliehor, 1975), *Myth* (later entitled *Masque of Separation*; mus. Burt Alcantara, 1975), *Place of Change* (mus. Schoenberg, 1975), *Stabat Mater* (mus. Vivaldi, 1975), *Nympheas* (mus. Debussy, 1976), *Khamsin* (mus. Bob Downes, 1976), *Forest* (mus. Brian Hodgson, 1977), *Nightwatch* (with Micha Bergese, Siobhan Davies, Robert North; mus. Bob Downes, 1977),

Job (for television; mus. Vaughan Williams, 1977), *Genesis Reconsidered* (mus. Zvi Avni, 1977), *Falling Man* (mus. Barrington Phelonng, 1978), *Ice* (mus. Morton Subotnick, 1978), *Eos* (mus. Barry Guy, 1978), *Rondo* (mus. John Herbert McDowell, 1979), *Songs, Lamentations and Praises* (mus. Geoffrey Burgon, 1979), *Field* (mus. Brian Hodgson, 1980), *Dances of Love and Death* (mus. Carl Davis, Conlon Nancarrow, 1981), *Chamber Dances* (mus. Geoffrey Burgon, 1982), *Agora* (mus. J.S. Bach, Barrington Pheloung, 1984), *A Mass for Man* (mus. Geoffrey Burgon, 1985), *Ceremony: Slow Dance on a Burial Ground* (mus. Stephen Montague, 1986), *Interrogations* (mus. Barrington Pheloung, 1986), *Video Life* (mus. Barry Guy, 1986), *Phantasmagoria* (mus. Barrington Pheloung, with Darshen Singh and Tom Jobe, 1987), *In Memory* (mus. Hans Werner Henze, 1989), *Stone Garden* (mus. Nigel Osborne, 1989), *Metamorphosis* (mus. Britten, 1989), *Crescendo* (mus. David Bedford, 1989), *A Midsummer Night's Dream* (mus. Mendelssohn, Barrington Pheloung, 1993), *Four Seasons* (mus. Vivaldi, 1995), *Pandora Liberante* (mus. Claudio Ambrosini, 1997).

Further reading

Interviews in 'Robert Cohan Talks to *Dance and Dancers* on Contemporary Dance in Britain', *Dance and Dancers*, September 1967; in 'Survial: Contemporary Dance', *Dance and Dancers*, February 1972; in 'Getting to Know You', *Dance and Dancers*, April 1976; with Gordon Gow, in 'London Contemporary Dance Theatre Residencies', *Dancing Times*, April 1976; with Chris de Marigny, in 'LCDT and Robert Cohan', *Dance Theatre Journal*, Winter 1985; with Mike Dixon, *Dance Europe*, October-November 1996.

Articles John Percival, 'London's Own Contemporary Dance Theatre', *Dance Magazine*, April 1983; Noël Godwin, 'Based on Love', *Ballet News*, April 1983; Noël Goodwin, 'An Adventurous Farewell' (on Cohan's last pieces for LCDT), *Dance and Dancers*, June 1989.

Books Janet Adshead and Richard Mansfield, *London Contemporary Dance Theatre, 1967–1975: Company Resource Pack No. 1*, Guildford, Surrey, 1985; Richard Mansfield, 'London Contemporary Dance Theatre', in *Twentieth-Century Dance in Britain: A History of Major Dance Companies in Britain*, edited by Joan W. White, London, 1985; Mary Clarke and Clement Crisp, *London Contemporary Dance Theatre: The First 21 Years*, London, 1987.

MERCE CUNNINGHAM

Reminiscing at the time of his seventy-fifth birthday on a national general-interest programme shown on US morning television, Merce Cunningham recalled that, according to his mother, he used to go dancing up the aisle in church as a child. With his sparse, crinkled grey hair framing his lined face like a platinum halo, the still-active choreographer gave his anecdote with a simplicity and directness that are the hallmarks of his career.

Cunningham's smiling recall of his happy first dance steps bespoke the love he has displayed over the years for both performing and creating dances. The year he turned seventy-five also marked the fiftieth anniversary of his career as choreographer. He began his actual dance training at the age of twelve with Mrs J.W. Barrett, in what might be called all-round theatrical dancing. His entry into the then-budding world of modern dance had come by way of the Cornish School in Seattle, Washington, an institute for the performing and plastic arts where Cunningham had been studying to be an actor. There, dance teacher Bonnie Bird and composer John Cage – then a Cornish School faculty member and eventually Cunningham's lifelong partner in art and life – suggested that Cunningham study at the Bennington School of Dance, which was spending a summer at Mills College in California. Martha Graham was on its faculty and she subsequently encouraged Cunningham to move east, where he became a member of Graham's dance troupe.

Graham first cast Cunningham in the role of 'Acrobat' for *Every Soul Is a Circus* (1939), next as the 'Christ Figure' in *El Penitente* (1940), and as 'March', the personification of spring, in *Letter to the World* and 'Pegasus' in *Punch and Judy* (both 1941), as 'Yankee, an orator' in *Land Be Bright* (1942), as 'The Poetic Beloved' in *Deaths and Entrances* (1943), and finally as 'The

'Revivalist' in *Appalachian Spring* (1944). In looking back on his years with Graham, Cunningham repudiated some of her premises, taking issue with the idea 'that a particular movement meant something specific. I thought that was nonsense'. Still, when looking at Cunningham's far-reaching career, Graham's characterization of him in her dances provides a helpful guide to his various facets. The acrobatic, charismatic, aerial, American, poetic, and intense lights in which Graham saw Cunningham continued to pertain to his own special qualities in his dancing and dances.

Cunningham traces the start of his career as choreographer to 1944. The specific programme marking this beginning was a solo dance concert he performed on an evening shared with John Cage and his music. Characterizing the overall effect of both Cage's and Cunningham's work in this debut concert as 'extreme elegance in isolation', the critic Edwin Denby noted that he had 'never seen a first recital that combined such taste, such technical finish, such originality of dance material, and so sure a manner of presentation.' However much these artistic partners and individual artists developed over the next fifty-odd years (Cage died in 1992), the perceptions in Denby's initial reaction to their work have remained consistently apt, particularly with regard to Cunningham.

From 1953 onwards, Cunningham had his own company of dancers on which to work. His variously constituted ensemble of male and female dancers grew more or less steadily in size over the years. In 1953, the troupe numbered five, including Cunningham; in 1994, there were seventeen, again including the choreographer. Numerous alumna from the company have gone on to dancer-and-choreographer careers of their own, starting with Paul Taylor, who was part of the first five-dancer unit. Remy Charlip, Viola Farber, Margaret Jenkins, Douglas Dunn, Gus Solomons, Jr, Karole Armitage, and Ulysses Dove – to name but seven more of these – might be called (to borrow a term coined by Arlene Croce) 'Mercists'. But, however high the various members of Cunningham's 'flock' have soared, none has yet flown quite so high and majestically as the mentor himself, except possibly Taylor, who has flown in a non-Mercist direction very much his own.

As he began exploring ways of working dancers and dancing, Cunningham aimed for a modernism that was not anti-ballet, as was so much of modern dance at this point, but somehow beyond ballet. His desire was to combine what he saw as the pronounced use of legs in ballet techniques with the strong emphasis on the upper body in modern dance methods. One of his technical advancements, related to ballet's five positions of the feet, he referred to as Five Positions of the Back: upright, curve, arch, twist, and tilt.

For all those who have found the product of Cunningham's career richly poetic and deeply rewarding, there have been perhaps an equal number who have found it otherwise, to say the least. 'What would a Cunningham season be,' the Cunningham devotee's query goes 'without a number of individuals fleeing the theatre, mid-programme or mid-dance, in semi-annoyed bewilderment?' Such may often be the knowing fan's lordly pleasure, but it doesn't seem to reflect Cunningham's view. 'No, no,' he once said when asked if he was interested in shocking people; rather, he elaborated, citing an aim of Cage's: 'I'm out to bring poetry into their lives'.

A good many viewers trying to put their finger on what bothers people about Cunningham's dances point accusingly at the unconventional sound element. In about the 1950s, this element became more and more unconventional, once the Cage (or school-of-Cage) scores Cunningham worked with stopped coming from piano or prepared-piano sources and started to come from every corner of 'left field' – that is, from nowhere predictable. Sometimes electronic sound sources screeched and/or blared at high decibel levels, but it seems doubtful that the individuals put off by the works in which such sound effects occurred would find them much more agreeable had they some equally random, but more gently toned, sonic base.

Much has also been made, both for and against Cunningham, of his use of chance procedures. Like the stress on his dances' unconventional sound dimension, the focus on chance can also be overemphasized. Whatever part is played by this way of making artistic decisions – that is, the use of forces outside the choreographer himself, such as tossed coins or a throw of the *I Ching*, to find a needed option – too much stress on it leads to thoughts of randomness, ambivalence, and shapelessness. On the evidence of decades'-worth of Cunningham's performing and choreography, three less Cunningham attributes are hard to imagine. As Denby noted instantly in 1944, taste, technical finish, originality, and sureness of manner all intermingle undeniably in Cunningham's art.

Another of Cunningham's ways of working, while undoubtedly practised in the course of his dancemaking, can also be dwelt upon so narrowly as to miss the effect of the end result in the effort of recalling the process. This is the oft-noted independence of traditionally interdependent theatrical elements – music, décor, and movement. Without doubt this is Cunningham's way of working: neither the composer nor the designer creates his part in close collaboration with the choreographer. But this does not mean that a clash is desired or that Cunningham cannot veto results that would obstruct the integrity of his dance. Just as he said he was not interested in shocking audiences, Cunningham said he was not actively being mysterious with his composers or designers: 'If they have questions, I try to answer them.' The list of visual artists who found Cunningham's way of working rewarding is long; among the most successful of these were Robert Rauschenberg, Jasper

Johns, Charles Atlas, Mark Lancaster and Marsha Skinner.

Cunningham's consistency of working methods and his eager striving for some unknown ('Every artist should ask,' he suggested in 1992, 'What is the point of doing what you already know?') have yielded a repertory of dances that reveals rewarding change amid singular artistic vision. In 1990, the dancemaker began devising ideas for dance movement on a computer, with a program called 'Life Forms'. *Trackers* (1991) was partly the result of Cunningham's computer experimentation; its inclusion of unusually dense, complex grouping moves and of unfamiliar positions for the arms indicated how the choreographer was able to put computer 'choices' into the scheme of dance.

Essentially Cunningham's philosophy precludes any nostalgic looking back. Few of the dances we can read about in the substantial body of literature around Cunningham are available for us to see nowadays. Since the later 1970s, however, Cunningham has been imaginatively involved with the making of moving picture dances (first on film, nowadays mostly video tape). Therefore, beyond the odd exception, here and there, of a 'revived' dance (*Septet*, a 1953 work, and *Rain Forest*, from 1968, have both been revived and kept in repertory over the past ten years), Cunningham's canon has been given a 'retrospective' dimension by the presence of film and video dances, all directed in part by Cunningham himself.

Another practical and yet unconventional way in which Cunningham recalls his own rich past while showcasing the dancers of his present ensemble is to create what he calls 'Events'. The first of these, *Museum Event No. 1*, was made in 1964 for a non-theatre space in a Vienna museum. Since then over 500 'Events' have been given. In them Cunningham puts together segments of older dances as a continuous programme of 'original' dancing, lasting approximately

ninety minutes. For each presentation, given in a location that cannot accommodate full-scale theatrical presentation, Cunningham uses one-time-only music, lighting, and costume design. It is in such performances that those who are nostalgic to remember Cunningham things past can find favourite and/or familiar former dance moments.

It is next to impossible with an artist as accomplished and prolific as Cunningham to point towards one work that might sum up his accomplishments. Knowing full well the potential folly of such a gesture, this writer would still feel comfortable selecting *Roaratorio (An Irish Circus on Finnegans Wake)*, a full-company (fifteen-dancer) work that Cunningham first created in 1983. It had homely, percussive music by John Cage, with more than a little help from a sextet of Irish musicians, clear-colour designs by Mark Lancaster, and some of the most simply presented yet grandly scaled and ravishingly grouped choreographic inventions this century has seen.

Robert Greskovic

Biographical details

Born Mercier Cunningham in Centralia, Washington, United States, 16 April 1919. **Studied** tap and ballroom dancing with Maude M. Barrett; also attended George Washington University, Washington, DC; Cornish School (now Cornish Institute of Allied Arts), Seattle, Washington, 1937–39; Bennington College School of Dance summer session; Mills College, Oakland, California, 1939. **Career** Danced with Martha Graham Dance Company, New York, 1939–45; first work as independent choreographer (with Jean Erdman and Nina Fonaroff), 1942, and first solo concert with composer John Cage, 1944: frequently collaborated with Cage thereafter; toured Europe, with concerts in Paris, summer 1949; founder, Merce Cunningham Dance Company, at Black Mountain College, North Carolina, 1953, and has subsequently choreographed almost exclusively for the company, with regular composers Cage, David Tudor, and with designers Robert Rauschenberg (resident designer, 1954–64), Jasper Johns (artistic adviser, 1967–80), Mark Lancaster (artistic adviser from 1980), as well as other contemporary artists;

collaborated on series of dance videos with Charles Atlas, from 1974. Recent projects have included an ongoing series of 'Events' and choreography based on the random output of the 'Life Forms' computer program. **Awards and honours** include Guggenheim Fellowships, 1953 and 1959; Honorary D.Litt., University of Illinois, 1972; Samuel H. Scripps/American Dance Festival Award for Lifetime Achievement, 1982; Commandeur de l'Ordre des Arts et des Lettres (France), 1982; Honorary Membership of American Academy and Institute of Arts and Letters, 1984; MacArthur Foundation Fellowship, 1985; Kennedy Center Honors, 1985; Olivier Award, 1985; Algur H. Meadows Award, Southern Methodist University, Dallas, Texas, 1987; Légion d'honneur, France, 1989; National Medal of Arts (US), 1990; Digital Dance Award, 1990.

Works

Seeds of Brightness (with Jean Erdman; mus. Norman Lloyd, 1942), *Credo in Us* (with Jean Erdman; mus. Cage, 1942), *Ad Lib* (with Jean Erdman; mus. Gregory Tucker, Cage, 1942), *Renaissance Testimonials* (mus. Maxwell Powers, 1942), *Totem Ancestor* (mus. Cage, 1942), *In the Name of Holocaust* (mus. Cage, 1943), *Shimmera* (mus. Cage, 1943), *The Wind Remains* (mus. Paul Bowles, 1943), *Triple-Paced* (mus. Cage, 1944), *Root of an Unfocus* (mus. Cage, 1944), *Tossed as It is Untroubled* (mus. Cage, 1944), *The Unavailable Memory of* (mus. Cage, 1944), *Spontaneous Earth* (mus. Cage, 1944), *Four Walls* (mus. Cage, 1944), *Idyllic Song* (mus. Satie, arr. Cage, 1944), *Mysterious Adventure* (mus. Cage, 1945), *Experiences* (mus. Cage, Livingston Gearhart, 1945), *The Encounter* (mus. Cage, 1946), *Invocation to Vahakn* (mus. Alan Hovhaness, 1946), *Fast Blues* (mus. Baby Dodds, 1946), *The Princess Zondilda and Her Entourage* (mus. Alexei Haieff, 1946), *The Seasons* (mus. Cage, 1947), *The Open Road* (mus. Lou Harrison, 1947), *Dromenon* (mus. Cage, 1947), *Dream* (mus. Cage, 1948), *The Ruse of Medusa* (mus. and libretto Satie, 1948), *A Diversion* (mus. Cage, 1948), *Orestes* (mus. Cage, 1948), *Effusions avant l'heure* (later retitled *Games and Trio*; mus. Cage, 1949), *Amores* (mus. Cage, 1949), *Duet* (1949), *Two Step* (mus. Satie, 1949), *Pool of Darkness* (mus. Weber, 1950), *Before Dawn* (1950), *Waltz* (mus. Satie, 1950), *Sixteen Dances for Soloist and Company of Three* (mus. Cage, 1951), *Variation* (mus. Morton Feldman, 1951), *Boy Who Wanted to Be a Bird* (1951), *Suite of Six Short Dances* (mus. various, 1952), *Excerpts from Symphonie pour un homme seul* (later retitled *Collage*; mus.

Pierre Schaeffer, Pierre Henry, 1952), *Les Noces* (mus. Stravinsky, 1952), *Theater Piece* (mus. David Tudor, 1952), *Suite by Chance* (mus. Christian Wolff, 1953), *Solo Suite in Space and Time* (mus. Cage, 1953), *Demonstration Piece* (1953), *Epilogue* (mus. Satie, 1953), *Banjo* (mus. Louis Moreau Gottschalk, 1953), *Dime a Dance* (mus. various, arr. David Tudor, 1953), *Septet* (mus. Satie, 1953), *Untitled Solo* (mus. Christian Wolff, 1953), *Fragments* (mus. Pierre Boulez, 1953), *Minutiae* (mus. Cage, 1954), *Springweather and People* (mus. Earle Brown, 1955), *Lavish Escapade* (mus. Christian Wolff, 1956), *Galaxy* (mus. Earle Brown, 1956), *Suite for Five in Space and Time* (later called *Suite for Five*; mus. Cage, 1956), *Nocturnes* (mus. Satie, 1956), *Changeling* (mus. Christian Wolff, 1957), *Labyrinthian Dances* (mus. Josef Matthias Hauer, 1957), *Picnic Polka* (mus. Louis Moreau Gottschalk, 1957), *Antic Meet* (mus. Cage, 1958), *Summerspace* (mus. Morton Feldman, 1958), *Night Wandering* (mus. Bo Nilsson, 1958), *From the Poems of the White Stone* (mus. Chou Wen-Chung, 1959), *Gambit for Dancers and Orchestra* (mus. Ben Johnston, 1959), *Rune* (mus. Christian Wolff, 1959), *Theater Piece* (mus. Cage, 1960), *Crises* (mus. Conlon Nancarrow, 1960), *Hands Birds* (mus. Earle Brown, 1960), *Waka* (mus. Toshi Ichiyanagi, 1960), *Music Walk with Dancers* (mus. Cage, 1960), *Aeon* (mus. Cage, 1961), *Field Dances* (mus. Cage, 1963), *Story* (mus. Toshi Ichiyanagi, 1963), *Open Session* (1964), *Paired* (mus. Cage, 1964), *Winterbranch* (La Monte Young, 1964), *Cross Currents* (mus. Conlon Nancarrow, arr. Cage, 1964), *Museum Event No. 1* (1964), *Variations V* (mus. Cage, 1965), *How to Pass, Kick, Fall and Run* (mus. Cage, 1965), *Place* (mus. Gordon Mumma, 1966), *Scramble* (mus. Toshi Ichiyanagi, 1967), *Rain Forest* (mus. David Tudor, 1968), *Walkaround Time* (mus. David Behrman, 1968), *Canfield* (mus. Pauline Oliveros, 1969), *Tread* (mus. Christian Wolff, 1970), *Secondhand* (mus. Cage, 1970), *Signals* (mus. David Tudor, Gordon Mumma, Cage, 1970), *Objects* (mus. Alvin Lucier, 1970), *Loops* (mus. Gordon Mumma, 1971), *Landrover* (mus. Cage, Gordon Mumma, David Tudor, 1972), *TV Rerun* (mus. Gordon Mumma, 1972), *Borst Park* (mus. Christian Wolff, 1972), *Un jour ou deux* (mus. Cage, 1973), *Exercise Piece* (1975), *Rebus* (mus. David Behrman, 1975), *Changing Steps* (mus. Cage, 1975), *Solo* (mus. Cage, 1975), *Sounddance* (mus. David Tudor, 1975), *Torse* (mus. Maryanne Amacher, 1976), *Squaregame* (mus. Takehisa Kosugi, 1976), *Travelogue* (mus. Cage, 1977), *Inlets* (mus. Cage, 1977), *Fractions* (video, dir. Charles Atlas and Cunningham; mus. John Gibson, 1977), *Exercise Piece I* (mus. Meredith Monk, 1978), *Exercise*

Piece II (mus. Cage, 1978), *Exchange* (mus. David Tudor, 1978), *Tango* (mus. Cage, 1978), *Locale* (video, dir. Charles Atlas and Cunningham; mus. Takehisa Kosugi, 1979), *Roadrunners* (mus. Yasunao Tone, 1979), *Exercise Piece III* (mus. Cage, 1980), *Duets* (mus. Cage, 1980), *Fielding Sixes* (mus. Cage, 1980), *Channels/Inserts* (video, dir. Charles Atlas and Cunningham, 1980), *10's With Shoes* (mus. Martin Kalve, 1981), *Gallopade* (mus. Takehisa Kosugi, 1981), *Trails* (mus. Cage, 1982), *Quartet* (mus. David Tudor, 1982), *Coast Zone* (video, dir. Charles Atlas and Cunningham; mus. Larry Austin, 1983), *Roaratorio* (mus. Cage, 1983), *Inlets II* (mus. Cage, 1983), *Pictures* (mus. David Behrman, 1984), *Doubles* (mus. Takehisa Kosugi, 1984), *Phrases* (mus. David Tudor, 1984), *Native Green* (mus John King, 1985), *Arcade* (mus. Cage, 1985), *Grange Eve* (mus. Takehisa Kosugi, 1986), *Points in Space* (video, dir. Elliott Caplan and Cunningham; mus. Cage, 1986), *Fabrications* (mus. Emanuel Dimas de Melo Pimenta, 1987), *Shards* (mus. David Tudor, 1987), *Carousal* (mus. Takehisa Kosugi, 1987), *Eleven* (mus. Robert Ashley, 1988), *Five Stone* (mus. Cage, David Tudor, 1988), *Five Stone Wind* (mus. Cage, Takehisa Kosugi, David Tudor, 1988), *Cargo X* (mus. Takehisa Kosugi, 1989), *Field and Figures* (mus. Ivan Tcherepnin, 1989), *August Place* (mus. Michael Pugliese, 1989), *Inventions* (mus. Cage, 1989), *Polarity* (mus. David Tudor, 1990), *Neighbors* (mus. Takehisa Kosugi, 1991), *Trackers* (mus. Emanuel Dimas de Melo Pimenta, 1991), *Beachbirds* (mus. Cage, 1991), *Loosestrife* (mus. Michael Pugliese, 1991), *Change of Address* (mus. Walter Zimmerman, 1992), *Enter* (mus. David Tudor, 1992), *Touchbase* (mus. Michael Pugliese, 1992), *Doubletoss* (mus. Takehisa Kosugi, 1993), *CRWDSPCR* (mus. John King, 1993), *Breakers* (mus. John Driscoll, 1994,), *Ocean* (1994), *4'33* (mus. Cage, 1994), *Joyce Events* (mus. Stuart Dempster, Takehisa Kosugi, Ron Kuivila, David Tudor, 1994), *Signals* (mus. Cage, 1994), *Minevent* (mus. John Driscoll, John D.S. Adams, D'Arcy Philip Gray, Takehisa Kosugi, 1995), *Ground Level Overlay* (mus. Stuart Dempster, 1995), *Windows* (mus. Emanuel Dimas de Melo Pimenta, 1995), *Rondo* (mus. Cage, 1996), *Garnier Event* (1997), *Scenario* (us. Takehisa Kosugi, 1997).

Further reading

Interviews with Arlene Croce, in *Current Biography Yearbook 1966*; with Peter Grossman, *Dance Scope*, 1970; with Elinor Rogosin, in her *The Dance Makers: Conversations with American Choreographers*, New York, 1980; with Jacqueline Lesschaeve, in *The Dancer and the Dance*, London

and New York, 1985 (from the French edition of 1980); with R. Tracy in 'Bicycle in the Sky', *Ballet Review*, 20(3), 1992; with Christopher Cook, in 'Forms of Life', *Dance Now*, Summer 1997.

Articles Merce Cunningham, 'Space, Time and Dance', *trans/formation* (New York), 1952; Merce Cunningham, 'The Impermanent Art', *7 Arts* (Indian Hills, Colorado), 1955 (later in *Esthetics Contemporary*, edited by Richard Kostelanetz, Buffalo, New York, 1978); Michael Snell, 'Cunningham and the Critics', *Ballet Review*, 3(6), 1971; Jack Anderson, 'Dances about Everything and Dances about Some Things', *Ballet Review*, 5(6), 1975/76; Jill Silverman, 'Merce Cunningham on Broadway', *Performing Arts Journal*, Spring 1977; Holly Brubach, 'Cunningham Now', *Ballet Review*, 6(2), 1977/78; Stephanie Jordan, 'Freedom from the Music: Cunningham, Cage and Collaborations', *Contact*, Autumn 1979; David Vaughan, 'Merce Cunningham: Retrospect and Prospect', *Performing Arts Journal*, Winter 1979; Merce Cunningham, 'A Collaborative Process between Music and Dance', *TriQuarterly*, 54 (Evanston, Illinois), Spring 1982; Richard Kostelanetz, 'Avant-garde Establishment: Cunningham Revisited', *Dance Magazine*, July 1982; David Vaughan, 'Merce Cunningham: Origins and Influences', *Dance Theatre Journal*, Spring 1983; Robert Greskovic, 'Merce Cunningham as Sculptor', *Ballet Review*, Winter 1984; Marcia Siegel, 'Repertory in Spite of Itself', *Hudson Review*, Summer 1985; special Cunningham issue of *Dance Theatre Journal*, Summer 1985; 'The Forming of an Aesthetic: Merce Cunningham and John Cage' (discussion), *Ballet Review*, Fall 1985; David Vaughan, 'Cunningham, Cage, and James Joyce', *Dance Magazine*, October 1986; Alastair Macaulay, 'The Merce Experience', *The New Yorker*, 4 April 1988; 'Decision Making Dancers' (symposium), *Ballet Review*, Winter 1992; K. King, 'Space Dance and Galactic Matrix: An Appreciation of Merce Cunningham's Sounddance', *Chicago Review*, 37(4), 1992; Michelle Potter, 'A License to Do Anything: Robert Rauschenberg and the Merce Cunningham Dance Company' *Dance Chronicle*, 16(1), 1993; Bruce Fleming, 'Talking Merce' (conference report), *DanceView*, Spring 1994; Leslie Martin, 'Black Mountain College and Merce Cunningham in the Fifties: New Perspectives' (conference report), *Dance Research Journal*, Spring 1994; Nicole Dekle, 'Cunnningham's World', *Ballet Review*, Fall 1994; Lesley-Anne Sayers, 'Cunningham Revisited', *Dance Theatre Journal*, Autumn 1994; Alastair Macaulay, 'Merce Cunningham Dance Company', *Dancing Times*, December 1995.

Books Edwin Denby, *Looking at the Dance*, New York, 1949; Selma Jeanne Cohen (ed.), *Time to Walk in Space* (Dance Perspectives 34), New York, 1968; Merce Cunningham, *Changes: Notes on Choreography*, edited by Frances Starr, New York, 1968; Calvin Tompkins, *The Bride and the Bachelors: Five Masters of the Avant Garde*, New York, 1968; James Klosty (ed.), *Merce Cunningham*, New York, 1975; Moira Hodgson, *Quintet: Five American Dance Companies*, New York, 1976; Joseph H. Mazo, *Prime Movers: The Making of Modern Dance in America*, New York, 1977; Ann Livet (ed.), *Contemporary Dance*, New York, 1978; Marcia Siegel, *The Shapes of Change*, Boston, 1979; Merce Cunningham, 'Choreography and the Dance', in *The Dance Anthology*, edited by Cobbett Steinberg, New York and London, 1980; Sali A. Kriegsman, *Modern Dance in America: The Bennington Years*, Boston, 1981; Arlene Croce, *Going to the Dance*, New York, 1982; Robert Coe, *Dance in America*, New York, 1985; Susan Leigh Foster, *Reading Dance: Bodies and Subjects in Contemporary Dance*, Berkeley, California, 1986; Judy Adam (ed.), *Dancers on a Plane: Cage/Cunningham/Johns*, London, 1989; Kostelanetz, Richard (editor), *Merce Cunningham: Dancing in Space and Time*, Pennington, New Jersey, 1992; John Cage, *John Cage: Writer*, edited by Richard Kostelanetz, New York, 1993; Copeland, Roger, 'Beyond Expressionism: Merce Cunningham's Critique of "The Natural"', in *Dance History: An Introduction*, edited by Janet Adshead-Lansdale, London and New York, 1994 (2nd edition); David Vaughan (Cunningham company archivist), *Merce Cunningham: Fifty Years*, edited by Melissa Harris, no place indicated, 1997.

SIOBHAN DAVIES

Siobhan Davies, one of Britain's leading modern dance choreographers, encapsulates in her work the contemporary dilemma between meaning and abstraction, showing her relation to the modernist tradition of strong dance values (the tradition of, for instance, Merce Cunningham and Richard Alston), while sharing in dance's recent commitment to narrative. In the 1980s, Davies seemed to be developing her work in two directions concurrently. There were essays in which the pure dance values

emerged most strongly – like *New Galileo* (1984) for London Contemporary Dance Theatre and *Embarque* (1988) and *Sounding* (1989) for Rambert Dance Company – and there were works in which emotional states or progressions were more pronounced – like *Minor Characters* (1983), *Silent Partners* (1984), and *Wyoming* (1988), experiments using the intimacy of the small independent dance companies Second Stride and the Siobhan Davies Dance Company. Yet there was no firm border-line between these two polarities of her output, and, in the 1990s, the boundaries have become even further blurred. While Davies refuses to join the issue-based, politically overt tradition of the younger generation of choreographers, with its narrative-based structures, she also demonstrates the impossibility of abstraction in dance. Now, she celebrates the fact that the most movement-led structuring devices produce resonances of meaning, and that even straightforward conventional dance moves contain feeling. Indeed, in *Wanting to Tell Stories* (1993), her starting-point was to bring out the stories embedded within dance emotion itself, like the tenderness that a dancer might feel inherent in a particular dance gesture, or the joy or abandon within a dancerly jump. Two years later, *Wild Translations* (1995) continued Davies's preoccupation with 'eloquence that parallels but is still different to that of language'. Here the expressive and narrative potential of gesture is suggestive of people in relationships rather than dictating particular events or experiences. Yet Davies never surrenders the richness of the dance language that she has built up over the years, for the formal complexities and manipulation of movement material developed in her more abstract pieces can inform narrative and make subtle its personalities. Her conviction remains that 'dance can communicate on is own terms', and it is partly because of this commitment that her work has enjoyed a prominent position within the repertories of the large established dance companies.

Davies, in any case, has always kept narrative or 'plot' extremely simple. The first of the 'narrative' works, *Then You Can Only Sing* (1978), set to the words and music of Judyth Knight, was a sequence of statements by five women, expressing aspects of individual personality and circumstance – loneliness, humour, uncertainty, and confusion. It is significant that *Something to Tell* (1980) sprang from her response to the playwright Chekhov, developing out of what she perceived as his minimal plot development but extensive revelation of troubled personality. The dance was about a woman in loneliness and desolation: Davies and her partner joined in 'several conversations as in a play'. There is no action as such in the piece, no reason given for behaviour; there are simply feelings 'to tell' in movement. Later works developed the emotional base through gestural exploration, like *Silent Partners*, which tells of the history of a man and woman passing through a series of relationships until they meet one another in a duet of heightened passion and tenderness. But it is interesting that Davies puts forward a regular, symmetrical, formal proposition through which to develop the story, the man and woman taking 'learned' movement ideas from one encounter into the next.

Formal devices are often metaphors for the structuring of experience and character. A person's dance material establishes identity, that person's story, and sharing of material with other dancers often seems to suggest togetherness, harmony, and resolution. But this is where the manipulation of the materials of dance itself takes over – and over the years, Davies has developed sophisticated techniques of cross-referencing and weaving together material. A contrapuntal complexity is evident in an especially compelling duet style, independent lines setting up their own countertensions and resolutions. There are imaginative territorial concepts within the stage space too, like the bodies resting motionless in *Make-Make* (1992), which affect the group island of

action by their own stubborn lack of action. There is also the developing fluidity of her large structures – the irregular pacing and overlapping of events, solos, duets, ensembles – and of Davies's stage textures, involving brilliant regroupings and dissolves among clusters of dancers. These last aspects came to the fore most emphatically in big company pieces like *Embarque*, which is, in simple terms, a series of five accumulations of dancers and two major climaxes marked by exuberant cavalcades of dancers in canon threading around each other in a path around the stage. But this description does not convey the variety and speed of process by which accumulation of energy is achieved, nor the effect of breathless curtailment from the second climax as it is paced to occur sooner than expected.

The continuing tension between narrative and abstraction is clearly illuminated through Davies's developing vocabulary and syntax over the years. Following the path of many other choreographers, her first task in her earliest pieces was to find an alternative to the Graham-based language in which she was trained. Many of the most interesting explorations she carried out using her own body. Later, she was to incorporate moves from technique class, or from choreographers with whom she worked – for example Robert Cohan and Richard Alston – even from ballet. But by this time she had already established her own attitude to weight, allowing the body to yield to gravity as well as to resist it, and she had also located an unusual fluidity of motion (the turning point was 1977's *Sphinx*, in which she explored the qualities of animal movement). A new density of movement ideas developed, as she experimented with building a series of complex movement phrases as a starting-point before structuring a piece through time. In the 1980s, alongside her regular vocabulary there was the new richness of gesture introduced into her character pieces, freshly sparked off by working with Ian Spink, then her co-director of Second Stride;

and there were also the 'speaking' full-body movements selected to indicate personality. By now, her work incorporated a rich dynamic and emotional range, from the gentleness and quiet (but often intense) passion of small gestures to the boldness and abandonment of whole-body motion.

The sensuality and speaking quality of Davies's style comes across no more surely than in her work after her 1987 study trip to the United States. Determined to get still further behind the stylistic barrier of traditional dance technique, she adopted working processes from the tradition of release, concerned with making personal movement choices from images and sensations. Davies drew together a group of experienced dancers who, although new to image-based work (apart from Scott Clark, a Feldenkrais practitioner), were prepared to move from Graham-based technique to a more fluent style and make decisions based on their own artistry. Davies was able to work more democratically than ever before, and so her dancers, in particular Clark, had a significant influence on the emerging vocabulary, which took on a freshness and a new vitality while including more tactile qualities and deeper warmth and intimacy.

The new work used the principle that a private image behind the simplest movement makes it a sign, although that sign need not be developed further than a 'mood' ground (and Davies continues to start her working process by building a movement/mood ground). Here again is the tension between narrative and abstraction. In *Wyoming*, for instance, the dancers read the writing of Gretel Ehrlich, and there were images of huge landscape, subtle textures of ground surface, weather conditions, and the physical sensations produced by these external features. Although the inclusion of text suggests a more literal meaning, the dance concerns itself more with the play among areas of expansive space, and among intimate spaces in meetings between dancers. Davies rehearsed the piece with a variety of instructions: 'think of how it would feel to be working on an uneven floor surface' or 'imagine that you are dancing in an irregular space'. Thus, movement that is plain structurally could be infused with a particular liveliness and made strange.

More recent dances have continued to work from an image base, like *Signature* (1990), for the Rambert Dance Company, where the dancers were invited to develop their own marks, and *The Glass Blew In* (1994), which developed from calligraphy, which the dancers studied as starting material. But she has continued to borrow movement vocabulary from external sources – the sign language of the deaf, for instance, for *Different Trains* (1990), and mimetic working hand movements for *Make-Make*. Davies's dancers continue to demonstrate the positive values of respect, gentleness, caring for each other, as well as a sense of their own power. However, a striking new sinuousness characterizes her most recent movement, showing a generous giving of weight as dancers fold over and around each other, with a melting of small joints into body and floor surfaces. Davies comes to rehearsal with some physical ideas and structures in mind, like keys to unlock possibilities, but rarely with set material. This working process means the dancers take greater ownership of their roles and their movement material. The dancers' exploration of movement seems to bring out responses to an internal collective system of sensations, beginning deep in the body, and emphasizes the essentially functional experience of moving, concerned with the process of moving itself. Inner impulses flow outwards, driving the dancers through space. Davies's current approach is, therefore, far more collaborative; her dancers regularly create their own material, dynamics, and timing, and it seems that she now reaches movement images of extreme eloquence precisely because they are so deeply personal to the dancers. Her work then is to select, refine, and give form to the raw material provided for her, using her whole history of choreographic technique.

At the beginning of her choreographic career, it seemed logical for Davies neither to work from music as a basis, nor to integrate designs into her work. At first, she wanted her dance to establish its own rhythms, and to explore rhythms based on breath- or body-timing rather than on musical phrasing or motor pulse. Once she felt more secure in her own talents, though, she welcomed the challenge of other media. Early scores, therefore, provided primarily an atmospheric background and were created separately from the dance; several of them were tape scores. The collaborative process and musical style were typical of the rest of the London Contemporary Dance Theatre (LCDT) repertoire in the mid-1970s. With *Then You Can Only Sing*, Davies explored, for the first time, fitting dance rhythms to sound, and since that piece she has used both commissioned and existing scores, including several works by Britten. From the mid-1980s Davies has shown a major commitment to new music, seeing this as an important way of making her work truly contemporary, and on several occasions having the musicians on the stage as a visual element close to the actual dance. She has used a series of scores by minimalist composers such as John Adams, Brian Eno, and Steve Reich, although she has worked in closer collaboration with Kevin Volans (three of his scores to date, two of them commissions), Gerald Barry (whose score for 1992's *White Bird Featherless*, developed from his opera *The Intelligence Park*), and Gavin Bryars (using Roger Heaton's live and multi-track clarinet sound for *The Glass Blew In*).

Davies's recent modes of working have varied, from deriving initial ideas from the music – including, in the case of Barry's score, the nature of riddle that was at the centre of his opera, to close give-and-take of ideas, to accommodating the score when most of the dance has been completed. But Davies has become ready now for all these different challenges, and she maintains certain stylistic preferences, still to allow dance to develop its own rhythm and phrasing, not to enter into a tight, regular relationship with the music, and not to use musical counts that work against the rhythms of body weight. Indeed, in parts of *White Bird Featherless*, the dancers were invited to find their own points of contact with the music in another example of the recent creative freedoms given to Davies's dancers. She continues to bring her artist's eye and sensitivity to her response to music and is more often inspired by the colour and texture and layering of a score, rather than melody or rhythm. Occasionally, as seen in *Winnsboro Cotton Mill Blues* (1992) when the dancers reflected the mechanistic and repetitive qualities of industrial looms, Davies has worked with, or in counterpoint to, rhythmic patterns.

Reflecting Davies's interest in continually challenging her response to sound and texture, *The Art of Touch* (1995) was set to harpsichord sonatas by Scarlatti juxtaposed with Matteo Fargion's *Sette Canzoni* (Fargion is a former student of Volans). The speed and complexity of the harpsichord demands an increased dexterity and wit from the dancers and sets a feel for period both modern and ancient, imbued with a sense of courtliness. Wild, furious, and tightly structured at the start, *The Art of Touch* calms to a more contemplative, meditative conclusion.

Davies's minimal design element in the 1970s distinguished her from most other LCDT choreographers. It was when she began to introduce narrative into her work that design became more prominent, and the costumes, less dancerly and more human. *Something to Tell* was an important early collaboration with the theatre designer Antony McDonald, who devised a striking Venetian blind set as well as the costumes. McDonald has also contributed to recent pieces, but Davies has worked most frequently with the photographer David Buckland and lighting designer Peter Mumford. A series of pieces in the 1980s used Buckland's blown-up photo images, which interrelated with the narrative content of the choreography, most provocatively in *Silent Partners*, where a landscape of presences functioned as a kind of history into which most of the dancers were finally subsumed.

Other Buckland and Mumford collaborations have offered a more abstract, geometrical concept, like the set for *New Galileo*, which created the actual spatial and temporal framework for the choreography: a pair of light beams hung overhead, at first close together; but by the end the gap between them widened to encompass the whole width of the stage. In *Wanting to Tell Stories*, two huge mesh screens turned and slid to reveal a range of different rooms and corridors. Thus Davies's designers have integrated their contributions with her choreography, now tending to create simple structures which resonate with the dance to assume a potency of meaning. And recently, design played an even more significant role, in *Trespass* (1996). Here, Davies invited Buckland to design constructions as extensions to the dancers' bodies or to deliberately impose on and 'trespass', into the dancers' stage space.

Davies has now started to revisit selected earlier works, rarely to reconstruct the original faithfully, but rather to recreate or to reinvent, to explore ways in which setting material on different bodies, in different times, requires reworking in order to reproduce the original visual statement and effect. This is, on the one hand, an opportunity for new audiences to see earlier works, many now regarded as classics, and, on the other, for Davies to see her work live on, grow, and change as the dancers who perform it also grow and change.

In 1995, Davies set *Sphinx*, originally choreographed for LCDT, on 4D, the graduate company of the London Contemporary Dance School. In reviving the work, Davies was concerned that *Sphinx* should speak to present audiences and have a current dialogue with the new performers. The new version is imprinted with Davies's more fluid, sensuous, and rippling dynamic. The dance emphasizes physical sensation, out of which body shapes emerge, rather than beginning with the aerial, pictorial, shape-oriented material that audiences were more used to in 1977. Sections lost from the original were remade, providing the opportunity for Davies to explore partnering sections with the benefit of the dancers' and her own experience of contact improvisation/release methods. In the new version, weight is passed and shared, with different body parts more seamlessly and more delicately punctuated, and with considerably more use of the floor. There is more emphasis on the passage of movement through the body rather than on end shapes and positions. A more measured and considered use of pause and stillness is evident, and tension is created to a greater extent in the spaces between movements than in the dramatic or dynamic tension within the movements.

The recent revival and reworking of *White Man Sleeps* reveals another subtle shift in Davies's work. Performed by a largely new cast (Gill Glark and Catherine Quinn were by this time the only surviving members of the original ensemble) and to the original instrumentation of Volans's music for harpsichords, viola da gamba, and drums, the movement reveals a fresh dynamic. Phrasing, determined by the individual dancers' bodies and rhythm, means that movement seems more peripherally initiated, more shaped, more hurried and incisive. The expansive use of space and the fleet-footed, sinuous fluidity at the heart of the work remain; yet there is a new percussive edginess and fewer references to other cultures and ways of moving, confirming now the manner in which, almost ten years after the first *White Man Sleeps*, Davies has developed a living, vibrant dance language.

Another important choreographic statement came in 1996 when Davies rehearsed and toured two companion pieces, *Trespass* and *Affections*. Ideas in *Trespass*, the earlier work, were revisited, repeated, and sometimes changed in *Affections*. *Trespass* has all the distinctive features of Davies's work—a highly-charged dance that luxuriates in its physical substance and presence. Loose-limbed, generous, full-bodied, bold yet quirky, *Trespass* is a series of short episodes in which the dancers collide and disperse, and it shows another fruitful companionship between music and movement. Davies's dance does not simply illustrate Gerald Barry's music; it steers, and impels the dancers on. The dimensions of *Trespass* are echoed in *Affections*, but whereas in the former ideas splintered, came to an abrupt end, and were raced through, *Affections* takes more time, expanding earlier ideas into more personal statements; or, to use a linguistic metaphor sentences in the earlier work become chapters. While contrasting in mood and atmosphere, in both *Trespass* and *Affections* movement does not so much represent ideas or emotions as suggest and evoke textures and images.

The most recent repertoire is coloured by a disquiet, a feeling of unrest, as seen in *Bank* (1997). Here, movement is deliberately fragmented, angular, restless, yet pensive. Shards of movement and gesture suggest an inhuman quality – perhaps a metaphor for our increasingly technological age – as if the dancers are propelled and driven by forces beyond their control. *Bank* is another collaboration between Davies and composer Matteo Fargion, who this time has produced a dense and highly rhythmic, percussive score. Reminiscent of aspects of *Rushes* (1982), a much earlier work which signalled a move to a harsher, speedier quality, the dancers break up and then briefly regroup, eventually unable to maintain the community group or family unit.

As Davies celebrates twenty-five years of dancemaking she continues to hone her craft and develop her individual choreographic voice through rigorous exploration and

investigation, focusing on movement itself and its ability to reveal the human condition. Davies believes that her work should enable a dancer to be 'revealed' in a movement style that is developed directly from personal history and idiosyncrasy. This perspective is evident in her continuing respect for those whom she entrusts with making her vision real – her dancers. Initially regarded as a choreographer who made cool, intellectual, and abstract work, Davies now finds that critics respond to the warmth, humanity, and compassion that have, in fact, always been at the core of her work. Yet Davies continues to focus predominantly on movement vocabulary and compositional structures rather than on overt narratives or explicit political themes.

Clearly, Davies has shifted into new and bold directions at various stages during her career, most obviously after 1981 when she developed a dual career between large and small independent companies, and after 1987 in her pursuit of a richer, more complex and tactile movement vocabulary. Now, in maturity, she has reached a true distinctiveness of style, and her various concerns from across the years are often brought together in subtle fusion.

Stephanie Jordan and Sarah Whatley

Biographical details

Born Susan Davies in London, 18 September 1950. **Studied** at Hammersmith College of Art and Building, London, 1966–67, and with Robert Cohan, London School of Contemporary Dance, 1967–71. **Career** Apprentice dancer at The Place (which became the London Contemporary Dance Theatre), from 1969; danced with Ballet For All, London, 1971, and with London Contemporary Dance Theatre, from 1971; also performed with Richard Alston's company, 1976–78; staged first choreography in 1970; associate choreographer for London Contemporary Dance Theatre, 1974, becoming resident choreographer and member of company directorate (upon retirement as a dancer), 1983–87; founded own (part-time) company, Siobhan Davies and Dancers, 1981; joint director (with Ian Spink), Second Stride, 1981–86; founder and chief choreographer, Siobhan Davies

Dance Company, 1988. Has also choreographed for Rambert Dance Company (associate choreographer, 1989–93) and English National Ballet; has worked as teacher for London School of Contemporary Dance, as guest teacher for Ballet Moderne de Paris, and as choreographer in residence and Senior Research Fellow, Roehampton Institute, London (1995–96). **Awards and honours** Greater London Arts Association Arts Award, 1980; Arts Award from the Fulbright Commission, for travel and study in America, 1987; Digital Dance Award, 1988, 1989, 1990, 1992; Olivier Award, 1991, 1993, 1996; MBE (Medal of the British Empire), 1995; Prudential Award, 1996.

Works

Relay (mus. Colin Wood, Bernard Watson, 1972), *Pilot* (mus. Igg Welthy, Stephen Barker, 1974), *The Calm* (mus. Geoffrey Burgon, 1974), *Diary* (mus. Gregory Rose, 1975; new mus. Morris Pert, 1976), *Step at a Time* (mus. Geoffrey Burgon, 1976), *Nightwatch* (with Micha Bergese, Robert Cohan, and Robert North; mus. Bob Downes, 1977), *Sphinx* (mus. Barrington Pheloung, 1977), *Then You Can Only Sing* (mus. Judyth Knight, 1978), *Celebration* (mus. medieval, arr. Nicholas Carr, 1979), *Ley Line* (mus. Vincent Brown, 1979), *Something to Tell* (mus. Britten, 1980), *Recall* (mus. Vincent Brown, 1980), *If My Complaints Could Passions Move* (mus. Britten, 1980), *Plain Song* (mus. Satie, 1981; television version, 1983), *Standing Waves* (mus. Stuart Dempster, 1981), *Free Setting* (mus. Michael Finnissy, 1981), *Mazurka Elegaica* (mus. Britten, 1982), *Rushes* (mus. Michael Finnissy, 1982), *Carnival* (mus. Saint-Saëns, 1982; television version, 1983), *The Dancing Department* (mus. J.S. Bach, 1983), *Minor Characters* (text Barbara McLauren, 1983), *New Galileo* (mus. John Adams, 1984), *Silent Partners* (mostly silent, 1984), *Bridge the Distance* (mus. Britten, 1985; television version the same year), *The School for Lovers Danced* (mus. Mozart, 1985), *The Run to Earth* (mus. Brian Eno, 1986), *and do they do* (mus. Michael Nyman, 1986), *Red Steps* (mus. John Adams, 1987), *Embarque* (mus. Steve Reich, 1988), *White Man Sleeps* (mus. Kevin Volans, 1988; television version, 1989), *Wyoming* (mus. John-Marc Gowans, 1988; television version, 1989), *Sounding* (mus. Giacinto Scelsi, 1989), *Cover Him with Grass* (mus. Kevin Volans, 1989), *Drawn Breath* (mus. Andrew Poppy, 1989), *Signature* (mus. Kevin Volans, 1990), *Dancing Ledge* (mus. John Adams, 1990), *Different Trains* (mus. Steve Reich, 1990), *Arctic Heart* (mus. John-Marc Gowans, 1991), *Winnsboro Cotton Mill Blues* (mus. Frederick Rzewski, 1992), *White Bird Featherless* (mus.

Gerald Barry, 1992; television version, 1995), *Make-Make* (mus. soundtrack David Buckland, Russell Mills, from material by David Bradnum, 1992), *Wanting to Tell Stories* (mus. Kevin Volans, 1993), *The Glass Blew In* (mus. Gavin Bryars, 1994), *Between the National and the Bristol* (mus. Gavin Bryars, 1994), *Wild Translations* (mus. Kevin Volans, 1995), *The Art of Touch* (mus. Scarlatti, Matteo Fargion, 1995), *Trespass* (mus. Gerald Barry, 1996), *Affections* (mus. Handel, 1996); *Bank* (mus. Matteo Fargion, 1997).

Further reading

Interviews with Chris de Marigny, *Dance Theatre Journal*, Winter 1985; in 'The Artist's View: Two Contrasting Interviews', *Dance Theatre Journal*, Autumn 1989; with Nadine Meisner, in 'Sound, Mood and Motion from the Floor', *Sunday Times* (Section 5), 8 September 1991; with Sanjoy Roy, in 'Making a Dance, *Dance Now*, Spring 1997; in Jo Butterworth and Gill Clarke (eds.), *Dancemakers' Portfolio: Conversations with Choreographers*, Bretton Hall, 1998.

Articles Colin Nears, 'Bridging a Distance', *Dance Research*, Autumn 1987; Stephanie Jordan, 'Second Stride, The First Six Years', *Dance Theatre Journal*, Winter 1988; John Percival, 'Bouncing Back: On Siobhan Davies and her New Company', *Dance and Dancers*, February 1989; Stephanie Jordan, 'Siobhan Davies Company', *Dance Theatre Journal*, Spring 1989; Jann Parry, 'Watch Their Steps', *Observer Magazine*, 19 November 1989; Angela Kane, 'Siobhan Davies' (Dance Study Supplement 6), *Dancing Times*, March 1990; 'Choreographer on the Move', *Dance and Dancers*, October 1990; Allen Robertson, 'Letter from Europe', *Dance Ink*, December 1990; Helen Wallace, 'String Smiths', *Strad*, August 1991; Sophie Preston, 'Beyond Words', *Dance Now*, Winter 1992–93; Sanjoy Roy, 'From Studio to Stage', *Dance Now*, Winter 1995; Bill Bissell, 'Siobhan Davies in St Petersburg', *Dance Now*, Spring 1996; articles by John Drummond, Alan Franks, Richard Alston, Kevin Volans, David Buckland, in special Davies issue of *Dance Theatre Journal*, Spring 1996; special Davies issue of *Dance Now*, Spring 1997: includes Sanjoy Roy's, 'Expanding the Human Body', Christopher Cook's 'Evolving a Style', Sophia Preston's 'Counterpoints and References', Stephanie Jordan's 'Body and Voice' (on *Affections*), and Nick Kimberley's 'Musical Collaborations'.

Books Joan W. White (ed.), *Twentieth-Century Dance in Britain: A History of Major Dance*

Companies in Britain, London, 1985; Allen Robertson and Donald Hutera, *The Dance Handbook*, Harlow, Essex, 1988; Stephanie Jordan, *Striding Out: Aspects of Contemporary and New Dance in Britain*, London, 1992; Judith Mackrell, *Out of Line: The Story of British New Dance*, London, 1992; Jonathan Thrift (ed.), *Siobhan Davies in Residence: Summer Programme*, Roehampton Institute, London, 1996.

ANNE TERESA DE KEERSMAEKER

Since the Belgian choreographer Anne Teresa De Keersmaeker began making work, she has shown a steady and methodical progression of choreographic development. *Asch* (*I'm Tired*), made in 1980, was her first piece, but it was a brief, productive time in New York City that spurred the making of her second and more important work, *Fase: Four Movements* (1982). De Keersmaeker met and worked with members of Reich's ensemble – Edmund Niemann and Nurit Tilles (piano) and Shem Guibbory (violin) – during her stay in the United States. She choreographed 'Violin Phrase' and 'Come Out', the first two sections of *Fase*, in New York, and 'Piano Phrase' and 'Clapping Music', on her return to Belgium. This seminal piece was a duet for herself and another fine Belgian dancer, Michele Anne De Mey. An effective performer in *Fase*, De Mey, a choreographer herself, continued as an associate and dancer in other De Keersmaeker works well into the 1980s.

Fase had its premiere in Brussels. It was of monumental importance to the choreographer's artistic evolution, with the music and movement minimalism providing a strong basis for her future choreography. De Keersmaeker's keen rhythmic sense and intelligence in structuring complex movement phrasing was realized in this compelling dance. Reich's pulsing music phrasing was not mirrored in her movement, but rather was played against her own

unique configurations. The driving visual force and intense dramatic quality portrayed by these riveted women was a forecast of the tough expressionistic voice that was soon to emerge.

The European dance network beyond Belgium was quick to notice De Keersmaeker's work, as out of necessity countries frequently co-produced dance projects that toured to co-operating cultural centres around Europe. Co-production allows for companies on relatively small budgets to be included on many performance rosters. De Keersmaeker, De Mey, and the three musicians from Reich's group travelled with *Fase* to several countries. The trio playing live heightened the power of the score's shifting repetitive phrases and added further energy to the dancers' superb performance. The tour exposure brought many positive responses to the work of this intensely serious and ambitious young choreographer.

It was at the Brussels Kaaitheater festival in 1983 that De Keersmaeker's company, Rosas, formally made its debut with the premiere of the stunning *Rosas danst Rosas*. The piece was for De Keersmaeker and three other founding members – Fumiyo Ikeda, Michele Anne De Mey, and Adriana Borriello. The four young women had met at Mudra, the Training and Research Centre for the Performing Arts founded by Maurice Béjart. The music was composed by another important Belgian artist, Thierry De Mey, in collaboration with Peter Vermeersch. The music composed for Rosas was entitled *Habanera*.

Rosas danst Rosas, an intimate portrait of four women, was a signature piece. The work begins with clamouring industrial sounds and rhythmic clapping followed by silence. The first of five movements starts in darkness, with the four women crouching and then coiling down flat to the floor. Quick urgent gestures alternate with long, sustained movements. The imagery suggests women who are weary and beaten down. The second movement is performed with chairs and begins with careful placement and the putting on of shoes. (Chairs are frequently incorporated in De Keersmaeker's work; performers sit on them, lie on them, roll from one to another, fall off, roll and remount, stack them, and carry them to new locations.) Compulsively repeated gestures are a feature in *Rosas danst Rosas* and they include a hand running through hair, the breast cupped with one hand, arms clenched tightly around the abdomen, both hands deep into the crotch, arms flung, clothing being adjusted, and the neck wrung to the furthest extent physically possible. These exaggerated naturalistic responses to life's frustrations are powerful images and match the hard driving percussive score. Solos are performed in the third section, accompanied by the sound of clarinets. The fourth section of turning and travelling through varying floor patterns is mesmerizing in its repetitive complexity.

De Keersmaeker's urgent and continuous patterning for the quartet is meticulously executed. As a needed relief, there are moments when the dancers seem to find a new energy, and take subtle delight in their virtuosity and in their sense of community among themselves. A dancer can move out from the group's synchronization, establish her own identity through idiosyncratic gestures, and then return to the ongoing movement phrase without losing the overall unity. Eventually, the driving music stops. Each woman takes her position: one stands upstage right, tugging at her shirt and repeating the hand-through-the-hair gesture, another drops back down on the floor, a third collapses back on the chair, and the fourth, originally danced by De Keersmaeker, stands facing the audience and then turns upstage. The finale is short and, as in the beginning, it is in silence.

Elena's Aria (1984) was De Keersmaeker's third major work for her female ensemble, now numbering five. De Keersmaeker's choreography now featured the addition of classical music, including operatic arias from Di Capua, Bizet, and Donizetti; the inclusion of text, such as a tape of a Fidel Castro speech, or performers speaking passages from Tolstoy, Brecht, and Dostoyevsky on the woes of male/female love; and cinematic images projected on a screen. Still present were the repetitive movements and dramatic gestures of before, but because of the abundance of new ingredients, the work was less coherent. The dance critic Anna Kisselgoff, writing in *The New York Times* (19 May 1987), said, 'The overall result is a highly emotional social critique. The specifics are not clear but the general atmosphere, with the inclusion of political speeches, suggests that women's place in society is part of a larger political problem.' Indeed, there is an irony in De Keersmaeker's portrayal of women. While being shown as unhappy, lonely victims, her women also play *femmes fatales* in their short tight dresses, sexy stiletto heels, and unabashed display of upper thighs. The women of Rosas are provocative and send mixed messages.

Works that follow show De Keersmaeker continually addressing gender issues in her own abstract communication style. In *Verkommenes Ufer Medeamaterial Landschaft mit Argonauten* (1987), based on Heiner Müller's triptych on Medea, she used the 'Medea' characters to broaden her inspiration and expressiveness. This was a pivotal work in her use of manipulating a classic text.

She toured with sixteen performers in *Ottone, Ottone* (1988), a work based on Claudio Monteverdi's opera, *L'Incoronozione di Poppea*. The principal theme of *Poppea*, as the programme notes by Nikolaus Harnoncourt explained, is 'the destructive power – even in society – of Love. ... Monteverdi shows us what happens when Love has total power to rule.' The critic Alex Mallems has further explained,

> [De Keersmaeker] has chosen this work deliberately because of her affinity for both the music and the themes of the

opera but used the plot and characters rather flexibly – adding and changing character freely – slowed down music, improvised speeches in various languages and added quotations from other Rosas works.

(*Ballet International*, February 1991)

A performer in *Ottone, Ottone* commented that De Keersmaeker was never content with the work, constantly incorporating new ideas and material much in the way that the German director/choreographer Pina Bausch is known to do.

Gender identity is again important in *Achterland* (1990). But more interesting in this dance are the musical choices and the choreographer's expanded development of her circular fall-and-rebound floor material. Doris Humphrey's classic work, *Two Ecstatic Themes (Circular Descent and Pointed Ascent)*, is particularly brought to mind in this piece for five women and three men. Dressed in tailored business suits, with short skirts, high heels, and knee pads, the women execute urgent runs leading to a coiled fall into the floor, a roll, and immediate ascent to standing. These patterns are repeated over and over, suggesting a desperate whirlwind of physical struggle. The women seem to be driven by an evil force. In juxtaposition to the frantic dance activity is the presence of a pianist playing the music of Györgi Ligeti. When the men dance, we hear the music of the virtuoso soloist Eugene Ysaye playing his composition, 'Three Sonatas for Solo Viola'. The male dancers are slightly more violent in their rolling action, adding a jump at the top of their ascent. Arms, with upward pointed elbows, and powerful leg movements add to the momentum, and later in the piece, the use of chairs and other specific movement themes for the women are reminiscent of earlier pieces.

De Keersmaeker used the work of the Hungarian composer, György Ligeti, again for her work *Stella*, choreographed in 1990 for five women. 'Of all the arts,' Anne

Teresa De Keersmaeker once confided, 'music is for me the most important thing in life.' And, as Anna Kisselgoff wrote in 1991:

music is only one springboard in *Stella*, which is essentially a multilevel essay on how context changes meaning, especially with respect to how women are regarded by others and themselves. Nothing is direct here, yet everything is toughly stated, depending on Ms. de Keersmaeker's own cultural references.

(*The New York Times*, 19 October 1991)

De Keersmaeker's cultural references for this work are rich and include *Rashomon* by Runosuke Akutagawa, *Stella* by Goethe, and *A Streetcar Named Desire* by Tennesse Williams.

De Keersmaeker continually returns to her original themes of the mysteries of human behaviour, and, perhaps more poignantly, reveals her ambivalence about the nature and role of the female gender. Her works become more theatrical and her context more layered with literary and cultural references. As is her practice, she reconstitutes and embellishes her source material, and is not averse to recycling material or structure from previous pieces. (She has revived and reworked selected dances, including *Fase* and *Rosas danst Rosas*.)

The choreographer chose three of her favoured composers, including Thierry De Mey, for her 1994 work, *Kynok*. This was a work in three parts: *Rosa*, with music by Bartók, was reworked from the choreography to a short film by Peter Greenaway: 'Grosse Fuge', from *Erts* (1992), with music by Beethoven, was also reworked; and the section itself entitled *Kynok* was new choreography. The word 'Kynok' is Russian for eye movements and a term used by Russian *cinéma vérité* artists (to convey candid realism).

The United States premiere of *Woud* (Forest) took place at the Next Wave Festival at the Brooklyn Academy of Music in the Autumn of 1997. The production offered a large range of imagery inspired by love themes in the music of Alban Berg, Arnold Schoenberg, and Richard Wagner. The two-and-a-half-hour work began with a lengthy film entitled *Tippeke*, choreographed and performed by De Keersmaeker. Thierry De Mey directed as well as composed the film's taped score. In this, a solo figure wearing a dress and boots on the large screen staggered through a stark forest while, periodically, a dancer attired in identical costume echoed the same movement on stage – a shadow image. In a desperate voice, De Keersmaeker repeated phrases concerning a boy named Tippeke. There were unexplained headlights, seen from the highway in the distance. Immediately following the end of the surreal film was the start of a live performance of Berg's *Lyric Suite*. The music here, as in all De Keersmaeker's work, was crucial to the structural frame and expressionistic themes that unfolded in layers. The male and female partnering and lifts were turbulent, intense, and rich in movement material. The familiar vocabulary of spiral air turns into the floor and energetic rebounds were beautifully executed. The piece, exploring episodic love relationships, contained many thwarted climaxes.

A capable and persistent dance maker, De Keersmaeker has a wide-ranging intellect and vision unique in European experimental dance. Her influence is guaranteed: a Performing Arts Research and Training Studio (PARTS) has been established in Brussels as a collaboration between La Monnaie and Rosas under the artistic direction of De Keersmaeker, with the training conducted by ex-dancers of such innovative choreography as that by Trisha Brown, Pina Bausch, and William Forsythe, as well as De Keersmaeker herself. She has stated that PARTS will not in any interfere, though, with her work with Rosas. In Belgium, De Keersmaeker's strong presence and popularity are well established – Rosas has been a 'Cultural Ambassador of Flanders' since

January 1993. De Keersmaeker's larger place in dance history, however, is yet to be determined, although she has established a firm and fertile grounding thus far.

Sandra Genter

Biographical details

Born in Mechelen, Belgium, 11 June 1960. **Studied** at Maurice Béjart's Mudra school, Brussels, 1978–80; attended New York University's dance department, in the Tisch School of Arts, early 1980s. **Career** Dancer in New York, early 1980s, and worked with composer Steve Reich's group of musicians; returned to Belgium, 1982, then toured internationally with her work *Fase*; founder, Rosas dance company, 1983, for which she has both choreographed and performed; appointed artist-in-residence, with Rosas, at the Théâtre de la Monnaie, Brussels, 1992; founder and director, PARTS (Performing Arts Research and Training Studios) dance course in Brussels, 1995, which replaced Mudra. **Awards** New York Dance and Performance Award ('Bessie'), 1988; Grand Prix Video Danse (for *Hoppla*), 1990; Dance Screen Award, 1992, 1994; Grand Prix International Video Danse, 1997.

Works

Asch (mus. Christian Cuppia, Serge Biran, 1980), *Fase: Four Movements* (mus. Steve Reich, 1982), *Rosas danst Rosas* (mus. Thierry De Mey, Peter Vermeersch, 1983), *Elena's Aria* (mus. various, also spoken text, 1984), *Bartok/Aantekeningen* (mus. Bartók, 1986), *Verkommenes Ufer Medeamaterial Landschaft mit Argonauten* (play by Heiner Müller, 1987), *Mikrokosmos* (mus. Bartók, 1987), *Ottone, Ottone* (mus. Monteverdi, 1988), *Stella* (mus. György Ligeti, 1990), *Achterland [Hinterland]* (mus. György Ligeti, Eugène Ysaye, 1990), *Mozart/Concert Arias* (mus. Mozart, 1992), *Erts* (mus. Beethoven, Schnittke, Webern, 1992), *Rosa* (film, dir. Peter Greenaway, mus. Bartók, 1992), *Kynok* (includes reworkings of parts of *Erts* and *Rosa*; new mus. Thierry De Mey, 1994), *Toccata* (mus. J.S. Bach, 1993), *Creation: Amor constante mas alla de la muerte* (mus. Thierry De Mey, 1994), *Erwartung: Verklärte Nacht* (mus. Schoenberg, 1995), *Three Movements* (mus. Schoenberg, Wagner, Thierry De Mey, 1996), *Woud [Forest]* (includes film *Tippeke*, mus. Thierry De Mey; *Lyric Suite*, mus. Berg, and *Verklärte Nacht* (1995); 1997), *Just Before* (mus. John Cage, Steve Reich, Thierry De May, Magnus Lindberg, 1997).

Further reading

Interviews with David Hughes, in 'Stop Making Sense', *Dance Theatre Journal*, Summer 1991; with Julia Pascal, in 'On Her Avantgarde', *Sunday Times*, 12 April 1992; with Roslyn Sulcas, in 'Space and Energy', *Dance and Dancers*, April 1992; with Mårten Spangberg, in 'Organising Time and Space', *Ballett International*, June 1995.

Articles Dee Conway, 'Anne Teresa De Keersmaeker', *New Dance*, Winter/Spring, 1983/84; Jann Parry, 'De Keersmaeker', *Dance and Dancers*, February 1983; Marianne Van Kerkhoven, 'The Dance of Anne Teresa De Keersmaeker', *Drama Review*, Fall 1984; Ann Nugent, 'Anne Teresa De Keersmaeker', *Dance and Dancers*, April 1986; Pascale Tison, 'Belgium: Between Tradition and Innovation', *Ballett International*, July/August 1986; Isabelle Lanz, 'The Netherlands: De Keersmaeker, Undisputed Highlight of Holland Festival, '86', *Ballett International*, September 1986; Elizabeth Zimmer, 'Waiting for the End of the World: Downtown Dance', *Dance Magazine*, February 1987; Judith Mackrell, 'Umbrella Dance and Dancers', *Dance Theatre Journal*, Spring 1988; Nadine Meisner, 'Anne Teresa De Keersmaeker', *Dance and Dancers*, February 1988; Alex Mallems, 'The Belgian Dance Explosion of the Eighties', *Ballett International*, February 1991; Sabrina Weldman, 'Belgian Dance: Fertile Ground', *Ballett International*, July/August 1991; Lesley-Anne Sayers, 'The Emperor's New Clothes', *Dance Theatre Journal*, Spring-Summer 1993; Sanjoy Roy, 'Toccata', *Dance Now*, Summer 1994; Ian Bramley, 'Turning World War I: Counterpointe', *Dance Theatre Journal*, Autumn 1994; Johannes Odenthal, 'The Beginnings of the Future' (on *Amor Constante*), *Ballett International*, January 1995; Janet Adshead-Lansdale, 'Empowered Expression from Bausch and De Keersmaeker', *Dance Theatre Journal*, Winter 1995/96; Nadine Meisner, 'Circular Moves', *Dance Theatre Journal*, 13(4), Summer 1997.

LAURA DEAN

Laura Dean established her choreographic reputation in the early 1970s with dances notable for their simplified structures, geometric floor patterns, minimal vocabulary, repeated movement phrases, and powerful rhythmic drive. She created a style so immediately recognizable as her own that some critics now accuse her of creating choreography that is a 'marketable commodity'. Typically categorized as 'minimalist' and 'postmodern', she both defines and defies the terms. Since 1980 she has been working increasingly with ballet companies and ballet vocabularies – one of many modern 'crossover' choreographers – developing work of increasing complexity and range.

She was born in Staten Island, New York. Her parents were not performing artists, but their professional interests – her father was an architect and her mother a mathematician – were certainly compatible with their daughter's future choreographic concerns. She received early training in both music and dance at the Third Street Settlement in New York City, later studying at the School of American Ballet. She continued training in ballet, modern, and jazz dance techniques at the High School of Performing Arts where she graduated with honours in 1963.

After two months at Boston College, it was clear that her life was not to take an academic direction. She resumed classes in New York City studios including those of Martha Graham and Merce Cunningham. She performed briefly with the Paul Taylor Dance Company, Paul Sanasardo, Kenneth King, Meredith Monk, and Robert Wilson. In the autumn of 1965 she presented a one-minute solo called *Medieval* which received favourable reviews for its 'discipline' and 'uncomplicated cheerfulness'. In 1967 and 1968 she presented a number of small-scale loft performances in a style typical of the times: mixed-media theatre works for small groups of friends, which evoked ritual by means of incense and candles.

In 1968 she went to San Francisco for two weeks and stayed for two years. Working alone in a studio, she made a 'discovery' that would guide her later work: in an effort to strip away the movements that characterized her previous training, she found herself reducing her motion to the 'simple' act of spinning. Although there is ample precedent for spinning in ritual dance and on the theatrical stage, Dean was adamant about having discovered and developed her style of spinning on her own. This style was characterized by an even distribution of weight across both feet, with the body and arms free to take a variety of positions as the dancer spins. An *Hour in Silence* (1970) consisted of an hour of solo spinning; *Spinning Dance* (1973) developed the same material for an ensemble. Extended passages of spinning would become a signature motif of Dean's dances – at one point she called it as essential to her work as a contraction is to the work of Martha Graham. It was an early manifestation of her interest in ritualistic and trance-like activities that embodied the seemingly contradictory qualities of both touching and distancing an audience – touching them by drawing them into the motion, distancing them by its introverted focus.

When Dean returned to New York City, she began making dances that were extreme in their simplicity. In addition to the above-mentioned spinning dances, in the early 1970s she did works such as *Stamping Dance*, *Jumping Dance*, and *Circle Dance*. She worked closely with Steve Reich, a composer who shared her interest in minimalist structures, repetition, and driving rhythms. Although Dean would argue that there is in reality no such thing as 'repetition', and that attempts to 'repeat' material in fact demonstrate the uniqueness and variety that are inherent in all human activities, she was making a fine philosophical point. Some audience members found her work and its repetitive elements to be mesmerizing and often healing or cathartic; others found it boring and intolerable. The effect of the carefully planned repetitions could be surprisingly visceral, with the slightest shift or change suggesting something powerful or exciting.

Although Dean claims not to have studied, or been influenced by, folk-dancing forms, her work frequently recalls or is compared to them in their emphasis on group dancing with evolving geometric floor patterns, simple vocabularies, and grounded footwork. The body vocabulary seems to draw from many sources, with the arms making subtle evocations of other cultural styles, especially the Eastern and oriental. The critic Tobi Tobias has noted that the kinds of things Dean frequently has her dancers do evoke the thrill of one's own play as a child, and Dean herself has acknowledged that she wants her dances to have a vitality that is innocent exhilaration. Despite their simple appearance, her dances require a high degree of training, technical skill, stamina, and mental acuity on the part of her performers.

In 1971 Dean officially formed her own company. She continued to develop signature elements and motifs. In addition to spinning passages, there were little hip-swaying shuffling walks, flat face falls, spread-eagle on the ground, little hops, canon forms, interweaving lines and modules. She created many works of long duration, such as *Drumming* (1975) (seventy minutes) and *Music* (1979) (seventy-five minutes). As 'minimal' as the works were, there was surprising complexity in them (more than one critic called them 'maximally minimal'); as 'formalist' as they were, critics commented on the distilled messages they contained and the emotions they evoked. For example, simply having all her dancers remain on stage, a quality characteristic of her early works, seemed to convey a sense of wholeness and community.

The setting and costumes for her works were distinctive. Many of her earliest works were performed in non-proscenium settings. The awareness of horizontal patterning has been sustained even as she adapted to the more frontal perspective of traditional theatres. However, she rarely uses scenic devices: her collaboration with the artist Michael Graves for the Joffrey Ballet's *Fire* (1982) was an unusual experiment. She has collaborated to positive effect, though, with lighting designers, notably with the late Tom Skelton.

Dean's costumes are mostly of her own design. Their simplicity and clarity have always carried a strong visual and even metaphoric impact. Characteristic would be simple loose white trousers, tunic tops, and unobtrusive jazz shoes. This look suggested harmony and unity, with white representing all colours blended. Later she glamorized the look by using shiny fabric and sequins. Even later she varied the style by having women wear skirts and sometimes heeled shoes or, in many ballet works, *pointe* shoes. But when she dressed the cast of *Impact* (1985) in sleek leotards, the press was in shock.

In 1976 Dean began writing the music for her own works, with the creation of a dance called *Song*. She has subsequently written the music for many of her works. She no longer likes to be called a 'choreographer', but prefers instead the title 'choreographer *and* composer' (in response to which one writer has suggested she use the term 'composographer'). She considers music and dance to be inseparable, and is fond of noting that many world traditions do not separate them. Her company, which was originally called the Laura Dean Dance Company, became Laura Dean Dancers and Musicians, and then, Laura Dean Musicians and Dancers (to discourage the press from dropping 'Musicians' out of the title).

Her music is also of what would be called the minimalist school, basic and fundamental, responding to rhythmic drive. Her instruments have included voice, percussion, piano, and now various electronic synthesizers. Although she had early training in music, she feels that music critics have not taken her seriously because she does not have traditional or advanced musical credentials.

Although Dean prefers to write her own music and has expressed mixed feelings about the relative success of various collaborations, she has continued to choreograph works to pre-composed and commissioned scores by other composers, including members of the minimalist school such as Reich, Philip Glass, and Terry Riley; jazz composer Anthony Davis; rock musician Prince; and most recently John Zeretzke, the music director of Aman World Music and Dance Ensemble, a troupe that performs a wide range of folk-dance repertories.

In 1980 Dean began her work with ballet companies when the Joffrey Ballet commissioned her to create a work for them. The result, *Night*, was a critical success, and other commissions have followed, including more for the Joffrey Ballet (*Fire*, *Force Field* (1986), *Structure/Light Field* (1992), and a section of *Billboards* (1993)), several for the Ohio Ballet, and two for the Royal Danish Ballet. In 1988, for the New York City Ballet's American Music Festival, she created *Space*, a work which incorporated four principal dancers and an ensemble of 36.

One of the few avant-garde dancers to have had a ballet background (a year at the School of American Ballet as a teenager, more years at the Joffrey School and with various teachers including Mia Slavenska), Dean was in a good position to do crossover work. As she began to use ballet vocabulary, she first confronted the difficulty of achieving her 'look' in ballet and the corollary problem, that of exploring a ballet 'look' with her own company. She also had to confront the issue of spinning – her signature style, with its grounded quality, did not look the same for dancers on *pointe* shoes and for dancers not trained in her style. Eventually she abandoned long spinning passages in her ballets; she began to explore instead the use of various ballet turns, such as pirouettes, *chaîné* turns, and *piqué* turns. Her ballet choreography has become increasingly virtuosic, and Dean has become more interested in explorations of partnering and individual solos. She had great success with her portion of the Joffrey Ballet's *Billboards*, entitled *Sometimes It Snows in April*, to the music of the rock star Prince (three other sections were choreographed by others). The section 'Trust', included in the videotape version of the ballet, includes many characteristic motifs and distinguishes itself by its formal clarity, its explicit exploration of the concept of 'trust' as it applies to partnership in ballet technique and hence in life, and its success at taking advantage of the company's casual, youthful, and virtuosic qualities.

She has also created several works for ice skating companies. The visionary John Curry, who was dedicated to bringing more choreographic sophistication to ice dancing, commissioned her to do *Burn* in 1983. She has also created works for the Next Ice Age Skating Company and for the Ice Theatre of New York. Although her choreographic style was already suited to the excitement of skating's sweep and spins and the pleasure of seeing evolving patterns, she has been praised for her ability to exploit the specific vocabularies of ice skating, especially its complex jumps.

Many would argue that Dean's work is without content, purely formalist. This assessment underestimates the level of thought that informs her work. One of its strengths is the ability to reduce to essences, a quality suggested by the evocative single-word titles she has applied to many of her dances: *Song, Dance* (1976), *Spiral* (1977), *Music* (1979), *Night, Fire, Impact, Magnetic* (1986), *Gravity* (1987), *Space* (1988), *Infinity* (1990), *Ecstacy* (1993). Some compare her work to pure music, and place her in the tradition of the music visualizations of Ruth St Denis and Doris Humphrey. Her dances touch on the visceral and emotional level of music more than on the level of ideas or thought. Descriptions of her work are often much like descriptions of music, or even abstract art. She is aware of how spatial elements like pattern and colour can touch our emotions, and that simple patterns can have larger implications.

But dance is also human. And while Einstein is one of her heroes, so is Jung. She is dealing with human bodies and thus evokes images and feelings and emotions.

She is certainly not telling stories, creating dramatic scenaria, using text, or doing performance art. But she is aware of the impact of an image, and part of what touches the viewer is her distillation of content into resonating archetype. Her early works frequently implied a 'content' about the nature of community; and the partnering work in *Billboards* has much to say about the nature of 'trust' between two people. In *Tympani* (1980) a group of spinning dancers make a gesture of cradling something in front of themselves, then shift their hands behind themselves to form an image of flying. Although the dance itself is not really about cradling, or flying, the images do touch us with their connotations.

Earth, created in 1993 for the Ohio Ballet, features a ritualistic movement sequence that includes kneeling, lying face down on the ground, then standing and opening the arms to the sky. The pattern – set in silhouette against a fiery orb – is performed early in the dance by a soloist, later by the same soloist with a partner, and finally, at the dance's close, with the whole group of ten dancers in a circle. Far from abstract, these repetitions clearly reinforce the dance's stated dedication, based on 'profound respect for all life on this earth'.

Lately, Dean's work seems to have been striving for increasing complexity. Tobi Tobias has complained that some of Dean's recent work is encumbered by 'gobs of material'. Deborah Jowitt has noted that the culminating solos in *Cloud* (1994) seem garish and crowd-pleasing. Although some critics feel that she has thus abandoned the very territory she had staked out, others see her development as indicative of an unexpected capacity for formal sophistication, recalling the more abstract work of master ballet choreographers such as Petipa and Balanchine. Balanchine once noted that it was with his early work with Stravinsky on *Apollo* that he recognized the importance of 'reducing what seemed to be multiple possibilities to the one that is inevitable'. He then

91

went on to create works of extraordinary texture, variety, and richness, built around that awareness. In a review of Dean's choreography, critic Joan Acocella noted that Dean's work seems to be in such a period of refocusing, but at the point the lens is adjusted, the picture inevitably blurs. We must wait a bit longer to see what direction Dean's more recent interests take her choreography.

Katy Matheson

Biographical details

Born in Staten Island, New York, 3 December 1945. **Studied** at the School of American Ballet for a year, the High School of Performing Arts (graduated 1963), and with Mia Slavenska, Lukas Hoving, Paul Sanasardo, Merce Cunningham, in New York. **Career** Danced with Paul Taylor Company, 1965–66, and for short periods with Sanasardo, Meredith Monk, Robert Wilson, and Kenneth King; founded Laura Dean Dance Company, 1971; began collaboration with composer Steve Reich in the early 1970s; renamed her company Laura Dean Dancers and Musicians (1976), subsequently changing it to Laura Dean Musicians and Dancers. Has also choreographed for Joffrey Ballet, Ohio Ballet, Concert Dance Company (Boston), Royal Danish Ballet, New York City Ballet, Berkshire Ballet, Bat-Dor Company (Israel), and for several ice-dance companies, including the John Curry Skaters and the Ice Theatre of New York; has also taught, including at the University of Texas, University of Rhode Island, and Pratt Institute, New York. **Awards** include *Dance Magazine* Award (1982), two Guggenheim Fellowships, a New York Dance and Performance ('Bessie') Award, and a Brandeis University Creative Arts Award.

Works

For many of the following pieces Dean also created the musical scores.

Medieval (1965), *3 Minutes and Ten Seconds* (1966), *Christmas Piece* (1967), *Hush Little Baby* (mus. Bob Dylan and Dean, 1968), *Life is All Around You* (mus. the Mamas and the Papas and Dean, 1968), *Sitting, Spinning, Stamping (Red-White-Black)* (mus. Dean, Gordon Lightfoot, 1968), *Farewell* (text: Teilhard de Chardin, 1968), *No Title* (1968), *At Alan Saret's* (1970), *An Hour*

in Silence (1970), *Bach Preludes* (mus. Bach, 1971), *A Dance Concert* (mus. African hand bell maracas, 1971), *Stamping Dance* (1971), *Jumping Dance* (1972), *Quartet Squared (Phase Patterns)* (mus. Steve Reich, 1972), *Piano Phase* (1972), *Circle Dance* (1972), *Square Dance* (mus. Steve Reich, 1972), *Walking Dance* (mus. Steve Reich, clapping 1973), *Changing Pattern Steady Pulse* (mus. Tim Ferchen, 1973), *Spinning Dance* (1973), *Response Dance* (1974), *Changing* (mus. drums, 1974), *Drumming* (mus. Steve Reich, 1975), *Solo Performance* (1976), *Song* (1976), *Dance* (1976), *Spiral* (1977), *Music* (1979), *Pattern* (1979), *Night* (1980), *Pattern II* (1980), *Tympani* (1980; film version the same year), *Sky Light* (1982), *Solo in Red* (1982), *Fire* (mus. Dean, 1982; revised version, 1989), *Inner Circle* (1983), *Enochian* (1983), *Burn* (ice dance; mus. Jean-Michel Jarre, 1983), *Trio* (1984), *Tehillim* (mus. Steve Reich, 1984), *Patterns of Change* (mus. Philip Glass, 1985), *Transformer* (mus. Anthony Davis, 1985), *Impact* (mus. Steve Reich, 1985), *Force Field* (mus. Steve Reich, 1986), *Magnetic* (1986), *Shaman II* (1987), *Gravity* (mus. Philip Glass, 1987), *For Two* (duet; mus. Jean-Baptiste Breval, 1987), *Dream Collector* (mus. Terry Riley, 1987), *Space* (mus. Steve Reich, 1988), *Equator* (1988), *Arrow of Time* (1989), *Ocean* (ice dance, 1989), *Memory* (1989), *Quantum* (1990), *Infinity* (1990), *Delta* (mus. Gary Brooker, 1990), *Sacred Dances* (1991), *Sedona Sunrise* (ice dance, 1991), *Structure/Light Field* (1992), *Sometimes It Snows in April* (part of the collaborative *Billboards*; mus. Prince, 1993), *Ecstasy* (1993), *Earth* (mus. Richard Kosinski and John Zeretzke, 1993), *Light* (1993), *Night Wind* (1993), *Reflections* (ice dance, 1993), *Cloud* (1994).

Further reading

Interviews with Mark Steinbrink, in 'Interview with Laura Dean', *Ballet News*, October 1981; Deborah Rawson, in 'New Laura Dean?', *Ballet News*, December 1982; with Jody Dalton, in 'Laura Dean, Composeographer?', *Ear Magazine*, October 1990.

Articles Marcia B. Siegel, 'Up from Minimalism', *Dance Magazine*, February 1974; Marcia B. Siegel, 'New Dance: Individuality, Image and the Demise of the Coterie', *Dance Magazine*, April 1974; Laura Dean, 'Notes on Choreography', *Dance Scope*, Fall/Winter 1974–75; Laura Dean, '7 Dances by Laura Dean and Company', *Drama Review*, March 1975; Jack Anderson, 'Rudolf and Laura: Nureyev', *Dance Magazine*, June 1977; Rob Baker, 'Geometrics: The Song and Dance of Laura Dean', *Dance Magazine*, November 1977;

Tullia Bohen, 'Making Television Dance', *Ballet News*, May 1980; Allen Robertson, 'Newer Than New: The Post-modern Choreographers', *Ballet News*, October 1981; Susan Reiter, 'What's Newer Than Modern: Two Festivals of New American Dance', *Dance and Dancers*, February 1982; '*Dance Magazine* Awards '82', *Dance Magazine*, August 1982; Deborah Rawson, 'A New Laura Dean?', *Ballet News*, December 1982; Noël Caroll, 'Introducing Laura Dean', *Dance Theatre Journal*, May 1983; Barry Laine, 'Form Clarifying Space: The Choreography of Laura Dean', *On the Next Wave* (published by the Brooklyn Academy of Music), October 1985; Gus Solomons Jr, 'New Wave: Ups and Downs', *Ballet News*, March 1986; Gary Parks, 'DeanMusicDance [*sic*]: Changing Pattern with a Steady Pulse', *Dance Magazine*, April 1987; 'Laura Dean', in *Contemporary Biography Yearbook 1988*; Marilyn Hunt, 'Laura Dean Meets the Royal Danish Ballet', *Dance Magazine*, March 1991.

Books Don McDonagh, *The Complete Guide to Modern Dance*, New York, 1976; Arlene Croce, *Going to the Dance*, New York, 1982; Anne Livet (ed.), *Contemporary Dance*, New York, 1978; Deborah Jowitt, *The Dance in Mind*, Boston, 1985.

DOUGLAS DUNN

In the search for a category in which to place Douglas Dunn, the term 'postmodern' remains appropriate, years after the term was first applied to dance. As a member of the first generation of postmodernist dancers and choreographers, Dunn retains qualities associated with the New York City avant-garde that was shaped in the 1960s and 1970s. Dunn is the sneaker-clad dancer caught in mid-air on the cover of Sally Banes's seminal book, *Terpsichore in Sneakers* (1980). Cool, elegant, graceful, a lanky blond dancer often compared in looks and style to Merce Cunningham (with whom he performed from 1968–73), Dunn, and his aesthetic, continue to challenge the viewer to delve into the work and uncover its meaning.

A California native, Dunn became intrigued with dance during his junior year of study at Princeton University. Abandoning art history for dance, Dunn moved to New York and performed with Yvonne Rainer in the late 1960s. Rainer's work, *Continuous Project – Altered Daily*, formed the basis of the Grand Union, a collaborative performance group which challenged theatrical and dance conventions. For several years, Dunn participated in the Grand Union's unique performances, which drew on a range of theatrical devices beyond mainstream notions of dance and theatre, combining mundane, everyday elements of life with dance. Although in 1980 he denied the Grand Union's influence on his work, echoes of the group's use of improvisation are evident throughout Dunn's career.

Douglas Dunn's years dancing with Merce Cunningham's Company, however, provided a more distinctive influence than his years with the Grand Union. The critic David Vaughan has commented that Cunningham's former dancers are able to find out what sort of dancers they want to be, because his 'discovery of his dancers' particular ways of moving gives them a basis on which to build their own choreographic style when they come to the point of breaking away'.[1] Dunn's break away was partial, his involvement beyond The Grand Union during the early 1970s extending to the creation of solos and group works while he was still dancing with Cunningham.

Dunn came into the dance world just as challenges were being set to redefine the very character of dance. Dance about dancing, movement as self-reflexive yet inherently expressive, expanded the range of challenges to dance set in place by Merce Cunningham. Dunn explained,

> You put your attention on the structure and then the feeling ... emerges immediately in the form of the structure. And the feeling, whatever it is, remains ... open. So I can do my dance, and I can feel one thing, and the audience can see it and feel another. ... It gives everybody a lot of room.[2]

Meaning is left open for interpretation, if one chooses to construct one.

Deborah Jowitt noted that Dunn's early works encompassed a period of examining the 'fact of performance', and had little dancing in them.[3] At its extreme, this approach was crystallized in 1974 by reducing human movement to complete stillness. Over a period, at four-hour intervals, Dunn objectified himself, putting his still body on display in *101* ('A Performance Exhibit'). Lying on top of an intricate wooden structure in his New York City loft, Dunn presented a performance exhibition that relied on the inquisitiveness of the spectator to search him out atop the structure, to decide how long to stay, and therefore, to establish the fundamental parameters of the 'performance'. A lack of obvious motion obscured the energy of keeping the heart pumping, or the intense range of activity necessary to build the structure on which he lay.[4] Although the performance appeared to be about the absence of motion, a spectator could approach the work within different frameworks, attending either to the actions implicit in the living body, or to the necessity of the viewer's active involvement to view Dunn. The avant-garde moment was captured on film in *Exhibit 101*, created by Charles Atlas, with close-up camera work fragmenting perception of the stationary body.

In an approach which prioritizes dancing about dancing, movement phrases are performed in a matter-of-fact, task-oriented attitude. Juxtaposition of emotion-evoking or at times mundane gestural actions within a detached context provides flashes of recognition for the audience which Sally Banes termed the 'Dunn phenomenon'.[5] Later works also exemplify the 'Dunn phenomenon', as Jack Anderson noted in *Elbow Room* (1984). In this, stamping, fist-shaking, and nervous gestures toward the head held no particular dramatic significance: 'they were simply gestures that fascinated Mr Dunn'.[6] This detached approach and consequent openness of meaning can result in widely differing perceptions of the same work, potentially even distancing the viewer from the piece.

Dunn's interest in improvisation – from dancers and, on occasion, audience members – emerges from a difference in attention demanded out of the process of decision-making. Choices made in the immediate moment, or in response to decisions made by fellow performers, keep the focus of both dancers and viewers constantly shifting. Dunn's works combine structured improvisations with phrases of movement exploration, integrating rather than rejecting dance technique. Dunn feels that the term 'making' dances rather than 'choreographing' more accurately reflects the processes which result in performance.[7] Dancers are offered costume choices in addition to movement ones; for example, in *Foot Rules* (1979) and *Stucco Moon* (1994), dancers added or removed articles of clothing and accessories, and even appeared in the nude during some performances.

Dunn developed *Lazy Madge*, an ongoing choreographic project, on a group of dancers over a period of two years between 1976 and 1978. The number of dancers fluctuated from around eight to ten, depending on schedules. Different aspects of the piece, generally specific duets or solo sections, were set and then integrated into performance, with the dancers drawing from a pool of movements, thereby enabling choreographed movement to be used without complete predetermination.[8] Thus, as Marcia Siegel explained in 1976, Dunn 'sees his work as an immediate and evolving process, not a job of creating fixed, repeatable stage works.'[9] Performances were shaped in part by the specifics of venue, and each unique manifestation was further enhanced by choices made by dancers. For example, on one occasion at the Brooklyn Academy of Music in 1978, *Lazy Madge* had the audience onstage, and the dancers in the auditorium, with no sound or musical accompaniment.

Moments of the absurd punctuate Dunn's works, creating a Dadaist aura at times. In *Celeste* (1977) at Connecticut College, a parachute jump was part of the performance, along with the repacking of the chutes. In *Octopus* (1974), the audience was prompted repeatedly to sing 'Happy Birthday' to Dunn and to participate in throwing balls back to the dancers. A subversion of expectations occurs, adding to the appearance of the extraordinary within a dance. Although Deborah Jowitt has, for example, focused on Dunn's attention to the 'niceties of form' in *Game Tree* (1982), she emphasized that 'nothing is slick or predictable'. This may be partly because there's nothing predictable about the movement. As you watch, you begin to believe that you'll never pin this down, that anything *could* occur.[10] Sally Banes, in her insightful overview of Dunn's work during the 1970s, significantly begins many paragraphs of her analysis with the work 'sometimes'. Dunn resists easy classification, as his emphasis is on the evolution of a piece, continuing to challenge audience expectations and moving from one extreme to another. As Banes explains, '[in] Dunn's aesthetic program, movement possibilities run the gamut from utter stillness to rapid, constant, protean motion.'[11]

The relationship between dance and other arts is constantly reinforced in high relief within Dunn's dances. Collaborations highlight Dunn's career, as he has drawn on the talents of musicians, painters, designers, and filmmakers in addition to dancers such as Sara Rudner and David Gordon. There have been no set rules in terms of collaborative method. John Driscoll's music for *Foot Rules* (1979) was created independently of the dance, while Dunn worked with jazz musician Bill Cole and filmmaker Jacob Burckhardt for the music and sound score of *Rubble Dance* (1991/93). In a 1986 work, *Dances for Men and Women and Moving Door*, the moving door by David Ireland was absent, although it was an integral component in the conceptual framework of the dance. It ultimately proved impractical in performance and hindered the choreography.

So, what do Douglas Dunn's dances look like? It depends upon which one you watch. What are they about? Again, it depends upon which one you watch. While Dunn's work is grounded in a postmodern aesthetic, its avant-garde elements have shifted over the decades. Jennifer Dunning has described the development of Dunn's modern dance classicism by explaining that he 'veered between extremes of formalism and expressionism with notable simplicity. He later settled into creating distinct dances made of pure, Cunninghamesque movement interpreted most vividly in his own easy way of moving.'[12] And Jowitt has explained that Dunn 'won't allow himself to forget that the point isn't so much to formulate answers as it is to keep asking new questions'.[13] When Dunn revitalizes works from previous years for new performances, fresh insight is provided, and his new questions continue to intrigue and challenge his viewers.

Stacey Prickett

Notes

1 Vaughan, David, 'Review', *Dance Magazine*, November 1982, p. 46.
2 Hanna, Judith Lynne, *Dance, Sex and Gender*, Chicago: University of Chicago Press, 1988, p. 155.
3 Jowitt, Deborah, 'Where Chance and Choice Collide', *The Dance in Mind: Profiles and Reviews, 1976–83*, Boston: David R. Godine, 1985, p. 83.
4 Banes, Sally, *Terpsichore in Sneakers*, Boston: Houghton Miflin, 1970, p. 195.
5 Banes, op. cit., p. 196.
6 Anderson, Jack, 'Dance: Dunn and Troupe Perform', *The New York Times*, 1 April 1985, I, 14.
7 Hanna, Judith Lynne, *The Performer–Audience Connection: Emotion to Metaphor in Dance and Society*, Austin, University of Texas Press, 1983, p. 98. Hanna devotes an entire chapter to the interpretation of meaning in Dunn's work.
8 Siegel, Marcia B., *Tail of the Dragon: New Dance, 1976–1982*, Durham: Duke University Press, 1991, p. 187.

9 Ibid., p. 196.
10 Jowitt, Deborah, 'Still Changing the Rules', op. cit., p. 87.
11 Banes, Sally, op. cit., pp. 192–93.
12 Dunning, Jennifer, 'Douglas Dunn and his Dancing Door', *The New York Times*, 13 June 1986, C3.
13 Jowitt, Deborah, 'Where Chance and Choice Collide', op. cit., p. 82.

Biographical details

Born in Palo Alto, California, United States, 19 October 1942. **Studied** with Lila Bruner, Maggie Black, Roland Guerard, at Princeton Regional Ballet Company, New Jersey, 1962–64; with Robert Cohan and others, at the Martha Graham Summer School, 1962; at Jacob's Pillow, 1962; with Françoise Martinet and Hector Zaraspe, at the American Ballet Center (Joffrey School), 1965; with Joseph Albano, at the Hartford Ballet Company, Connecticut, 1967; at the Margaret Jenkins Studio, 1968–69; with Richard Thomas at the New York School of Ballet, 1968–70; at the Merce Cunningham Studio, 1968–73. **Career** Dancer with Yvonne Rainer and Group, 1968–70, and with the Merce Cunningham Dance Company, 1968–73; founding member and performer, Grand Union, 1970–76; began choreographing in 1970; founded Douglas Dunn and Dancers in 1977, often performing solo pieces. Has also choreographed for Paris Opéra Ballet, GRCOP (Groupe de Recherche Chorégraphique de l'Opéra de Paris), Ballet de Nancy, New Dance Ensemble, Repertory Dance Theater (Salt Lake City), and several other groups and university dance theatres.

Works

One Thing Leads to Another (with Sara Rudner, 1971), *Dancing Here* (with Pat Catterson, 1971), *Co-incidents* (with David Gordon, 1972), *Eight Lanes, Four Approaches* (with Sara Rudner, 1972), *Mayonnaise, Part I* (film, dir. Charles Atlas, 1972), *Nevada* (solo, 1973), *Orange My Darling Lime* (solo, 1973), *Time Out* (solo, 1973), *Four for Nothing* (1974), *101* (solo performance exhibit, 1974; filmed by Amy Greenfield, 1974), *Octopus* (sound tape Dunn, 1974), *Part I Part II* (with David Woodberry, 1975), *Gestures in Red* (with live music, 1975), *Lazy Madge* (1976, and later revisions), *Early and Late* (solo, with Annabel Levitt, 1976), *Celeste* (1977), *Solo Film and Dance* (incorporating films of *Mayonnaise* and *101*, 1977), *Rille* (1978; short version later same year), *Relief* (1978), *Coquina* (mus. Robert Ashley, 1978), *Lazy Madge II* (short version of original, 1978), *Foot*

Rules (mus. John Driscoll, 1979), *Echo* (solo; mus. John Driscoll, 1979), *Suite de Suite* (mus. Eliane Radigue, 1980), *Echo* (mus. John Driscoll, 1980), *Pulcinella* (mus. Stravinsky, 1980), *Cycles* (mus. Steve Lacy, 1981), *Walking Back* (mus. John Driscoll, 1981), *Holds* (mus. John Driscoll, 1981), *Châteauvallonesque* (mus. John Driscoll, 1981), *Skid* (mus. John Driscoll, 1981), *View* (mus. John Driscoll, 1981), *Hitch* (mus. Linda Fisher, 1981), *Terri's Dance* (sound John Driscoll, 1981), *Game Tree* (mus. Linda Fisher, 1982), *Second Mesa* (mus. John Driscoll, Richard Lerman, 1983), *Secret of the Waterfall* (video, dir. Charles Atlas; text Reed Bye, Anne Waldman, 1982; adapted for live performance in 1983), *Elbow Room* (mus. Linda Fisher, 1984), *Pulcinella* (revised version, 1984), *Naropa East* (1984), *1st Rotation* (mus. Steve Kramer, 1984), *Futurities* (mus. Steve Lacy, 1984), *2nd Rotation* (mus. Linda Fisher, 1984), *Jig Jag* (mus. Ron Kuivila, 1985), *3rd Rotation* (mus. Linda Fisher, 1985), *Pacific Shores* (1985), *Lift* (1985), *Dances for Men, Women, and Moving Door* (mus. Alvin Lucier, 1986), *Light, O Tease* (mus. various, 1987), *Operia* (mus. various classical, 1987), *The Perfect Summer Dress* (mus. various, 1987), *Peepstone* (mus. various, 1987; revised version, 1989), *Gondolages* (mus. various, 1988), *Haole* (solo; mus. various; text Niles Eldredge, Ian Tattersall, 1988), *November Duet* (1988), *Wildwood* (mus. Gavin Bryars, 1989, revised version same year), *Sky Eye* (mus. various, 1989), *The Great Dinosaur Rescue* (mus. various, 1989), *Ahoy* (1989), *Roses* (mus. Rachmaninov, 1990), *Don't Cry Now* (mus. pop songs, 1990), *Blocs* (mus. Tom Waits, Mahler, Marianne Faithful, 1990), *The Myth of Modern Dance* (video, based on *Haole*; dir. Charles Atlas, 1990), *Unrest* (mus. Bill Cole, 1990), *Let's Get Busy* (mus. John Adams, 1991), *Hurry Up* (to sound of dancers' voices, 1991), *Rubble Dance, Long Island City* (film, dir. Rudy Burckhardt; mus. Bill Cole, Warren Smith, Robert Black, 1991), *Rubble Variations* (solo; mus. Soviet Army Chorus and Band, 1991), *Double Bond* (mus. Robert Elam, 1991), *Stucco Moon* (Minneapolis and Washington, DC, versions: mus. David Ireland, 1992; Portland, Oregon, version: mus. various, 1992), *Octopus* (sound tape and text Dunn, 1992), *The Star Thrower* (script John Cimino; mus. Cimino, Richard Albagli, Jon Klibonott, 1992), *Rubble Dance* (sound tape Jacob Burckhardt, 1992), *Landing* (mus. Steve Lacy, 1992), *Rock Walk* (mus. Yaz Shehab, 1993), *Empty Reel* (mus. Scottish folk music, 1993), *Dance for a Past Time* (mus. Lindsey Vickery, Jonathan Mustard, 1993), *Tangling* (mus. David Pye, 1993), *Pulcinella* (revised version, mus. Stravinsky, 1993), *Stucco Moon* (New York version, mus. David Ireland,

1994), *Dance for New Dance* (video; mus. Noel Quinlan, 1994), *Disappearances* (outdoor dance, 1994), *Caracole* (mus. various, 1995).

Further reading

Interviews in 'Dialogue on Dance' (with Trisha Brown), *Performing Arts Journal*, Fall 1976 (also in *The Vision of Modern Dance*, edited by Jean Morrison Brown, Princeton and London, 1980); with John Howell, *Live Performance Art*, 4, 1980; with Connie Kreemer, in her *Further Steps: Fifteen Choreographers on Modern Dance*, New York, 1987.

Articles Rob Baker, 'Grand Union: Taking a Chance on Dance', *Dance Magazine*, October 1973; Marcia B. Siegel, 'New Dance: Individuality, Image and the Demise of the Coterie', *Dance Magazine*, April 1974; Nancy Moore, 'Perspectives: Douglas Dunn', *Dance Magazine*, June 1974; Elizabeth Kendall, 'The Grand Union: Our Gang', *Ballet Review*, 5(4), 1975/76; Richard Schechner, 'Selective Inattention', *Performing Arts Journal*, Spring 1976; Sally Banes, 'Cool Symmetries/Douglas Dunn', *Dance Scope*, Spring/Summer 1978; Tobi Tobias, 'Ins, Outs, Dunn, Spaces, etc.', *Dance Magazine*, December 1979; John Percival, 'Douglas Dunn', *Dance and Dancers*, June 1984; Robert Sandla, 'Downtown: Vets', *Dance Magazine*, December 1990.

Books Sally Banes, *Terpsichore in Sneakers: Postmodern Dance*, Boston, 1980; Judith Lynne Hanna, *The Performer-Audience Connection*, Austin, Texas, 1983; Deborah Jowitt, *The Dance in Mind*, Boston, 1985; Allen Robertson and Donald Hutera, *The Dance Handbook*, Harlow, Essex, 1988; Margaret Hupp Ramsay, *The Grand Union*, New York, 1991; Marcia Siegel, *Tail of the Dragon: New Dance 1976–1982*, Durham, North Carolina, 1991.

EIKO AND KOMA

The parallels between 'Fred and Ginger' of 1930s Hollywood musical fame and 'Eiko and Koma' are not many – but they do exist. From the beginning of their career as a team of theatre artists, the Japanese-born couple has chosen to be known by their first names. Regularly their biographical sketches explain that the Eiko is the female half of the duo and Koma the male. No last names are ever mentioned. In real life, this man and woman are a married couple, suggesting the rapport inherent to the 'perfect partnership' recognized almost universally in the Fred-and-Ginger label. Theoretically, the physical and temperamental rapport that Eiko and Koma display on stage is every bit as practised and harmonious as that of the ballroom/show-dancing duos – but there, more or less, is where such similarity ends.

The art of Eiko and Koma is as introspective and tragic in tone as that of Fred Astaire and Ginger Rogers is extrovert and ebullient. Their art exists in a world of nearly infinite shadow and of infinitesimally calibrated motion, much of which is painstakingly slow. The mainstay of their 'movement theatre' comes as close to being a persistence of stillness as movement can get without actually standing still. Fred and Ginger came to the forefront of American culture during the aftermath of a crushing economic depression; Eiko and Koma came to maturity as artists out of the post-nuclear-holocaust era of the Japanese empire. The dance-theatre artform that springs most readily to mind in the picture of Eiko and Koma's Japan is that known as 'Butoh', or 'dance of utter darkness'. After a time as students of law and political science, Eiko and Koma began their dance studies with Tatsumi Hijikata in 1971 and then with Kazuo Ohno. Both these teachers are described by Eiko and Koma in their background information as central figures in the 'Japanese avant-garde theatrical movement of the 1960s'. No mention is made of Butoh, even though this form of Japanese 'new' dance is closely associated with both Hijikata and Ohno, who are sometimes thought of as the founders of Butoh.

Similar to the artistic route taken by Ohno, Eiko and Koma developed an interest in *Neue Tanz* and studied in Germany in 1972 with Manja Chmiel, a disciple of Mary Wigman. After a move to Amsterdam and some touring around Europe, the couple began working in the United States, where they became citizens and have continued to work. From the outset of their partnership, Eiko and Koma have chosen to perform only their own works. The earliest in the canon of works, as it is now described by the artists, is *White Dance*, from 1976. In those beginning years, Eiko and Koma performed isolated stints, often in out-of-the-way, non-proscenium spaces. Soon, however, their brand of seemingly unmodulated, austere, and unrelenting unclimactic theatre caught the public's imagination, or at least a part of the public, and by the mid-1980s the couple was being featured as part of the so-called 'Next Wave Festival' presented by New York's Brooklyn Academy of Music. There, and at two subsequent festivals, the duo in its snail-paced creations played alongside the troupes of such dance theatre big-timers as Merce Cunningham, David Gordon, Karole Armitage, Mark Morris, and Pina Bausch.

By starting out with poetically phrased titles for their works (*Fur Seal* (1976), *Before the Cock Crows* (1978), and *Fluttering Black* (1979), for example), Eiko and Koma felt their way, so to speak, towards their maturity. By the 1980s they had hit their stride with regard to naming the essences in their creations. They proceeded to deepen their explorations of poetic occurrences for humankind in its natural-cum-manmade environment. *Trilogy*, *Grain*, *Beam*, *Elegy*, *Night Trade*, *Shadows*, *Thirst*, *Tree*, *Canal*, *Rust*, *Memory*, and *Passage*, *Land*, *Wind*, and *River* followed in the 1980s and 1990s.

Though these two performing artists had initial backgrounds in the methodology of Butoh, their creations, when seen against those of proclaimed Butoh proponents, are different enough to show why they wish to separate themselves from that aesthetic movement. Much of Butoh outwardly declares itself to be antithetical to the decorous, reticent, impassive strains in much traditional Japanese performing art, such as Bugaku, Kabuki, and Noh, for example.

Instead, the Butoh aesthetic accentuates the graphically grotesque, the intentionally ugly, and the pointedly disturbing.

For all the anti-pretty aims of Eiko and Koma, there remains in their art little of Butoh's creepy grotesquerie: no madly rolling eyes, quivering lips, and vampire-like bared teeth. Eiko and Koma's world in art is not one describing man's uplifting triumph over the animal forces in the universe. Mostly it conveys a heroic but futile battle against overwhelming forces, almost always constructed in the form of a cycle, which we somehow chance upon, already in progress, at the beginning of each work and then seem to leave, at its end, in an advanced state of progression. The tone of these exquisitely gauged works is one of a high-wire act unrelentingly poised between hopefulness and hopelessness. Eiko and Koma specialize in the art of elegy rather than that of poster protest or sensational statement. They accomplish their elegiac vision with means and methods that owe debts to the trappings of true Butoh – rice-powdered, pallid, or mummified skin, for example, and blatant nudity. However, their individually varied results are unique to them. For décor, the two sometimes commission outside artists, even while they carefully oversee and incorporate that contribution into their very personal view of the world. For music, the contributions of various composers or sound engineers are also delicately set into the tapestry of their singular vision. In effect, the soundscapes that resonate in Eiko and Koma works are akin to the atmospheric sounds that one imagines would play about in the air during the dramatic, 'poetic' occurrences they make the subject of their art.

For their first appearance on Brooklyn Academy's 'next wave' series in 1986, Eiko and Koma performed four separate works, *Night Tide*, *Beam*, *Shadows*, and *Elegy*, under the umbrella title of *New Moon Stories*. This 'full-evening' work fairly summed up the vision, scope, and depth of their aesthetic. As a quartet they showed the range, integrity, and interrelationship of one Eiko and Koma piece to another. In the course of the evening, one might have been given to ponder the four seasons or the four corners of the earth or, perhaps most aptly, the four elements of nature: air, earth, fire, and water. In the first segment, Eiko and Koma appeared to float, inertly, high above the space, and almost imperceptibly approach and blindly bypass one another. In the next, fixed atop a mound of earth, they remained one jumbled, intertwined mass, until Eiko slid numbly down and out of Koma's crude grasp. Next, more as opposing characters, rather then dumbly instinctive equals, Koma smotheringly accosted Eiko, who put up no resistance to his seemingly overpowering strength. Finally, as separate individuals with no thought whatsoever of coming together, the two stood, like golden shells of humanity, and hauntingly descended from contorted vertical stances to listless horizontal heaps, into shiningly lit thin pools of water.

Eiko and Koma's methods of movement are both carefully selective and richly reductive. In an immediate sense they appear to be doing absolutely nothing, when all the while, it becomes evident that they are never not doing something. When the couple conduct teaching sessions about theatrical composition and techniques, they call their meetings 'Delicious Movement Workshops'. This almost jolly-sounding name for an exploration of rigorous, serious, and shadowy ways of moving explains succinctly why Eiko and Koma do not consider themselves proponents of Butoh.

In the spectacular piece called *Passage* (1989), Eiko and Koma threaded their dramatic ways through what seemed the inside of a human organism pulsating with intensely saturated reds and blacks, the whole gnarled landscape dripping wet all the while. Another evening-long work, *Wind* (1993), was as filled with air as *Passage* was airless and included an added player, Yuta Otake, the couple's eight-year-old son, as a wondrous figure of new life in a bleak but not utterly barren world.

Distant (1994), a twelve-minute solo for Koma, and a longer piece, *Echo* (1995), accompanied by traditional Japanese music, were performed during residencies at Art Awareness in Lexington, New York. Both were also supported financially by the duo's loyal backers, the Japan Foundation, who first brought them to the United States. That organization also partly funded the ambitious *River* (1995), a one-hour 'outdoor environmental collaboration' with naturalist and visual artist Judd Weisberg, which took place after sunset amid flowing water, and involved the use of film – a typical example of Eiko and Koma's mingling of natural and artificial elements. A more portable reworking of *River* appeared in 1997. Restaged for an indoor theatre, the musical collage of the 1995 version was replaced by a specially commissioned score by composer Somei Satoh, played by the famous Kronos Quartet.

Robert Greskovic

Biographical details

Eiko and Koma are a domestic partnership who choreograph and dance together. Koma Otake (male) was born in Niigata, Japan, 27 September 1948. Eiko Otake (female) was born in Tokyo, 14 February 1952. Both studied law and political science at Waseda University, where they met, before turning to professional dance. **Career** Both joined Tatsumi Hijikata dance company, Tokyo, 1971, where their partnership was established; began working independently in 1972 while also studying with Kazuo Ohno; moved to Germany, studying with Manja Chmiel, 1972–73, and toured in Germany, the Netherlands, Switzerland and Tunisia, 1973–75; moved to the United States in 1976, where they later established permanent residence: currently based in New York City, where, as well as performing, they present occasional 'Delicious Movement' Workshops. They have also choreographed for CoDanceCo and Dance Alloy (Pittsburgh). **Awards** include several grants from charitable foundations and the National Endowment for the Arts; Guggenheim Fellowship, 1984; New York Dance and Performance Award ('Bessie'), 1984, 1990; MacArthur Fellowship, 1996.

Works

Sound/music by Eiko and Koma unless otherwise indicated.

White Dance (mus. J.S. Bach and medieval, 1976), *Fur Seal* (mus. Schubert, Alan Hovhaness, the Beatles, 1976), *Before the Cock Crows* (mus. Middle-Eastern, 1978), *Fluttering Black* (mus. Glenn Branca, 1979), *Trilogy* (includes *Cell, Fisson, Entropy*; mus. Andean folk, 1979–81), *Nurse's Song* (poetry William Blake; mus. Allen Ginsberg, 1981), *Grain* (mus. Japanese, Tibetan, Indonesian folk, 1983), *Beam* (mus. Asian folk, 1983), *Tentacle* (video; mus. Japanese folk music, 1983), *Night Tide* (1984), *Elegy* (1984), *Wallow* (video version of *Fur Seal*; silent, 1984), *Thirst* (silent, 1985), *Bone Dream* (video; 1985), *By the River* (1986), *Broken Pieces* (1986), *New Moon Stories* (includes *Beam, Shadows, Night Tide, Elegy*; 1986), *Lament* (video, parts from *Elegy*, 1986), *Husk* (video; solo by Eiko, 1987), *Tree* (1988), *Undertow* (video; 1988), *Canal* (mus. Los Jaivas, 1989), *Rust* (1989), *Memory* (mus. Deuter, 1989), *Passage* (1989), *Land* (mus. Robert Mirabel, 1991), *Wind* (sound score by Robert Mirabel, Eiko and Koma, vocal score based on music by Francisco Guerrero, 1993), *Dream* (mus. Jon Gibson, 1994), *Distant* (solo for Koma; mus. Ushio Torikai, 1994), *River* (outdoor version in collaboration with visual artist Judd Weisberg; mus. traditional Japanese, 1995), *Echo* (mus. traditional Japanese, 1995), *River* (indoor theatre version, mus. Somei Satoh, 1997).

Further reading

Interviews with Merry Dufton, *New Dance*, January 1988; with Leslie Windham, in 'A Conversation with Eiko and Koma', *Ballet Review*, Summer 1988.

Articles Susan Reiter, 'Moving on from Dance', *Dance and Dancers*, May 1982; Jochen Schmidt, 'What Moves Them and How', *Ballett International*, June/July 1982; 'Looking for a Pattern', *Dance and Dancers*, January 1982; Effie Mihopoulos, 'Eiko and Koma', *Salome*, 32/33, 1983; Margaret O'Keefe, 'Eiko and Koma', *Attitude*, January/April 1984; Paula Josa-Jones, 'Delicious Moving', *Contact Quarterly*, Winter 1986; Lynn Garafola, 'Variations on a Theme of Butoh', *Dance Magazine*, April 1989.

Books Deborah Jowitt, *The Dance in Mind*, Boston, 1985.

MATS EK

Mats Ek is a prominent, and controversial, figure in twentieth century European choreography. In less than twenty years he has developed and established a personal choreographic style; yet his actual contribution to contemporary dance is contested, particularly when works such as the remade *Giselle* (1982) and *Swan Lake* (1987) – unanimously considered his most representative creations – are taken into account. Ek is the first European contemporary dance choreographer to have successfully revisited the masterworks of ballet history, by modifying the means of expression – namely the dance idiom – and updating the subject-matter. His adaptations are often saluted as more accessible artforms than their antecedents in terms of style, vocabulary, and content. On the other hand, some regard such translations of the nineteenth-century classics of ballet into contemporary dance as either desecration or lack of inventiveness.

In reworking ballet classics, Ek's aim is 'to render the characters alive, providing a clear description of their inner emotions and contrasts'.[1] The psychological characterization of the roles is thus enlarged; the characters' relationships and their emotional response to the development of the action are considered in greater depth. Although the transposition entails a careful process of revision and updating, the original essence and the original content of the work are neither betrayed nor altered; and as far as the music is concerned, the original score is also retained, although partly rearranged to suit the new dramatic structure. The outcome is a performance, prompted by an analytical reading of the old scenario, that aims to present the original message in an approachable way to contemporary audiences, addressing current issues. 'Clarity' is the choreographer's key word, as opposed to what he calls 'the ambiguity of the conventions and the clichés of classical bal-let'.[2] In Ek's case, however, 'clarity' should not be mistaken for simplicity. In both *Giselle* and *Swan Lake*, there lies beneath an accessible, straightforward dramatic con-struction an intricate amalgam of social, political, cultural, and literary references. This is a characteristic trait and a constant component of his choreographic produc-tions. Political, social, racial, and sexual concerns informed Ek's first three creations, *The Batman* (based on Büchner's unfinished play *Woyzeck*), *St George and the Dragon* (both 1976), and *Soweto* (1977); psycholog-ical themes and gender issues played a part in both *The House of Bernada Alba* (1978) and *Antigone* (1979), long before *Giselle* and *Swan Lake*. Because of these themes, dance scholars and critics have often labelled Ek as a 'politically committed' choreographer. The definition, however, is not entirely appropriate, for none of Ek's works can be regarded as a political manifesto. This is par-ticularly evident in *Soweto*, inspired by the 1976 repression of a black students' revolt in Johannesburg. A little mechanical doll, representing white power, runs endlessly in a predesignated pattern, shaking her head after witnessing the dramatic revolt, as con-veyed by the dancers' stylized movements and gestures. The mechanical, repetitive movements of the doll symbolize the entrenched attitudes of the whites towards the blacks. Despite the immediacy of the theme and the metaphors, the work is imbued with a sense of detachment – as if the choreographer were merely an observer – lending a subtle, sombre irony to his vision.

Irony is a characteristic element of Ek's choreography, in which strong images and dramatic situations often contrast with brief, humorous episodes. Examples can be found in the first act of *Giselle*, wherein two male peasants dance a comic duet in front of Albrecht's fiancée, or in the many slapstick antics of the three jesters in *Swan Lake*. In the first instance, the comic duet is placed within one of the most dramatic scenes

before the conclusion of the act, heralded by the arrival of the aristocratic party. The dance, however, does not loosen the tension. On the contrary, it accentuates the theme of social conflict between one class and the other, as the dancers' humorous movements can be interpreted as mocking and irreverent gestures directed at the aristocrats.

Similarly, the three jesters in *Swan Lake* appear on stage whenever a dramatic situa-tion reaches its climax, such as at the end of the lakeside scene. Their earthy antics can be seen as a reminder of reality, as opposed to Prince Siegfried's confused dream-world, which reflects his uncertain sexuality. The juxtaposition heightens the sense of the principal character's introspective detach-ment, felt throughout the work. Human psychology, in all its varied facets, is one of Ek's more recurring preoccupations. In his works he has managed to encompass and to explore virtually every possible form and variation of human relationship – man/ woman, parent/child, rich/poor, white/black, society/outsider.

Ek's wider interests – for example his career as puppeteer, actor, and director – have influenced the development of his choreography, especially in terms of subject-matter. The significant role played by dramatic elements within the choreography can be detected in every one of his creations. Some of his works derive both their title and their subject-matter explicitly from well-known masterworks of theatre history, such as Sophocles' *Antigone*, García Lorca's *The House of Bernada Alba*, and Büchner's *Woyzeck*, mentioned above. References to Shakespeare's *Hamlet* are to be found in *Swan Lake*, where Siegfried is portrayed as the Danish prince, and the Queen as Gertrude; in both *Old Children* (1989) and *Light Beings* (1991), respectively dedicated to his mother and to his father, there is an echo of Ingmar Bergman, with whom Ek worked as assistant director (not to mention the fact that his father, Anders Ek, was one of Bergman's favourite actors).

Ek's distinctive movement vocabulary derives mainly from the combination of his ballet training, his dancing experience with his mother, Birgit Cullberg, and his collaboration with the Nederlands Danse Theater. Although Ek may reject the conventional codes of ballet, his choreographic idiom clearly stems from principles of balletic technique. Evidence can be found in the whole range of jumps and turns, in the footwork, and in the constant use of basic positions – such as *plié à la second* – which recur in Ek's compositions. At the same time, these elements are treated from a contemporary perspective and interwoven with fundamentals of contemporary dance technique, such as freer pelvis movements, and the use of the floor and of the body weight.

Another important influence is that of his mother, Birgit Cullberg. In 1969, Ek contributed some group dances to Cullberg's *Romeo and Juliet*. That marked the beginning of a collaboration with the Cullberg Ballet, which was consolidated with his appointment as resident dancer, and eventually co-director. A comparison between Cullberg's major works, such as *Miss Julie* (1950) and those by Ek reveals the extent to which her work influenced Ek's development. Although Cullberg's vocabulary is often strictly balletic, some features of her choreographic style recur as characteristic components in Ek's choreography. The attention to psychological characterization, the sensitive portrayal of human feeling, the juxtaposition of strong images and humorous episodes – all can be seen as typical attributes of both Cullberg's and Ek's creations.

Finally, his work as a choreographer for the Nederlands Danse Theater, which began in 1980, has contributed to the realization of Ek's choreographic style. Although Jiří Kylián's artistic formulae differ considerably from those of Mats Ek, there are some similarities between Kylián's works and those created by Ek after that date, particularly in terms of movement vocabulary. The

fundamentals of what has generally become known as 'Northern European contemporary dance' have influenced, if not moulded, Ek's *œuvre*. The stylized, yet still dramatically expressive language of gesture, the use of the scenic space in terms of choreographic patterns, the particular sensitivity to the music, and the fluidity of the movement with no apparent solution of continuity are elements of Ek's choreography that are not exclusive to his work, but represent some of the common traits of that dance form. It is, however, the combination of these elements and their personal use within the choreographic texture that give a unique imprint to Ek's choreography. If Ek is considered part of the contemporary dance tradition, then his own individual dance style represents one of its most interesting expressions.

Giannandrea Poesio

Notes

1 Ek, M., in Vaccarino, E. (ed.) (1993) 'Giselle di Mats Ek', *I grandi protagonisti della danza*, 13, Novara: Instituto Geografico de Agostini, 1.
2 Ibid.

Biographical details

Born in Malmö, Sweden, 18 April 1945 (son of choreographer Birgit Cullberg and actor Anders Ek). **Studied** dance with Donya Feuier on a summer course, 1962; undertook theatrical training at Marieborg Volks College; returned to dance training at Stockholm Ballet Academy, 1972. **Career** Dance debut at Riksteater, Stockholm, 1963; director at the Stockholm Puppet Theatre, 1966–73; also directed in the conventional theatre: worked at the Stockholm Stadsteater and the Dramaten [Royal Dramatic Theatre], collaborating with Ingmar Bergman and Alf Sjöberg; director at the Dramaten, 1968–72; dancer with his mother's Cullberg Ballet, 1973–74, and Düsseldorf Ballet, 1974–75, returning to Cullberg Ballet in 1975: began choreographing there, 1976, and became its joint artistic director with his mother, 1978; also dancer and choreographer, Nederlands Dans Theater, 1980–81; sole artistic director of the Cullberg Ballet on Birgit Cullberg's retirement, 1985–93; freelance choreographer since 1993, including for television, and recently writer and choreographer of theatre works for actors and dancers. Has also choreographed for the National Theatre in Oslo, Stuttgart Ballet, Hamburg Ballet, Paris Opéra Ballet, and for dancer Sylvie Guillem. Awards Grand Prix de Video-Danse, 1988; two Emmy Awards since 1993; Dance Screen Award, 1996; Prix Italia, 1997.

Works

Kalfaktorn [The 'Batman' or Officer's Servant] (mus. Bartók, 1976), *St George and the Dragon* (mus. pop and folk, 1976), *Soweto* (mus. various, 1977), *The House of Bernarda Alba* (mus. J.S. Bach, Spanish folk music, 1978), *The Four Seaons* (mus. Vivaldi, 1978), *Antigone* (mus. Mikis Theodorakis, Iannis Xenakis, 1979), *Memories of Youth* (mus. Bartók, 1980), *Cain and Abel* (mus. George Crumb and others, 1982), *Giselle* (mus. Adam, 1982; later staged for television), *Rite of Spring* (mus. Stravinsky, 1984), *På Norrbotten* [Up North] (mus. Scandinavian folk, arr. J.P.N. Nyströms, 1985), *Eldstad* (mus. Philip Glass, D.V. Bausznern, 1985), *Gräs* [Grass] (mus. Rachmaninov, 1987), *Swan Lake* (mus. Tchaikovsky, 1987), *Like Antigone* (mus. Manos Hadjidakakis, Greek folk music, 1988), *Gamla Barn* [Old Children] (mus. various, 1989), *Over There* (1990), *Light Beings* (mus. various, 1991), *Journey* (mus. Steve Reich, 1991), *Carmen* (mus. Bizet, Schredrin, 1992; later staged for television), *Pointless Pastures* (1993), *Dans med nästen* [Dancing with One's Neighbour] (drama/dance work, 1993), *She Was Black* (mus. Górecki, 1995), *Wet Woman* (solo; video, 1995), *Smoke* (solo; video, 1995), *Sleeping Beauty* (mus. Tchaikovsky, 1996), *Solo for Two* (stage version of *Smoke*, mus. Arvo Pärt, 1996); *A Sort of* (mus. Górecki, 1997); *På Malta* [On Malta] (drama/dance work, based on Christopher Marlowe's play *The Jew of Malta*, 1997).

Further reading

Interviews with Ulrich Tegeder, in 'Mats Ek's *Giselle*: Create Characters, Special People', *Ballett International*, May 1983; with Rolf Garske, in 'Searching for a New Complexity', *Ballett International*, March 1989; with Marinella Guatterina, in 'Ora pensa a *Carmen*', *Danza e danza*, February 1992.

Articles Mårten Spangberg, 'The Pyschological Dimension of Classical Dance', *Ballett International*, March 1996; Horst Vollmer, 'Irreverently Classical' (on *Sleeping Beauty*), *Ballett International*, July 1996; Gunilla Jensen, 'Mats Ek and the Cullberg Ballet', *Dancing Times*, August 1997.

GARTH FAGAN

With quiet but absolute dedication, Garth Fagan throughout the 1970s was nurturing one of the most exciting sensibilities in contemporary dance. The career of Jamaican-born Fagan had followed a circuitous route: touring with Ivy Baxter's Jamaican National Dance Company while still in his teens; attending college in the United States, where he studied with the likes of José Limón, Martha Graham, and Alvin Ailey; and involvement with a handful of Detroit companies as dancer, choreographer, or artistic director. Soon after joining the faculty of the State University of New York, he began teaching dance in nearby Rochester, to young adults more familiar with baseball pitches and inner-city streets than the stage. At about the same time, Arthur Mitchell was embarking on a similar adventure, shaping untrained urbanites into his Dance Theater of Harlem. But Mitchell's goal had been to create classical ballet dancers who would excel particularly in the *œuvre* and style of choreographer George Balanchine. Fagan, on the other hand, had something else entirely in mind. His fledgling dancers were trained in a style all his own, a stunning synthesis of modern, jazz, and Afro-Caribbean influences with just a tincture of balletic élan.

Fagan began calling his budding company 'The Bottom of the Bucket, But ... Dance Theater', with a mixture of penurious apology and high hopes. By the mid-1980s the bottom had dropped out, so to speak, as Fagan's troupe, redubbed the Bucket Dance Theater, was acclaimed one of the major dance discoveries of the decade. Now that they are secure in their status as a leading force in contemporary dance, the name is simply Garth Fagan Dance. Fagan is, naturally, the company patriarch, working diligently to create intelligent artists capable of interpreting his choreography fully rather than dancers slavishly duplicating the master's steps in 'monkey see-monkey do' manner. From the beginning, his dancers' education extended beyond the studio, with Fagan both encouraging their exposure to all other art forms and inviting group discussion of what they experienced.

As a dancemaker, Fagan draws from a similarly broad background, blending together the grounded, passionate inner expressiveness and corporeal isolations of classic modern dance pioneers like Graham, Limón, and Doris Humphrey; the expansive theatrical buzz of Alvin Ailey's company; the abstract, yet dramatic, detachment of Merce Cunningham's work; the windmill arms, rubbery jumps, and syncopated footwork of African dance; and the more undulant rhythms propagated by Baxter and her fellow Caribbean dancer-teachers Pearl Primus and Lavinia Williams. This is not eclecticism for its own sake, but an integral fusion of a multitude of disparate Afro-European dance elements.

Fagan's impeccable ensemble bears the weight of this complex lineage with effortless control and protean authority. The almost mystical air of concentration in which they dance is partly owed to Fagan's unusual rehearsal studio set-up: he believes that mirrors promote narcissism, whereas in their absence dancers are forced to perform more honestly, 'from the inside out'. His dancers possess a natural refinement and unadorned but eloquent power; they're absorbed in the work, not in themselves. The men show a vulnerability and the women a resourcefulness that melt into virile grace in both sexes. They come across as real people capable of executing monumental actions, thanks to their strong backs, streamlined limbs, muscular amplitude, and seemingly boneless flexibility.

Fagan's choreography allows them the opportunity to shift expressively between a gamut of states, from lyrical stately serenity to skittering mania, to sheer joyful exuberance. His impish wit is evident in *Traipsing Through the May* (1987), an ensemble throwaway tuned to Vivaldi. In the total tonal contrast is the long, dark solo, created for the company's superb 'benchmark' dancer Norwood Pennewell, that opens *Passion Distanced* (1987), a brooding, enigmatic sextet made the same year. The moodswings in Fagan's dances are aligned with the sharp changes in dynamics and shapes the dancers must register. They are celebrated for their high, sometimes jagged, preparationless jumps followed by the softest of landings; their smoothly-held, crouching or asymmetrical balances and elegiac extensions; and their prayerful stillness, disturbed by the most unexpected, unbridled bursts of energy. Fagan's ordering of these characteristic moves marks him out as a voluptuously original formalist. The richness of his choreographic language seems to appeal, physically and spiritually, to dance audiences and intellectuals alike.

The company's standard introductory piece is *Prelude* (1981), the subtitle of which, 'Discipline is Freedom', serves as a collective philosophy. The piece is a perpetual flow of discontinuous movement, flecked with luxuriant oddities and propelled by Fagan's love of speed. It is his version of a company class-cum-showcase, climaxing with dancers fearlessly spilling, rocketing, and spinning across the stage on diagonal paths. *Oatka Trail* (1979), a more adagio male trio set to Dvořák's moving Cello Concerto, is a fine example of Fagan's unpredictable musicality. Never content merely to ape rhythms, he eschews both the obvious and the sentimental, preferring instead to get under the music's skin. The dance closes with the three men in alternately desperate opposition to, or physical harmony with, the music. *Easter Freeway Processional* (1983) weds exultant dramatic characterizations to the persistent rhythms of composer Philip Glass. *Never Top 40 (Juke Box)*, from 1985, is a kaleidoscopic suite of dances made in response to some of Fagan's favourite music (Puccinni, Keith Jarrett, reggae). *Mask Mix Masque* (1986) is an intriguing and affectionate homage to Fagan's friend and fellow Jamaican, the pop singer Grace Jones.

The 1978 company signature piece *From Before* trades in kineticized tribal ideas relevant to Fagan's background as a dark-skinned man influenced by white twentieth-century Westernism. Ten years later he made *Time After Before Place*, a piece taking those ideas further to an even more sophisticated, primal, multi-cultural plane. A majority of Fagan's dancers are African-American, but to label the troupe 'black', he feels, is seriously to limit its reach and to narrow its possibilities. In 1995's *Earth Eagle First Circle*, Fagan celebrated the common ingredients of human cultures globally via an improbable, but exultant, fusion of the African-Latin rhythms of the late jazz pianist Don Pullen, the powerful chants, drumming and dances of native Americans, and his own variegated choreography.

Griot New York (1991) is one of the best demonstrations of Fagan's belief that his work must be about culture rather than folklore, ethnicity instead of race. In West African society a griot is an oral historian and entertainer. Made in collaboration with jazz trumpeter-composer Wynton Marsalis and sculptor-turned-designer Martin Puryear, Fagan's *Griot* is a wise, roomy embrace of a city's heritage in all its uplifting, or ugly, glory. Exhilarating in its breadth and depth, it is one of Fagan's crowning achievements.

Fagan has choreographed for theatre, devising some particularly vibrant, earthy movement for the hit adaptation of Disney's animated feature *The Lion King* in 1997. A decade earlier, in 1986, he directed *Queenie Pie*, an unfinished street opera by Duke Ellington (to whom Fagan paid playful tribute in the 1983 duet *Postscript Posthumous: Ellington*). Like Cunningham, Twyla Tharp, Mark Morris, and other modern choreographers, he has tried his hand at devising a ballet. Probably his more extraordinary creative stretch yet is *Footprints Dressed in Red*, a large-cast piece *en*

pointe made for the Dance Theater of Harlem in 1986. A rigorous work of eccentric, searching intelligence, it challenges familiar classical syntax without violating it. The elimination of conventional transitions between steps, the brilliant contrasts, and Fagan's creative use of space justify the praise he has received as an artist who 'reinvents the ordinary'.

Donald Hutera

Biographical details

Born in Kingston, Jamaica, 3 May 1940. **Studied** African-Caribbean dance with Pearl Primus and Lavinia Williams; attended Wayne State Univeristy, Detroit, majoring in psychology, graduated 1968: also took masterclasses from Merce Cunningham, José Limón, Lucas Hoving, Sophie Maslow, and Jean Erdman; studied in New York with Martha Graham, Mary Hinkson, Alvin Ailey, and Limón. **Career** Danced with Ivy Baxter and Rex Nettleford's Jamaican National Dance Company, touring Latin American from 1957; studied and performed 1960–70 in Detroit, where he founded the East Side All-City Dance Company, co-founded Detroit Contemporary Dance Company, and was principal soloist and choreographer for Dance Theater of Detroit (1968); moved to Rochester, New York, to become professor of dance (awarded title Distinguished Professor, 1986) at the State University of New York at Brockport, 1970; founded, as chief choreographer and artistic director, The Bottom of the Bucket, But ... Dance Theatre, Rochester, 1970, which later became Bucket Dance Theatre, and then Garth Fagan Dance in 1991: has regularly collaborated on productions with sculptor Martin Puryear. Has also choreographed for the Dance Theater of Harlem, Alvin Ailey American Dance Theater, José Limón Company, and Lyon Opéra Ballet. **Awards and honours** National Endowment for the Arts (3-year) Choreography Fellowship, 1983; New York Dance and Performance ('Bessie') Award, 1984; Wayne State University Arts Achievement Award, 1985; New York State Governor's Arts Award, 1986; Guggenheim Fellowship, 1989; *Dance Magazine* Award, 1990; Fulbright 50th Anniversary Distinguished Fellowship, 1996; honorary doctorates from Juilliard School (New York), University of Rochester, Nazareth College (Rochester), and Hobart and William Smith Colleges (Geneva, New York).

Works

Life Forms/Death Shapes (mus. Carlos Surinach, 1967), *From Before* (mus. Ralph MacDonald, 1978), *Oatka Trail* (mus. Dvořák, 1979), *Of Night, Light and Melanin* (mus. Keith Jarrett, 1981; video version, 1982), *Prelude: Discipline is Freedom* (mus. Abdullah Ibrahim, Max Roach, 1981; revised version, 1983), *Touring Jubilee 1924 (Professional)* (mus. Preservation Hall Jazz Band, 1982), *Daylight Savings Time* (mus. Jaco Pastorius, Dona Alais; includes duet *Spring Yaounde*, 1982), *Easter Freeway Processional* (mus. Philip Glass, 1983), *Postscript Posthumous: Ellington* (mus. Duke Ellington, 1983), *Never Top 40 (Juke Box)* (mus. various; includes *Court Dance Contemporary, Dance Rainbow Revisited, Dance Psalmody 137, Dance Psalmody 69, Rainbow and Ballroom Romp*; 1985), *Mask Mix Masque* (mus. Grace Jones, Trevor Horn, 1986), *Footprints Dressed in Red* (mus. John Adams, 1986), *Queenie Pie* (dances for opera by Duke Ellington, 1986), *Traipsing Through the May* (mus. Vivaldi, 1987), *Passion Distanced* (mus. Arvo Pärt, 1987), *Scene Seen* (solo for Judith Jamison; mus. Dollar Brand with Archie Shepp, 1988), *Time After Before Place* (mus. Art Ensemble of Chicago, 1988), *Landscape for 10* (mus. Brahms, 1988), *Telling a Story* (includes *A Shorthand of Sensation, A Précis of Privilege*; mus. Miles Davis, 1989), *Until, By & If* (mus. Don Pullen, 1990), *Griot New York* (mus. Wynton Marsalis; includes *City Court Dance, Bayou Baroque, Spring Yaounde, Sand Painting, The Disenfranchised, Down Under, Waltz Détente, Oracabessa Sea, High Rise Riff*; 1991), *Moth Dreams* (mus. André Jolivet, Thelonius Monk, Wynton Marsalis, 1992), *Jukebox for Alvin* (mus. various, 1993), *Postcards: Pressures and Possibilities* (mus. David N. Baker, 1994), *Draft of Shadows* (mus. David Diamond, 1994), *Never No Lament* (mus. Kronos Quartet, 1994), *Postcards: Pressures and Possibilities* (mus. David N. Baker, 1994), *Earth Eagle First Circle* (mus. Don Pullen, 1995), *Mix 25* (mus. various, 1996), *Nkanyit* (mus. various, 1997), *The Lion King* (stage version of Disney musical, mus. Elton John, 1997).

Further reading

Interview with Francis Mason, in 'A Conversation with Garth Fagan', *Ballet Review*, Spring 1995.

Articles Joan Acocella, 'The Bucket Dance Theatre, But No Longer at the Bottom', *Dance Magazine*, March 1986; Herbert Simpson, 'Quest for Perfection', *Ballet News*, March 1986; Kate Regan, 'Of the Bucket that Rose like a Rocket', *Connoisseur*, October 1987; Rex Nettleford, 'Afro-Caribbean Dance' (Dance Study Supplement 8), *Dancing Times*, May 1990; David Vaughan, 'Two Leaders: Mark Morris & Garth Fagan', *Ballet Review*, Summer 1990; David Vaughan, 'Fagan Dance: Discipline is Freedom', *Dance Magazine*, November 1990; Tobi Tobias, 'Beauty and the Beast', *New York Magazine*, January 6, 1992; Helen Dudar, '*Griot New York* Sets the City's Rhythm to Dance', *Smithsonian*, September 1992.

Books Jamake Highwater, *Rituals of Experience*, New York, 1978, 3rd edition, 1992; Allen Robertson and Donald Hutera, *The Dance Handbook*, Harlow, Essex, 1988; Selma Jeanne Cohen (ed.), *Dance as a Theatre Art: Source Readings in Dance History from 1591 to the Present*, 2nd edition (with new section by Katy Matheson), Princeton, New Jersey, 1992.

ELIOT FELD

Americans love to proclaim the next king even though the present one is alive and kicking. This over-eager, often foolish impulse had a reasonableness about it when applied to Eliot Feld. The occasion was the premiere of his first ballet, *Harbinger*, in May 1967, by American Ballet Theatre (ABT), the troupe Feld danced with at the time. Two months later came a second fine ballet, *At Midnight*, also presented by ABT. Feld was immediately and unanimously hailed as the genuine article, and for genuine reasons. Both ballets were absolutely fresh and original in choreographic style, yet they also felt within the historical continuum of ballet. They affirmed the cherished belief that an artist could recycle old ideas and make them new, that, in fact, this is what the best art did. Two other qualities in these ballets made Feld all the more impressive. They were very musical and very different in feeling from each other. *Harbinger*, set to a Prokofiev piano concerto, was youthful, frisky, and optimistic. *At Midnight*, set to Mahler songs, was a darker piece, centred upon an anguished Christ figure.

Within the next four years Feld had more than a dozen ballets to his credit, just about all of them first-rate. While Feld's career started out as the quintessential overnight success story, he was to be no flash in the pan. He was downright prolific. Moreover, this early bundle of work enriched the diversity that his first two pieces had promised. *Intermezzo No. 1* (1969, set to Brahms) was rapturously lyrical, while pieces like *A Poem Forgotten* (1970) and *Theatre* (1971) had raw, expressionistic power. These latter two works incorporated strong narrative elements, while *Intermezzo No. 1*, *Early Songs* (1970) and many others followed a suite form of contrasting moods, conveyed primarily through movement and inspired by Feld's intelligent ear for music.

Feld's fecundity has never abandoned him. By the end of 1997, he had presented almost 100 works. The individualistic style that characterized his ballets thirty years earlier remains as individualistic and, quite remarkably, unchanged.

The unique 'look' of a Feld dancer derives from Antony Tudor. But whereas Tudor's style usually expressed a repressed state of mind, Feld's is able to sustain both happy and sad moods. What for Tudor was psychologically necessary is for Feld aesthetically pleasing.

The most characteristic aspect of this style is the *contraposto* line. While a Feld dancer's body is not always as twisted as Hagar's in Tudor's *Pillar of Fire*, his or her head and shoulders are often posed in opposition to the trunk. In place of the traditional *effacé*, or open, line of ballet, Feld favours the *croisé* line pushed into corkscrew complications. Like the Tudor torso, the Feld torso is held tightly. The body breaks at the joints; there is little bend. Feld's use of the *pointe* shoe is also influenced by Tudor. In more traditional ballet modes (namely, by Petipa, Ashton, and Balanchine), the action of the foot as it goes up and down is a focus of movement. A Feld woman sneaks up onto her toes; it's a rather shadowy business how

and when she gets up there. Again, like Tudor, Feld likes to invent very convoluted and hence difficult ways of moving, yet he avoids virtuoso dancing. And when he does go in for some show-off tactics, it is usually to satirize virtuosity, *à la* Tudor's *Gala Performance*.

Feld's love of *contraposto* lines, his ambivalence toward *pointe* work, and his hatred of audience-pleasing virtuosity are a few of the reasons why some observers wonder whether Feld can be viewed as a *bona fide* ballet choreographer. Another source of confusion is the fact that Feld never uses the traditional hierarchy of *corps de ballet* and soloists. All of his dances are conceived for an ensemble; accordingly stage centre is nor necessarily the most important part of the stage. It is also true that, having seriously studied modern dance as well as ballet in his youth, Feld has more authentic access to modern dance movement than most ballet choreographers, and it sometimes figures importantly in his ballets.

The difficulty some find in categorizing Feld's work is probably the best proof of Feld's major achievement: he has indeed taken ballet in a new direction and in a profound way, not only by giving his dancers a contemporary physical profile but by moving the very structure of a dance away from the nineteenth century and Balanchinian conventions. Radical in his avoidance of the chorus line and ballerina construct, he is nevertheless traditional in his use of music as prime motivation and in his adherence to theme and variations as the basic building blocks of his dances.

Feld's reliance on theme and variations has, in fact, grown over the years – unfortunately, to detrimental effect, for what was originally a useful tool has now become an end in itself. Whereas his earlier works were concerned with evocations of atmosphere and feelings arising from music, his more recent body of work is about the number of ways a core movement can be manipulated. Feld's fascination with the mechanics of theme and variations was seen as early as 1974, in *The Real McCoy*, where the focus of this Gershwin dance was a *chaise-longue*. In how many ways could it be made to glide? Feld counted them, all right. It was Feld's discovery of Steve Reich's modular music, however, that sealed the bond between Feld and the theme-and-variations device. Since that first Reich work in 1984, *The Grand Canon*, Feld has made eleven works to Reich, the most recent being *Tongue and Groove* (1995). In almost all his other works as well, be they set to Stephen Foster, Satie, or Mozart, Feld's approach has basically been squeezing as many variations as possible out of a basic theme.

An extraordinarily inventive manipulator, Feld has always found a few more variations than one would think possible – and than one would want. The passion with which he has pursued his game borders on the obsessional, which in turn makes the experience of watching a Feld ballet troubling to the mind as well as exhausting to the eye.

Quite aside from the issue of obsession, Feld's ballets are generally not the food for the conventional ballet audience. (Who knows whether he ever wanted them to be, although he did want to have artistic control over the mainstream ABT when he started choreographing for that troupe.) Feld's aversion to virtuosity and to choreography that brings individual personalities to the fore, and his preference for a more introverted, Tudoresque style over the more expansive, brilliant style embodied by Balanchine preclude his success within opera-house conditions.

Feld Ballets/NY has not toured as much as similar troupes and is virtually unknown abroad. It last visited Europe in 1986, and has never appeared in England. When it does tour it plays the college circuit rather than large theatres in big cities. And its repertoire is practically wholly by Feld, which often makes the company less appealing to audiences than the eclectic programming offered by other ballet groups.

Feld is unique in the ballet world because he has survived and flourished on his own terms and without the institutional backing of an umbrella company. Instead, he has developed his own institutional protections. In 1982 he and his then executive director, Cora Cahan, raised funds to renovate a rundown movie theatre to form the superb Joyce Theater. Feld Ballets/NY is now guaranteed seven weeks of theatre time in New York, an advantage few other troupes have. In 1986 Feld Ballets and ABT worked out a deal in which they were able to purchase the building in which they had been renting rehearsal space. Feld Ballets, as well as ABT, is thus in the envious position of being landlords of prime real estate. Yet another coup has been the development of a ballet school, which opened in 1977. It is a tuition-free academy for students of New York's public school system, and has played an increasingly important role in Feld's endeavours. By the late 1980s several members of Feld Ballets/NY were graduates of the school. In 1994, Kids Dance was launched, consisting of pre-professional students who performed in programmes designed for young audiences. In 1997, the name of the professional company was changed to Ballet Tech, with most of its roster drawn from the school. The six ballets Feld made for Ballet Tech have so far tended to be less classically based than earlier works.

In August 1997, Feld was also the choreographer for a highly publicized revival of the Leonard Bernstein musical *On The Town*, produced by the New York Shakespeare Festival.

Nancy Goldner

Biographical details

Born in Brooklyn, New York, 5 July 1942. **Studied** at the High School of Performing Arts and the School of American Ballet; also trained with Richard Thomas, New York. **Career** Made first professional stage appearances in off-Broadway productions, 1954, and then in Broadway musicals; also danced in Balanchine's *Nutcracker*, 1954;

performed in modern dance companies under Pearl Lang, Sophie Maslow, Donald McKayle; danced with the American Ballet Theatre, 1963–68, and 1971–72, and choreographed his first work for the company in 1967; founder, director, and choreographer, American Ballet Company, 1969–71; founder, Eliot Feld Ballet, 1974, remaining principal choreographer and artistic director: company renamed Feld Ballet, 1980, Feld Ballets/NY, 1990, and Ballet Tech – using only Feld-trained dancers – in 1997; established the New Ballet School to train children in 1977. Has also choreographed for Royal Winnipeg Ballet, London Festival Ballet, New York City Ballet, Royal Swedish Ballet, and Royal Danish Ballet. **Awards** include *Dance Magazine* Award, 1990; Honorary Doctorate, Juilliard School, 1991.

Works

Harbinger (mus. Prokofiev, 1967), *At Midnight* (mus. Mahler, 1967), *Meadowlark* (mus. Haydn, 1968), *Intermezzo No.1* (mus. Brahms, 1969), *Cortège Burlesque* (mus. Emmanuel Chabrier, 1969), *Pagan Spring* (mus. Bartók, 1969), *Early Songs* (mus. Richard Strauss, 1970), *A Poem Forgotten* (mus. Wallingford Riegger, 1970), *Cortège Parisien* (mus. Emmanuel Chabrier, 1970), *The Consort* (mus. various, 1970), *Romance* (mus. Brahms, 1971), *Theatre* (mus. Richard Strauss, 1971), *The Gods Amused* (mus. Debussy, 1971), *A Soldier's Tale* (mus. Stravinsky, 1971), *Eccentrique* (mus. Stravinsky, 1971), *Winter's Court* (mus. Elizabethan lute songs, 1972), *Jive* (mus. Morton Gould, 1973), *Tzaddik* (mus. Copland, 1974), *Sephardic Songs* (mus. traditional, arranged Manuel Valls, 1974), *The Real McCoy* (mus. Gershwin, 1974), *Mazurka* (mus. Chopin, 1975), *Excursions* (mus. Samuel Barber, 1975), *Impromptu* (mus. Albert Roussel, 1976), *Variations on 'America'* (mus. Charles Ives, William Schumann, 1977), *A Footstep of Air* (mus. Beethoven, Scottish and Irish folk, 1977), *Santa Fé Saga* (mus. Morton Gould, 1977), *La Vida* (mus. Copland, 1978), *Danzón Cubano* (mus. Copland, 1978), *Half Time* (mus. Morton Gould, 1978), *Papillon* (mus. Offenbach, 1979), *Circa* (mus. Hindemith, 1980), *Anatomic Balm* (mus. ragtime, 1980), *Scenes for the Theater* (later retitled *Scenes*; mus. Copland, 1980), *Song of Norway* (mus. Grieg, adapted by R. Wright and G. Forrest, 1981), *Play Bach* (mus. J.S. Bach, 1982), *Over the Pavement* (mus. Charles Ives, 1982), *Straw Hearts* (mus. various, 1982), *Summer's Lease* (mus. Mahler, 1983), *Three Dances* (mus. John Cage, 1983), *The Jig is Up* (mus. The Bothy Band, John Cunningham, 1984), *Adieu* (mus. Hugo Wolf, 1984), *Moon Skate* (mus. Ravel, 1984), *The Grand Canon* (mus. Steve Reich, 1984), *Intermezzo No. 2* (mus. Brahms, 1985), *Against the Sky* (mus. Bartók, 1985), *Medium: Rare* (mus. Steve Reich, 1985), *Aurora I* (mus. Steve Reich, 1985), *Aurora II* (mus. Steve Reich, 1985), *Echo* (mus. Steve Reich, 1986), *Skara Brae* (mus. traditional Irish, Scottish, and Breton, 1986), *Bent Planes* (mus. Steve Reich, 1986), *Embraced Waltzes* (mus. Chopin, 1987), *A Dance for Two* (mus. Haydn, 1987), *Shadow's Breath* (mus. Mozart, 1988), *The Unanswered Question* (mus. Charles Ives, 1988), *Kore* (mus. Steve Reich, 1988), *Petipa Notwithstanding* (mus. Terry Riley, 1988), *Asia* (mus. Ravel, 1989), *Love Song Waltzes* (mus. Brahms, 1989), *Ah Scarlatti* (mus. Scarlatti, 1989), *Mother Nature* (mus. Monteverdi, 1989), *Contra Pose* (mus. C.P.E. Bach, 1990), *Charmed Lives* (mus. Ravel, 1990), *Ion* (solo; mus. Steve Reich, 1991), *Fauna* (mus. Debussy, 1991), *Common Ground* (mus. J.S. Bach, 1991), *Savage Glance* (mus. Shostakovitch, 1991), *Clave* (mus. Steve Reich, 1992), *Evoe* (mus. Debussy, 1992), *Endsong* (mus. Richard Strauss, 1992), *Wolfgang Strategies* (mus. Mozart, 1992), *To the Naked Eye* (mus. Stravinsky, 1992), *Hello Fancy* (mus. traditional, from John Playford, 1992), *Hadji* (mus. Lou Harrison, 1992), *Frets and Women* (mus. Lou Harrison, 1992), *The Relative Disposition of the Parts* (mus. J.S. Bach, 1993), *Blooms Wake* (mus. Scriabin, 1993), *M. R. I.* (mus. Varèse, 1993), *Doo Dah Day* (mus. Stephen Foster, 1993), *Doghead and Godcatchers* (mus. Haydn, 1994), *23 Skidoo* (mus. Martinů, 1994), *Gnossiennes* (mus. Satie, 1994), *Ogive* (mus. Satie, 1994), *Ludwig Gambits* (mus. Beethoven, 1995), *Chi* (mus. Steve Reich, 1994), *Tongue and Groove* (mus. Steve Reich, 1995), *Meshungana Dance* (mus. klezmer music, 1996), *Paper Tiger* (mus. Leon Redbone, 1996), *Paen* (mus. Henry Cowell, 1996), *Shuffle* (mus. Michael Gordon, 1996), *Industry* (mus. Michael Gordon, 1996), *Yo Shakespeare* (mus. Michael Gordon, 1996), *Evening Chant* (mus. William Doerrfeld, 1996); *Re:x* (mus. Julian Wolfe, 1997), *Joggers* (mus. Dick Koomans, 1997), *Umbra Blues* (mus. Detta Blues, 1997), *Juke Box* (mus. Jerry Leiber and Mike Stoller, 1997), *Partita for Two* (mus. J.S. Bach, 1997), *The Last Sonata* (mus. Debussy, 1997), *On the Town* (musical by Bernstein, 1997).

Further reading

Interviews with Charles E. France, 'A Conversation with Eliot Feld', *Ballet Review*, 3(6), 1971; in John Gruen's *The Private World of Ballet*, New York, 1975; in Elinor Ragosin's *The Dance Makers: Conversations with American Choreographers*, New York, 1980; with R.L. Cowser, in

'Eliot Feld Talks', *Dance Scope*, September 1980; with Joseph Mazo, in 'After 25 Years', *Elle*, March 1992.

Articles 'Eliot Feld', *Contemporary Biography Yearbook, 1971*; Doris Hering, 'Two Eliot Felds?', *Dance Magazine*, January 1971; Marcia Siegel, 'Feld Re-Fielded', *Dance Magazine*, March 1974; Jack Anderson, 'Talking to Myself about Eliot Feld', *Dance Magazine*, February 1975 (reprinted in Anderson's *Choreography Observed*, Iowa City, 1987); Claudia Roth Pierpont, 'Contradictions in Eliot Feld', *Dance Life*, Summer 1976; Tobi Tobias, 'Plus ça Change . . . ', *New York*, 19 June 1990; Clive Barnes, 'A Modern Classic: Eliot Feld', *Dance Magazine*, February 1992; Ken Emerson, 'Feld's Foster', *Ballet Review*, Fall 1994.

Books John Gruen, *The Private World of Ballet*, New York, 1975; Moira Hodgson, *Quintet: Five American Dance Companies*, New York, 1976; Robert Coe, *Dance in America*, New York, 1985; Deborah Jowitt, *The Dance in Mind*, Boston, 1985.

WILLIAM FORSYTHE

From a high school rock-'n'-roller in Manhasset on Long Island, New York, William Forsythe propelled himself along an upward path leading to the directorship of the Frankfurt Ballet in Germany. His passion as a dancer was established early in his teens, his talent authenticated by winning high school dance contests. The gyrating, disjointed, energetic movements he performed in the 1960s have filtered into his own unconventional and convoluted ballet lexicon. Forsythe formally trained in ballet and performed with Joffrey Ballet II in New York City. During his brief time with the Joffrey, he had some opportunities as an understudy to perform with the senior company. The young dancer's charismatic nature did not take long to surface: Robert Joffrey himself commented on how quickly Forsythe's ideas flowed. In 1973, Forsythe won director John Cranko's approval and performed with the famed Stuttgart Ballet: his first piece, *Urlicht*, was made for that company in 1976. Soon his early choreographic success with the Stuttgart and Basel Ballet companies brought him recognition as an important, upcoming creative artist.

Since 1984 Forsythe has been Frankfurt Ballet's artistic director and chief choreographer. His large company is based in a traditional German opera house, but there is nothing traditional about this controversial, risk-taking choreographer. Inheriting a government-supported opera house has enabled him to make grand-scale productions with ambitious production possibilities. Forsythe's intelligence has guided his artistic decisions as to what the Frankfurt community will tolerate and accept. In his experimentation with classical ballet, *Swan Lake* has not been on his agenda, and it is doubtful that it ever will be, at least in its traditional form. In a Spring 1990 interview in *Ballet Review* Forsythe said, 'I have a good sense of the German culture, what might work for them . . .'. He has proved his point by developing a large, new, and younger audience. He has been able to balance the Frankfurt community's intellectual tradition with still having his own contemporary vision realized. Unconventional ways of moving dancers' bodies within a context of *non-sequitur* images that seldom result in a logical conclusion can infuriate, confuse, or excite his audiences. Although his work has been seen in America, it is in the countries of Western Europe where Forsythe has had greatest popularity and financial support. It is understandable in view of his success that his artistic sensibilities are more akin to those found in Germany, Italy, France, Belgium, and Holland than to those found in North America. France, a great supporter of new dance, has commissioned his choreography and has generously bestowed prestigious venues, such as the Théâtre Musical de Châtelet, for extended company residencies. A 1997 United States tour was squelched owing to production strictures and lack of an appropriate venue. Forsythe's large-scale theatrical requirements are difficult to accommodate, but by late 1997 plans for a 1998 Next Wave Festival at the Brooklyn Academy of Music were in the making.

Forsythe is a modern-day theatrical wizard, a man of many talents. Choreography for his own and other companies (such as San Francisco Ballet, New York City Ballet, Nederlands Dans Theater, Joffrey Ballet, Britain's Royal Ballet, and Paris Opéra Ballet) are only part of his *œuvre*. As in the *auteur* tradition of European filmmakers, Forsythe the scenographer controls many aspects of his ballets. These include lighting and costume designs; conceiving and writing texts (often spoken in performance); creating the music (principally with Dutch composer Thom Willems) and/ or sound effects; and sometimes directing through microphones an entire work as it is happening. Idiosyncratic theatrical devices and eclectic activities are commonly employed in his pieces, such as a fire curtain thudding to the floor – leaving the house in total darkness until it is lifted again to expose a complete change of stage activity. A curtain drop was repeated periodically throughout *Artifact* (1984), a piece seen at the Pepsico Summerfare Festival in Purchase, New York in 1987. (*Artifact* was the first Frankfurt Ballet work seen in America and made strong but varied critical impressions.) *New Sleep* (1987), created for the San Francisco Ballet, reflected the range of Forsythe's activity: it had choreography, lighting, costumes, and stage design all by Forsythe. The lighting design split the stage into quarters on diagonal lines, with the lighting downstage right/upstage left very dark and that downstage left/upstage right very bright. A reviewer for the German newspaper *Suddeutsche Zeitung* found that 'With *New Sleep*, Forsythe presents his audience a surrealistic puzzle in lighting, that has possibly not been seen on any other stage yet. Forsythe expresses his scepticism about the techniques he operates . . . in the form of an extremely entertaining masterpiece

packed with energy'. His involvement in so many aspects of his dances has not, however, won universal admiration. Some critics have been harsh about Forsythe's overindulgence in sound volume, in spoken (or screaming) text, and in extremes in the intensity of the lighting.

Forsythe's subject matter has also divided critics; in particular there has been controversy over his depiction of brutality towards women, specifically in *Side 2 – Love Songs* (1979), set to music of Aretha Franklin and Dionne Warwick. This work prompted polarized responses of applause or shock at the misogynistic treatment involved in the male/female partnering. The choreographer responds to his critics by simply saying that various companies dance his work differently, and in cities around the world, audiences react differently. *Love Songs* was originally created for his own company where the dancers were just executing the movement; the 'love' duets were taken less seriously. Forsythe's work has since developed far beyond this early dramaturgy of love songs. The furious explosive dancing is still seen, but the context of his later works is far more developed and complex.

Alie/nA(c)tion (1992) showed further development in his high-tech, fragmented dance theatre. It has been described as one of his most difficult pieces to comprehend. The deconstructed title alone is cause for puzzlement. Forsythe here engages his audience in what is happening on the stage both in the construction and the deconstruction of the work process. During this work, his viewers are privy to benches being pushed around into place, seconds being counted for several minutes over a loudspeaker by a man with headphones, breathing sounds, gasps, squeals, and sobs of performers equipped with personal microphones, the smell of smoke from a man's cigarette, the sound of rappers rapping and shouting obscenities, a man pretending to be a walrus, and electric dancing that is exhilarating. Experiencing

Alie/nA(c)tion was likened by one young dancer to an assault on one's entire physical being; some critics were not so enthusiastic. However, Rolf Michaelis wrote in *Ballett International*, 'Even when Forsythe suspends the audience's comprehension – where else is the expressive range of contemporary dance being as vigorously extended as in Frankfurt?'

Conventional linear narrative is not part of Forsythe's repertory; a receptive audience has more than enough to feast their eyes on in his maze of activity. Yet Forsythe's work is not always hard-edged and highly charged. His *Quintet* (1993) makes no use of high-tech feats, and has an atypical musical score, in quality if not in structure, by Gavin Bryars (entitled 'Jesus's blood never failed me yet'). The song's words are continually repeated with subtle musical variations that can be hauntingly beautiful or, for some, tedious. The choreography has been described as having falling, swooping, and skimming movement. A trapdoor with stairs leading below the stage, through which the dancers can move in and out of the audience's view, gives, along with the music, a dramatic context to explore.

Full-length evening pieces such as *France/Dance* (1983), *Impressing the Czar* (1988), and *Artifact* have been likened to the creations of the American director Robert Wilson, who is also embraced enthusiastically by European cultural communities. The major difference between the two men lies in Forsythe's interest in movement structure for his dancers and in how they produce the material in performance. His dancers have necessary qualities beyond a strong ballet technique. The shape and size of his dancers are not as important to him as their ability to co-ordinate their head and arms and their rhythmic sense. In a 1989 interview with Burt Supree, the former senior dance editor of *The Village Voice* (published in the *Proceedings of the Dance Critics Association Conference*, 1990), Forsythe said, 'I've discovered there are two kinds of people who are dancing: there are dancers, and there are people who have learned to dance ... people who are just dancers [have] danced since they were this big [he gestures, child high], and then can dance, will always dance, and probably must dance ...'. These are the dancers (like himself) that Forsythe wants because he needs people who can organize their bodies for whatever is necessary and commit themselves to the act of dancing. The company does, however, take a straightforward daily ballet class as a centring base. Yet the choreographic work does not adhere to strict classical format. Forsythe pushes the ballet line far beyond the norm, especially for his women *en pointe* who jet out of verticality into wonderfully odd and impossible-looking silhouettes. Ballerinas are seen in daring off-centre lifts with legs rotated at 180 degrees, or being dragged across the stage *en pointe*. It is also not unusual for the arms to have a more inventive motion than the legs. To increase possibilities, the dancer's footwear can vary from *pointe* shoes, to work-boots, socks, to anything that might fit the bill. Performing movement at frantic speeds and blatantly showing strong physicality are elements that dominate Forsythe's work. Audiences who admire him are thrilled at the daring style of movement, while others are annoyed at his bold departure from a 'pure' dance art.

Forsythe has attributed his creative inspiration to diverse branches of cultural and intellectual influences. He has read Rudolf Laban and Roland Barthes, along with many other philosophical and intellectual notables. He became interested in the movement theorist Laban after studying and experiencing his spatial concepts in relation to the body's movement possibilities. His dancers are not considered instruments to be moulded by his whim, but an integral part of his creative process. For example, Forsythe says, 'I give the dancers my thoughts and not the results of them. I don't tell anyone what to do. I just tell them how they should do it. I've only created the conditions, but the movements are made manifest by the dancers themselves' (*Ballett International*, February 1994). Dancers might, for example, be given a responsibility or task within a musical section to phrase the movement and be ready for the succeeding section. As with Merce Cunningham, mastering a sophisticated computer system and other technological theatre tools has been an important learning requirement for Forsythe: he uses them to enhance his own realm of creative possibilities.

A 1995 project for the London Royal Ballet was an example of the difficulties involved in working with a company alien to Forsythe's choreographic process. The choreographer was dissatisfied with the progress of a promised new work. The company members were not prepared for Forsythe's 'choreographic association with the dancers' method of creating a work. He then divested the project to two of his own experienced company members, Dana Caspersen and Antony Rizzi, and worked with them to create *Firstext* and *Steptext*. In this, the earlier *Steptext* (1984) was joined to the new *Firstext* and, originally, a section of *Artifact*. (It is not unusual for Forsythe to detach a section of a multiple-part piece for presentation on its own.) Dancers in the United States have also experienced Forsythe's approach to making movement. Both Leslie Carothers (Joffrey Ballet) in *Square Deal* (1983) and Lourdes Lopez (New York City Ballet) in *Behind the China Dogs* (1988) have spoken of the creatively productive time they had with Forsythe. But his improvisational work is not a customary practice with traditional ballet dancers and their choreographers.

In keeping with Barthes' philosophy of the goals of an artist, Forsythe is a man of his time and place, never dwelling on whether past projects were or were not well received. He has said that dancing has nothing to do with closure or exclusion of movement possibilities. With unfailing

energy, the artist continues to choreograph work that excites his vast audiences, providing them with eye-riveting movement action, challenges to the mind, stimuli to the senses, and a desire in the spectators to come back for more. As Anna Kisselgoff noted once in *The New York Times* (4 November 1983), Forsythe 'has married highbrow ideas with lowbrow imagery and done so with high class intelligence.'

Sandra Genter

Biographical details

Born in New York, 30 December 1949. **Studied** with Jonathan Watts, Maggie Black, Finis Jhung at the Joffrey Ballet School, New York, from 1969. **Career** Danced with Joffrey Ballet, 1971–73, Stuttgart Ballet, 1973–80. First choreography was for the Noverre Society Young Choreographers' Workshop, Stuttgart, 1976; choreographer for Stuttgart Ballet, 1976–80; freelance choreographer, staging ballets in Germany, Austria, Italy, and the Netherlands, 1980–82; choreographer, Frankfurt Ballet, 1982, then its director and chief choreographer, from 1984. Has also choreographed for many other companies, including Basel (Basle) Ballet, Munich Ballet, Nederlands Dans Theater, German Opera Ballet (Berlin), Royal Ballet (London), Joffrey Ballet, Paris Opéra Ballet, Aterballetto (Italy), San Francisco Ballet, and New York City Ballet. **Awards and honours** Olivier Award for *In the Middle, Somewhat Elevated*, 1992; Chevalier de l'Ordre des Arts et des Lettres (France), 1992; Hessen Arts Prize (Germany), 1995; International Theatre Institute Award, 1996; Grand Prix Carina ARI (for *Solo*), 1996.

Works

Urlicht (mus. Mahler, 1976), *Daphne* (mus. Dvořák, 1977), *Bach Violin Concerto in A-Minor* (mus. J.S. Bach, 1977), *Flore Subsimplici-Suit* (mus. Handel, 1977), *From the Most Distant* (mus. György Ligeti, 1978), *Dream of Galilei* (mus. Penderecki), *Folia* (mus. Hans Werner Henze, 1978), *Orpheus* (with playwright Edward Bond, mus. Hans Werner Henze, 1979), *Side 2 – Love Songs* (mus. Aretha Franklin, Dionne Warwick, 1979), *Time Cycle* (mus. Lukas Foss, 1979), *Joyleen Gets Up, Gets Down, Goes Out* (mus. Boris Blacher, 1980), *'Tis a Pity She's a Whore* (mus. Thomas Jahn, 1980), *Famous Mothers Club* (solo, 1980), *Say Bye Bye* (mus. various, 1980),

Die Nacht aus Blei (mus. von Bose, 1981), *Whisper Moon* (mus. William Bolcom, 1981), *Event 1, 2, 3* (mus. various, 1981), *Gänge 1 – Ein Stück über Ballett* (mus. Forsythe, Michael Simon, 1982), *Gänge* (mus. Michael Simon, Thomas Jahn, 1983), *Mental Model* (mus. Stravinsky, 1983), *Square Deal* (mus. Forsythe, 1983), *France/Dance* (mus. J.S. Bach, collage by Forsythe, 1983), *Berg AB* (film; mus. Berg, 1984), *Artifact* (includes *Artifact II*; mus. J.S. Bach, Eva Crossman-Hecht, 1984), *Steptext* (mus. J.S. Bach, 1984), *LDC* (mus. Thom Willems, 1985), *Isabelle's Dance* (musical by Forsythe and Eva Crossman-Hecht, 1986), *Skinny* (mus. Thom Willems, Forsythe 1986), *Die Befragung des Robert Scott* (mus. Thom Willems, 1986), *Big White Baby Dog* (mus. Thom Willems, 1986), *Baby Sam* (mus. Thom Willems, 1986), *Pizza Girl* (with others; mus. Thom Willems, 1986), *New Sleep* (mus. Thom Willems, 1987), *Same Old Story* (mus. Thom Willems, 1987), *The Loss Of Small Detail* (mus. Thom Willems, 1987; revised version, 1991), *Impressing the Czar* (mus. Beethoven, Eva Crossman-Hecht, Leslie Stuck, and includes *In The Middle, Somewhat Elevated*, mus. Thom Willems, 1988), *Behind the China Dogs* (mus. Leslie Stuck, 1988), *The Vile Parody of Address* (mus. J.S. Bach, 1988), *Enemy in the Figure* (mus. Thom Willems, 1989), *Slingerland I* (mus. Gavin Bryars, 1989), *Limb's Theorem* (includes *Enemy in the Figure*; mus. Thom Willems, 1990), *Slingerland II and III* (mus. Thom Willems, 1990), *Slingerland IV* (mus. Gavin Bryars, 1990), *Marion/Marion* (mus. Bernard Herrmann's soundtrack for film *Psycho*, 1991), *The Second Detail* (mus. Thom Willems, 1991), *Snap, Woven Effort* (mus. Thom Willems, 1991), *Alie/nA(c)tion* (mus. Thom Willems, Schoenberg, 1992; revised version, 1993), *Quintet* (mus. Gavin Bryars, 1993), *Hermann Schmerman* (mus. Thom Willems, 1992; revised version, 1993), *As a Garden in This Setting* (mus. Thom Willems, 1993), *Self Meant to Govern* (mus. Thom Willems, Maxim Franke, 1994), *Pivot House* (mus. Kraton Surakarta, 1994), *Four Point Counter* (mus. Thom Willems, 1995), *Firstext* (mus. Thom Willems, 1995), *Invisible Film* (mus. J.S. Bach, Handel, Purcell, 1995), *Of Any If And* (mus. Thom Willems, 1995), *The The* (with Dana Caspersen, no music, 1995), *Eidos: Telos* (with the company; mus. Thom Willems, 1995), *Solo* (video, dir. Thomas Lovell; mus. Thom Willems, 1995), *Six Counter Points* (includes *The The*; *Duo*, mus. Thom Willems; *Trio*, mus. Beethoven, Berg; *Four Point Counter*, mus. Thom Willems; *Approximate Sonata* and *The Vertiginous Thrill of Exactitude*, mus. Thom Willems; 1996), *Sleepers Guts* (with the company; mus. Thom Willems and Joel Ryan, 1996), *Tight Roaring Circle* (with Dana Caspersen, 1997).

Further reading

Interviews with Birgit Kirchner, in 'Good Theatre of a Different Kind', *Ballett International*, August 1984; with Elisa Vaccarino, in *Balletto oggi*, November 1989; with Senta Driver *et al.*, in 'A Conversation with William Forsythe', *Ballet Review*, Spring 1990; with Johannes Odenthal, in 'Conversation with William Forsythe', *Ballett International*, February 1994; with William Anthony, in 'William Forsythe Talks to William Anthony', *Dance Europe*, December/January 1996/97.

Articles L. Shyer, 'Stuttgart Orpheus', *Theater*, Spring 1980; Mary Whitney, 'Prodigal Son', *Ballet News*, October 1983; R. Langer and R. Sikes, 'New Directors, Part II: William Forsythe', *Dance Magazine*, January 1986; Otis Stuart, 'Forsythe's Follies', *Ballet Review*, Fall 1987; Marcel Michel, 'Billy Side Story', *Pour la Danse*, February 1989; Arlene Croce, 'Wise Guys', *The New Yorker*, 31 July 1989; Eva Elisabeth Fischer, 'Aesthetic Norms and Today's Social Taboos: The Effect of Innovation and Creativity', *Ballett International*, January 1990; Nadine Meisner, 'Choreographer for Today', *Dance and Dancers*, April 1990; Senta Driver, '2 or 3 Things That Might Be Considered Primary', *Ballet Review*, Spring 1990; Roslyn Sulcas, 'William Forsythe: The Poetry of Disappearance and the Great Tradition', *Dance Theatre Journal*, Summer 1991; Nadine Meisner, 'Dangerous Dancing', *Dance and Dancers*, January/February 1992; Claudia Jeschke, 'American Theatricality in Contemporary German Theater Dancing: John Neumeier and William Forsythe', *Society of Dance History Scholars Proceedings*, February 1992; Edith Boxberger, '. . . want to be hypnotized . . .', *Ballett International*, February 1994; Dorrell A. Wilkins, 'Aesthetics and Cultural Criticism in William Forsythe's *Impressing the Czar*', *Ballet Review*, Spring 1994; Nadine Meisner, 'Dangerous Beauty', *Opera House*, January 1995; Edith Boxberger, 'Breaking New Ground from Deconstruction' (on *Eidos: Telos*), *Ballett International*, March 1995; William Anthony, 'Forsythe in Frankfurt' (on *Six Counter Points*), *Dancing Times*, March 1996; Ann Nugent, 'Confounding Expectations' (on *Solo*), *Dance Theatre Journal*, Summer 1996; Roslyn Sulcas, 'Theorems and Counterpoints' (on *Limb's Theorem* and *Six Counter Points*), *Dance Now*, Summer 1996; Paige Perry, 'Sleepers Guts in Frankfurt', *Dance Europe*, December/January 1996/97; Roslyn Sulcas, 'The Continuing Evolution of Mr Forsythe' (on *Sleepers Guts*), *Dance Magazine*, January 1997; William Anthony, 'Forsythe's New Ballet: Sleepers Guts', *Dancing Times*, March 1997.

JEAN-CLAUDE GALLOTTA

Jean-Claude Gallotta, enigmatic poet, philosopher and 'auteur' of the *nouvelle danse* in France, has been called 'the most controversial, loved, hated and wooed choreographer in France today' (*L'Unità*, October 1986). Perhaps it is dangerous to talk about any choreographer in terms of superlatives. However, certain aspects of the quotation deserve consideration in the light of Gallotta's artistic output and his role in contemporary French dance.

Gallotta is undoubtedly a controversial figure. It is difficult to categorize his work, and as a result he puts critics on the spot by challenging their terms of reference. A Gallotta work usually covers a wide range of movement, from the most pedestrian to the most highly technical, with an ample dose of personal input that defies any sort of definition.

It is this unorthodox approach to dance that has made Gallotta one of the leading exponents of the *nouvelle danse*, or New Dance, in France – a label that has been given to those dance phenomena that began to appear in the 1970s. *Nouvelle danse* has a shorter history than modern or post-modern dance in America, and the main reason for this is commonly considered to be the predominance in France of ballet, in particular at the Paris Opéra, often seen to be resistant to change. Such resistance was common to all artforms at a time when the neoclassical aesthetic flourished in the fine arts and music after the First World War. Those forms that did challenge this aesthetic, such as *Ausdruckstanz* in Germany, were crushed by the weight of political events, and it was not until the 1970s that dance once again found its voice and its cultural identity in the forceful and extraordinary figure of Pina Bausch.

In France in turn, it was the force of the student revolt of 1968 which finally broke down social barriers; young people questioned the whole structure of the so-called Establishment, while the authority of universities, church, and family all came in for strong criticism. A set of values that had been the basis of postwar society – such as paternal authority, male dominance, patriotism, and sexual fidelity – no longer held sway. This climate, it has been argued, was the perfect stimulus for the New Dance expression in France.

At first, the great influences were American. Guest performances by the Graham, Cunningham, and Nikolais companies brought new ideas to French audiences, while some dancers (such as Susan Buirge and Carolyn Carlson) settled in France and had a great impact on the dance scene. Béjart, too, contributed to a new approach by offering a new style within the ballet genre, and, above all, by opening the doors to a much larger dance audience by showing his works in parks, stadiums, and other unorthodox performance spaces.

The general climate of change meant that the old rules no longer applied to dance. This situation was to give an opportunity to a whole new generation of artists, who approached dance without necessarily going through the (previously obligatory) route of lengthy academic study and training before performing. In this context Gallotta serves as a prime example of his time. He was born in Grenoble in 1950, of an Italian father and Italian–Austrian mother. His works are often about (or include) groups of people who can be seen as immigrants, survivors, or the more marginalized and despised elements of society in general. His first experience of dance was when he entered a dance school in his home town looking for models as inspiration for his studies as a fine arts student. The impact that this casual event had upon him changed the whole course of his artistic life, for he subsequently decided to dedicate himself to what was, for him, a previously unknown art form. Despite his age (twenty), he began attending various dance classes, including ballet, before going to the United States to study with Cunningham – an influence that is still to be seen in his use of pure, clean lines, wide backs, and long arms. However, an accident and subsequent forced inactivity made him think again about technique and the use of the body. The results of these reflections can often be seen in the small, quivering, dithering, little movements that appear in his works.

In 1979 Gallotta returned to Grenoble and, with Leo Standard, a sculptor and scenographer, and Henri Torgue, a musician, he founded the Group Emile Dubois, a name as enigmatic as the choreographer and his works. (Musician Serge Houppin joined in 1982.) In fact, 'Emile Dubois' could be anyone, someone, or no one at all. 'Anyone', argues Norbert Servos, critic of *Ballett International*, because the rough equivalent in English would be the 'John Smith Group'.[1] 'Someone', we are told by Nadine Meisner, because Emile Dubois was a painter who tried to create modern dances in Paris during the Diaghilev era.[2] 'No one', we might conclude, because Gallotta has stated that Dubois is entirely a creature of his own imagination.[3]

The very mysteriousness of his company name reveals a great deal about Gallotta. It suggests his sense of humour, his love of myths and the creation of mysterious worlds inhabited by whole tribes, with their customs, rites, and rituals – a sort of dance equivalent of *Lord of the Rings*, as Bentivoglio wrote in 1990. *Ulysse* (1981), *Les Survivants* (1982), *Les Aventures d'Ivan Vaffan* (1984), *Mammame* (1984–86), and *Les Mystères de Subal* (1990) all belong to this genre. The dancers themselves reflect such an approach. They have been called 'a tight-knit family of appealingly unglamorous dancers'[4] or defined as 'strange because they are too human, too ordinary, too like us common mortals'. It is also clear that they are rarely chosen for their technical abilities even if Gallotta uses highly technical movements at certain moments.

In other works, such as *Daphnis et Chloé* (1982), *Les Louves et Pandora* (1986), and *Docteur Labus* (1988), the choreographer faces time and again the problem of relationships (above all sexual relationships) between people. Using duets, trios, and groups of four dancers, he expresses all the emotion, confusion, and even violence of personal communication in modern society.

Gallotta has another source of inspiration which clearly places him among the new generation of choreographers: his love and use of film. This has led him to coin the phrase 'danse d'auteur' for a certain type of choreography which not only uses rhythms, methods, and structures common to cinema (such as flashbacks, reordered sequences, unconventional angles, and so on), but which is clearly the hallmark of a single choreographer in the same way that certain films can only be the work of one director. Gallotta also regularly rechoreographs his works for the film medium. *Un Chant presque éteint* (1986) is one such piece and can be used as an example here to consider several of Gallotta's characteristics. First, its reworking of the choreography of *Mammame* reflects the basis of much of his artistic output, a need for an ongoing choreographic development throughout a series of works. Second, Gallotta chose the location for filming, the Gare de l'Est railway station in Paris, because he saw it as both a 'cathedral of the new humanity'[5] and a place of great isolation, as evident in his shots of the 'fringe' elements of society – older people, workers, immigrants and babies – all passively waiting and watching, never leaving, never moving. The station is also seen as a place of brief encounters of every kind, which end quickly, even violently. In this setting Gallotta places his dancers so that they are barely distinguishable from the *bona fide* passengers, and so creates an ambience for them and their dramas which they play out using a mixture of pedestrian and dance-like movements.

Gallotta's own contribution to his works has been described as to 'direct the traffic of the dancers'[6] and 'to guide and sustain',[7] and in *Un Chant...* he remains true to those roles. He is the observer, the initiator, the orchestrator involved with the happenings of the others while remaining apart. His movements filter and change or initiate those of the others: he is a true conductor.

In a long interview between Gallotta and Marinella Guatterini in 1993, Gallotta explained several of his views on dance, including the opinion that dance should be freed from choreography in the same way as music has been freed from harmony and painting from representation. Non-dancer, 'non-choreographer', poet and philosopher of the French New Dance scene, Gallotta has, with intelligence, artistic flair, and humour, won world-wide recognition for his particular way of seeing dance.

Ann Veronica Turnbull

Notes

1 Servos Norbert, 'Past ecstasy: Jean-Claude Gallotta's *Les Survivants*, Part II of his *Hommage à Yves P.* at the Berlin Festival, *Ballett International*, December 1983, p. 24.
2 Nadine Meisner, 'Le Groupe Emile Dubois', *Dance and Dancers*, February 1986, p. 26.
3 Marinella Guatterini, *Discorsi sulla Danza*, Milan, Ubulibri, 1994.
4 Gus Solomons Jr, review in *Ballet News*, 6(11), May 1985, pp. 35–6.
5 In 1978 an exhibition dedicated to the railway station, 'a modern-day Tower of Babel', was mounted in the Pompidou Centre in Paris. This quotation comes from the exhibition catalogue.
6 Marinella Guatterini, 'Danza, da Grenoble con furore, *L'Unità*, 12 October 1986.
7 Leonetta Bentivoglio 'Gallotta dei misteri', *La Repubblica*, Milan, 8 March 1990.

Biographical details

Born to Italian parents in Grenoble, France, 7 April 1950. **Studied** visual arts at the Ecole des Beaux Arts, Grenoble, and dance with Merce Cunningham in the United States, 1978–79. **Career** Returned to Grenoble in 1979; founding director and choreographer, Groupe Emile Dubois, 1979; appointed director at the Maison de la Culture in Grenoble (the first choreographer to be appointed to such a position), 1986, and then artistic director, Centre Chorégraphique Emile Dubois. Has also written about his views and theories of dance. **Awards** include Bagnolet Festival Award, 1981; Prix de la Danse de la Societé des Auteurs, 1985; Grand Prix National de la Danse du Ministère de la Culture, 1985; Cannes Film Festival Prix Georges Sadoul (for video *Montalvo et l'enfant*), 1989.

Works

Pas de quatre (mus. Olivier Darcissac, Henri Torgue, Gilles Jaloustre, 1980), *Mouvements* (mus. Olivier Darcissac, Gilles Jaloustre, Henri Torgue, 1980), *Ulysse* (mus. Henri Torgue, Gilles Jaloustre, 1981), *Waslaw-Desirs: trittico* (includes revised *Pas de Quatre, Mouvements, Ulysse*, 1981), *Grandeur nature* (mus. Henri Torgue, Gilles Jaloustre, 1982), *Daphnis et Chloé* (mus. Henri Torgue, 1982), *Hommage à Yves P.* (includes *Yves P., Les Survivants, Solo de Yves P.*; mus. Henri Torgue, Serge Houppin, 1982), *Les Aventures d'Ivan Vaffan* (mus. Henri Torgue, Serge Houppin, 1984), *Mammame I: Le Désert d'Arkadine* (mus. Henri Torgue, Serge Houppin, 1985), *Les Louves et Pandora* (mus. Henri Torgue, Serge Houppin, 1986), *Mammame II: Les Enfants qui toussent* (mus. Henri Torgue, Serge Houppin, 1986), *Un Chant presque éteint* (film version of the two parts of *Mammame*, 1986), *Docteur Labus* (mus. Henri Torgue, Serge Houppin, 1988), *Montalvo et l'enfant* (film; dir. Claude Maurieras, 1989), *Rei Dom, ou la légende des Kreuls* (film; 1989), *Les Mystères de Subal* (mus. Henri Torgue, Serge Houppin, 1990), *La Légende de Romeo et Juliette* (text Henri Buffard, 1991), *L'Amour en deux* (film; 1991), *La Légende de Don Juan* (mus. local, 1992), *Les Solos des Orioines* (1992), *Prémonitions* (1994), *Les Variations d'Ulysse* (mus. Pierre Drouet, 1995),) *La Tête contre les fleurs* (mus. Alfred Schnittke, 1995), *Hommage à Pavel Haas* (mus. Pavel Hass, 1995), *Rue de Palanka* (solo; 1996).

Further reading

Interviews with Rolf Garske, in 'Dance Creates Its Own Handwriting', *Ballett International*, January 1985; with Andrew Lucre, in 'Child's Play with Adult Meanings', *The Sunday Times*, 8 October 1989; with Oonagh Duckworth, *Dance Theatre Journal*, Winter 1989.

Articles Jean-Marc Adolphe, 'Gallotta', *Dance Theatre Journal*, Summer 1989; Jean-Claude

Gallotta, 'Introducing Gallotta', *Dance and Dancers*, September 1989; Nadine Meisner, 'Different Sensibilities', *Dance and Dancers*, October 1989; Thomas Hahn, 'Choreographing out of Nothing', *Ballett International*, July 1996.

Books Laurence Louppe, Jean Louis Schefer, and Claude-Henri Buffard, *Gallotta: Groupe Emile Dubois*, Paris, 1988; Jean-Claude Gallotta, *Mémoires d'un dictaphone: Notes d'un chorégraphie*, Paris, 1990; Jean-Marc Adolphe, 'La Nouvelle Danse Française', in *The Dance Has Many Faces*, edited by Walter Sorrel, New York, 1992; Marinella Guatterini, *Discorsi sulla Danza*, Milan, 1994.

DAVID GORDON

David Gordon's dance works rarely fit neatly into the category 'choreography'. He is a brilliant manipulator of movement phrases, visual images, and verbal texts, who prefers to call himself a 'constructor' rather than a choreographer. The critic Allen Robertson has suggested the label 'plasario punographer' to capture Gordon's distinctive combination of traits as playwright, impresario, punster, and choreographer.

A typical Gordon work is a complex collage of performative materials – text, sometimes music, props, actions that range from everyday gestures to technically accomplished dance movements. The dance movements are deceptively casual, their difficulty masked by an uninflected flow. What distinguished Gordon's work from the many creators who mix media is that the materials are interwoven in an extraordinarily rich way. Sally Banes has commented that his work reminds her of that of a cubist painter who 'accumulates and organizes multiple views of a single phenomenon into one composition'. And Arlene Croce has commented that no matter how much Gordon extends a piece, one comes away feeling 'refreshed'.

Gordon takes on the most fundamental and difficult of life's questions with a wry sense of humour; in other words, he is

serious without taking himself too seriously. He loves to undercut his material, to unmask illusions and delusions at the same time as he is creating them. A gesture might illustrate or contradict a statement; an interaction with a prop or between dancers might illuminate or obscure a consideration. He has created works for his own company, for other dance companies – including several major ballet troupes – and more recently for theatre companies. He explores the territory where dance and theatre intersect, creating dazzling formal constructions (and deconstructions) that approach something of the state of music. The beauty of the structures themselves provides a sense of security, no matter how far out of control the world they are describing and confronting may seem. In this sense Gordon is both humanist and classicist, despite his roots in the rebellions of postmodernism.

Gordon's strong verbal and visual sensitivities were encouraged in his early studies. He entered Brooklyn College in New York with the intention of majoring in literature, but then switched to studies in visual design. He came to dance late in his life and by a series of almost accidental occurrences, which included following a pretty girl to her dance class and winning the lead in a school musical production while accompanying a friend. While sitting in a park one day in 1956, he was approached by a stranger who asked him to join his dance company. The stranger turned out to be James Waring, a witty and iconoclastic choreographer who combined both ballet and modern influences. Gordon danced with Waring's company from 1958 to 1962.

Gordon entered the dance world at a time of questioning and reassessment, and at a time when 'everyday' movement was beginning to be considered valid for performance. He was one of the founders and frequent participants in the experimental performances held at Judson Church in the early 1960s, where he presented his first work. He was also a member of the group of dancers who performed with Yvonne Rainer, and it is from her – specifically from her work *Trio A* – that he derived his interest in a way of moving that had an uninflected quality. He subsequently helped to form, and was a core member of, the Grand Union, that small but highly influential improvisational ensemble that emerged from Rainer's group. From 1970 to 1976 this company challenged many prevalent notions of what a dance performance could be, testing the boundaries from performance to performance, often with little advance preparation. The performances would frequently include verbal commentary on the dancers' activities, manipulation of props, and the evolution of motifs of items from one performance to the next – all of which became characteristic of Gordon's work as well. Gordon distinguished himself as a mischief-maker from the start, and as a frequent source of many humorous occurrences. Although once into dance he trained seriously, he never considered himself to have the technical accomplishment or prowess of other company members; he did, however, have an understanding of technique and a strong performing presence.

Gordon's own early work, seven pieces created from 1962 to 1966, were varied. The most memorable appears to have been a longer work called *Random Breakfast* (1963), a duet featuring Gordon and his wife Valda Setterfield, whom he had married in 1960. (British-born and ballet-trained, she was one of the early and enduring members of the Merce Cunningham Dance Company. She continues to play an integral role in much of Gordon's work.) One section of *Random Breakfast* involved a spoof of many different approaches to choreography. Like the other Judson participants, Gordon questioned traditional composition classes, such as those of Louis Horst. He also went a step further and questioned the methods of his fellow rebels and of their mentor and composition teacher Robert Dunn.

Gordon stopped creating his own work in 1966 for a period of five years, when one

experimental piece received negative audience reaction and some very harsh reviews. By his own admission he knew the material he was using was unpleasant – it included gestures like holding his crotch and spitting – and he wasn't quite sure why he was doing it. He resumed choreography in 1972. For the next several years he created work with Setterfield, sometimes with his colleagues, and added on other dancers as needed. He didn't really want a formal company, or one under his name, so in 1978 he compromised by creating a company called 'David Gordon/Pick-Up Company', legitimizing the ad-hoc groups he had been using.

His work in the 1970s established some of the concerns that interest him throughout his career. He realized that although many of the Judson generation, especially Yvonne Rainer, used everyday events and commentary, their purpose in doing so was to diminish theatricality. Gordon realized he loved theatricality and he wanted to use 'mundane means to a magical end'. In his works, running commentaries on process or everyday events would begin to take on almost epic proportion and autobiographical details would achieve the impact of universal truth.

As many of his titles indicate, he would often incorporate bits of one work into another or elaborate on earlier themes. He began to explore the ways in which a seemingly simple movement, such as a hand gesture, could be repeated, refracted, and reorganized into a surprisingly complex and witty structure. He became fascinated with the stop-action photographs of Eadweard Muybridge, creating a solo for Setterfield based on forty-four poses in *One Part of the Matter* (1972). In 1974, he explored a wide range of possible ways to dance with a simple folding chair in the aptly titled *Chair*. Although chairs would show up in many later works, becoming almost a signature prop, he approached other props with similarly thorough explorations, such as a frame (in *Framework*, 1983), cloth banners

119

(in *My Folks*, 1984), and a ladder (in versions of *Punch and Judy*, 1992).

Gordon had been supporting himself financially by designing windows, chiefly for a chain of Japanese stores, Azuma, a job that offered him ample opportunity to manipulate and have fun with visual designs and materials and which won him an underground reputation for his wit and style. In the mid-1970s he began to participate as a consultant on government grants panels, including the New York State Council for the Arts and the National Endowment for the Arts, for which he also served several years as Dance Chairman. He had begun to win the approval of distinguished critics such as David Vaughan, Dale Harris, and *The New Yorker*'s Arlene Croce. He also began to win grant money which enabled him to concentrate his full energy on creating new work.

During the 1980s he was exceptionally prolific, creating as many as six works in a year. In 1981 he had his first three commissions outside America – *Counter Revolution* for the Extemporary Dance Theatre in London, *Big Eyes* for Werkcentrum Dans in the Netherlands, and *Pas et Par* for Théâtre du Silence in Lyon. Noting that everything in his career had been ephemeral, he began to explore video documentation as well as the creation of new material for video. In 1982 he created *TV Reel*, a richly complex work which involved the interaction of live dancers with video projections of the same dancers.

In 1983, in addition to creating *Framework* – a complex visual manipulation with prop design by Power Boothe – for his own company, and four works for other companies, he embarked on his first major collaboration, *The Photographer*, a full-evening work devoted to the life and career of Muybridge, which was a prestigious commission for the Brooklyn Academy of Music's Next Wave Festival. As choreographer, Gordon collaborated with distinguished colleagues, including the composer

Philip Glass and the stage director Joanne Akailaitis.

Gordon created, in 1984, his first piece for a ballet company – *Piano Movers* for the Dance Theater of Harlem, set to music by Thelonius Monk. The following year he created *Field, Chair, and Mountain* for the American Ballet Theatre (ABT). It was set to the music of the nineteenth-century Irish composer John Field. Each of its twenty dancers – two principals, six soloists, and a corps of twelve – had a simple folding chair. This familiar Gordon prop was now being manipulated and danced upon by ballet dancers doing ballet steps. The 'mountain' was part of the scenery, a large picture which rose up at the back of the dancers towards the end of the ballet. Another important scenic element (by designer Santo Loquasto) was a continuously evolving scroll with an oriental tone. Though this was a very beautiful and poetic work, its stylistic qualities riled some audience members sufficiently to elicit at least one angry and much-commented-about 'boo' on opening night. In general, however, both audience and critical reaction was highly favourable.

Gordon was invited to do further work for ABT and for its virtuosic director, Mikhail Baryshnikov. In 1986 he created a witty comedic piece, *Murder*, a send-up of various ballet genres in the form of a detective story, with sets and costumes by Edward Gorey, the famed master of gothic parody. The plot involved characters each of whom had a form of the name 'Smith' (e.g. Smythe, Lady Smith, Psmith, Granny Smith, etc.) with Baryshnikov in several pivotal roles, including that of a mad scientist, the butler (a prime suspect), and the heroine/victim who, once 'killed', would not stay put in her coffin. (This ballet was featured in a television production, *David Gordon's Made in U.S.A.*, which also included a new duet for Baryshnikov and Setterfield.)

In 1987 Gordon began work on his ambitious project *United States*. Although most critics called its funding plan ingenious, their reaction to its artistry was less enthusiastic. Twenty-seven organizations in sixteen states had agreed to fund sections of the work each of which was to feature local talent and references. The first full evening included material representing Minnesota (*Minnesota*), San Francisco (*Sang and Sang*), and New York City (*Pounding the Beat*, and *Slaughter*). New England material – a recording of a discussion with poet Robert Frost about the process of writing poetry – was used to introduce the other sections and provide transitions. Although massive research had been involved in preparing the material, some critics felt the material may have overwhelmed Gordon. His creation seemed to lack the clockwork precision they had come to admire, and some of his artistic choices were criticized for being too obvious or pat (for example, representing New York by a mock mugging and San Francisco with the Tony Bennett song). Perhaps in response to their reaction, the second full evening of material, which premiered a year later, drew on music, incidents, and readings from many geographic regions, but was organized into more complex conglomerates titled 'Birds, Trees and the Birthday of Congress' and 'Weather'. Perhaps the work was meant to be looser, more exploratory, mysterious, and evocative, an associative collage rather than a cubist painting, a different sort of poetry from that which he had created before.

Much of Gordon's work in the 1990s moved more explicitly into the realm of pure theatre. *The Mysteries And What's So Funny?* (1990–91), with wildly imaginative sets and costumes by Red Grooms and music by Philip Glass, featured Setterfield in the role of Marcel Duchamp, icon of the surrealist avant-garde. It addressed the question 'What is art?' (recalling a final exam Gordon had once been given by one of his favourite art teachers, Ad Reinhardt, which asked three questions: 'What is art?', 'What is is?' and 'What is what?'). Gordon's text for the

work was later published in the anthology *Grove New American Theater* (1993).

One of the subplots of *The Mysteries* was family dynamics. Gordon addressed this theme explicitly in his remarkable *The Family Business* (1994), which featured his own real family – himself, Setterfield, and their son Ain Gordon – in a comic story about a semi-functional family. The work was in fact a collaboration with his son, who had already been establishing himself as a successful writer, director, and performer. Rather than responding competitively or jealously, Gordon placed his son's work in the context of other family businesses, such as the plumbing family in the story, in which it is quite usual for a son to follow in his father's footsteps (or theatrical family traditions in many cultures where generations of family members are in the profession).

Also in 1994, at the invitation of Robert Brustein (himself an outspoken and controversial theatrical director, writer and educator), Gordon directed and 'choreographed' *Schlemiel, the First*, a play by Brustein based on stories by Isaac Bashevis Singer. It featured a klezmer band playing traditional Jewish songs onstage. Gordon's 'everyday'-movement manipulations worked beautifully on professional actors. John Lahr, writing in *The New Yorker*, praised the work as 'fresh and elegant' and claimed it put the joy back into musical theatre, noting it 'dares the musical to go back to its beginnings and start again'.

Some observers continue to find Gordon's work difficult to watch. Although dance can often be a universal language, communicating in ways that cross boundaries of culture and tradition, *theatrical* dance sometimes communicates in a dialect that is almost limited to its creator. Gordon is a complex and individual poet of the performing arts at a time when much of the dance audience is still barely literate or only able to tolerate the most traditional or linear of narratives. Gordon is fond of saying that just because *Sleeping Beauty*, one of the great classics of the ballet reper- tory, is a beautiful ballet, does not mean that it is the only thing we should ever watch. Some of his contemporaries who were also rebels felt it necessary to destroy the past in order to move into the future. Gordon, however, can see the value of traditions even as he questions them. He likes having it both ways, and shows us that we can.

Katy Matheson

Biographical details

Born in Brooklyn, New York, 14 July 1936. **Studied** fine arts and visual design at Brooklyn College (now part of City University of New York): BA in 1957; studied dance with James Waring from 1956. **Career** Danced with the James Waring Dance Company, 1958–62; co-founder of Judson Dance Theater, 1962; dancer with Yvonne Rainer's company, 1966–70; began as choreographer in 1960, showing own work at the Living Theatre and with first Judson Dance perfor- mances, 1962–66; did no choreography, 1966–71; founding member, Grand Union, 1970 (company disbanded, 1976); presented work as David Gordon/Pick Up Co. from 1971: group incorpo- rated as the Pick Up Performance Company, 1978. Has also staged work for Extemporary Dance Theatre, Werkcentrum Dans (Netherlands), Théâtre du Silence (Lyon), Dance Theater of Harlem, Group Recherche Chorégraphique de l'Opéra de Paris (GRCOP), American Ballet Theatre, Rambert Dance Company, and Baryshnikov's White Oak Dance Project. Married dancer Valda Setterfield in 1960. **Awards** Guggenheim Fellowship, 1981 and 1987; New York Dance and Performance Award ('Bessie'), 1984 and 1991; Obie Award, 1992 and 1994.

Works

Gordon's works have often used live or prere- corded language as well as (or instead of) musical compositions.

Helen's Dance (mus. Satie, 1962), *Mannequin Dance* (1962), *Mama Goes Where Papa Goes* (1962), *Honey Sweetie Dust Dance* (1963), *Random Breakfast* (1963), *Silver Pieces (Fragments)* (1964), *Walks and Digressions* (1966), *Sleepwalking* (1971), *David Gordon Doing Windows* (1972), *Co-Incidents* (with Douglas Dunn, 1972), *Oh Yes* (1972), *One Part of the Matter* (1972), *The Matter (I)* (1972), *The Matter*

(II) (including *Oh Yes, Men's Dance, One Part, Mannequin;* 1972), *Liberty* (1972), *Chair, Alternatives 1 Through 5* (1974), *One Act Play* (1974), *Spilled Milk Variations* (1974), *Chair* (includes *Symmetrical Form,* 1975), *Times Four* (1976; revised version later the same year), *Personal Inventory* (1976), *Wordsworth and the Motor* (1977), *Mixed Solo* (1978), *What Happened* (1978), *Not Necessarily Recognizable Objects* (or *Wordsworth Rides Again;* 1978), *Lifting Duet* (1979), *Solo Score* (1979), *Song and Dance* (1979), *Close Up* (1979), *The Matter (Plus and Minus)* (1979), *An Audience with the Pope, or This Is Where I Came In* (1979), *Soft Broil* (1980), *Double Identity Part One* (1980), *Untitled Solo* (1980), *Dorothy and Eileen* (1980), *Untitled Solo* (as a trio, 1980), *By Two* (1980), *Counter Revolution* (1981), *Profile* (1981), *Double Identity Part Two* (1981), *Phone Call* (1981), *Grote Ogen [Big Eyes]* (1981), *Pas et Par* (1981), *Big Eyes II* (1982), *Trying Times* (1982), *10 Minute TV* (1982), *TV Reel* (1982), *Passing Sentence* (1983), *Short Order* (1983), *Framework* (1983), *The Photographer* (1983), *Limited Partnership* (1983), *Passing Through* (1983), *A Plain Romance Explained* (1984), *My Folks* (1984), *Piano Movers* (mus. Thelonius Monk, 1984), *Field Study* (1984), *Negotiable Bonds* (1984), *Eleven Women in Reduced Circumstances* (1985), *Four Man Nine Lives* (1985), *Nine Lives* (1985), *Offenbach Suite* (1985), *Four Cornered Moon* (1985), *Beethoven and Boothe* (1985), *Field, Chair, and Mountain* (mus. John Field, 1985), *Bach and Offenbach* (1986), *Murder* (1986), *The Seasons* (1986; revised version, 1987), *Transparent Means for Travelling Light* (1986), *Renard* (opera by Stravinsky, 1986), *Panel* (for television, 1986), *Minnesota* (part of *United States,* 1987), *David Gordon's Made in U.S.A.* (for television, 1987), *Four Stories* (1988), *Sang and Sang* (part of *United States,* 1988), *Mates* (1988), *My Folks* (for television, 1988), *Pounding the Beat, and Slaughter* (part of *United States,* 1988), *Weather* (part of *United States,* 1989), *Birds, Trees and the Birthday of Congress* (part of *United States,* 1989), *United States* (full version, 1989), *The Mysteries and What's So Funny?* (text Gordon; mus. Philip Glass, 1990–91), *Punch and Judy* (1992), *Punch and Judy Get Divorced* (for televi- sion, 1992), *The Family Business* (with son Ain Gordon, 1994), *Schlemiel, the First* (musical play by Robert Brustein, 1994), *Punch and Judy Get Divorced* (theatre version, 1996).

Further reading

Interviews with Sally Banes, in 'An Interview with David Gordon', *Eddy* (New York), Winter 1977; with Nancy Stark Smith, in 'David Gordon and

Valda Setterfield Talk about Labels, Madmen, Vanity, and More' and 'Part 2: Talking about Making Work, Not Making Work, Teaching, and More', *Contact Quarterly*, Winter 1979 and Spring/Summer 1980; with Allen Robertson, in 'Clever Cookie', *Ballet News*, March 1982; with Chris de Marigny, in 'Newfield – New Horizons', *Dance Theatre Journal*, Winter 1984.

Articles Karen Smith, 'David Gordon's *The Matter*', *Drama Review*, September 1972; Robb Baker, 'Grand Union: Taking a Chance on Dance', *Dance Magazine*, October 1973; David Gordon, 'It's about Time', *Drama Review* (postmodern dance issue), March 1975; Elizabeth Kendall, 'The Grand Union: Our Gang', *Ballet Review*, 5(4), 1975/76; Jennifer Dunning, 'Something Old, Something New', *Dance Magazine*, July 1977; B. Barr, 'David Gordon's *What Happened*', *Drama Review*, September 1979; Amanda Smith, 'David Gordon: Keeping the Options Open', *Dance Magazine*, February 1981; John Percival, 'Atlantic Crossing', *Dance and Dancers*, September 1981; Arlene Croce, 'Making Work', *The New Yorker*, 29 November 1982; Alastair Macaulay, 'Not Actually Extemporising', *Dance Theatre Journal*, May 1983; Amanda Smith, 'Autobiography and the Avant-Garde', *Dance Magazine*, January 1985; Valda Setterfield, 'The Making of *Field, Chair, and Mountain*', *Ballet Review*, Spring 1985; Susan Reiter, 'Man in Demand', *Ballet News*, May 1985; Judith Mackrell, 'Words Words Words', *Dance Theatre Journal*, Spring 1985; Alastair Macaulay, 'Umbrellosis: Karole Armitage, David Gordon, Mark Morris, and Then the Rest', *Dancing Times*, January 1986; 'David Gordon', in *Contemporary Biography Yearbook*, 1994.

Books Don McDonagh, *The Complete Guide to Modern Dance*, New York, 1976; Sally Banes, 'David Gordon: The Ambiguities', in her *Terpsichore in Sneakers: Post-modern Dance*, Boston, 1980; Arlene Croce, *Going to the Dance*, New York, 1982; Deborah Jowitt, *The Dance in Mind*, Boston, 1985; Arlene Croce, *Sight Lines*, New York, 1987; David Gordon, *The Mysteries and What's so Funny?* (text of the work), in *Grove New American Theater*, edited by Michael Feingold, New York, 1993.

BILL T. JONES

Bill T. Jones's significance as a choreographer is virtually inseparable from his eloquence as a performer. In both fields he exhibits a soul-searching, missionary zeal. He is a humanist with a multifarious political agenda, using dance to ask passionate questions about life.

It is impossible to consider Jones's output as a dancemaker without taking into account the late Arnie Zane. Jones has described himself and Zane, partners in every sense of the word, as 'a continent of two'. Jones's career can be divided into roughly three phases: first, his early work with Zane; second, the pieces produced in the company, formed in 1982, that still bears both their names; and finally, all that Jones has done both for and independent of the company since 1988, when half of that continent submerged as a result of Zane's AIDS-related death.

A prime component of their creative relationship was the attraction of, and tension between, opposites. Zane was short and springy, with a speedy agility and pugilistic directness that bounced off the tall, muscular Jones's dark silkiness. They met at the State University of New York, Binghampton, in 1971. Jones, a college athlete who was the tenth of twelve children born to Baptist-Methodist migrant farm workers, was hoping to become a professional actor. Zane, of Italian-Catholic and Lithuanian-Jewish extraction, had a degree in art history with a particular focus on photography. Their initial kinetic common ground was contact improvisation, an intimate, free-form method of movement (traces of it can still be detected in Jones's work) that dovetailed arrestingly with their highly autobiographical onstage dialogues.

Jones has always been a charismatic, even confrontational, talker who has apparently little problem making public his private thoughts or feelings. As recently as 1992, in the solo *Last Night on Earth*, Jones, clad only in white briefs, combined semi-spontaneous meditations on the history of his pin-up physique with gestures and poses abstracted into design. The result highlighted the fine line between self-aware honesty, a clarion issue for Jones, and attitudinizing self-indulgence, an accusation sometimes lobbed at him by critics.

In 1974, Jones and Zane co-founded American Dance Asylum in Binghampton. It served as a forum for a series of experimental solos and duets. Zane was initially discomfited by the kind of naked stream-of-consciousness storytelling and wordgames that Jones was pushing for. (In one of their early pieces he dealt with his fears by speaking in Dutch.) Jones eventually compromised, agreeing to a more scripted, less personal use of speech in their joint work. Between 1979 and 1980 the pair devised a trilogy – *Monkey Run Road, Blauvelt Mountain* and *Valley Cottage* – that put them on the international dance map. These were pieces marked by an intellectual rigour and purposeful physical vitality, overlaid with their own mutual warmth and candour.

Given the notoriety generated by their work, the logical next step was to form a company of dancers. The new recruits were selected as much for individual personalities as for their technical strengths and stamina; differences and contrasts remain key company watchwords. Jones's and Zane's own differences, however stormy, served them well as co-artistic leaders. Zane was the organized thinker and director, while Jones tended toward the intuitive, concentrating on developing shapes and phrases into a cohesive yet diverse movement vocabulary.

In 1983, Jones scored a hit with *Fever Swamp*, a celebratory, crowd-pleasing all-male sextet fashioned for the Alvin Ailey American Dance Theater. Ailey, arch-populist and founder of America's first completely multi-racial dance company, figures prominently among Jones's influences, along with Martha Graham, José Limón, and the great wave of postmodernism that stretches from Merce Cunningham, through the Judson Dance Theater and Grand Union,

and beyond. In addition, Jones, who has sometimes referred to himself as a poet, has admitted an affinity with fragmentary forms or artistic expression such as modern music and structuralist filmmaking. *Fever Swamp* is one of his 'danciest' dances, proving that, as he put it, 'I don't have to wear my ideology on my sleeve'. When the dance was incorporated into his and Zane's troupe, the casting became gender-blind both by necessity (there weren't six men in the company to do it) and philosophy (Jones and Zane believed in breaking down male/female dance stereotypes).

Together they received even more attention with *Secret Pastures* (1984), an aggressively hip, wacky company collaboration with the graffiti artist Keith Haring, fashion designer Willi Smith, and art-rock composer Peter Gordon and his Love of Life Orchestra. Add to this trendy line-up the gymnastic, jazzy, and decidedly eclectic choreography, plus the semblance of a wildly allegorical, neo-Frankenstein plot, and you have a frank bid for commercial viability and accessibility. Jones danced the role of the Fabricated Man, the literal brainchild of Zane's Mad Scientist, fêted by society and, in turn, adopting its tenets of greed, lust, and violence. The casting carried its own oblique commentary about a black man's role in a predominantly white creative milieu.

To some, the gutsy, uncompromising daring of the intense first phase of the Jones/Zane partnership seemed to have given way to a more streamlined urban chic. Their raw energy was refined to accommodate bigger stages, an increasingly global audience, and the duo's broadened comprehension of what their art could do. The company is still known for its risky, edgy, all-out style, but the theatricality now carries an extra emotional charge. Zane's premature death, and Jones's own HIV-positive status, has lent a greater urgency and depth to the latter's choreography. Rather than disband the company, Jones decided to keep it going as a living memorial to Zane. He has injected his personal understanding of grief and survival into the spectrum of social and aesthetic concerns once shared with Zane.

The year following Zane's death, Jones produced three works, all of which dealt, directly or indirectly, with loss. White sheets and draperies set the tone in *Absence* (1989), a slow, sombre piece about mourning and isolation, which uses statuesque silhouettes, waltzing, mime, and crawling. *D-Man in the Waters* (1989), its polar opposite, is a sporty, joyous display of ensemble virtuosity, set to a Mendelssohn octet and dedicated to another company member who died of AIDS. The music of Kurt Weill and Bessie Smith permeates *Soon* (1988), five duets infused with feelings of romantic and sexual longing and separation that may be performed by one or two pairs of dancers of the same or opposite sex.

Mortality plays a part in Jones's later works. A death-like figure wearing a white hooded jacket stalks and capers about the emotional landscape of *Love Defined*, commissioned by Lyon Opéra Ballet in 1992. (Jones was appointed resident choreographer there in 1994–95.) In this dance a balletic spin is given to expressive, syncopated street rhythms cued by the plaintive pop music of Daniel Johnston, an eccentric Texan whose voice might best be described as scrawny. *Achilles Loved Patroclus*, a 1993 *tour-de-force* solo for Arthur Aviles, a former company dancer with a compact power similar to Zane's, weds together notions of heroism, homoeroticism, and death.

One of Jones's most comprehensive, accomplished pieces to date is the evening-length epic, *Last Supper at Uncle Tom's Cabin/ The Promise Land* (1990). This controversial examination of racism, sexuality, and faith was inspired by a mixed bag of sources: Leonardo Da Vinci's painting; Harriet Beecher Stowe's nineteenth-century novel about slavery during the American Civil War; African-American vaudeville, particularly c. 1920s Harlem; and a deck of soft-core porn cards. The actual artistic

ingredients were equally varied: saxophonist/composer Julius Hemphill's dissonant yet elegiac score; text, including excerpts from playwright Leroi Jones' *Dutchman*, a blistering two-hander from 1964, and fragments of Martin Luther King's 'I have a dream' speech (1968), recited backwards; and movement ranging from ironic variations of popular steps to pungent modern dance. Combining the sweep of opera with the impact of political statement, the show presented images of power, struggle, sacrifice, humiliation, and oppression. By the finale, however, the fury and desperation fuelling the whole piece were set aside and overcome, as a swarm of dancers of all shapes and sizes filled and filed back and forth across the stage, united by their complete or (in some performances) partial nudity.

Jones has since choreographed and directed opera and theatre productions. In the early 1990s, he launched the survival project, which culminated in a full-length dance-theatre work called *Still/Here* (1994). The subject was mortality, with content culled from workshops held in eleven American cities with people coping with life-threatening illnesses. It is at once his most controversial and acclaimed work to date.

Still/Here, as its title indicates, is split into two distinct parts. The first and more elegiac half, relating to reactions to a diagnosis, utilizes the workshop members' own words, set to music by composer Kenneth Frazelle and sung by folk singer Odetta in a voice crackling with hard-won wisdom. The tone is internalized and spiritual, with the dancers clad in white, grey, and pale blue outfits. The second, more corporeal and affirmative section is about living with the prospect of death. The performers wear identical costumes, only dyed red. The choreography is correspondingly more driven and dynamic, fuelled by the music of rock guitarist Vernon Reid. The kinetic vocabulary blends the odd balletic step with colloquial gestures and bold contemporary moves. Nothing the dancers do is conventionally literal, yet the shapes, forms, and rhythms Jones uses convey tremendous feeling.

Jones has insisted that *Still/Here*, which features Gretchen Bender's extensive and haunting video footage of the workshop participants, was not about death but rather was intended as a tool for learning 'how we can become more alive'. In most quarters it was regarded as an unqualified artistic triumph. Arlene Croce, dance critic of the prestigious *New Yorker* magazine, was the loudest voice of dissension. Her refusal even to see the production, on the grounds that as 'victim art' it begged her sympathy and therefore made itself impossible to be written about objectively, engendered both enormous debate within the arts world and additional publicity for the show itself.

Jones's subsequent dances have leaned towards the lyrical and abstract, although never at the expense of drama. For Lyon he made the evening-length *24 Frames per Second* (1995), an impressionistic tribute to the 100th anniversary of the Lumière brothers' invention of the cinema, and the smaller-scale *Green and Blue* (1997), a subtle and ghostly response to two lesser-known string works of Mozart. Poetry provided a life-affirming source for two 1996 pieces for Jones's own company. *Ballad*, a suite of ensemble and fleeting solo dances, is set to Dylan Thomas's readings of four of his own poems, while *Ursonate*, co-choreographed with dancer Darla Villani, draws on a 1928 sound-poem by Dada master Kurt Schwitters to impart an exciting sense of structured disconnection. The collage-like quality spilled over into the engaging, and deliberately disorientating, *Lisbon* (1997), virtually a choreographic retrospective marked by jarring changes of action, speed, light, and music ranging from hard-driving rock to undulant Latin folk rhythms.

In 1997 Jones embarked on another evening-length work. *We Set Out Early ... Visibility Was Poor*, unlike *Last Supper ...* or *Still/Here*, opts for a kind of mysterious communal adventure in lieu of 'in-your-face' polemics. Hard to pin down but seamlessly constructed, and loaded with vibrant movement, this cryptic, polished piece invites an intuitive response. Whether it points to a new direction in the unpredictable Jones's ongoing body of work is anybody's guess.

Donald Hutera

Biographical details

Born in Bunnell, Florida, United States, 15 February 1952. **Studied** African dance with Percival Borde, ballet with Ernest Paganano and Maggie Black, contact improvisation with Lois Welk, modern dance technique with Linda Grande and Humphrey Weidman, improvisation with Birchard Bull, and jazz ballet with Cova Pullman; also attended State University of New York at Binghampton and State University College at Brockport, 1970–73. **Career** Cofounder, with dancer-choreographer Arnie Zane, American Dance Asylum in Binghampton, New York, 1974–76; toured independently as dancer-choreographer; co-founder (again with Zane), Bill T. Jones/Arnie Zane Dancers, 1982, continuing as sole artistic director of Bill T. Jones/Arnie Zane Dance Company after Zane's death in 1988; resident choreographer (honorific title) for Lyon Opéra Ballet, 1994–97. Has also choreographed for the Alvin Ailey dancers, and worked as choreographer and director for opera companies, including Houston Grand Opera, Glyndebourne Festival Opera, New York City Opera, Boston Lyric Opera, as well as Lyon Opéra Ballet. **Awards and honours** Choreographic Fellowship from the National Endowment for the Arts, 1980, 1981, 1982; New York Dance and Performance Award ('Bessie'), 1986 and 1989; Dorothy B. Chandler Performing Arts Award, 1991; *Dance Magazine* Award, 1993; MacArthur 'Genius' Award, 1994; Bard College (Annandale-on-Hudson, New York) honorary doctorate, 1996.

Works

Pas de Deux (with Arnie Zane, 1971), *Pas de Deux for Two* (with Arnie Zane, 1973), *A Dance with Durga Devi* (mus. Tibetan temple chants, Bessie Smith, 1974), *Negroes for Sale* (sound-tape Jones, 1974), *Entrances* (1974), *Track Dance* (mus. Lou Grassi, 1974), *Could Be Dance* (1975), *Across the Street There is a Highway* (text Jones, mus. percussion, 1975), *Woman in Drought* (1975), *Impersonations* (1975), *Everybody Works/All*

Beasts Count (mus. Jessye Fuller songs, 1975), *For You* (1977), *Stomps* (1977), *Walk* (1977), *A Man* (1977), *Asymmetry: Every Which Way* (mus. Lou Grassi, 1977), *Da Sweet Streak ta Love Land* (mus. Otis Redding, 1977), *Floating the Tongue* (text Jones, 1978), *Naming Things is Only the Intention to Make Things* (text Jones, singing Jeanne Lee, 1978), *Progresso* (1978), *By the Water* (texts by Jones and Sheryll Sutton, 1978), *Echo* (mus. Helen Thorington, 1979), *Addition* (1979), *Circle in Distance* (text and choreography with Sheryl Sutton, 1979), *Monkey Run Road* (with Arnie Zane; mus. Helen Thorington, 1979), *Blauvelt Mountain* (with Arnie Zane; mus. Helen Thorington, 1979), *Dance in the Trees* (mus. Jeff Cohan, Pete Simonson, 1980), *Open Places: A Dance in June* (mus. Dan Hummel, Mark Gaurmond, Thomas Berry, 1980), *Untitled Duet* (with Sarry Satenstrom; mus. Dan Hummel, Marcia Miget, Dartanyan Brown, 1980), *Valley Cottage* (with Arnie Zane; mus. Helen Thorington, 1980), *Balancing the World* (1980), *Sisyphus* (solo; mus. Helen Thorington, 1980), *Social Intercourse: Pilgrim's Progress* (mus. Joe Hannon, text and lyrics Jones, 1981), *Break* (mus. George Lewis, 1981), *10: Prologue Performance* (text Jones, 1981), *Ah! Break It!* (mus. Ualalu Calvert Nelson, recorded chants by Jones, 1981), *Three Dances* (mus. Mozart, Peter Gordon; text Jones, 1982), *Shared Distance* (1982), *Duet × 2* (mus. J.S. Bach, 1982), *Continuous Replay* (with Arnie Zane; mus. Bryan Rulon, 1982), *Rotary Action* (with Arnie Zane; mus. Peter Gordon, 1982), *Fever Swamp* (mus. Peter Gordon, 1983), *Naming Things* (with Phillip Mallory Jones and David Hammons; mus. Miles Davis, funeral dirge, 1983), *Intuitive Momentum* (with Arnie Zane; mus. Max Roach, Connie Crothers, 1983), *21* (1983; video version, dir. Tom Bowes, 1984), *Corporate Whimsy* (mus. Bryan Rulon, 1983), *Casino* (mus. Peter Gordon, 1983), *Dances with Brahms* (mus. Brahms, 1984), *Freedom of Information* (with Arnie Zane; mus. David Cunningham, 1984), *Secret Pastures* (with Arnie Zane; mus. Peter Gordon, 1984), *1, 2, 3* (mus. Carl Stone, 1985), *Holzer Duet ... Truisms* (with Lawrence Goldhuber; text Jenny Holzer, soundtape Jones, 1985), *M.A.K.E.* (text Jones and Arnie Zane, 1985), *Pastiche* (mus. James Brown, Eric Dolphy; text Jones, Shakespeare, Edith Sitwell, 1985), *Virgil Thompson Etudes* (mus. Virgil Thompson, 1986), *Animal Trilogy* (with Arnie Zane; includes *How to Walk an Elephant*, *Water Buffalo: An Acquired Taste*, and *Sacred Cow: Lifting a Calf Every Day Until It Becomes an Ox*; mus. Conlon Nancarrow, 1986), *Red Room* (mus. Stuart Arbright, Robert Longo, 1987), *Chatter* (mus. Paul Lansky, 1988), *Soon* (mus. Kurt Weill,

Bessie Smith, 1988), *History of Collage Revisited* (with Arnie Zane; mus. Charles R. Amirkhanian, 'Blue' Gene Tyranny, 1988), *Don't Lost Your Eye* (mus. Sonny Boy Williamson, Paul Lansky, 1989), *Forsythia* (text soundtape of Zane, mus. Dufay, 1989), *La Grande Fête* (mus. Paul Lansky, 1989), *It Takes Two* (mus. Ray Charles, Betty Carter, 1989), *Absence* (mus. Penderecki, Berlioz, 1989), *D-Man in the Waters* (mus. Mendelssohn, 1989), *Last Supper at Uncle Tom's Cabin/The Promised Land* (mus. Julius Hemphill, 1990), *New Year* (opera by Tippett, 1989; also television production), *Mother of Three Sons* (opera by Leroy Jenkins, 1990), *Havoc in Heaven* (mus. John Bergamo, 1991), *Broken Wedding* (mus. Klezmer Conservatory Band, 1992), *Die Offnung* (mus. John Oswald, 1992), *Love Defined* (mus. Daniel Johnson, 1992), *Our Respected Dead* (mus. Daniel Johnson, 1992), *Aria* (1992), *Fête* (mus. Rich Goodheart, Paul Lansky, 1992), *Last Night on Earth* (solo; mus. Kurt Weill, Bessie Smith, 1992), *Lost in the Stars* (opera by Kurt Weill, 1992), *After Black Room* (mus. Sarah Plant, 1993), *Achilles Loved Patroclus* (mus. John Oswald, 1993), *War Between the States* (mus. Charles Ives, 1993), *There were so many ...* (mus. John Cage, 1993), *And the Maiden* (mus. Bessie Jones and accompaniment, 1993), *Just You* (mus. various, 1993), *Still/Here* (mus. Kenneth Frazelle, Vernon Reid, 1994), *I Want to Cross Over* (mus. gospel, 1994), *24 Images/Seconde (24 Frames per Second)* (mus. John Oswald, 1995), *Degga* (with drummer Max Roach and writer Toni Morrison, 1995), *Ursonate* (with Darla Villani; sound poem by Kurt Schwitters, 1996), *Ballad* (soundtape of Dylan Thomas reading his poetry, 1996), *Soon* (duet; mus. Weill, Bessie Smith, 1996), *New Duet* (mus. John Oswald and Laurie McDonald, 1996), *Some Songs* (mus. Jacques Brel, 1996), *Bill and Laurie: About the Rounds* (mus. Laurie Anderson, 1996), *Blue Phrase* (mus. Eric Dolphy, 1996), *Love Redefined* (revised version of *Love Defined*; mus. Daniel Johnston, 1996); *Green and Blue* (mus. Mozart, 1997), *Lisbon* (mus. Portuguese folk, Negrito, 1997), *We Set Out Early ...Visibility Was Poor* (mus. Stravinsky, John Cage, Peteris Vasks, 1997).

Further reading

Interviews in *Further Steps: Fifteen Choreographers on Modern Dance*, edited by Connie Kreemer, New York, 1987; with Maya Wallach, in 'A Conversation with Bill T. Jones', *Ballet Review*, Winter 1990/91.

Articles J. Lewis, 'Making Dances from the Soul: The Warm and Startling Images of Bill T. Jones,

Dance Magazine, November 1981; Elizabeth Zimmer, 'Bill T. Jones and Arnie Zane: Solid Citizens of Post-Modernism', *Dance Magazine*, October 1984; B. Laine, 'Trendy Twosome', *Ballet News*, August 1985; Donald Hutera, 'Bill T. Jones Going Naked', *Dance Theatre Journal*, Autumn 1990; Robert Sandla, 'Terra Nova', *Opera News*, October 1991; Maya Wallach, 'Bill T. Jones: In Search of the Promised Land', *Dance Magazine*, October 1991; R. Tracy, 'Bill T. Jones: Full Circle', *Dance Magazine*, October 1992; 'Bill T. Jones', in *Current Biography Yearbook 1993*; Henry Louis Gates, Jr, 'The Body Politic', *The New Yorker*, 28 November 1994; Arlene Croce, 'Discussing the Undiscussable', *The New Yorker*, 26 December 1994 and 2 January 1995 (double issue); Raymond T. Ricketts, 'Working with Bill T. Jones', *Dance Now*, Autumn 1995.

Books Allen Robertson and Donald Hutera, *The Dance Handbook*, Harlow, Essex, 1988; Elizabeth Zimmer and Susan Quasha (eds), *Body Against Body: The Dance and Other Collaborations of Bill T. Jones and Arnie Zane*, Barrytown, New York, 1989; Bill T. Jones, with Peggy Gillespie, *Last Night on Earth* (autobiography), Harmondsworth and New York, 1995.

JAMES KUDELKA

Creating dance for me is a way of being less afraid of life.

(James Kudelka, 1995[1])

A child prodigy is a rare thing among choreographers, but Kudelka produced his first piece at the age of fourteen, and by twenty-one he had created the deeply disturbing, utterly adult ballet, *A Party* (1976). This prompted the Toronto dance critic Penelope Doob to ask in 1977, 'How many choreographers, especially at twenty-one, can make convincingly realistic ballets about grown-ups? ... [H]e just might turn out to be the special choreographer we have been waiting for.'[2] He was. According to Canadian ballerina Karen Kain, Kudelka 'has become the foremost choreographer in this country',[3] and by 1997, at the age of forty-two, he had already made over sixty works, and acquired a rising international reputation.

But *A Party* already exhibited in embryo the essential Kudelkian characteristics: 'physical drive' (to quote the first-cast dancer, Frank Augustyn), sculptural form, precarious weight-sharing between partners, psychological depth, and a troubling theme. (In the 'date rape' *pas de deux*, for instance, Nadia Potts had to support herself arched backwards on one arm, while clinging to her 'rapist' (Augustyn) with the other: the effect was both sculpturally striking and all too sadly appropriate to the nature of date rape itself.)[4] As David Earle has said of Kudelka's work generally, 'Freeze-frame any part of his dances, and you'll have a gorgeous three-dimensional sculpture'[5] – and this is true even in this early piece.

In 1965 Kudelka had arrived at Toronto's National Ballet School, in the words of dancer Victoria Bertram, a 'ten-year-old adult',[6] having lost his grandfather on the same day and having left his large, extended, protective family of chamber musicians for the loneliness of a school dormitory.[7] Kudelka was an intellectual, passionately serious child, given to dark moods; David Earle (who taught Kudelka the Graham technique which has been so influential in his work), says 'James never recovered from the pressures of the school, where he had been ridiculed by his peers but prized for his intelligence by the staff.' Robert Sirman of the National Ballet School has suggested that the theme of humiliation and loneliness that runs through much of this choreography is related to this experience.

Kudelka's time in the company, from 1972, was memorable for his strikingly innovative interpretations of hitherto unnoticed characters, and his skill at mime and his intense stage presence won him ever more important roles (like the lead in Rudi van Dantzig's, *Monument for a Dead Boy*).[8] But it was also claustrophobic and emotionally damaging: the company was under the directorship of Alexander Grant, whose fixation on the Ashton repertoire Kudelka found stifling; he increasingly sought relief in

Graham classes at Toronto Dance Theater (forming a lifelong friendship with David Earle, with whom he has co-choreographed). The chance to work with Les Grands Ballets Canadiens in Montreal (1984–91) was revivifying, and it was there that he produced his first works to win international acclaim, like *In Paradisum* (1983). The then artistic co-director, Daniel Jackson says, 'We not only gave him *carte blanche* to experiment, we made him a principal dancer so he would be challenged both ways ... My head still floats with the images of his invention.'[9]

Kudelka the choreographer still thinks like a dancer: 'I hate the idea of becoming one of *them* – the Artistic Staff', he said in 1995,[10] but by 1996 the luxury of rebellion was vanishing fast, as he progressed from artist in residence to artistic director of the National Ballet of Canada at bewildering speed. Half nostalgic for the days when a corps of six (*The Actress* of 1994) was his largest staging headache, he was now worrying about how to put 120 people on stage in a new *Nutcracker* (1995).[11] Having to 'work to order' to mount a large classic and yet make it his own, he felt he had 'finally earned the right to be a resident choreographer'. And now he was artistic director, he was 'looking around for someone to be artist in residence, to play the role of court jester and give frank feedback, as he did with Reid [Anderson]'. Whether less comfortable as king than as court jester, Kudelka has learned quickly how to make the productions both 'a challenge for me and attractive for an audience'. As his responsibilities have become larger, so has his sense of duty to history: interested now (perforce) in what he calls '"takes" on classical form', he asks questions like, 'if it's a tutu ballet, what should a tutu look like now, and how should you dance in it?'

But perhaps most revealing of Kudelka the man is his concern to 'care about every dancer'[12] in the company he now directs so conscientiously. This might have been predictable from a knowledge of how this most empathetic of choreographers works *with* his dancers during the choreographic process.[13] Karen Kain says that he is 'enigmatic' in rehearsal, that he tells his dancers very little to begin with, but that his 'enormous intelligence and talent' causes her to

> turn myself over to him completely ... he wants us to use our own intelligence and instincts to the fullest ... and then suddenly there will be a moment of discovery far more intense and satisfying than what you might experience at the denouement of a mystery story.[14]

Kudelka's choreography, however, is notoriously and deliberately difficult (he prefers his dancers to be *thinking* constantly). Ballet mistress Anita Paciotti of San Francisco Ballet has said that

> It was clear ... that he had been influenced by modern dance, because he challenges the classical notion of dance as balanced and vertical. James isn't interested in watching something comfortable ... he loves using off-balance, with dancers sharing weight, which is precarious in *pointe* shoes.[15]

She also described Kudelka's choreography as 'the most dangerous' she'd ever worked with, 'but also the most exciting'. Kudelka himself speaks of his penchant for off-balance *pas de deux* work as 'sculptural opportunity', a way of exploring risk because 'having a partner allows you to be off-balance'. His daring technical experimentation translates into immediate emotional impact on stage, as in, for instance, the slow, tense off-balance turn on *pointe* in the Kain/Anderson *pas de deux* from *The Actress*: at this moment the relationship, hitherto enigmatic, between the actress and a former acquaintance takes on a startlingly menacing quality effected by the physics of uneasy dependence.

Among Kudelka's major works, apart from *A Party*, are *Washington Square* (from

1977, an ambitious rendering of the Henry James novel done when Kudelka was only twenty-two), *In Paradisum* (about terminal illness and the process of dying), *Fifteen Heterosexual Duets* (1991, a modern piece made for Toronto Dance Theatre), *The Miraculous Mandarin* (1993, about child abuse within a dysfunctional family), and *The Actress* (flashback vignettes of a dancer-actress's life, choreographed semi-biographically for Karen Kain). One is struck, looking over this list, by several things: first, only two of these works (*In Paradisum* and *Fifteen Heterosexual Duets*) are off-*pointe*. Second, many of them are narrative ballets and many deal with serious social or psychological issues. These points are not unrelated: Kudelka himself notes the scarcity in North America of contemporary choreographers working in the classical idiom, and he attributes this to the 'all-encompassing' and 'unhelpful'[16] influence of Balanchine's detached aestheticism. A choreographer more opposite to Balanchine would be hard to imagine. Although he has had many offers to go to the United States and Europe, and has worked in both places, Kudelka's is a distinctively Canadian 'voice', which the United States companies (like the Joffrey and San Francisco Ballet) apparently find appealing: 'They invite me to do what *I* do', he says.

But what exactly does Kudelka do? And what is Canadian about his 'voice'? A sense of inferiority, victimization, and emotional repression are Canadian themes, and they proliferate in Kudelka's ballets: programme notes to *The Miraculous Mandarin*, for instance, describe this narrative ballet as dramatizing 'the salvation and ultimate empowerment of the youngest son', and much (perhaps too much) has been made of the autobiographical implications of that theme for its choreographer.[17] But the theme can also work on a national level, too, as the painful rescue and emergence from cultural colonialism (both European and American) that has taken place precisely in Kudelka's

generation. As for what Kudelka does choreographically, critics often complain that he has no consistent style. He has no visible lineage (although he has been compared to Massine,[18] whose works he does not know). Graham technique, however, encouraged and supplemented by David Earl's gift for mime, has been the most visible influence on the 'contemporary' side of this otherwise innately classical (though never conservative) choreographer. Perhaps a closer look at the off-*pointe* work for which he has become most famous will illustrate the unique character of his work better than labels and generalizations.

In Paradisum is quintessential Kudelka, the natural flexibility and range of modern dance here supported, not emasculated, by the classical precision. As such it is worth some detailed investigation, as exemplifying the elusive Kudelka approach. The piece is also a complex blend of his rare intellectual and interdisciplinary range, with raw emotional and absolutely autobiographical conflict. (Inspired both by the books of Dr Elizabeth Kuebler-Ross on the five stages of dying, and by Kaethe Kollwitz's stark drawings of death and communal grief in wartime Germany, it was also created out of his devastation at his own mother's death).[19] It combines driving and turbulent movement with emphatic gesture, memorable tableaux, and (surprising) moments of ethereal serenity. The sharp changes in mood throughout *In Paradisum* are partly a response to composer Michael Baker's deceptively neutral minimalistic music, periodically disturbed by bursts of quick chromatic half-scales, urgently repeated upwards and downwards, giving the piece its alternatingly frantic and controlled sensibilities. Its use of the modern idiom is so pure and effortless it could have been choreographed by Graham herself, although its appearance is more like the work of contemporary choreographers such as Jiří Kylián or even Nacho Duato. The costumes are Grahamesque, with their simple, tailored lines and flowing skirts; designer

Denis Joffre has deftly captured something of the universality Kudelka strives for in the choreography, the slightly Grecian full-length tunics evoking a classical and timeless dignity and stoicism. Yet there is also a strong sense of Christian tradition – both angelic and monastic – in the overall effect. Both men and women are dressed in full-length skirts, and the lead roles – indeed all the roles – are interchangeably performed by men or women. On consecutive nights the three lead roles (that of the dying person, his or her beloved, and the angelic guide) have been performed either by a woman, a man and a woman (respectively), or by three men. The differences in casting have been striking: the often photographed moment of 'Pietá' (in which the beloved holds the dying person in his lap), for instance, looks very different when both are male. Kudelka has explained that in the male/female casting, the piece takes on a 'more domestic' air; however, in the three-male cast (perhaps most memorably danced by Edward Hillyer, Sylvain LaFortune, and Kudelka himself), the piece takes on a 'more universal' quality: 'the male cast creates something more abstract that people can identify with'.[20] This is what Kudelka was striving for: in response to terminal illness, he says, 'we have to look inside ourselves to see how vast the damage is – one life is many lives.' This is in fact the essence of In Paradisum's message; rarely do choreographers speak so articulately on their own works.

In Paradisum has the Kudelka trademark of demanding, fast-paced intricate movement pattern and natural emotional power. Yet in spite of its emotional resonance for its choreographer, the work finds control through its immersion in pure technique, which in turn transforms, even masks, the emotionalism for the dancers especially.

The piece begins in the initial phase of Kuebler-Ross's five stages of dying: Denial and Isolation, when in Kudelka's words, the 'whole family or community boils up' in shock and resistance to the news of a death,

and then proceeds recognizably, though never slavishly, through the other stages (Anger, Bargaining, Depression, Acceptance). Kudelka's gifts as a mime artist emerge in several leitmotif gestures: the centuries-old one for grief, for instance, of holding one's head in one's hands, is stylized by Kudelka so that the fingers are fanned out to convey starkness and the hands don't quite touch the head – a brilliant suggestion of abstraction and distraction blended in one gesture. The same stylization of gesture occurs when the dying and the beloved embrace each other with starkly straight arms so that the arms (and the dancers' gaze) extend to, but also beyond, the reach of the partner – simultaneously capturing the sense of mutual support yet individual loneliness in the preparation for death or bereavement. Other leitmotifs, especially for the 'family or community', include repeated pirouettes in arabesque performed with swooping arm movements and fists clenched in rage, or open pirouettes in second with awkwardly flexed foot.

The most important leitmotif, again often photographed, is the tableau that begins and ends the piece, in which the dying man reaches upwards (with fingers fanned open), while his companion, one arm wrapped lovingly around him, nevertheless turns away, his head buried in grief, while the 'community' swirls about them. The same tableau ends the piece, but this time with the addition of the third principal, the angelic guide, who kneels beside, with both arms wrapped around the dying man. The guide figure only comes onstage towards the end of the piece, distinguished by (in the all-male cast) the same white skirts as the other two leads, except that he is bare-chested. He has a unique mimic gesture – an arm fully extended to the side with hand sharply angled upwards from the wrist, performing a series of rigid fluttering motions, as if a single wing. Is Kudelka's angel so powerful as to need only one wing – or is he slightly crippled? Each viewer must decide for him- or herself.

Whatever fear of life (or death) Kudelka is exorcising through his choreography, the single most important emotion in all his works is courage. As he has said himself, 'safe is not one of the words you use to describe a dancer or choreographer because you are always at risk', and *In Paradisum* epitomizes the combination of sacrifice, pain and courage that represent at once the cost and the beauty of Kudelka's creativity.

Kathryn Kerby-Fulton

Notes

1 Quoted from the interview in 'Originals in Art', executive producer, Mozes Znaimer (Sleeping Giant Productions, in association with Bravo Television, copyright 1995).
2 'Spotlight on James Kudelka', *Dance Magazine*, March 1977, pp. 72–3.
3 *Movement Never Lies: An Autobiography*, by Karen Kain, with Stephen Godfrey and Penelope Reed Doob (Toronto: McClellend and Stewart, 1994), p. 19.
4 See the photo of this moment in *Kain and Augustyn: A Photographic Study* by Christopher Darling, text by John Fraser, foreword by Rudolf Nureyev (Toronto: Macmillan of Canada, 1977), pp. 118, and 114 for Augustyn's comment.
5 Quoted by Paula Citron in 'James Kudelka: Out of the Depths', *Dance Magazine*, February 1994, p. 96.
6 Quoted in Doob, 'Spotlight on James Kudelka', p. 71.
7 From 'Originals in Art'.
8 The best account of Kudelka's career as a *dancer* is Doob's (see below).
9 Quoted in Citron, p. 96.
10 'Originals in Art'.
11 Penelope Doob, 'Balancing Virtue and Necessity: The Dual Roles of James Kudelka', *Performance*, February 12–16 (1997), pp. 11–17; pp. 13–14 for the quotations from Kudelka which follow in the remainder of this paragraph.
12 Doob, p. 13.
13 From 'Originals in Art'; a good demonstration of Kudelka's sensitive studio manner during the choreographic process can be seen in 'Dance for Modern Times', written and produced by Moze Mossanen (with participation of CBC, Telefilm Canada, the Ontario Film Development Corporation and TV Ontario), copyright Mossanen Productions, 1987) – even in contrast to other choreographers in the same file.

14 *Movement Never Lies*, p. 254.
15 Cited in Citron, p. 97.
16 From 'Originals in Art'.
17 See, for instance, Leland Windreich, 'Full Circle: Love, Sex and Death in James Kudelka's *The Miraculous Mandarin*', *Dance International*, Fall 1993, pp. 10–15, which is typical of Kudelka criticism in stressing the autobiographical.
18 Windreich, p. 14.
19 Complete programme notes can be found in the October 1983 issue of *Performance* (O'Keefe Center for the Performing Arts, Toronto), p. 11. On the five stages, see Kuebler-Ross's, *On Death and Dying* (New York: Macmillan, 1969); there are many reproductions of Kollwitz's drawings, but I consulted those in Ida Katharine Rigby, *War-Revolution-Weimar* (San Diego University Press, 1983). I would like to thank my colleague, Edward Zeitlow, for advice about Kuebler-Ross and Kollwitz. *In Paradisum* may be seen in Mossanen's film, 'Dance for Modern Times'.
20 All the following comments by Kudelka and Hillyer on *In Paradisum* are quoted from the interview segments of Mossanen's 'Dance for Modern Times'.

Biographical details

Born in Newmarket, Ontario, Canada, 10 September 1955. **Studied** as a child at the National Ballet School (director Alexander Grant), Toronto, 1965–72; also studied Martha Graham technique at the Toronto Dance Theatre, under David Earle. **Career** Danced with the National Ballet of Canada, Toronto, from 1972, becoming soloist in 1976, and principal dancer from 1981 to 1986; early choreography was for the National Ballet of Canada workshops, 1973–80; then company choreographer in Toronto, 1980–82; principal dancer and (from 1984) resident choreographer, Les Grands Ballets Canadiens, Montreal, 1984–91; artist in residence, from 1992, then artistic director (succeeding Reid Anderson), National Ballet of Canada, from June 1996. Has also choreographed for Joffrey Ballet, San Francisco Ballet, Montréal Danse, Toronto Dance Theatre, Margie Gillis, Les Ballets Jazz de Montréal, American Ballet Theatre, Birmingham Royal Ballet, Hubbard Street Dance (Chicago), Peggy Baker, and the Joyce Trisler Company. **Awards** Jean Chalmers Award (National Ballet of Canada), 1975; Isadora Duncan Award, San Francisco, 1988; Dora Mavor Moore Award, 1992.

Works

Sonata (Moods of Intimacy) (mus. Franck, 1973), *Apples* (mus. Tchaikovsky, 1974), *Sonata* (mus. Franck, 1974), *A Party* (mus. Britten, 1976), *Washington Square* (mus. Michael Conway Baker, 1977; revised version, 1979), *Bach Pas de Deux* (mus. J.S. Bach, 1979), *Windsor Pas de Deux* (mus. Copland, 1979), *The Rape of Lucrece* (mus. Frank Martin, 1980), *Playhouse* (mus. Shostakovich, 1980), *All Night Wonder* (mus. Britten, 1981), *Passage* (mus. Tallis, 1981), *Intimate Letter* (mus. Janáček, 1981), *Genesis* (mus. Stravinsky, 1982), *Dido and Aeneas* (with David Earle and others; mus. Purcell, 1982), *Hedda* (mus. Norma Beecroft, 1983), *In Paradisium* (mus. Michael J. Baker, 1983), *Court of Miracles* (with David Earle, Christopher House, and others; 1983), *Alliances* (mus. Brahms, 1984), *unfinished business* (mus. Michael J. Baker, 1984), *Dracula* (mus. Michael J. Baker, 1985), *Death of an Old Queen* (mus. Tallis, 1985), *Diversion* (mus. Britten, 1985), *The Heart of the Matter* (mus. Prokofiev, 1986), *Vers la glace* (with Margie and Christopher Gillis; mus. Eugene Friesen, 1986), *Collisions* (mus. Henry Kucharzyk, 1986), *Soudain l'hiver dernier* (mus. Gavin Bryars, 1987), *Dreams of Harmony* (mus. Schumann, 1987), *Le Sacre du Printemps* (mus. Stravinsky, 1987), *'the wakey nights'* (solo; mus. Michael J. Baker, 1987), *Concerto Grosso* (mus. Jean Papineau-Couture, 1988), *In Camera* (mus. Kevin Volans, 1988), *La Salle des pas perdus* (mus. Brahms, 1988), *Signatures* (mus. Beethoven, 1988), *Love, Dracula* (mus. Michael J. Baker, 1989), *The Comfort Zone* (mus. Beethoven, 1989), *Ouverture Russe* (mus. Glinka, 1989), *There, Below* (mus. Vaughan Williams, 1989), *Divertissement Schumann* (mus. Schumann, 1989), *Schéhérazade* (with David Earle; mus. Rimsky-Korsakov, 1989), *Romance* (mus. Dvořák, 1990), *C.V.* (mus. Michael J. Baker, 1990), *Pastorale* (mus. Beethoven, 1990), *Romeo and Juliet before Parting* (mus. Prokofiev, 1990; also video, 1990), *Violin Concerto (Misfits)* (mus. Prokofiev, 1990), *This Isn't the End* (sound John Oswald, 1991), *The Kiss of Death* (sound John Oswald, 1991), *Musings (Fare Well)* (mus. Mozart, 1991), *Mirror* (mus. Mozart, 1991), *Mixed Program* (mus. Schubert, arr. Michael J. Baker, 1991), *Fifteen Heterosexual Duets* (mus. Beethoven, 1991), *Desir* (mus. Prokofiev, 1991), *The First Dance* (duet; mus. John Oswald, 1992), *The End* (mus. Brahms, 1992), *Making Ballet* (silent, 1993), *New York* (duet; mus. Schubert, 1993), *Ghosts* (mus. the Beatles, 1993), *The Miraculous Mandarin* (Bartók, 1993), *Vittoria Pas de Deux*(mus. Tchaikovsky, 1993), *Vestiges, ou, Les Ratées du coeur, or Six Tableaux for the Sexually Challenged* (mus. Henrich Biber,

Beethoven, Gavin Bryars, Antoine Dessane, 1993), *Spring Awakening* (mus. Michael J. Baker, 1994), *Heroes* (mus. John Adams, 1994), *Cruel World* (mus. Tchaikovsky, 1994), *The Actress* (mus. Chopin, 1994), *Gluck Pas de Deux* (mus. Gluck, 1994), *The Nutcracker* (mus. Tchaikovsky, 1995), *Missing* (mus. Copland, 1995), *States of Grace* (mus. Hindemith, 1995), *Terra Firma* (mus. Michael Torke, 1995), *Solo for Rex* (mus. Purcell, 1995), *Daisy's Dead* (mus. Spirit of the West, 1996), *A Piece for Walter* (mus. Prokofiev, 1996), *Le Baiser de la fée* (mus. Stravinsky, 1996), *I'm a Stranger Here Myself* (for television; mus. Weill, 1996), *The Four Seasons* (mus. Vivaldi, 1997).

Further reading

Interview with Penelope Doob, in 'Spotlight on James Kudelka', *Dance Magazine*, March 1977.

Articles Ellen Shearer, 'James Kudelka', *Dance in Canada*, Summer 1979; Linda Howe-Beck, 'Kudelka Charts the Land of Heart's Desire', *Dance Magazine*, May 1991; Leland Windreich, 'Full Circle: Love, Sex and Death in James Kudelka's *The Miraculous Mandarin*', *Dance International*, Fall 1993; Paula Citron, 'James Kudelka: Out of the Depths', *Dance Magazine*, February 1994; 'James Kudelka', in *Current Biography Yearbook, 1995*.

Books Karen Kain, with Stephen Godfrey and Penelope Reed Doob, *Movement Never Lies: An Autobiography*, Toronto, 1994; James Neufeld, *Power to Rise: The Story of the National Ballet of Canada*, Toronto, 1996.

JIŘÍ KYLIÁN

It has become the custom to think of great choreographers as those who are particularly innovative with the language of movement, who have provided what can be called a new language for dance. Jiří Kylián, then, is perhaps something of a throwback to an earlier age, one that was less thirsty for the 'new' than now; for if Kylián has a claim to greatness, it is not so much as a starkly original formal innovator but as a master craftsman contributing to the overall evolution of his art. Whatever his comparative standing, Kylián has undeniably strengthened the art of dance by building on its foundations, and will therefore hand on not just the products of an individual creative talent but an enriched heritage.

Kylián certainly has something in common with all the most significant creators, and that is that his formative years took place at a special time and in a special place. The place was Stuttgart and the time became known as the 'Ballet Boom'. Kylián joined the Stuttgart Ballet in 1968 in the middle years of John Cranko's remarkable directorship, when choreographers Cranko, Maurice Béjart, and Hans Van Manen were providing a lively new approach to ballet characterized by athletic, theatrical movement.

Kylián began choreographing prolifically from 1970, occasionally working for Nederlands Dans Theater (NDT), a company that had come to the forefront of the contemporary dance revolution in Europe during the 1960s. Founded in 1959, NDT was the first European ballet company to institute a regular modern dance class and thus was a pioneer in the combination of classical and modern dance traditions within one company. In its early days its prime mover was Hans Van Manen, whose choreography for the company drew on a wide range of composers including Stravinsky, Satie, Stockhausen, and Cage. After Van Manen resigned as artistic director in 1970, the company entered a period of decline and it was Kylián who brought it back to international prominence, during the 1970s and 1980s.

Kylián brought to NDT the ethos of Stuttgart, an approach to ballet that was firmly based in the classical technique and neo-classical style. In addition, however, Kylián's work teems with references to folk dance, which can add another textual level to the dance, like old dialect breaking through the sophisticated, highly evolved, and constraining balletic language he has adopted and made his own. His vocabulary is convoluted and dense; the vision from which he forms his steps and gestures is driven by expressionism but schooled in neo-classicism, and informed by a profound musicality.

Ballet's straight, sharp leg extensions coupled with the contracted body of the Graham technique has made the female body a particularly potent expressive tool for embodying dualism and conflict, and this has been powerfully exploited by Kylián. Like many diverse choreographers working in ballet since the 1960s, Kylián uses the balletically trained body at its extremes. Yet his motivation does not appear theatrical or virtuosic, or purely abstract; it comes from within, from an emotion or idea which resonates outwards. Kylián is a master of tension, providing potent, dramatic ballet, inventive and profound. He has proved himself prolific and diverse, one of the most consistently stimulating but also one of the most accessible of contemporary choreographers.

Kylián's normal *métier* is the non-narrative, dramatic ballet, though he has made ventures into other terrains such as narrative in *L'Histoire du soldat* (1986) and explorations of aboriginal rituals in *Nomaden* (*Nomads*) (1981), *Stamping Ground* (1983), and *Dreamtime* (1983). Just as you fix him in one rich interior, Kylián will undoubtedly show you another. In general, however, it could be said that Kylián's vocabulary is informed by a basically modernist consciousness; certainly his vivid descriptive talent deals well with a range of human emotions and with a complexity that is unusual in ballet.

As If Never Been (1992), for example, explores a sense of nihilism and despair. Two dancers are locked together in an internal drama based on dependency and exploitation. Against a background of silent, abstractly gestural commentators, who provide something of a Greek chorus, a hellish duet of mounting tension takes place – a kind of expressionistic *paso doble*. The woman is manipulated by her partner into various contorted shapes and exaggerated extensions, or thrown into passages of forced abandon, her legs flying around his head like windmills. The shapes they make together are typical of Kylián's style and evocative power, such as when she wraps around his body and with her bony arms and legs gives him skeletal wings, or when he walks her up the proscenium arch and over on to her back to pose in the air like an upturned cockroach.

Kylián can deal equally well with classical sublimity. If Tudor's *Dark Elegies* is ballet's *Paradise Lost* then Kylián's *Sinfonietta* (1978) is surely its *Paradise Regained*. This is Kylián at his most optimistic and life-affirming. To the uplifting brass opening of Janáček's score, Kylián sets six men in tights and billowing shirts against a painted land-scape. With simple leaps, runs, and turns they announce and celebrate the musical theme. When only two are left on stage they are joined by two women who, rushing across the stage, are stopped by the men and pose for a moment in a detached halted run. Although the couples are interchangeable partners, often passed from one to the other, (in Kylián's work there is very little sense of the dancers as individuals), the work is essentially romantic, sensual, and supremely lyrical. Undercurrents of folk rhythms run through the music and when they break out in the choreography they momentarily add another dimension, taking away any sense of pre-Fall innocence from these otherwise joyous creatures. Overall the mood is wonderfully serene. One of the loveliest moments is perhaps when four dancers lie down centre-stage, one behind the other, and in unison raise their arms in a slow, broad sweep that brings to mind the tail of a whale waving in the air before plunging into the deep.

Kylián's dancers can be classically sublime, as in *Sinfonietta*, and then again they can sculpt themselves into space in a way that has conflict and angst screaming

out of the contortions; Kylián can uplift your spirit one minute, and set your teeth on edge the next. In watching his ballets one enters a strongly defined world; the dancers are not characters as such but they certainly embody ideas. What makes his work particularly accessible is that it is dramatically expres-sive, lyrical, virtuosic, and profoundly musical. He is renowned particularly for his use of late Romantic composers, but has in fact worked with quite a wide variety of scores and soundscapes.

For example, *Falling Angels* (1989), set to Part One of Steve Reich's *Drumming* (1971), consists of one basic rhythmic pattern which is varied only in terms of phrase position, pitch, and timbre. It is simple but labyrinthian and so dominating in its power and density, so overwhelming an aural experience, that one might think it would leave no room for choreography. Kylián shows us otherwise. *Drumming* is compelling because it is such a wildly inven-tive exploration of a single isolated and confined idea. The tension inherent in this combination of contradictory qualities is similarly exploited by Kylián; the choreog-raphy is tightly controlled, a mesmeric use of choral movement and repeated phrases but with an exhilarating sense of wildly creative energy.

Falling Angels begins with a group of dancers slowly walking towards the audience out of the darkness; they are all women. They contort on the beat and retreat a couple of steps, all in unison. They look like a cross between the figures on an Egyptian frieze, in terms of their angular two dimen-sional shapes and, with their red lipstick, fixed focus, strong projection, and black swimsuits, something more Germanic – a Pina Bausch-style line-up with a touch of cabaret. They flash an angular figure of eight with a dreamlike flow of crisscrossing arms and legs. Hands slap, caress, cover, flick, move body parts, splay. Flat-footed jumps with bent knees recall Nijinsky's faun. In spirit it is primitive, ritualistic; they look rather like displaying insects totally in command of their prey. Dancers break free, duets break out, but the group always reclaims them. Contrasting moments of dramatic stillness create a surreal sense of space, even in the midst of this frenzied drumming. They are pious one minute, military another, but can then subvert it all with a fey lean to the side, hands draping diagonally across their bodies, or by flirtatiously pulling their swimsuits away from their flesh as if to taunt the audience.

In a very different style we can find a similar musicality and mastery of choral movement in Kylián's earlier work, *Symphony of Psalms* (1978), set to the driving rhythms of Stravinsky's score. The music is concerned with praising God; however, Kylián's choreography, sublime as it is, is rather more earthily sensual, set against a sumptuous background of oriental carpets. Again he does far more than visualize the music; his dialogue with it brings out the music's subtleties but then insists upon its own contrasting statements. Perhaps most breathtaking of all in this work is Kylián's use of deep space. Space is always emotionally resonant with Kylián; dancers reach out to it rather than simply stretch into it, but here the pleasure is also intellectual, a visual feast of layered movement. The eye moves from the lucidity of the dancers' individual bodies out to the larger scale of the mass and back again. Curves counter angles in the body, mesmerizing flow counters stark shape (it is difficult to believe that so many parts can move in so many different directions), creating a complex message of joy and sorrow, sensual pleasure and anxiety even within one movement. Kylián calls for a dramatic power in his dancers that they can switch on and off whenever the piece warrants it; they must be detached but involved, expressive but not 'acting' – everything is in the movement and apparently every muscle can be choreographed.

There is in Kylián's work a celebration of the creative spirit that spills over into a kind of joyous playfulness. His ability to be witty is well represented by two works set to Mozart, *Six Dances* (1986) and *Petite Mort* (1991). These works are an amusing romp through the music of the great composer but are intended as more than merry dances of bawds and cuckolds. For all their foppish wigs, headless crinolines on wheels, sword play and bubbles, there is a level of social comment without which they would not be Kylián but some other choreographer.

Kylián's moral consciousness and his intelligence are easily located within his work; he is accessible without being a popularist, and there is a depth to his ballets that makes them among the most rewarding to watch. His dancers are not presented as extraordinary performers to be physically admired for their virtuosity, but as expressive figures in a landscape or situation which has dramatic and social resonance. Judith Lynne Hanna notes that *Symphony in D* (1976) reverses the partnering conventions of classical ballet and challenges the *status quo* (J.L. Hanna, *Dance, Sex and Gender: Signs of Identity, Dominance, Defiance, and Desire*, University of Chicago Press, 1988, p. 213). Kylián's social and political consciousness, however, runs deeper than simple reversals of the norm. *Fallen Angels*, for example, has been read as a profound examination of the struggling female psyche. (See Ann Nugent: 'Two Radicals in Europe', *Dance Now*, 1(4), Winter 1992/3.)

There are a number of ways in which Kylián could be said to have questioned, and gently shifted, the norms of Western theatre dance. For example, the superficiality of an art-form shackled to youth and good looks for its splendours is something that he has directly addressed. Recognizing the power of the older, experienced dancer, and the profound eloquence that can be the product of a career spent working with a wide range of choreographers, Kylián established NDT3 in 1991, giving a new lease of life to dancers whose careers would normally have come to an end around the age of forty. This has been an important step in developing a deeper, more sophisticated appreciation of dancers.

In terms of his choreography, Kylián's morality, spirituality, and bouts of existentialism can seem rather old-fashioned today, though his work is none the weaker for that. The sensuality and sexuality of his works can also appear a little dated when compared to many contemporary choreographers. Yet there are passages of his work where its tremendous physicality moves towards the starker terrain of a more brutal and violent eroticism, which has been explored more fully by choreographers such as Lloyd Newson and Michael Clark. Examples are the male duet from *La Cathédrale engloutie* (1975) or passages of *Torso* (1975). But it is doubtful that Kylián could simply explore images of today's brutalized consciousness without intellectually commenting upon it and setting it in some form of moral and social framework. This is perhaps central to what makes him a great choreographer, as opposed to merely a strong contemporary voice.

Kylián's work often presents us with a potent dialogue between classical (and perhaps also Christian) ideals and the contorted angularity of modernism. He can choreograph the divine light and equally well explore our fractured twentieth-century consciousness full of angst and godless doubt. While not directly religious, his works often embrace the kind of duality that is a part of Christian consciousness: a sense of the double possibility of elation and despair, agony and ecstasy, heaven and hell, the sacred and profane, order and meaninglessness. As bodies sink down to earth, eyes often search upwards. There are shapes that seem shot through with Christian imagery (for example, there is a photograph of dancer Bryony Brind hanging down from outstretched arms in a crucifixion-like pose from the Royal Ballet's 1975 production of his *Return to a Strange Land*). Above all else Kylián is a great humanist; he is not

concerned with abstraction; he sites his ideas firmly within the human sphere. He presents human struggles, passions and prayers, elation and despair; he is a choreographer of potent dualisms lucidly expressed through his mixture of classical sublimity and contemporary expressionism. Although the medium in which Kylián works – this combination of classical and modern dance languages – is familiar rather than formally innovative, it is difficult to think of a more *eloquent* living choreographer.

Lesley-Anne Sayers

Note: Parts of this essay first appeared as a review of NDT's 1992 Bradford Season in *Dance Theatre Journal*, 10(2), 1993.

Biographical details

Born in Prague, Czechoslovakia (now Czech Republic), 21 March 1947. **Studied** at the National Ballet School, Prague Conservatory from 1962, and at the Royal Ballet School in London from 1967. **Career** Danced with Stuttgart Ballet, Germany, becoming soloist 1968–75; choreographed first work for Stuttgart Ballet in 1970; co-artistic director at Nederlands Dans Theater (NDT), 1975, becoming artistic director in 1977; established NDT 3 in 1991 for dancers over the age of 40. Most of his works have had their first performances with the NDT, though many have been reproduced by other companies, notably in the United States and Germany, and in the United Kingdom by Scottish Ballet, Ballet Rambert, and the Royal Ballet. **Awards** include Carina Ari Medal (Sweden); Society of West End Theatre Award (London); Netherlands Choreography Prize; Hans Christian Andersen Ballet Award (Denmark); Grand Prix International Video-Danse (France); Sonia Gaskell Prize (Netherlands); and a 1994 *Dance Magazine* Award.

Works

Paradox (mus. Kylián, 1970), *Kommen und Gehen* (mus. Bartók, 1970), *Incantations* (mus. André Jolivet, 1971), *Der Einzeiganger* (mus. Kylián, 1972), *Der stumme Orpheus* (mus. Toru Takemitsu, 1972), *Viewers* (mus. Frank Martin, 1973), *Blue Skin* (mus. traditional, 1974), *Der Morgen danach* (mus. Bártok, 1974), *Rückkehr ins fremde Land* [*Return to the Strange Land*] (mus.

Janáček, 1974; extended version, 1975), *Stoolgame* [*The Odd One*] (mus. Arne Nordheim, 1974), *La Cathédrale engloutie* (mus. Debussy, 1975), *Verklärte Nacht* [*Transfigured Night*] (mus. Schoenberg, 1975), *Torso* (mus. Toru Takemitsu, 1975), *Nuages* (mus. Debussy, 1976), *Elegia* (mus. Shostakovich, 1976), *Symfonie in D* (two-part version; mus. Haydn, 1976), *November Steps* (mus. Toru Takemitsu, 1977), *Ariadne* (mus. Arne Nordheim, 1977), *Symfonie in D* (three-part version; mus. Haydn, 1977), *Kinderspelen* [*Children's Games*] (mus. Mahler, Carpenter 1978), *Sinfonietta* (mus. Janáček, 1978), *Intimate Pages* (mus. Janáček, 1978), *Rainbow Snake* (mus. Erik Norby, 1978), *Symphony of Psalms* (mus. Stravinsky, 1978), *Glagolitic Mass* (mus. Janáček, 1978), *Dream Dances* (mus. Luciano Berio, 1978), *Field Mass* (mus. Martinů, 1980), *Overgrown Path* (mus. Janáček, 1980), *Forgotten Land* (mus. Britten, 1981), *Nomaden* [*Nomads*] (mus. Stravinsky, 1981), *Symfonie in D* (four-part version; mus. Haydn, 1981), *Svadebka* [*Les Noces*] (mus. Stravinsky, 1982), *Lieder eines fahrenden Gesellen* (mus. Mahler, 1982), *Stamping Ground* (mus. Carlos Chavez, 1983), *Dreamtime* (mus. Toru Takemitsu, 1983), *Curses and Blessings* (with Christopher Bruce; mus. Petr Eben, 1983), *Wiegelied* (mus. Berg, 1983), *Valencia* (mus. Padilla, 1984), *L'Enfant et les sortilèges* (mus. Ravel, 1984), *Heart's Labyrinth I* (mus. Schoenberg, Webern, Dvořák, 1984), *Heart's Labyrinth II* (mus. Schoenberg, Webern, Witold Lutosławski, 1985), *Piccolo Mondo* (mus. Praetorius, 1985), *Silent Cries* (mus. Debussy, 1986), *L'Histoire du soldat* (mus. Stravinsky, 1986), *Six Dances/Sechs Tanze* (mus. Mozart, 1986), *Heart's Labyrinth* (new version; mus. Schoenberg, Webern, Dvořák, 1987), *Frankenstein!* (mus. Gruber, 1987), *Sint Joris rijdt uit* (mus. various, 1987), *Evenings Songs* (mus. Dvořák, 1987), *Kaguyahime* (mus. Maki Ishii, 1988), *No More Play* (mus. Webern, 1988), *Tantz-Schul* (mus. Mauricio Kagel, 1989), *Falling Angels* (mus. Steve Reich, 1989), *Sweet Dreams* (mus. Webern, 1990), *Sarabande* (mus. Bach, Electronic Sounds, 1990), *Petite Mort* (mus. Mozart, 1991), *Obscure Temptations* (mus. John Cage, 1991), *Stepping Stones* (mus. Webern, John Cage, 1991), *Un ballo* (mus. Ravel, 1991), *As If Never Been* (mus. Lukas Foss, 1992), *No Sleep Till Dawn of Day* (mus. Berceuse de Savo, Polynesian, 1992), *Whereabouts Unknown* (mus. Arvo Pärt, Steve Reich, Charles Ives, Webern, de Roo, 1994), *Double You* (solo; mus. J.S. Bach, 1994), *Tiger Lily* (mus. John Cage, György Kurtág, Webern, J.S. Bach, 1995), *Quando Corpus* (1995), *Arcimboldo* (with others; mus. various, 1995), *Bella Figura* (mus. Baroque, Pergolesi,

Lukas Foss, 1995), *Anna and Ostriches* (mus. Strauss polkas, Zbigniew Preisner, 1996), *Trompe l'oeil* (mus. various, 1996), *Compass* (1996), *If Only...* (1996), *Wings of Wax* (mus. Heinrich von Biber, John Cage, Philip Glass, J.S. Bach, 1997).

Further reading

Interviews with Sue Merrett, in 'Spotlight on Jiří Kylián', *Dancing Times*, May 1991; with Peta Koch, in 'Jiří Kylián: Outlining Dance', *Dance Australia*, December 1993.

Articles Norma McLain Stoop, 'Jiří Kylián of the Netherlands Dance Theatre', *Dance Magazine*, October 1979; Patricia Barnes, 'New Faces: Jiří Kilián', *Dance News*, December 1979; Norma McLain Stoop, 'Midsummer Nights' Dreams', *Dance Magazine*, July 1982; James Monaghan, 'Amsterdam and Kylián', *Dancing Times*, May 1984; Rolf Garske, 'In Love with Music and Movement', *Ballett International*, March 1987; Louisa Moffett, 'Kylián Changes Keys', *Dance Magazine*, May 1987; Horst Koegler, 'Pledged to the Spirit of Our Times: Nederlands Dans Theater, 1959–1989', *Ballett International*, May 1989; Rolf Garske, 'At the Crossroads: NDT – 1989', *Ballett International*, May 1989; Janet Sinclair, 'Choreographer's Luck', *Dance and Dancers*, June/July 1991; Jiří Kylián, 'What is Dance?', *Dance Now*, Winter 1992/93; Lesley-Anne Sayers, 'Dreams and Discontent: The Choreography of Jiří Kylián', *Dance Theatre Journal*, 10(2), 1992; Ann Nugent, 'Two Radicals in Europe', *Dance Now*, Winter 1992/93; Helmut Scheier, 'Choreographing in Symbols', *Ballett International*, October 1994; Ann Nugent, 'Ripe Tomatoes, Sweet Grapes – and *Arcimboldo*', *Dance Theatre Journal*, Summer 1995; Janet Sinclair and Leo Kersley, 'Celebration in The Hague', *Dancing Times*, June 1995; Eva van Schaik, 'Master of Ceremonies, Seeker of Truths', *Ballett International*, June 1995.

Books Arlene Croce, *Going to the Dance*, New York, 1982; Jack Anderson, *Choreography Observed*, Iowa City, 1987; Gerard Mannoni, *Kylián* (in French), Arles, 1989; Isabelle Lanz, *A Garden of Dance: A Monograph on the Work of Jiří Kylián* (in Dutch and English), Amsterdam, 1995.

DANIEL LARRIEU

Daniel Larrieu has been one of the leading figures of the French *nouvelle danse* scene since he and his tiny group Astrakan won the prestigious Prix Bagnolet choreography award in 1982. A dancemaker renowned for his witty ironic approach, Larrieu has since choreographed for some of Europe's leading companies, including Nederlands Dans Theater, Frankfurt Ballet, and the Paris Opéra itself.

Larrieu was a student at horticultural college when he began his dance training, and his early interest in things botanical has emerged in various ways ever since, perhaps most dramatically in *Attentat poétique* (1992), which, with the help of effective costumes and set designs provided by the Paris Opéra, used as its central motif the image of the rose through the ages. After college, Larrieu formed his company, Astrakan Recherches Chorégraphiques (usually shortened to 'Astrakan'), with just two other dancers, Pascale Houbin and Pascale Henrot. At first, lacking studio space, they rehearsed in the gardens of the Palais Royal in Paris, presumably a natural progression for Larrieu the gardener.

Larrieu's early work showed his commitment to a certain degree of formalism and line, but with a playful intellectualism that explored the many layers of meaning in ordinary movement and gesture, particularly of the upper body. A quirky, even absurd, sense of humour was revealed in incongruities and unexpected juxtapositions, as when a pot plant played a central role in the 1982 *Volte-face*. The piece that won the Prix Bagnolet, *Chiquenaudes* (1982) – or 'flicks of the finger' – declared Larrieu's interest in the smallest and most apparently banal aspects of body language, yet also revealed an intelligent awareness of the possibilities of theatre. Having at that point worked almost entirely *al fresco*, one reviewer pointed out, Larrieu therefore made original

use of the stage, 'playing a kind of Chinese puzzle game with entrances and exits'.[1]

Un Sucre ou deux?, from the same year, used only two dancers – Larrieu and Houbin – in a series of relatively sparse movements set to the familiar, swelling music of Prokofiev's *Romeo and Juliet*. In its intensive and often repetitive emphasis on everyday gesture, this piece frustrated more conventional viewers looking for a wider range of movement, especially to the evocative theme of Shakespeare's doomed lovers. But Larrieu appeared to delight in the very incongruity as the two dancers, dressed most unromantically in clownlike baggy trousers and bandaged feet, enacted an almost pathetic but strangely moving duet, with intensified, frantic hand gestures, synchronized to perfection, reaching a poignant climax of movement and atmosphere to match the music. When this piece was performed at the United Kingdom's Dance Umbrella festival in 1983, the critic Lesley-Anne Davis perceptively pointed out that Larrieu could be 'wonderfully eloquent with quite minimal movement content'. Summing up Larrieu's work at this time, she wrote, 'he is as anarchic as Pina Bausch with a sense of humour not unlike that of the late Jacques Tati.'[2]

But for all his concentration on small gesture and repetitive, sometimes even robotic movement, Larrieu has demonstrated an equal fascination with the flow of movement – especially underwater, and he is perhaps best known for his seminal 1986 work, *Waterproof*, which takes place in a swimming pool. Both performed live and captured in a film version that is critically acclaimed in its own right, *Waterproof* manages to be completely unlike the Esther Williams 'synchronized swimming' spectacle that one might expect. Rather, it is arguably the closest that a choreographer has yet come to creating pure dance in water.

The piece was composed for nine 'dancers' dressed in identical black costumes and swimming goggles, and lasts for about an hour. One of Larrieu's chief aims was obviously to explore the idea of continuous motion, something which is more or less impossible on dry land. Many critics have preferred the film version of *Waterproof*, as careful editing and joining of dance sequences can create even more effectively the sense of endless flow and weightlessness. During live performances of the work, video screens around the pool projected images from an underwater perspective in order to further this sense. In either the live or recorded medium, Larrieu's water choreography redefines time and space for the dancer, and suggests a kind of infinity through the presentation of ongoing ebb and flow, like water itself. As the critic Ann Nugent, responding to the film of *Waterproof*, put it,

'The effect was of calm, weightlessness, blue water and bright lights, and a maze of torsos, endlessly flowing, curving and curling. So fine was the editing that you were never quite certain about the beginnings and endings of sequences, never saw dancers gasping for air, but felt gripped instead by the silence of anonymous movement, and the way it was made to reach out into the mysterious unknown.'[3]

While Larrieu may have shown himself to be comfortable in such spaces as gardens and swimming pools, he is still at home in a more traditional theatrical environment. He has choreographed for opera (Weber's *Oberon* in 1986, Strauss's *Salome* in 1990) for the Opéra de Lyon, and has staged a postmodern 'ballet' for that bastion of classicism, the Paris Opéra. In *Attentat poétique*, commissioned by Patrick Dupond, Larrieu had the services of some of the Opéra's leading dancers – although some critics complained that he lacked either the interest or the capacity to make the best use of their talents. Such traditional constituents as *pas de deux*, a *corps de ballet* of sorts (representing roses), and named characters like 'Le Chevalier' or 'La Reine du bal de roses'

suggested a more conventional ballet structure, but ultimately the opera-house environment was judged to put Larrieu's iconoclastic gifts at a disadvantage. For many, there seemed to be no coherent dramatic conception behind the work's various components. Solo dances, particularly for the male characters, were of greater choreographic interest than the group ensembles, the effect of which one critic compared to a 'bored aerobics class'.[4]

Larrieu's principal works in the mid- to late 1990s remain his creations for his own company – now known as Compagnie Daniel Larrieu – such as *Un Gests ou deux* (1995), *Mobile, ou le miroir du château* (1995), *Delta* (1996), and *Delta +* (1997). Yet, as the commissions works suggest, Larrieu has found increasing acceptance in the French cultural establishment, earning the title of *Officier* from the Ordre des Arts et des Lettres and being selected as director of the Centre Chorégraphique National in Tours.

Virginia Christian

Notes

1 Ulrich Tegeder, 'Criticism from Within', *Ballett International*, June–July 1982, p. 30.
2 Lesley-Anne Davis, 'Dance Umbrella '83', *Dance Theatre Journal*, 2(1), p. 38.
3 Ann Nugent, 'Spring to Life', *Dance and Dancers*, June 1987, p. 30.
4 Roslyn Sulcas, 'Reviews: Odile Duboc, Daniel Larrieu', *Dance and Dancers*, July 1992, p. 31.

Biographical details

Born in Marseille, France, 23 November 1957. **Studied** at the Collège de Hyères, Provence, obtaining qualifications in horticulture and viticulture. **Career** Dancer with Wes Howard's Quatuor de Danse, 1978–80, Anne-Marie Reynaud and Odile Azagury's Le Four Solaire, 1980–81, and Régine Chopinot, 1982; founder and artistic director, Astrakan Recherches Chorégraphiques (commonly known as Astrakan), 1982, which acquired its first permanent base in the Ferme du Buisson, a cultural centre in Marne la Vallée outside Paris, 1990–92; group renamed Compagnie Daniel Larrieu on Larrieu's appointment as director of the Centre

Chorégraphique National de Tours, 1993. Has also choreographed for Extempory Dance Theatre, Frankfurt Ballet, Nederlands Dans Theater, Ballet de Nancy, Lyon Opéra Ballet, Paris Opéra Ballet, and Jeune Ballet de France. **Awards and honours** Bagnolet Festival Choreographic Prize, 1982; Grand Prix SACD, 1988; Chevalier de l'Ordre des Arts et des Lettres, 1988; Carte Blanche de la Danse, Avignon, 1989; Officier de l'Ordre des Arts et des Lettres, 1994; Grand Prix National de la Danse, 1994.

Works

Chiquenaudes (silent, 1982), *Volte-face* (mus. Catalan songs, extracts fron Bizet's *Carmen*, 1982), *Un Sucre ou deux?* (mus. Prokofiev, Liszt, 1982), *La Peau et les os* (mus. Hector Zazou, 1984), *Ombres électriques* (mus. Roger Sourd, Berlioz, 1984), *Romance en stuc* (mus. Jean-Jacques Palix, 1985), *Waterproof* (mus. Jean-Jacques Palix, Eve Couturier, 1986; film version the same year), *Quai Bourbon* (film, 1986), *Obéron* (opera by Carl Maria von Weber, 1986), *Terre Grenadine* (mus. Jean-Jacques Palix, 1986), *Jungle sur la planète Vénus* (sound collage Jean-Jacques Palix, 1987), *L'Eléphant et les faons* (mus. Jean-Jacques Palix and Eve Couturier, 1987), *Anima* (mus. various, 1988), *Les Anges protecteurs* (mus. Sibelius, 1988), *Les Marchands* (mus. Arvo Pärt, 1989), *Pour l'instant* (solo; soundtape Jean-Jacques Palix, 1989), *Vous qui habitez le temps* (silent, 1989), *Les Bâtisseurs* (mus. Thom Willems, 1989), *Hydmen* (1989), *Salomé* (opera by Richard Strauss, 1990), *Les Prophètes* (sound collage Jean-Jacques Palix and Eve Couturier, 1990), *Gravures* (sound collage Tapage atypique, 1991), *Attentat poétique* (sound collage Tapage atypique, 1992), *Rideaux ou les trois jours de décembre* (mus. Fauré and others, 1992), *L'Histoire du soldat* (mus. Stravinsky, 1993), *Mimi* (mus. Charles Trenet, 1993), *Emmy* (mus. Górecki, 1993), *Mica ou le sourire de l'eau* (mus. Egon Po, 1994), *'Père. Je remets mon esprit entre tes mains'* (solo in *Les Sept dernières paroles du Christ*; mus. Haydn, 1993), *Un Geste ou deux* (mus. various, 1995), *Mobile, ou le miroir du château* (mus. Thom Willems, 1995), *Jolie môme* and *Avec le temps* (with Pascale Houbin; mus. Léo Ferré, 1995), *Delta* (mus. Scanner, Robin Rimbaud, 1996), *Delta+* (mus. Scanner, Robin Rimbaud, 1997).

Further reading

Interviews with Patrick Bensard, in 'Entretien avec Daniel Larrieu', *Empreintes*, March 1983;

with Nini Candalino, in 'Entretien avec Larrieu', *Sotto Traccia*, June 1987; with Philippe Verrièle, in 'Daniel Larrieu', *Les Saisons de la Danse*, January 1995.

Articles Lesley-Anne Davis, 'Dance Umbrella '83', *Dance Theatre Journal*, January 1984; Alain Nahmais, 'Daniel Larrieu se jette à l'eau', *Danser*, December 1985; Ann Nugent, 'Spring to Life', *Dance and Dancers*, June 1987; Angela Kane, 'A Kingdom for a Stage', *Dancing Times*, January 1989; Noël Goodwin, 'A Matter of Form', *Dance and Dancers*, February 1989; Laurence Louppe, 'The Origins and Development of Contemporary Dance in France', *Dance Theatre Journal*, Summer 1989; Daniel Dobbels, 'Trial by Water – Daniel Larrieu's *Waterproof*', *Dance Theatre Journal*, Summer 1989; Bernadette Bonis, 'Trois chorégraphes français', *Danser*, September 1990; Nathalie Auger, 'Compagnie Astrakan', *Les Saisons de la Danse*, December 1990; Annie Bozzini, 'They Film as They Dance', *Ballett International*, January 1991; André Béchaz, 'Avant-première: La puissance de l'amour' (on *Gravures*), *Les Saisons de la Danse*, November 1991; Gilberte Cournand, 'Dix années de créations', *Les Saisons de la Danse*, September 1992; Thomas Hahn, 'Hypothetical Streams in the Bermuda Triangle' (part on *Delta*), *Ballett International*, March 1997.

Books Allen Robertson and Donald Hutera, *The Dance Handbook*, Harlow, Essex, 1988; Gilbert Lacault, Daniel Dobbels, and Nadia Tazi, *Larrieu* (in French), Paris, no date.

MURRAY LOUIS

Murray Louis, known in his own right as a witty and poetic choreographer of prolific output, grew to fame through his association with the great teacher and choreographer Alwin Nikolais. Since Nikolais's death in 1993, Louis has been director of the Nikolais-Murray Louis Dance Company in New York City.

Louis met Nikolais at the Hanya Holm Summer School of dance at Colorado College in 1946. There, in Nikolais's classes, as he tells it, he 'suddenly realized the huge scope of dance movement'. He joined Nikolais at the Henry Street Playhouse and became soloist at the Playhouse Dance Company (later renamed the Nikolais Dance Theater) when it was formed in 1949.

By 1951, he had earned a degree in speech and theatre and was named head of the children's dance department at the Playhouse. During this period he was also a guest teacher throughout the United States. When interviewed, Louis's students – children, adolescents, and adults – have said not that he taught them 'how to dance', but rather, that he showed them 'what dancing is all about'. As Tobi Tobias has written, his teaching has demonstrated two essential commitments: 'sentient awareness of movement for its own sake, and a deeply serious commitment to the art'.

Louis is an engaging choreographer and performer, noted for his timing, wit, and kinetic range. His works are highly theatrical, mimetic though not necessarily narrative. Although the stage is enchantingly designed and lit, dance is never subordinated to the other theatrical elements: the focus is on the dancers – on people, rather than things. The body's movement potential is fully explored. He often employs what some critics have called a 'childlike' vaudevillean approach to set humorous works. Trained in Bauhaus-influenced stage magic, which unites the visual magic of multi-media effects and kinetic imagery, Louis, especially in his solos, transcends the mimetic and transmits the emotion inherent in movement imagery. Marcia Siegel notes in *At the Vanishing Point* that John Martin, looking at a Louis dance piece called *Dark Corner* (1955), 'recognized that [Louis] was not dancing about how it felt to be in dark corner, he simply was dark corner.'

Louis was making his first works from 1950, but his official debut as choreographer was in 1953 on a programme of four works shared with Gladys Bailin. He gave his first one-man concert in 1955, starting with solos and later developing complex group works. There are over 100 pieces in the chronology of his works from over 40 years of

choreography. Notable dances in the first twenty years of his *œuvre* are *Man in Chair* (1955), *Bach Suite* (1956), *Reflections* (1956), *Journal* (1957), *Entre-act* (1959) *Calligraph for Martyrs* (1961), *Facets* (1962), *Interims* (1963), *Landscapes* (1964), *Junk Dances* (1964), *Chimera* (1966), and *Proximities* (1969).

Junk Dances was his signature piece for many years. The work is a comment on the 'junk' of everyday life pushed on the public by advertising. Husband, wife, and chorus of housewives are clichés of that 'I Love Lucy' time, in the 'underside of the sophisticated world where ordinary citizens live'. Using a collage of popular and operatic music and décor by Robert Wilson, Louis created a lively and funny dance soap opera that was part mime, part popular dance, and part cartoon.

Chimera is a solo demonstrating Louis's superb muscular control. Using a stage set of various sized openings, designed by Nikolais, he moves from one to another, allowing different parts of the body to appear in each. The movement in all moments is selected and detailed, revealing and concealing, releasing laughter and chagrin at the futility of disguise. In this, as in several other works, Louis explores the stage magic and a surprising, detailed vocabulary initiated by Nikolais and later developed by other dance companies, like Pilobolus.

Seven dances create the excitement of a three-ring circus in *Hoopla* (1972). Set to traditional music played by the Lisbon State Police Band with costumes by long-time associate Frank Garcia, the work is a series of episodes depicting moments in a fantasy carnival – an athletic duet for acrobats, an animal-taming number, a conjuring act, a puppet theatre. Once again, this work shows Louis's mastery of theatrical, eccentric movement.

Louis's solo works and performances have drawn special appreciation from audiences and critics for their 'freedom based on great control'. In *Moments* (1975), a work originally created for Rudolf Nureyev and set to three movements of Ravel's *String Quartet*, a central figure traces shapes in the air, like a conductor bouncing downbeats. Four male dancers support him, providing counter-movement in unison. By contrast, *The Disenchantment of Pierrot* (1986), cited by Anna Kisselgoff of *The New York Times* as a 'little everyman' solo, depicts a 'street-wise, wistful, Chaplinesque character', in turn very different from *Frail Demons* (1984), a suite of four dances presenting an inner state of emotion without conventional emotional gesture. His 1994 solo, *Alone*, is a tribute to Alwin Nikolais, who died in 1993.

Louis's group works of note include the jazzy romp *Four Brubeck Pieces* (1984), *The Station* (1985), a dramatic work set to Weimar songs, *Revels* (1986), a carnival fantasy with a score by Nikolais and David Gregory, and *Tides* (1994), a three-part work for four women. *Tides* continues the chore-ographic tradition inherent in Louis's works – lyric movement, exploring the boundaries of kinetic expression, hinting at the mimetic yet transcending it. The work creates the environment of the ocean floor, the shapes of sea creatures, the water's movement. Yet it always remains a kaleidoscope of these images, never a fixed presentation or montage. The choreography remains as fluid as the title, with locomotor patterns and grouped shapes formed and reformed through body contact and spatial exchange. The sound score is by Alwin Nikolais; the costume design by Frank Garcia. Louis, the choreographer, also did the lighting.

In 1992–93, a Nikolais/Louis Residency and Retrospective Program was presented under the sponsorship of the Mason Gross School of the Arts at Rutgers, the State University of New Jersey. The programme provided the opportunity to 'reconstruct' several of Nikolais's early works, including *Imago*, *Tower*, *Tent and kaleidoscope* and many of Louis's works, including *Index ('to a necessary neurosis')* (1973), *Four Brubeck Pieces*, *Bach Suite* and *Calligraph for*

Martyrs, *Journal*, and *Interims*. At the Conference on Dance REConstructed, Louis, who supervised the reconstructions, remarked that it is the aesthetic intent of the choreographer that is the guiding value of reconstruction.

> It is aesthetics, really, that feeds from one artist to another. I think that in the history and the continuity of this ephemeral art it is not so much the mechanics of a work, not so much the virtuosity of a work, not so much the hook of work that should be considered and will be remembered as what has that work said to you, what has it left you with, which is what I call its aesthetics.

In his lengthy career, Murray Louis has created works for leading modern dance and ballet companies and for leading individual artists such as Rudolf Nureyev, Erik Bruhn, and Patrick Dupond. He has worked closely with many major composers and musicians, including the jazz great Dave Brubeck, who scored several of his dances. Louis has received numerous awards and distinctions, and his company has performed worldwide, from Istanbul to Helsinki, Paris to New York, Israel to Italy. He is also the author of two books and an accomplished film-maker.

Joanna Harris

Biographical details

Born Murray Louis Fuchs in Brooklyn, New York City, 4 November 1926. **Studied** with Hanya Holm at Colorado College summer session, 1946, with Anna Halprin from 1947, and at Alwin Nikolais's Henry Street Playhouse, New York, from 1949; also attended New York University, receiving a BA in Dramatic Arts, 1951. **Career** Danced as a soloist with Alwin Nikolais's Playhouse Dance Company (later the Nikolais Dance Theater), from 1949, remaining with the Nikolais company until 1969; director of children's dance depart-ment at the Henry Street Playhouse from 1951, becoming associate director of the theatre under Nikolais; founded Murray Louis Dance Company in 1953; director of Nikolais–Murray Louis Dance

Company since 1993; has choreographed well over 100 works, and staged pieces for international companies including Royal Danish Ballet, José Limón Company, Hamburg Opera Ballet, Scottish Ballet, Berlin Opera Ballet, Cleveland Ballet, and Israel's Batsheva Dance Company; also created five-part film series, *Dance as an Art Form*, 1972. **Awards and honours** include Guggenheim Fellowship, 1973; *Dance Magazine* Award, 1977; Grande Médaille de la Ville de Paris, 1979; Chevalier de l'Ordre des Arts et des Lettres (France).

Works

Dragon Flower (1950), *Starbeam Journey* (1950), *The Sun is Stolen* (mus. percussion, 1951), *The Broken Mirror* (1952), *Milos Word* (mus. Bob Abrams, 1952), *Opening Dance* (mus. Malcolm Waliron, 1953), *Little Man* (mus. Britten, 1953), *Antechamber* (mus. percussion, 1953), *Star Crossed* (mus. David Diamond, 1953), *Pierre Patelin* (1953), *Affirmation* (mus. J.S. Bach 1954), *For Remembrance* (mus. Alfredo Cassella 1954), *Courtesan* (mus. Vivaldi, 1954), *Family Album* (mus. Norman Dello Joio, 1954), *Martyr* (mus. percussion, 1954), *Triptych* (mus. Satie, 1954), *Pata Pan* (1954), *Piper* (mus. Henri Dutilleux, 1955), *Court* (mus. Harold Faberman, 1955), *Dark Corner* (mus. percussion, 1955), *Monarch* (mus. Henri Dutilleux, 1955), *Night* (mus. Henri Dutilleux, 1955), *Polychrome* (mus. medieval, 1955), *Man in Chair* (mus. Satie, 1955), *Figure in Grey* (mus. Alan Hovhaness, 1955), *As the Day Darkens* (mus. medieval, 1955), *Small Illusions* (mus. Weill, 1955), *Frenetic Dances* (mus. Alan Hovhaness, 1955), *Improvisation* (mus. percussion, 1955), *Wizard of Oz* (dance play, 1955), *Warrior* (1956), *Bach Suite* (mus. J.S. Bach, 1956), *Incredible Garden* (mus. Fassett, Hovhaness, 1956), *Reflections* (formerly *Harmonica Suite*; mus. Eddy, Manson, 1956), *Pied Piper* (1956), *The Little Match Girl* (1956), *Belonging to the Moon* (mus. Alan Hovhaness, 1957), *Journal* (1957), *Jack and the Beanstalk* (1957), *The Midas Touch* (1959), *Entre-acte* (mus. Toch, Giuffre, Orff, 1959), *Rangda the Witch* (1959), *El amor brujo* (mus. Manuel de Falla, 1959), *Hansel and Gretel* (1959), *Tarievedy and Clorinda* (1959), *Odyssey* (mus. Ivan Fiedel, 1960), *Aladdin* (1960), *Calligraph for Martyrs* (mus. Alwin Nikolais, 1961), *Signal* (mus. Alwin Nikolais, 1961), *Sonatina* (mus. Alwin Nikolais, 1961), *Facets* (mus. Alwin Nikolais, 1962), *Interims* (mus. Lukas Foss, 1963), *Suite for Divers Performers* (mus. Vivaldi, 1963), *Canto* (mus. Albéniz, 1963), *Duet* (mus. J.S. Bach, 1963), *The King's Necklace* (1963), *Rialto* (1963), *Transcendencies* (mus. Pierre Schaeffer,

Alwin Nikolais, 1964), *Junk Dances* (1964), *Landscapes* (mus. Alvin Walker, 1964), *A Gothic Tale* (mus. Alwin Nikolais, 1964), *Cinder-Eyelid* (dance play for children, 1965), *Chimera* (mus. Alwin Nikolais, 1966), *Chorus I* (mus. Alwin Nikolais, 1966), *Concerto* (mus. J.S. Bach, 1966), *Illume* (mus. Toshiro Mayuzumi, 1966), *Go-Six* (mus. Heinrich, 1968), *Tribute* (1968), *Proximities* (mus. Brahms, 1969), *Intersection* (mus. Harold Faberman, 1969), *Uptied* (1970), *Personnae* (mus. Free Life Communications, 1971), *Continuum* (mus. Corky Siegel Blues Band, Alwin Nikolais, 1971), *Disguise* (mus. Corky Siegel Blues Band, Alwin Nikolais, 1971), *Hoopla* (mus. traditional, Lisbon State Police Band, 1972), *Index* (mus. Oregon Ensemble, 1973), *Scheherazade* (mus. Rimsky-Korsakov, Alwin Nikolais, Free Life Communications, 1974), *Geometrics* (mus. Alwin Nikolais, 1974), *Porcelain Dialogues* (mus. Tchaikovsky, 1974), *Catalogue* (mus. Hugo, 1975), *Moments* (mus. Ravel, 1975), *Cleopatra* (1976), *Glances* (mus. Dave Brubeck, 1976), *Schubert* (mus. Schubert, 1977), *Ceremony* (mus. Alwin Nikolais, 1977), *Déjà Vu* (mus. various, 1977), *Vivace* (mus. J.S. Bach, 1978), *Canarsie Venus* (mus. Cole Porter, William Bolcom, 1978), *Figura* (mus. Paul Winter Consort, 1978), *Dance for Lisa* (mus. Dvořák, 1979), *Promenade* (mus. Ted Kalmon, 1979), *Five Haikus* (mus. Scriabin, 1979), *Afternoon* (mus. various, 1979), *The City* (mus. David Darling, 1980), *November Dances* (mus. David Darling, 1980), *Films: Solos* (1980), *Pulcinella* (mus. Stravinsky, 1981), *Many Seasons* (mus. Alwin Nikolais, 1982), *Aperitif* (mus. Alexis Emmanuel Chabrier, Milhaud, 1982), *A Stravinsky Montage* (mus. Stravinsky, 1982), *Afterboat* (mus. David Gregory, 1983), *Lenny and the Heartbreakers* (mus. Scott Killian, 1983), *Four Brubeck Pieces* (mus. Dave Brubeck, 1984), *Pugs Land* (mus. Alwin Nikolais, 1984), *Frail Demons* (mus. Alwin Nikolais, 1984), *Tales of Cri-Cri* (1984), *The Station* (mus. David Gregory, 1985), *Butterfly* (mus. Glenn Moore, 1985), *Revels* (mus. Alwin Nikolais and David Gregory, 1986), *Black & White* (mus. Tigger Benford, Ben Hazard, 1986), *The Disenchantment of Pierrot* (mus. Alwin Nikolais, J.S. Bach, Riccardo Drigo, 1986), *By George* (mus. Gershwin, 1987), *Return to Go* (mus. Alwin Nikolais, 1987), *Act I* (mus. Dave Brubeck, 1987), *Glyphics* (mus. David Gregory, Tigger Benford, 1987), *Bach II* (mus. J.S. Bach, 1987), *Asides* (1987), *A.T. & T.* (film; mus. Dave Brubeck, 1988), *ML in Concert* (film; 1989), *Ten Legs* (mus. Alwin Nikolais, 1989), *Oracles* (mus. Alwin Nikolais, 1989), *Segue* (mus. Alwin Nikolais, 1990), *Appearances* (mus. Alwin Nikolais, 1990), *Ceremonies* (1991), *Where Phantoms Gather* (mus. Jon Scoville, 1992), *A Fine Line* (mus. Witold Lutosławski, 1992), *Blue Streak* (mus. Mendelsohn, 1992), Alone (1994), *Tides* (Mus. Nikolais, 1994), *Homage to the Swedish Ballet* (1995), *Symphony* (mus. Nikolais, 1996), *Sinners All* (1996), *Création du Monde* (mus. Milhaud, 1996), *Tips* (mus. Scott Killian, 1997), *Venus* (mus. Copland, 1997).

Further reading

Interviews in 'Two American Choreographers', *Dance and Dancers*, May 1972; with Cynthia Lyle, in her *Dancers on Dancing*, New York and London, 1977; with Kitty Cunningham, in her *Conversations with a Dancer*, New York, 1980; in *People Who Dance*, edited by John Gruen, Princeton, New Jersey, 1988.

Articles Doris Hering, 'Who Knows How I Appear?', *Dance Magazine*, November 1963; Marcia Marks, 'Murray Louis Dance Company', *Dance Magazine*, January 1964; Phyllis W. Manchester, 'Murray Louis: Great American Dancer', *Dancing Times*, September 1966; Doris Hering, 'Two Works by Murray Louis', *Dance Magazine*, January 1958; Bill Hooks, Robert Miller, and W.H. Stephen, 'The Dance in New York', *Dance Digest*, February 1958; Claire Williams, W.H. Stephen, and James Damian Holmes, 'The Dance in New York', *Dance Digest*, June 1958; Clive Barnes, 'Murray Louis: On His Own', *The New York Times*, February 23 1969; Tobi Tobias, 'Nikolais and Louis: A New Space', *Dance Magazine*, February 1971; Peter Williams and John Percival, 'Two American Dancer-Creators', *Dance and Dancers*, August 1972; Joseph Gale, 'The Grand Tours: A Year with Murray Louis Alwin Nikolais', *Dance Magazine*, February 1973; Alan J. Shaw, 'A Proportion for Misproportion', *Dance Magazine*, March 1975; Elizabeth Kendall, 'Dancers and Audiences, and Thoughts about Entertainment', *Dance Magazine*, May 1975; Moira Hodgson, 'Inside Murray's Pinball Machine', *Dance Magazine*, March 1976; Clive Barnes, 'Barnes on . . . Murray Louis', *Ballet News*, October 1980; Murray Louis, 'Anatomy of a Production', *Dance Magazine*, November 1989; Anne Tobias, 'Murray Louis and Nikolais Dance: Staying Power', *Dance Magazine*, February 1997.

Books Marcia Siegal, *At the Vanishing Point*, New York, 1972; Don McDonagh, *The Complete Guide to Modern Dance*, New York, 1976; Murray Louis, *Inside Dance: Essays by Murray Louis*, New York, 1980; Murray Louis, *Murray Louis on Dance*, Pennington, New Jersey, 1992.

LAR LUBOVITCH

Lar Lubovitch's dances evoke descriptions such as exuberant, energetic, sweeping, luscious, and impassioned. He transcends the boundaries between ballet and modern dance, choreographing for prominent companies of both genres. In the United States the list includes the New York City Ballet, American Ballet Theatre, Alvin Ailey Dance Theater, the White Oak Dance Project, and his own Lar Lubovitch Dance Company. The Paris Opera Ballet and Israel's Bat-Dor Dance company represent the diversity of his appeal abroad. Despite dissenting opinions from some critics, audiences respond vociferously to his works, making Lar Lubovitch an internationally praised choreographer.

An artistic background in painting, combined with an underlying urge to dance since childhood, meant that Lubovitch came into the professional dance world through the higher education system, as have numerous American choreographers and performers. A visit by the José Limón Company while Lubovitch was studying art at Iowa State University fuelled his desire to dance professionally. Abandoning his brushes for the dance studio, Lubovitch attended Connecticut College briefly before entering the Juilliard School under a full scholarship. The lineage of those who contributed to Lubovitch's initial years of formalized dance training would rank among the *Who's Who* of twentieth-century dance – Anna Sokolow, Louis Horst, Lucas Hoving, and Antony Tudor among them.

Lubovitch choreographed his first full work in 1968, in the midst of a performance career encompassing both modern dance and ballet. (Members of his company, then and now, reflect the diversity of training evident in Lubovitch's own background. He has worked with dancers of both ballet and modern dance techniques who are known for their strength and versatility;

145

notable dancers over the years include Rob Besserer and Mark Morris.) In 1998, the Lar Lubovitch Dance Company celebrated its thirtieth anniversary. Financial success has fluctuated over the years, but the company has survived despite a brief year-long hiatus in 1974.

Distinct choreographic phases are evident over Lubovitch's career. He began with works such as *The Time Before the Time After (After the Time Before)* (1972), a duet about a tortured relationship in which the lovers are constantly hurting each other yet are unable to walk away. *Scherzo for Massah Jack* (1973), an evocation of the deep South, combined figurative and abstract movement. Other dances – *Whirligogs* (1969), *Some of the reactions of some of the people some of the time on hearing reports on the coming of the Messiah* (1971), and *Joy of Man's Desiring* (1972) – link movement and music to create 'a teeming meeting of the psychological and the physical' resulting in 'high-voltage aesthetic results'.[1] In contrast, Marcia B. Siegel characterized the early works as rhythmic with 'huge simultaneous body changes', without 'lightness or upward swing to this choreography, no sense of flying out into space'.[2]

Photographs of *Cavalcade* (1980), a signature work of Lubovitch's company for years, epitomize a second phase of his choreographic development which began in the late 1970s. With limbs stretched taut in explosive leaps, beautiful bodies caught mid-air in stylized all-in-one leotards, the message is the movement. Rhythmically driven by the scores of the minimalist Steve Reich in *Marimba* (1976) and *Cavalcade*, and of Philip Glass in *North Star* (1978), dancers responded directly to the music, passing on undulations through bodies and each other, 'ricocheting a movement phrase through a line of dancers'.[3] Trance-like flowing and circular qualities dominated some dance sections during this phase, while in others a controlled energy built up until the dancers burst out in leaps across the stage.

Harnessing what he termed 'energy reverberations' in *Calvacade*, Lubovitch draws on the individual strengths of his dancers, shaping them into a fast-paced virtuosic 'parade of dancers'.[4] Yet the mass, the contemporary *corps* of eight, retain their individuality as dancers step out to perform solos and duets.

Lubovitch described the middle years of working as taking 'the theoretical approach rather than the exclusively physical approach' to creating movement.[5] In contrast to his audience appeal, critical responses were not unanimously favourable, as some found Lubovitch's work repetitive and derivative during this phase. Arlene Croce focused on the music and movement relationship, which she found simplistic in terms of a direct correlation. The repetitive character of Steve Reich and Philip Glass's scores lay the foundation for movement repetition, but Croce felt the dance 'never transcends procedural mechanics, and it always seems to begin and end in the same spot without having gone anywhere in between'.[6]

Brahms Symphony marked a transformative phase in 1985, as Lubovitch turned back to early composers for inspiration in his search for a 'primal spirit of movement'.[7] Post-*Cavalcade* works evoked positive praise from a number of prominent critics in the United States and abroad who remarked on Lubovitch's impassioned movement. Jennifer Dunning wrote that 'Mr Lubovitch has created dances so warm and sensuous and pretty, he seems to have created a new category – dance to bask in',[8] highlighting the intricate patterns, tilting torsos, and lifts of surging motion which compel the dancers in *Brahms Symphony*. A revitalized confidence was noted by Jack Anderson in a paring down, the use of fewer steps.[9] Significantly, Lubovitch explained that his return to the intuitive and the physical occurred when he became reintegrated into the choreographic process by moving his own body.

Lubovitch distinguishes between the creation of movement and dance technique itself, although his works demand high levels of technical skill. 'Movement is what dance is about', focusing on transitions rather than static poses.[10] Traditionally, Lubovitch sets the structure of the dance in relation to the music first, although he ventures away from the familiar on occasion. He explains that choreographing a dance is like solving a problem approachable through various methods.

The movement questions Lubovitch set lead to unexpected results, with varying degrees of success. In *Of My Soul* (1987), Lubovitch drew from the text of J.S. Bach's *Cantata No. 78* in shaping the dance to the extent that American sign-language for the deaf is integrated into the choreography. Here, the character of The Sermon admonishes The Fallen (a role taken by either a female or male dancer) set against a chorus, combining gestures specific to signing with dancerly movement. For *Fandango* (1990), Lubovitch eschewed the critical musical relationship during the work's creation, turning instead to verbal descriptions of drawn abstract shapes to evoke movement material from his dancers. In performance, the piece was danced to Ravel's *Bolero*.

Beau Danube (1981), a humorous piece set to Johann Strauss's music, *Rhapsody in Blue* commissioned by the New York City Ballet for its 1988 American Music Festival, and *American Gesture* (1992) for the Pacific Northwest Ballet, set to Charles Ives, represent the range of composers used over the years. Rather than commissioning new scores, Lubovitch draws on existing works, establishing a critical relationship between the music and movement. An emphasis on structure informs the vision which shapes his work rather than setting out to tell a specific story, although messages also emerge:

I work first from a structural standpoint. ... I begin to build shapes, separate from the music, separate from the ego states

that the dancers or I bring in at that moment. I just work on pure visual shape. Then, from that shape, I build motive. ... I search for the relationship between my shape and the music. ... Then the combination of the shape, emotional suggestions and musical correlation is the finished phrase.[11]

Increasingly linked with the music of Mozart, Lubovitch creates highly popular dances on a range of themes. Undaunted by the complex beauty of the symphonies and concertos of the master composers, Lubovitch responds to musical impulses in 'kinetic feasts for the eye'.[12] Anna Kisselgoff remarked that Lubovitch hears the music in his own way, highlighting musical passages in unexpected ways instead of through musical equivalents.[13] France's Centre National de Danse Contemporaine commissioned one of the most well known of Lubovitch's works, inspired by Mozart's *Concerto for Clarinet and Orchestra* (K. 622). The first and third movements of *Concerto Six-Twenty-Two* (1985) create and celebrate a sense of community which frames a male duet performed to the adagio movement. Often performed independently, the duet was created in response to the AIDS crisis, but is 'more about love than lovers'.[14] In setting out to celebrate friendship between men, Lubovitch decided to focus on the dignity of male friendship rather than the agony of death and loss which has devastated society. One partner's physical support translates into an emotional basis upon which a caring relationship is framed between men, yet it speaks beyond a friendship of two.

Success on Broadway has also marked Lubovitch's career, as choreographer for Steven Sondheim and James Lapine's *Into the Woods* (1987), a musical based on fairy-tale characters, and for new dances in Rodgers and Hammerstein's *The King and I* (1996). And despite the 1993 critical failure of the Broadway musical adaptation of the movie, *The Red Shoes*, American Ballet Theatre (ABT) bought the performance rights to Lubovitch's choreography. In a further collaboration with ABT (as well as San Francisco Ballet), Lubovitch's major work of 1997 was a version of *Othello*, exceptionally – for Lubovitch – danced to a newly commissioned score, by Elliot Goldenthal. Collaborations with Olympic ice skaters John Curry and Peggy Fleming in *Tilt-a-Whirl* (1979), which was followed by *The Sleeping Beauty* for Robin Cousins and Rosalyn Sumners (1987), have extended Lubovitch's expertise beyond the proscenium frame. He has since choreographed further ice dances, for Paul Wylie (*Adagio* and *Touch Me*), Roca and Sur (*I'll Be Seeing You*), and for the Ice Theatre of New York (*Gershwin Variations*), all in 1996.

The international appeal of Lar Lubovitch's dances is found in those themes that celebrate humanity and its range of emotional states, through an emphasis on the music/movement relationship, which transcends national boundaries. As Lubovitch has explained 'All of my dances are about dancing. Dancing is really a superior metaphor for humanity and emotions'.[15]

Stacey Prickett

Notes

1 Gruen, John, *People Who Dance: 22 Dancers Tell Their Own Stories*, Princeton, New Jersey, 1988, p. 80.
2 Siegel, Marcia B., *At the Vanishing Point: A Critic Looks at Dance*, New York: Saturday Review, 1972, p. 126.
3 Sommers, Sally R., 'Review', *Dance Magazine*, June 1981, p. 46.
4 Luger, Eleanor Rachel, 'Lar Lubovitch: in Command of Method and Madness', *Dance Magazine*, March 1981, p. 68.
5 Gruen, John, 'Confrontation with Dance: Lyricism and Craft, Lar Lubovitch', *Dance Magazine*, February 1990, p. 48.
6 Croce, Arlene, *Going to the Dance*, New York: Alfred A. Knopf, 1982, p. 364.
7 Quoted in Parks, Gary, 'New Lease on Lar', *Dance Magazine*, November 1986, p. 55.
8 Dunning, Jennifer, 'Dance: Premiere by Lar Lubovitch', *The New York Times*, 9 May 1985.
9 Anderson, Jack, 'Lubovitch and Brahms: Exuberant Partnership', *The New York Times*, 22 March 1988, C20.
10 Lubovitch, quoted in Parks, op. cit., p. 54.
11 Lubovitch in Gruen 1988, p. 87.
12 Tobias, Anne, 'Lar Lubovitch Dance Company', *Dance Magazine*, September 1992, p. 71.
13 Kisselgoff, Anna, 'Lubovitch the Earth-Shaker Takes a Breather', *The New York Times*, 17 March 1988, III, p. 23.
14 Kisselgoff, Anna, 'The Wider Dimension of Lubovitch's Male Duet', *The New York Times*, 13 May 1993, p. C15.
15 Harris, William, 'For Lubovitch, Dance is a Verbal Art', *The New York Times*, 25 February 1990, II, p. 1.

Biographical details

Born in Chicago, United States, 9 April 1943. **Studied** art at Chicago's Art Institute and Iowa State University; studied dance at Connecticut College, New London, with José Limón and Alvin Ailey, and at New York's Juilliard School of Performing Arts from 1964, and with Anna Sokolow, Martha Graham, Louis Horst, Lucas Hoving, Antony Tudor, and Leon Danielian; also attended classes at the Joffrey Ballet School and the Martha Graham School. **Career** Danced with several ballet, modern, and jazz companies, including Pearl Lang Company, 1964, Manhattan Festival Ballet (soloist), and Harkness Ballet (soloist), 1967–69; first choreography for opera productions, 1965; formed own group, the Lar Lubovitch Dance Company, in 1968: company disbanded 1974, but reformed in 1975; has been guest choreographer for various companies, including Pennsylvania Ballet, Bat-Dor-Dance Company (Israel), Gulbenkian Ballet, Dutch National Ballet, Paris Opéra Ballet, Ballet Rambert, Baryshnikov's White Oak Dance Project, Pacific Northwest Ballet, New York City Ballet, Alvin Ailey Dance Theater, and American Ballet Theatre. Has also choreographed a number of works for ice dancers, and for Broadway and West End musicals. **Awards and honours** include International Emmy Award (for film of *Fandango*), 1992; National Education Film and Video Festival Golden Apple, 1993; Astaire Award (Theater Development Fund), 1993–94; US International Film and Video Festival Gold Camera Award, 1995; Worldfest Gold Award (Houston, Texas), 1995; Gemini Award (Canada, for ice-dance film *The Planets*), 1996.

Works

Don Giovanni (opera by Mozart, 1965), *The Marriage of Figaro* (opera by Mozart, 1965), *Carmen* (opera by Mozart, 1965), *Blue* (1968), *Freddie's Bag* (1968), *The Journey Back* (mus. Akira Miyoshi, 1968), *Greeting Sampler* (mus. Toru Takemitsu, 1969), *Transcendant Passage* (mus. Pierre Henry, Morton Subotnick, 1969), *Unremembered Time – Forgotten Place* (mus. Tony Scott, Kimio Eto, 1969), *Incident at Lee* (mus. tape collage, 1969), *Whirligogs* (mus. Luciano Berio, 1969), *Variations and Fugue on the Theme of a Dream* (mus. 'Ramayana monkey chant', 1970), *In a Clearing* (mus. J.S. Bach, 1970), *Sam Nearlydeadman* (mus. collage by Lubovitch, 1970), *Social* (mus. J.S. Bach, 1971), *Clear Lake* (mus. Mendelssohn, 1971), *Some of the reactions of some of the people some of the time upon hearing reports of the coming of the Messiah* (mus. Handel, 1971), *The Time Before the Time After (After the Time Before)* (mus. Stravinsky, 1972), *Joy* (mus. J.S. Bach, 1972), *Air* (mus. J.S. Bach, 1972), *Considering the Lilies (Joy of Man's Desiring)* (mus. J.S. Bach, 1972), *Sans titre* (mus. Stravinsky, 1972), *Scherzo for Massah Jack* (mus. Charles Ives, 1973), *Chariot Light Night* (mus. J.S. Bach; television version, 1973; stage version, 1974), *Three Essays* (mus. Charles Ives, 1974), *Zig Zag* (mus. Stravinsky, 1974), *Eight Easy Pieces* (mus. Stravinsky, 1974), *Prelude in C Minor (Avalanche*; mus. J.S. Bach, 1975), *Girl on Fire* (mus. Britten, 1975), *Rapid Transit* (mus. Stravinsky, 1975), *Session* (silent, 1975), *Marimba: A Trance Dance* (mus. Steve Reich, 1976), *Les Noces* (mus. Stravinsky, 1976), *Cite Veron* (retitled version of *Session*, 1977), *Exultate, Jubilate* (mus. Mozart, 1977), *Scriabin Dances* (mus. Scriabin, 1977), *North Star* (mus. Philip Glass, 1978), *Valley* (mus. Beethoven, 1978), *Tilt-a-Whirl* (ice dance; mus. Philip Glass, 1979), *Up Jump* (mus. Duke Ellington, 1979), *Mistral* (for television; mus. Philip Glass, Brian Eno, 1979), *Calvacade* (mus. Steve Reich, 1980), *American Gesture* (mus. Charles Ives, 1981; expanded version, 1992), *Beau Danube* (mus. Johann Strauss, 1981), *Big Shoulders* (silent, 1983; revised version, with sound collage, 1985), *Tabernacle* (mus. Steve Reich, 1983), *Adagio and Rondo for Glass Harmonica* (mus. Mozart, 1984), *Court of Ice* (ice dance; mus. J.S. Bach, 1984), *Brahms Symphony* (mus. Brahms, 1985; revised version, as *A Brahms Symphony*, 1995), *Concerto Six Twenty-two* (mus. Mozart, 1985), *Blood* (mus. George Antheil, 1986), *Of My Soul* (mus. J.S. Bach, 1987), *Sleeping Beauty* (ice dance; mus. Tchaikovsky, 1987), *Into the Woods* (musical by

Steven Sondheim and James Lapine, 1987), *Musette* (mus. Poulenc, 1988), *Rhapsody in Blue* (mus. Gershwin, 1988), *Fandango* (mus. Ravel, 1990), *From Paris to Jupiter* (mus. Mozart; 1990; later retitled *Just Before Jupiter*), *Quartet for Oboe and Strings* (mus. Mozart, 1990), *Hautbois* (mus. Mozart, 1990), *Sinfonia Concertante* (mus. Mozart, 1991), *Waiting for Sunrise* (mus. Les Paul, Mary Ford, Johnny Puleo and his Harmonica Gang, 1991), *Dance of the Seven Veils* (for play *Salomé* by Oscar Wilde, 1992), *The Red Shoes* (adpatation of film musical by Jule Styne, 1993), *So in Love* (mus. Cole Porter, 1994), *The Planets* (ice dance for television; mus. Holst, 1994), *Oklahoma* (musical by Rodgers and Hammerstein, 1994), *The King and I* (musical by Rodgers and Hammerstein, 1996), *Touch Me* (ice dance; mus. the Doors, 1996), *Adagio* (ice dance; mus. J.S. Bach, 1996), *I'll Be Seeing You* (ice dance; mus. Mel Tormé, 1996), *Gershwin Variations* (ice dance; mus. Gershwin, 1996), *Othello* (mus. Elliott Goldenthal, 1997).

Further reading

Interviews in 'Lar Lubovitch: American Dancer and Choreographer', *Dance and Dancers*, October 1972; with John Gruen, in 'Confrontation with Dance: Lar Lubovitch', *Dance Magazine*, February 1990.

Articles Doris Hering, 'Choreography by Lar Lubovitch', *Dance Magazine*, February 1970; Norma McLain Stoop, 'A Human Being Who Dances: Lar Lubovitch', *Dance Magazine*, April 1972; Horst Koegler, 'The Lisbon Story – Part One', *Dance and Dancers*, August 1972; John Gruen, 'Lar Lubovitch: Choreographer in Search of Meaning', *Dance Magazine*, February 1977; Eleanor Rachel Luger, 'Lar Lubovitch: In Command of Method and Madness', *Dance Magazine*, March 1981; Allen Robertson, 'Right on Target', *Ballet News*, February 1984; Alastair Macaulay, 'Umbrellissima', *Dancing Times*, December 1984; Gary Parks, 'New Lease on Lar: Passion's Progress', *Dance Magazine*, November 1986; Clive Barnes, 'Outsiders Moving In', *Dance and Dancers*, February 1987; Kevin Boyd Grubb, 'Broadway and Beyond', *Dance Magazine*, April 1988; Maya Wallach, 'Lubovitch Strikes Out', *Attitude*, Winter 1989/90; Tobi Tobias, 'Rites of Passage', *New York Magazine*, 7 January 1991; 'Lar Lubovitch', in *Current Biography Yearbook 1992*.

Books Max Niehaus, *Ballett Faszination*, Munich, 1972; John Gruen, *The Private World of Ballet*, New York, 1975; Don McDonagh, *The Complete*

Guide to Modern Dance, Garden City, New York, 1976; Cynthia Lyle (ed.), *Dancers on Dancing*, New York and London, 1977; Arlene Croce, *Going to the Dance*, New York, 1982; John Gruen (ed.), *People Who Dance: 22 Dancers Tell Their Own Stories*, Princeton, New Jersey, 1988.

MAGUY MARIN

Although it is generally acknowledged that *Tanztheater* is a genre exclusive to German culture, its equivalent in English, the term 'dance-theatre', is conventionally used to designate contemporary productions that do not rely on the language of dance as the sole means of expression. If considered from this standpoint, the works of Maguy Marin are fitting examples of 'dance-theatre', for the dance medium is often circumscribed by the concomitance of other elements, including aural, vocal, and visual ones. It is not incidental, therefore, that some dance historians and reviewers have labelled Marin's choreography the 'French answer to *Tanztheater*'. At the same time, her formulae differ considerably from those of, for example, Pina Bausch and Susanne Linke, whose works refer more or less explicitly to the canons of German Expressionism, and indeed do not stem from any specific artistic or cultural movement.

An overview of Marin's works reveals that, through the years, she has constantly changed her artistic principles, approaching the art of dance from different angles and experimenting with different forms of expression. In her early works, such as *La jeune fille et la mort* [Death and the Maiden] (1979) and *Cante* (1980), the movement vocabulary, stemming from the combination of classical dance with contemporary techniques, and her choice of subject-matter reflected her experience as a member of both Mudra and Béjart's Ballet du XXème Siècle. After 1981, a deeper investigation of theatre led Marin to the creation of some of her most distinctive dances, such as *May B.* (1981), *Babel*

Babel (1982), and *Hymen* (1984). It is possible that these works were conceived under the influence of *Tanztheater*, which significantly affected European choreography in the early 1980s. Yet, it should be remembered that the combination of theatre elements with dance was also one of the characteristic traits of Béjart's spectacular performances. Finally, the rediscovery of ballet – which had constituted an integral part of Marin's dance training – has been the impetus behind more recent works, such as *Cendrillon* [Cinderella] (1985), *Groosland* (1990), and *Coppélia* (1993).

Despite such a varied *œuvre*, it is still possible to identify some recurring elements in Marin's choreography. Perhaps the most characteristic aspect is her ability to create metaphorical and allegorical images. The symbolism that permeates Marin's works is neither obscure nor self-indulgent but reflects the choreographer's wide range of thematic concerns. In *La jeune fille et la mort*, considered Marin's first major creation, Schubert's quartet provided the inspiration for a dance that focused on the difficulty of existing and of communicating. Similarly, in *May B.*, unanimously regarded as the work that confirmed her pre-eminence within European contemporary choreography, Marin alluded to Samuel Beckett, particularly to some of his most significant plays, in order to explore and to portray the 'tortuous paths of human relationships'.[1] One year after the creation of *May B.*, the biblical myth of Babel prompted *Babel Babel*, which dealt with the contrast between the simple language of an idealized, original world – to which societies will eventually revert – and the restrictive, often absurd conventions of the various idioms created by man through different eras of civilization. *Hymen*, perhaps the least narrative and most allegorical of Marin's creations, was a celebration of mystical love through a sequence of contrasting images derived from well-known, recognizable sources, such as the paintings of Velásquez and the films of Fellini. In *Cendrillon* the familiar fairytale of Cinderella became the pretext for a psychological investigation of a child's world, addressing issues such as children's innate cruelty and children's vision of love and parenthood. More recently, with *Coppélia*, Marin explored the constraints and oddities of male erotic ideals, as analysed from a witty feminist perspective.

Marin's symbols and metaphorical images rely on a complex combination of different means of expression. At the beginning of *Babel Babel*, for example, the dancers appeared in the nude (thus conveying that idealized, pure, original world) and performed, to music by Mahler, steps and sequences derived from the combination of contemporary dance and ballet. Then, in a rapid crescendo of images, various stages of human history were shown: a rural community moving to the rhythmic sounds of rustic tools; a fashionable beach with body-builders posing; a rock group singing tunes from the 1960s; the advent of the punk movement. After a cathartic explosion, the action reverted to the opening sequence, as a message of hope. The members of the company, including the choreographer (who appeared as one of the rock singers, thus referring ironically to her previous artistic experiences) expressed themselves through a variety of means, exploiting all their possibilities as actors, singers, mimes, and musicians.

The use of masks, created by Monserrat Casanova – one of Marin's loyal artistic collaborators – characterized *Cendrillon*; according to the choreographer, their purpose was to 'transcend the limits of traditional pantomime'.[2] The set resembled a doll's house, divided in several compartments corresponding to the locations of the action. Prokofiev's ballet score was interpolated both with recordings of electronic sounds, to accompany the movements of the fairy godmother, portrayed as a science-fiction character, and with sounds of children's voices, underlining some of the most dramatic moments, such as the ballroom scene, where the party-goers ended up fighting over lollipops.

In *Coppélia*, the action took place both on stage and on a screen. *Coppélia*, the doll, was portrayed as a celluloid sex-symbol, starring in movies that Frantz and Coppelius enjoyed watching in private. Her image was suddenly multiplied into twelve identical starlets, who came out of the screen to haunt the two men, as the Wilis do in the Romantic ballet *Giselle*.

Because of the presence of diverse theatre idioms in such works, dance critics have often considered Marin more a 'director' than a choreographer. But that definition is inappropriate, for the language of dance remains the distinctive common denominator of all her works, whereas other means of expression are used only occasionally, depending on their compatibility with either particular subjects or with particular moments in the action. It is not difficult to identify the principles of Marin's dance style, much as the movement vocabulary may vary in relation to dramatic, musical, and cultural context. What the choreographer refers to as 'my language'[3] is a personal adaptation of the dance style absorbed from Mudra, Carolyn Carlson (with whom she worked briefly) and Béjart's company, a style that was itself derived from a concoction of combining contemporary technique and modern ballet. In Marin's works, the dance movement is always smooth and fluid, interwoven with contrasting angular motions and an often predominant language of gesture.

Indeed, gesture is a significant element in Marin's choreography. If her dance vocabulary is the constant, then different types of gesture represent the variants that distinguish, both technically and stylistically, each work. In *May B.*, for example, the fast, neurotic movements echoed Beckett's writing, whereas in *Cendrillon* gestures provided a stylized portrayal of children's physical behaviour. These gestures, however, never become trite pantomime. Indeed it is the perfect balance between diverse elements that is the successful formula of Marin's creations, and reveals her in-depth knowledge of theatre arts.

Giannandrea Poesio

Notes

1 Dienis, J.C. (1985), 'Maguy Marin, femme on the rock', *Danser*, Paris, no. 28, p. 40.
2 Marin, M. in ibid., p. 43.
3 Marin, M. in ibid., p. 43.

Biographical details

Born in Toulouse, France, 2 June 1951. **Studied** classical ballet at the Toulouse Conservatoire from 1959, with Nina Vyroubova in Paris, and at Maurice Béjart's newly created Mudra school in Brussels, 1970–73. **Career** Danced with Strasbourg Opéra Ballet, c.1969; joined the Chandra group (directed by Micha van Hoecke), which split away from the Mudra school in 1974; joined Béjart's Ballet du XXième Siècle in 1972 as dancer: first choreography for the company, 1976; together with Daniel Ambash formed her own company, Le Ballet Théâtre de l'Arche, 1978: based in Créteil from 1981; renamed Compagnie Maguy Marin, 1984, it became a Centre Chorégraphique National in 1990. Has also choreographed for the Groupe de Recherche Chorégraphique de l'Opéra de Paris (GRCOP), Paris Opéra Ballet, Lyon Opéra Ballet, Dutch National Ballet, and Nederlands Dans Theater. **Awards and honours** First Prize, Nyon Choreography Competition, 1977; First Prize, Bagnolet Festival International Choreography Competition, 1978; Grand Prix National de Chorégraphie, 1983; Chevalier de l'Ordre des Arts et des Lettres.

Works

Yu-ku-ri (mus. Alain Louafi, 1976), *Evocation* (mus. Brahms *Lieder*, 1977), *Nieblas de Niño* (mus. Spanish folk music; text: poetry by García Lorca, 1978), *L'Adieu* (with Daniel Ambash; mus. Stephane Dosse, 1978), *Dernier Geste* (mus. J.S. Bach, 1978), *Puzzle* (mus. Steve Reich, 1978), *Instantané-Simultané* (mus. Pierre Henry, 1978), *Zoo* (mus. Stravinsky, 1979), *La jeune fille et la mort* (mus. Schubert, 1979), *Cante* (mus. Spanish folk music, Charlie Haden, 1980), *Réveillon* (mus. Marino Marini, 1980), *Contrastes* (mus. Bartók, 1980), *Jodl* (mus. traditional African, 1980), *May*

B. (mus. Schubert, Gilles de Binche, Gavin Bryars, 1981), *Babel Babel* (mus. Mahler, 1960s pop, 1982), *Jaleo* (mus. Gitanes de Stes-Maries-de-la-Mer, 1983), *Hymen* (mus. various, 1984), *Cendrillon* (mus. Prokofiev, Johan Schwarz, 1985), *Calambre* (mus. Arturo Rayon, 1985), *Eden* (mus. Marin, Yves Bouche, Pierre Colomer, 1986), *Leçons de ténèbres* (mus. Couperin, 1987), *Otello* (opera by Verdi, 1987), ... *Des petits bourgeois Les sept pechés capitaux* (mus. Weill, Bernard Barras, text Bertolt Brecht, 1987), *Coups d'états* (mus. Bernard Barras, 1987), *Groosland* (mus. J.S. Bach, 1988), *Eh, qu'est-ce que ça m'fait à moi!?* (mus. Michel Bertier, Philippe Madile, Jean-Marc Sohier, 1989), *Cortex* (mus. Denis Mariotte, 1991), *Ay Dios* (mus. Denis Mariotte, 1992), *Made in France* (mus. Denis Mariotte, 1992), *Coppélia* (mus. Delibes, 1993; also film version), *Waterzooi* (mus. Denis Mariotte, 1993), *RamDam* (mus. Denis Mariotte, 1995), *Aujourd'hui peut-être* (mus. Volapük, 1996).

Further reading

Interview with Martine Plenells, in 'Moi, Je fais du spectacle', *Danser*, March 1991.

Articles Danielle Gregoire, 'Micha van Hoecke et Maguy Marin', *Pour la Danse*, November 1975; Laure Pental, 'Maguy Marin et Pierre Henry', *Pour la Danse*, November 1978; Raphael de Gubernatis, 'Maguy Marin', *Danser*, April 1983; Allen Robertson, 'Danse Nouvelle: The New Wave of French Modern Dance', *Ballet News*, July 1983; Norbert Servos, 'Vintage Avant-garde', *Ballett International*, January 1985; Jean Claude Diénis, 'Maguy Marin, Femme on the Rock', *Danser*, November 1985; Malve Gradinger, 'Surface Values: French Dance Theatre', *Ballett International*, February 1986; Bruce Merrill, 'France's Marin', *Dance Magazine*, March 1986; Malve Gradinger, 'Punk Counterworlds', *Ballett International*, April 1986; Claudia Roth Pierpont, 'Nouvelles *Cendrillons*', *Ballet Review*, Summer 1987; Bernadette Bonis, 'French Choreographers Creating New Worlds', *Ballett International*, November 1989; Jean-Marc Adolphe, 'The Source and the Destination: Concepts of Memory, Movement, and Perception in French Dance', *Ballett International*, January 1991; André Philippe Hersin, 'Avant-premières: Marin/ Hoffmann/Eifman', *Les Saisons de la Danse*, February 1991.

Books Allen Robertson and Donald Hutera, *The Dance Handbook*, Harlow, Essex, 1988.

SUSAN MARSHALL

To choreographer Susan Marshall, dance is about real people, not about performers. Marshall designs movement choices that encourage audiences to see modern dance in terms of real men and women, conveying a sense of the struggle involved in intimate relationships. As such, her choreographies, Marshall says, are 'a sequence of interior states', telling audiences about 'interaction and relation and response', and revealing human intent. As one critic has commented, the 'intelligently calibrated constructions reveal nuances of human emotions, complexities of intimate relationships, absurdities and hidden hostilities that form part of even the tenderest friendship'.[1]

Her dances are also commentaries on American life, 'with its headlong drive for individual distinction and achievement'.[2] They are icons of our ravenous need to be loved and our undeniable fear of loneliness. So we see lovers who cannot quite live together, but cannot bear to be separated, we experience friends giving the impression that they are trying to ignore, yet also impress, each other; we witness duets rooted to the spot, or suspended in air, defying gravity or sinking under the weight of weakness. Marshall's characters express helplessness through arm movements that embrace, fondle, and support while gripping, manipulating, and repelling space or each other, in dances where gestures register alternately as lethal blows and tender caresses.

Male–female relations became a very natural subject matter for Marshall. They formed the subject matter of family dinner-time conversations between her father, a behavioural scientist and scholar, and her mother, a leading feminist writer. Later, in preparation for a career in dance, Marshall studied at the Juilliard School of Music in New York City. After two years she decided to explore the craft of choreography on her own. In the early 1980s, Susan Marshall & Company was formed, and with it she gained recognition and acceptance.

Marshall's first evening-length work, *Interior With Seven Figures*, had its premiere in 1988 at the Brooklyn Academy of Music. In this piece, austere black figures enter a harshly lit stage, inhabiting a frigid landscape consisting of a massive, empty metal frame hanging at the back and a matching square of mauve laid on the floor. The seven dancers behave like participants in a series of arduous contests, whose goals remain ambiguous, but which are propelled by the 'dash to seize, the grab of manipulative hands, the slap of body against body against the floor ... The most potent imagery seems subtly derived from drowning, rescuing, and ... from those frightening early swimming lessons that plague many adult nightmares'.[3] In this and other works Marshall has examined what has been described as 'the dualities and complexities of a troubled and often unsympathetic society',[4] combining social comment with psychological insight. And her work has emerged in an era characterized by a social shift from a concern solely with oneness to pluralism.

In her working methods, Marshall reflects the influence and lineage of notable choreographers of the 1960s and 1970s, such as Trisha Brown, Yvonne Rainer, David Gordon, Steve Paxton, and Meredith Monk. What critic Jack Anderson views as her 'tight, bare-bones structure and vocabulary strictly limited to pedestrian moves' are put to a purpose that is unique among contemporaries. In her early pieces, Marshall contrived an 'action and response' technique to illustrate the way in which narrative functioned in her dances. Each character would achieve a definition, as one dancer would react to another's movements, in a collaborative volleying that became a method to 'create and sculpt movement'.

In rehearsal, Marshall is not a mercurial worker, but draws on her dancers' reactions and input, systematically videotaping each rehearsal, then studying the tapes between rehearsals. She extracts or condenses a recorded movement motif and develops it further in later sessions. 'there's a lot of give and take with the dancers in the creation of the work and they give a great deal of material and feedback', Marshall says. 'I outline the structure and tell them what I think the work is about . . . [they] bring to the process their personal lives and stories as well . . . There is another layer which is our lives together as a company – this feeds into the work as well . . . The dance [becomes] steeped with all these different layers of individual experiences and contributions and . . . it ends up being very tangible to an audience'.[5] Ultimately, Marshall provides the 'narrative units' for the viewer to experience. In the finished works, non-traditional movement and everyday action become elevated into theatrically expressive gestures while retaining a formalistic sense of architecture and an emotional edge.

A good example of her working technique is *Contenders* (1990), set to a musical score by Pauline Oliveros. It is a piece that provides a metaphor for many of life's challenges. The dancers appear as 'generic jocks . . . sprinters, long-distance runners, wrestlers, swimmers, acrobats . . . relentless strivers',[6] attempting to surpass their own capabilities. Dressed in workout apparel, they line up repeatedly, moving forward through a series of sporty physical manoeuvres in competitive postures. They strut, vogue, and rough-neck. Their manic behaviour makes strong social statements, compelling us to view them as attention seekers. Yet *Contenders* is also about heroic effort, about not giving up – about 'going for it, making it, pushing beyond all reasonable limits of strength, speed, endurance and courage'.[7]

Marshall's dance vocabulary, as well as her themes, are deliberately limited and pragmatic. As she says:

I'm taken by all kinds of simple everyday movements, say the way someone might leave or enter a room . . . [or] two people walking toward each other in a corridor . . . all movement is there for me to use as material, just as with a writer all language is there for them to use as their medium . . . [Choreographers] often use embraces, kisses, touches, things of this nature as punctuation – as meaningful signifiers . . . I might use an embrace, over and over and over again with subtle variations as you see it repeated. The embrace becomes recognizable again as something other than a cliché – a gesture with depth and possibilities . . . [A] familiar gesture takes on more shades of meaning than if it were used as a theatrical punctuation.[8]

She thinks not only of defining parameters of the art of dance (What is it? Who does it, where, and how?), but also concentrates rigorously on individuals reacting, on motivation. Marshall describes her approach as one of wanting the 'audience thinking about the dancers as characters, thinking, "what's happening here?"'[9] In elaborating on her narrative themes, Marshall often uses the same characters – or character types – through different dances. Within a single choreography, role reversal and examples of mutual dependency are also evident. Examples are *Ward* (1983), *Interior With Seven Figures* (1988), *Untitled (Detail)* (1992), and *Standing Duet* (1993).

Often a movement motif will thread itself through several pieces. For instance, the concluding segment of *Trio in Four Parts* (1983) became the thematic motif of *Arms* (1984), one of the company's signature works. Repeated use of arm gestures, for example, has taken on different dramatic and emotional connotations in different theatrical contexts, in works such as *Trio in Four Parts* (1983), *Arms* (1984), *Interior With Seven Figures*, and *Contenders*. Such vocabularies of arm and torso movements help audiences to 'read' a Marshall choreography.

In recent works, however, Marshall has begun to move away from a concentration on a kind of narrative. *Fields of View* (1994), with its emphasis on swirling movement, visual designs, and compelling music (Philip Glass's *Fourth String Quartet*), was the first of these. It offered several visually arresting theatrical images, such as dancers walking backwards against falling 'snow'. Marshall provided a context for this piece, though, by pointing out that:

at the center of [the] work was the tangled relationship between experience and time . . . our interior lives move fluidly through time uninterrupted by barriers . . . [even] as we live in the present, we revisit and rethink the past. We dream and rearrange the future. This dance unfurled like a scroll containing many smaller dances that recurred, advanced, receded and co-existed.[10]

In creating other works in the mid-1990s, such as *Spectators at an Event* (1994), Marshall presented complex situations that could be frozen into a moment or made to float in our minds as solitary memories. *Spectators* drew its inspiration from the 1940s journalistic photographer, WeeGee (Arthur Fellig), a theme-and-variation photographer who depicted a wide range of emotions. Marshall's interest was in WeeGee's stark realism, which captured the reactions of individuals and groups at the exact moments of witnessing images of murder, disorder, and other dramatic events in New York City during the 1930s and 1940s. His images have been described as 'dramatic close-ups [and] brightly lit shots of spectators' which 'blurred the dividing line between being a participant in the action and spectator to it'.[11] Thus Marshall structured *Spectators* with multiple layers of images of 'people watching, watching people', describing it as being about 'those who are left behind. How their lives go on and how some people's lives don't go on'.[12]

A literary rather than a photographic source inspired Marshall's major 1996 work. Jean Cocteau's 1929 novel *Les Enfants terribles*, a surreal and menacing story about the complex psychological tragedy of two siblings, prompted Marshall, in collaboration with composer Philip Glass, to construct a dance-opera entitled *Les Enfants terribles: Children of the Game*. The performers consisted of a mixture of singers, dancers, musicians, who, together with a projected text, created a rich aural and visual amalgam expressing Cocteau's belief in the tranformative powers of the imagination. The success of the work earned Marshall and Glass a 1997 'Bessie' award.

Marshall's most recent work has been a collaborative dance project with composer David Lang, performed by the Bang on the Can All-Stars Band. This piece, *The Most Dangerous Room in the House* (premiering in 1998), a full evening's performance in three acts, investigates 'the fears of the people, forces, and events that influence and shape the directions our lives take', according to Marshall. Her idea for the work began with her anticipation of becoming a mother and 'the fear that accompanies my knowledge that I would not be able to control the world (or my child, for that matter) in attempting to bring him fulfillment and security'. Such a fear of vulnerability – along with strivings for self-sufficiency, the craving of companionship, the discovery of intoxicating love, and hostility towards self and others form the emotional range that constitute the richness of so much of Marshall's choreography.

Jennifer Predock-Linnell

Notes

1 T. Tobias, *The New York Magazine*, 4 January 1988.
2 A. Kriegsman, 'The Drive of *Contenders*', *Washington Post*, 2 February 1991.
3 D. Jowitt, 'Love is a Knockout', *Village Voice*, 27 December 1988.
4 B. Deresiewicz, 'Susan Marshall's Small Pleasures', *Dance View*, Summer 1993.
5 S. Marshall, *An Interview with Susan Marshall*, published by the Kreisberg Group, 1 June 1994.
6 T. Tobias, 'Down for the Count: Dance', *The New York Magazine*, 17 December 1990.

SUSAN MARSHALL

7 A. Kriegsman, op. cit.
8 S. Marshall, op. cit.
9 M.J. Cowell, *Dance about People* programme
   notes, Washington DC, 1990.
10 S. Marshall, op. cit.
11 B. Lifson, *WeeGee's Passion*, 1997.
12 S. Marshall, op. cit.

Biographical details

Born in Pensacola, Florida, United States, 17
October 1958. **Studied** at the Dance Department
of the Juilliard School of Music (having first
trained as a gymnast), New York, 1976–78. **Career**
began as choreographer in 1982, founding her
own small performing group, Susan Marshall &
Company; residency at The Yard, 1982. Has
choreographed works for New York company
CoDanceCo, Boston Ballet, Dallas Ballet, Groupe
de Recherche Chorégraphique de l'Opéra de Paris
(GRCOP), Frankfurt Ballet, Montréal Danse, and
Lyon Opéra Ballet. Has also staged dances for
Los Angeles Opera and New York City Opera.
Awards New York Dance and Performance
Award ('Bessie'), 1985, 1997; fellowships from
New York Foundation for the Arts, 1985, and
National Endowment for the Arts, 1986–91;
Guggenheim Fellowship, 1990; American Chore-
ographer Award, 1988; Brandeis University
Creative Arts Citation, 1988; *Dance Magazine*
Award, 1994, 1995.

Works

Eighteen Marbles (mus. Robert Kaplan, 1982),
Fault Line (mus. Robert Kaplan, 1982), *Trio in
Four Parts* (mus. Luis Resto, 1983), *Ward* (mus.
Linda Fisher, 1983), *Arms* (mus. Luis Resto,
1984), *Routine and Variations* (mus. Scott Killian,
1984), *Opening Gambits* (mus. Luis Resto, 1985),
Common Run (mus. Luis Resto, 1985), *Kin* (mus.
A. Leroy, 1985), *Arena* (mus. ballroom/big band
music, 1986), *Gifts* (mus. Schumann, Widor, Saint-
Saëns, 1986), *The Refrain* (mus. Luis Resto, 1986),
Overture (mus. Luis Resto, 1987), *Kiss* (mus. Arvo
Pärt, 1987), *The Aerialist* (mus. Luis Resto, 1987),
Companion Pieces (mus. Luis Resto, Jackie
Wilson, Percy Sledge, 1987), *Interior with Seven
Figures* (mus. Luis Resto, 1988), *Figures in
Opposition* (mus. Schubert, 1989), *In Media Res*
(mus. Beethoven, 1989), *Articles of Faith* (mus.
Linda Fisher, 1990), *Contenders* (mus. Pauline
Oliveros, 1990; film version, dir Mark Obernhaus,
1991; revised version, 1992), *Dances in Les
Troyens* (opera by Berlioz; 1991), *Untitled (Detail)*
(mus. Beethoven, 1992), *Standing Duet* (mus. Luis
Resto, 1993), *Solo* (mus. Victor Cavini, 1993),

Walter's Finest Hours (mus. Pauline Oliveros,
1993), *Entr'acte I* (mus. Philip Glass, 1993),
Entr'acte II (mus. Philip Glass, 1993), dances in
The Midsummmer's Marriage (opera by Tippett;
1993), *Central Figure* (mus. Philip Glass, 1994),
Private Worlds in Public View (mus. various,
1994), *Fields of View* (mus. Philip Glass, 1994),
Spectators at an Event (mus. Górecki, 1994), *Lines
from Memory* (mus. Philip Glass, 1995), *Les
Enfants terribles: Children of the Game* (mus.
Philip Glass, 1996); The Most Dangerous Room
in the House (mus. David Lang, 1998).

Further reading

Articles Elizabeth Zimmer, 'Susan Marshall &
Company', *Dance Magazine*, April 1985; Sally
Sommer, 'Susan Marshall & Company', *Dance
Magazine*, May 1986; Otis Stuart, 'Susan Marshall
and Company at BAM: Marshalling the Next
Wave', *Dance Magazine*, December 1988;
Robert Sandla, 'Freedom of Expression', *Dance
Magazine*, February 1990; Sally Sommer, 'Susan
Marshall & Company', *Dance Magazine*, August
1990; Tobi Tobias, 'Down for the Count', *New
York Magazine*, 17 December 1990; David
Hughes, 'The Poetics of Exhaustion', *Dance
Theatre Journal*, Spring 1991; Judith Mackrell,
'Post-Modern Dance in Britain: An Historical
Essay', *Dance Research*, Spring 1991; Sally Banes,
'American Postmodern Choreography', *Choreo-
graphy and Dance*, 1(2), 1992; Bill Deresiewicz,
'Susan Marshall's Small Pleasures', *Dance View*,
Summer 1993; L. Traiger, 'Gender Bending',
Dance View, Autumn 1992; Doris Hering, 'Susan
Marshall and Company', *Dance Magazine*, March
1993; Ann Tobias, 'Susan Marshall: A Place
Beyond', *Dance Ink*, Summer 1994.

BEBE MILLER

Bebe Miller, one of the best, most unpretentious exponents of downtown New York
dance, works in the postmodern idiom with
confidence. Her work, steeped in urban
sensibility, frequently employs everyday
movement, but it is always grounded in
Miller's impressive understanding of her
craft. Her choreography, which could be
called semi-narrative, is never merely abstract for its own sake. She devises movement
that is deeply rooted in recognizably human

dynamics. For her there is a direct, visceral link between mind and motion. The result is the creation of warm, urgent, kinetic drama.

Miller does not make an issue of being an African-American woman. She is far more keen to make dances than feminist or ethnic manifestos. Born in Brooklyn, she began taking dance workshops as a child on Manhattan's Lower East Side. Her tutors included Murray Louis and Alwin Nikolais. Composition and improvisation were the strong suits of her training, factors still evident in Miller's work today: her dancers' seemingly off-the-cuff, stream-of-consciousness spontaneity is usually supported by a strong structure. She majored in art at Indiana's Earlham College, before securing a dance fellowship at Ohio State University College, where she encountered Nina Wiener, a dance-choreographer in the Twyla Tharp mould. (Wiener was a member of Tharp's company in the early 1970s.) Miller signed on with Wiener's troupe for six years. By the time she left, she had begun to make dances of her own. She toured with Dana Reitz, another Tharp alumna and a maverick minimalist, before forming her own eponymous company in 1984.

As a performer, Miller is compelling, compact, and essentially without any apparent ego. She favours fast, clear moves, but is also capable of great, idiosyncratic delicacy: witness her 1985 signature solo, *Spending Time Doing Things*. This pensive, private, highly gestural piece begins and ends in silence. Miller's beautifully modulated phrasing seems to summon up the music, Duke Ellington's *In My Solitude*. When the music, as it were, vanishes, Miller is alone again, with her body and her thoughts.

If *Spending Time* is an ingenious dance equivalent of a soliloquy, *Two* (1986) is an anguished dialogue. In this small masterpiece, a collaboration with Ralph Lemon, Miller explores the terrible weight of wanting, but being unable, to connect with another person. The man and woman in this haunting dance wage a gripping, compulsively watchable war of see-sawing need and rejection. Their emotional agitation is at once explicit and fraught with ambiguity. In Miller's best works, the atmosphere may be charged with feeling, yet some mystery is preserved. This makes viewing her dances a discovery of, rather than a lesson in, human behaviour, and is a source of their wisdom.

Miller is a dancer's dancer-choreographer, who extracts a high degree of input from dancers, whether they are part of her company or merely the living material she is working with on commissioned pieces. Miller treats them as individuals whose virtual duty is to make her movement their own. Consequently, they tend to exhibit an unforced alertness, as they must, given the precisely inflected, unexpected shifts of weight, tone, energy, and nuance she demands from them. Miller's dancers boldly glide on complexity. They thrash, pause, wander, and whip themselves about, swooping, hopping, crashing to the floor and rising again in vertical jumps. There are quiet moments, too, of tenderness and trust. To negotiate all this lush, galvanizing turbulence requires considerable control while pulling out all the stops.

Miller's ensemble pieces run the gamut from infernally dark to red-hot to irrepressibly playful. She drew on her experiences as a waitress to make *Working Order*, a 1986 study in blue-collar despair and survival. *The Hendrix Project* is her exuberant, exhaustive 1991 response to guitarist Jimi Hendrix's music. (Miller's aural selections lean towards jazz, rock, or electronics.) The group moves are sleek, ample, loopy, and filigreed. Like many choreographers who dance, from Merce Cunningham to Trisha Brown, Miller planted into the piece a central solo for herself, full of airborne splits, slicing arm thrusts, and circular rhythms. Then there is the strung-out but amiable belligerence of *Trapped in Queens* (1984), the high, partying rhythms of *Gypsy Pie* from the same year, the rollicking fluidity of *Cantos Gordos*

(1994), and a big, liquid fingerpaint of a dance called *Thick Sleep* (1989).

These fun (and much more) works may all ultimately be of less interest than the 1987–88 trilogy of *Hell Dances*, in which Miller marks out every available inch of space in the prison of interpersonal intimacy. *This Room Has No Windows and I Can't Find You Anywhere* (1988) is an entangled tango of ruthless relationships, with the dancers cruising each other, offering occasional support minus affection. The double-duet *Habit of Attraction* 1987) amplifies *Two*, counterpointing the struggles of couples for whom conflict is a bond. *Simple Tales* (1988) brings the power-playing elements of eroticism and aggression from the other two dances to a head.

Miller's dances sometimes meander and doodle, as if the intentions behind them are temporarily lost. The 1994 female quartet *Tiny Sisters*, her response to the strange and poignant real-life story of the 'silent twins', a pair of West Indian siblings living in Wales who developed their own secret language, is more of a tantalizing fragment than a finished work. Miller took even greater risks with *Nothing Can Happen Only Once* (1993), her most overtly theatrical, and frustratingly unfulfilled, experiment to date. This seventy-minute piece used text, and fairly elaborate settings and effects, as much as movement to examine the arbitrary nature of memory. As an attempt to put the thought process on stage it failed, but honourably so. Embedded in the half-baked ideas and the characteristically alternating floppy/sharp choreography was at least one gorgeous duet.

Miller was the first American choreographer to work in post-apartheid South Africa. She drew upon this experience for the 1996 *Yard Dance*, a piece incorporating her readings of passages from the journal she kept during her month-long residency there. Her dancers' joyous stomps are inspired by the percussive boot dances of street children she observed in Soweto and Johannesburg.

Miller seems to be moving in the direction of larger-scale theatrical and collaborative projects. Working with a composer and videographer, she created *Drummin': The Rhythms of Miami* (1997), a multi-media, interdisciplinary performance revolving around ethnic drumming traditions in communities throughout greater Miami. With text and choreography by Miller, 1998's *Going to the Wall* is a highly physical examination of race, culture and identity. The piece is planned as a touring performance with residency activities involving both local artists and the community at large. Miller is just the person to spearhead this blending of the socio-political and the creative.

Donald Hutera

Biographical details

Born Beryl Adele Miller, in New York City, 20 September 1950. **Studied** with Murray Louis at Henry Street Settlement, New York, 1954–62; attended Earlham College, Richmond, Indiana, 1967–71, receiving BA degree; trained at the Louis Nikolais Dance Theater Lab, 1972–73, and at Ohio State University, 1973–75 (MA in dance). **Career** Danced with Nina Wiener Company, 1976–82, and with Dana Reitz Company, touring, 1983; first choreographic work, 1978, and regular choreographer from 1981; formed own group, the Bebe Miller Company, in 1984. Has also choreographed for Concert Dance Company, Zenon Dance Company, Creach/Koester Company, Alvin Ailey Repertory Ensemble, Boston Ballet, Phoenix Dance Company (Leeds, England), Dayton Contemporary Dance Company, Pennsylvania Dance Company, Oregon Ballet Theater, PACT Dance Theatre (Johannesburg), and other groups. Has served as board-member of Dance Theater Workshop, Gotham Dance, Wexner Center for the Arts International Advisory Council, Bates Dance Festival, and Colloquium, Contemporary Dance Exchange. **Awards** Creative Artists' Public Service Fellowship, 1984; New York Foundation for the Arts Fellowship, 1984, 1991; National Endowment for the Arts Fellowship, 1985–88; New York Dance and Performance Award ('Bessie'), 1986, 1987; Guggenheim Fellowship, 1988; American Choreographer Award, 1988; Earlham College Outstanding Alumni Award, 1988; Dewar's Emerging Artist Award, 1990.

Works

Tune (mus. Van Morrison, 1978), *Square Business* (mus. 'M', 1981), *Task/Force* (mus. David Bowie, Brian Eno, 1981), *Jammin'* (mus. reggae, 1981), *Task/Force (solo)* (silent, 1981), *Vespers* (mus. Linda Gibbs, 1982), *Story Beach* (mus. Hearn Gadbois, 1982), *Gotham* (mus. Hearn Gadbois, 1983), *Guardian Angels* (mus. Gregorian chanting, 1983), *Trapped in Queens* (mus. Scott Killian, Jonathan Kane, 1984), *Reet City* (mus. Hearn Gadbois, 1984), *Spending Time Doing Things* (solo; mus. Duke Ellington, 1985), *Gypsy Pie* (mus. Mike Vargas, 1985), *No Evidence* (mus. Lenny Pickett, 1985), *Walt's* (mus. Scott Killian, 1986), *A Haven for Restless Angels of Mercy* (mus. Saqqara Dogs, George Sempepos, 1986), *Working Order* (mus. Hearn Gadbois, Jonathan Kane, J.S. Bach, 1986), *Heart, Heart* (mus. Ladysmith Black Mombazo, text John Cheever, 1986), *Two* (with Ralph Lemon; mus. Christopher Hyams-Hart, 1986), *The Habit of Attraction* (mus. Christopher Hyams-Hart, 1987), *This Room Has No Windows and I Can't Find You Anywhere* (mus. Christopher Hyams-Hart, 1987), *Butte* (mus. J.S. Bach, 1987), *Simple Tales* (mus. Christopher Hyams-Hart, Jay Bolotion, text Holly Anderson, 1988), *Hell Dances* (trilogy comprising *The Habit of Attraction*, *This Room . . .* and *Simple Tales*, 1988), *Cracklin' Blue* (mus. Patsy Cline, 1988), *Thick Sleep* (mus. Lenny Pickett, 1989), *Allies* (mus. Fred Frith, 1989), *Rain* (mus. Hearn Gadbois, Heitor Villa-Lobos, 1989), *Vital Boulevard of Love* (mus. Lou Reed, 1989), *The Hidden Boy: Incidents from a Stressed Memory* (mus. Jay Bolotin, 1990), *The Hendrix Project* (mus. Jimi Hendrix, Bob Dylan, 1991), *Sanctuary* (mus. Marianne Faithful, Gospel at Colonus, 1991), *Paisley Sky* (mus. Jimi Hendrix, 1992), *Spartan Reels* (mus. Jonathan Kane, George Sempepos, 1992), *Nothing Can Happen Only Once* (mus. Christian Marclay, text Ain Gordon, 1993), *Things I Have Not Forgotten* (mus. Fred Frith, 1993), *Cantos Gordos* (mus. Don Byron, 1994), *Daughter* (mus. Robin Holcomb, 1994), *Tiny Sisters* (mus. Robin Holcomb, 1994), *Heaven + Earth* (solo, mus. Ellen Fullman; company version, mus. various, 1994), *A Certain Depth of Heart, Also Love* (mus. various, 1994), *Arena* (mus. Led Zeppelin, 1994), *Tiny Sisters in the Enormous Land* (mus. Robin Holcomb, text Holly Anderson; video Kit Fitzgerald, 1995), *Blessed* (mus. Café of the Gate of Salvation, 1996), *Yard Dance* (soundtape animal noises, mus. James Brown, Vusi Mahlasela, 1996), *Voyages plein d'espoir* (mus. various, 1997), *Roses in a Righteous Garden* (mus. various, 1997), *Drummin': The Rhythms of Miami* (mus. drumming, 1997), *Field* (mus. John Adams, 1997), *Going to the Wall* (1998).

Further reading

Articles E. Zimmer, 'Bebe Miller Comes Home', *Dance Magazine*, December 1989; Jann Parry, 'Bebe Miller and Company', *Dance Theatre Journal*, Autumn 1989; Jann Parry, 'Now for Something Completely Different', *Observer*, 8 November 1992.

Books Allen Robertson and Donald Hutera, *The Dance Handbook*, Harlow, Essex, 1988.

MEREDITH MONK

I definitely feel that I am a humanist. I really am involved with trying to figure and deal with how we, as people, are going to survive in this environment on a large scale. I want every element of the human being to be utilized – the spiritual, the instinctive, the emotional, the intellectual, and I feel that if a piece doesn't have all of these things, at least for me, it's not complete.

(*Thrust*, March 1970, p. 2)

When the Houston Grand Opera presented the premiere of Meredith Monk's opera *Atlas* in 1991, many of the varied aspects of her career were brought together: here was a large-scale work of musical theatre for which Monk had prepared the scenario, organized the text, composed the music and movement, and overseen the production, in addition to singing the leading role. Indeed, the only major aspect of her work that wasn't prominently represented was filmmaking.

The story of the explorer Alexandra Daniels (loosely based on the explorer Alexandra David-Néel) presents a voyage of self-exploration that takes us into spiritual realms only hinted at in earlier works, but reflecting Monk's long interest in the writings of Gurdjieff and Eastern mysticism. Combining scenic spectacle (including music and dance to shape the dramatic situations) with great simplicity in a journey toward inner truth, *Atlas* recalls elements from such earlier works as *Vessel* (1971), *Education of the Girlchild* (1972–73), *Quarry* (1976), and *The Games* (1983), all of them products of collaborations with close associates whose contributions inextricably became part of the works' richness.

Above all, Monk is a musician and a choreographer, a maker of movement. 'I think of myself as a composer: of music, of movement, and of images', Monk has said. 'There are actually three branches of my work: the music concerts, the large multi-media performance pieces, and the films. The concerns of one overlap into another.' Most of her work grows from her efforts as composer-choreographer-performer, whether alone or with members of the collective known as The House. Although each work bears her unmistakable imprint, she has consistently worked with collaborators who share her vision while bringing highly individual qualities to the work. Monk's associates are as physically disparate (conventional notions of beauty seldom being relevant) as they are multi-talented. Over the years, members of The House come to seem like parts of one's family – perhaps like distant relatives seen on special occasions – and as familiar faces disappear new ones gradually join the group. As music has become increasingly central to her work, singing has become one of the expected skills of a Monk performer, in the wide-ranging vibrato-less style she developed. Yet each must have the physical control of the actor/dancer. In this way a social and spiritual ideal of the 1960s – the idea of the collective – becomes merged with Monk's musical/dramatic vision. (In 1972, after a Liverpool performance, she told the *Guardian* about The House: 'We don't want our life and work to be separate. We want our work to be an expression of our lives, which are striving to be good.')

Gesture in Monk's work may derive from familiar movements, but it is selected, slowed, abstracted, sometimes framed, so

that the characters seem archetypes: a sick child, an old woman, a group of women sitting at a table, perhaps pouring coffee. The movements of the Inuit couple which Monk and Robert Een enact (and sing) in *Facing North* (1990) are circumscribed by their bulky garments, but their solemn gaiety shows that they are at one with their demanding world. 'Narrators' sometimes appear framing works (often wordlessly), like the two who hop through *The Girlchild*.

Blending music and dance came naturally to Monk, whose early training combined both. Her mother was a singer, her maternal grandparents musicians, and a greatgrandfather a cantor who sang for the Tsar. In addition to music, Monk studied Dalcroze Eurythmics, ballet, and later modern dance. At Sarah Lawrence College she fortunately found the right mentor in Bessie Shoenberg, who encouraged her students to become the very best of whatever they were. Therefore, when coming on to the New York dance/music/art scene in the early 1960s, Monk moved easily into the performing and creative world that was beginning to show work at the Judson Church and other spaces, those alternatives to the established theatres and studios where more traditional modern dance was seen. Along with newcomers like Phoebe Neville and Kenneth King, and the slightly older Yvonne Rainer and Trisha Brown, Monk performed in 'happenings' and avant-garde events that broke the formal constraints of dance as practised by Martha Graham, José Limón, and even Merce Cunningham. On the West Coast Anna Halprin was another influence, especially through her task-oriented, site-specific works, which often incorporated performers without prior dance training.

Monk was soon recognized as a choreographer with a highly individual way of combining theatrical elements, usually in a non-proscenium space, while controlling and distancing powerful emotional overtones. Thus, *Duet with Cat's Scream and Locomotive* (1966) was a non-erotic *pas de deux* that stressed physicality through large close-ups of mouths rocking around the area and a taped score associating the locomotive with him, the cat with her. The long solo *16 Millimeter Earrings* (1966) introduced singing (her first original score) and film, with images of her face projected onto a paper globe covering her head. The piece moved from a film of a burning doll to the projection of flames on Monk's nude body as she crumpled into a trunk, in an image combining martyrdom and desire.

In these early works one can see the basis of Monk's fascination with the narrow line between the real and artificial, and her involvement with space that makes the later works designed for conventional theatres so striking. *Blueprint* (1967) moved among usually private and public spaces within the large Judson Church complex, where one saw things close-up, then framed at a distance through a doorway or window. At one point, Monk, in traditional costume, danced *The Dying Swan* (not badly), shaking real feathers from a pillow. *Juice* (1969) began in Frank Lloyd Wright's Guggenheim Museum, with its great spiral ramp, and concentrated first on the viewers at the bottom looking up into the light, and then on the viewers on the ramp looking down. Later the audience shifted to a small theatre, and the third night ended in Monk's studio, where no performers were present, only photographs of what had been seen. *Vessel* (1970) derived from the idea of Joan of Arc, moving from the confines of Monk's studio, where everyday activities took place in slowed time, to a theatre where 'medieval' figures clambered around an obviously artificial cloth mountain, to a vast parking lot where armies seemed to sweep across the space, figures appeared on the steps of a distant church, motorcycles churned around the area, and finally Joan was immolated in the light of a welder's torch. These spectacles brought together a dazzling array of elements from life, theatre, dance, music, and village pageants, but were always controlled by a sensibility that gave them shape, depth, and focus.

Education of the Girlchild, *Paris/Chacon* (1972/1974) and *Quarry* began the body of musical/dramatic works that have formed the core of a repertory that leads towards *Atlas*. *The Girlchild* began as a remarkable solo in which a crone-like figure, cackling with glee at having thus far evaded death, begins a journey down a white cloth path that reverses time, ending as a numinously innocent child. The first part, added later, includes a favourite Monk image: women of various ages and shapes sitting at a table engaged in ordinary activities, 'the tribe of companions'. Each is distinct, yet part of a defined group. Monk's feminism, like her mysticism, is simple and practical, never doctrinaire.

Paris/Chacon (made with a frequent collaborator, Ping Chong) contrasted a Parisian couple enjoying a stroll (why Monk wore both a dress and a moustache, typically, was never explained) with a community of dancers actually larger than tiny Chacon, New Mexico. In *Quarry*, however, the dreams of a sick child reveal modern horrors: 'The sick child, in a sense, is a metaphor for the diseased world', Monk says. The ordinary events of life are transformed by gesticulating dictators into an endless emigration (covering centuries), leading toward inevitable death, while a crowd carrying artificial clouds returns with airplanes, instruments of death. Through music, spectacle, and the carefully recalled details of daily life, she has dug deeply in the uneasy foundations of modern life. On a smaller scale, *Recent Ruins* (1979) suggests similar concerns as we become archaeologists patiently reconstructing our lives. *Specimen Days: A Civil War Opera* (1981) put this in a specifically American context, presenting a museum of scenes from Walt Whitman's time, representing the quintessentially American struggle for freedom, political and spiritual. *The Games* (again with Ping Chong) takes us into a future world in which simple pleasures of life are only memories to be recreated ritually. The concerns of the moral and physical world are evident in Monk's work, although she is seldom tendentious.

Since forming a vocal ensemble in 1978, Monk's music has become richer in its textures, more contrapuntal in the clarity of its interweaving lines, often suggesting medieval music without literally imitating it. (She especially admires the twelfth-century French composer Pérotin Le Grand.) Her own voice is a pure soprano with a remarkable three-octave range and no vibrato, a cool pure sound that would be ideal for 'early music', yet can cackle, keen, or croon as easily as soar. (An evening of art songs at the Whitney Museum in 1974 called *Raw Recital* was as remarkable for its musical variety and vocal purity as for the way she and her pianist circled the space on a small platform.) Not one to compromise artistically, Monk is now able to support some of her large-scale ventures by solo recitals, although these can be carefully planned theatrically, like the 1994 programme *Volcano Songs*, where visual images proved as memorable as the music.

Although Monk has often been ranked with Steve Reich and Philip Glass as a minimalist, her use of *ostinato* is not to create clock-like structures, but to provide a foundation for the vocal lines, which develop above and beyond its harmonic implications. A synthesizer often provides that basic continuity, blending with the voices while asserting its own independence. Like the music, the vocal techniques draw on many sources, from medieval organum and hocketing through African music to Mongolian *hoomi* (to produce very high fundamentals and overtones). Supporting instruments range from the jew's harp and glass harmonica (*Our Lady of Late*, 1973) to the shawm, sheng recorder and didgeridoo played by Wayne Hankin, who conducted *Atlas*.

Her film, *Ellis Island*, made for *Recent Ruins*, juxtaposed past and present with images of immigrants coming through the dusty, decaying halls of the great building where so many, like Monk's ancestors, first set foot in America. In *Turtle Dreams* (1983), the turtle crawls across maps, a creature from the past totally out of scale, finally filling the empty streets of a deserted city, an image of desolation. *Book of Days*, her 1989 feature-length film, expands this intertwining of present and past when a fourteenth-century Jewish girl has visions of the future, such as the silver bird she draws that we recognize as an airplane. Her grandfather interprets her visions through the past – the Bible – and only a madwoman with compassion for suffering (played by Monk) understands her clairvoyance. The past is shown in black and white. Only when modern workmen rediscover her village, which was overtaken by plague, do we have colour, the sense of our own lives.

Returning to where we began, *Atlas* reveals many stages of Monk's archetypal journey, after the girl who is its central character is prepared for exploration by the Spirit Guides. Her companions chosen, their way takes them through idyllic farm communities to the Forest, then to the seductive, terrifying hell of the Ice Demons and on to the Desert, until all but one can ascend to a timeless, radiant place of spiritual knowledge. At the end we return to that familiar, but now extraordinary image, a woman quietly pouring and drinking a cup of coffee. The true journey is not without, but within. To convey such a vision in musical and dramatic terms is Monk's achievement.

George Dorris

Biographical details

Born in New York City, 20 November 1942. **Studied** Dalcroze movement, ballet, and music from childhood; technique and composition at Sarah Lawrence College, Bronxville, New York, receiving BA degree in 1964; studied dance in New York with Mia Slavenska, Merce Cunningham, Martha Graham, and at Ruth Mata/Eugene Hari studio and the Joffrey School.

Career Performance debut in 1963, and subsequent career has been as choreographer, composer, singer, performer, film director, and recording artist, frequently combining several of these capacities in individual projects. Performed briefly with Judson Dance Theater, New York, 1960s; founded own interdisciplinary arts group, The House, 1968, remaining as artistic director and chief choreographer and composer. Has directed several video and film projects (including some versions of stage works), and recorded several albums of her music. **Awards and honours** Guggenheim Fellowship, 1972, 1986; Obie Award, 1972, 1976, 1985; Venice Biennale First Prize, 1975; New York Dance Festival Merit Award, 1980; *Ciné* Golden Eagle Award, 1981; New York Dance and Performance Award ('Bessie'), 1985; Creative Omega Award, 1987; Rockefeller Foundation Distinguished Choreographer Award, 1987; Honorary Doctorate, Bard College (Annandale-on-Hudson, New York), 1988; Honorary Doctorate, University of the Arts (Philadelphia), 1989; *Dance Magazine* Award, 1992; Samuel H. Scripps American Dance Festival Award, 1996; Sarah Lawrence College Distinguished Alumnae Award, 1996; New York Foundation for the Arts Fellowship, 1996.

Works

Me (silent, 1963), *Timestop* (sound Glen Mack, 1964), *Untitled* (mus. Daniel Pinkham, 1964), *Diploid* (with Elizabeth Keen; mus. Copland, 1964), *Arm's Length* (sound collage, 1964), *Cowell Suite* (mus. Henry Cowell, 1964), *Break* (tape collage Monk, 1964), *Cartoon* (live sounds, 1965), *The Beach* (tape collage Monk, 1965; revised version, 1969), *Relache* (with Dick Higgins; mus. Satie, 1965), *Blackboard* (silent, 1965), *Radar* (mus. Jackson Mac Low, 1965), *Portable* (tape collage Monk, mus. Bob Dylan, Monteverdi, 1966), *Duet with Cat's Scream and Locomotive* (tape collage Monk, 1966), *16 Millimeter Earrings* (mus. Monk, 1966; film version the same year), *Blueprint (1)* (mus. Monk, Don Preston, 1967), *Overload (Blueprint 2)* (mus. Monk, 1967), *Blueprint (3)* (mus. Monk, 1968), *Blueprint (4)* (mus. Monk, 1968), *Blueprint (5)* (soundtapes, 1968), *Co-op* (mus. Otis Redding, 1968), *Title: Title and Untidal: Movement Period* (1969), *Tour: Dedicated to Dinosaurs* (mus. Monk, 1969), *Tour 2: Barbershop* (mus. Monk, 1969), *Juice: A Theater Cantata* (mus. Monk, 1969), *Tour 4: Lounge* (mus. Monk, 1969), *Tour 5: Glass* (mus. Monk, 1970), *Tour 6: Organ* (mus. Monk, Don Preston, 1970), *Tour 7: Factory* (mus. Monk, Daniel Sverdlik, 1970), *Needle-Brain Lloyd and the Systems Kid: A Live Movie* (mus. Monk, 1970),

Tour 8: Castle (mus. Monk, 1971), *Vessel: An Opera Epic* (mus. Monk, 1971), *Education of the Girlchild* (solo; mus. Monk, 1972), *Paris* (with Ping Chong; mus. Monk, 1972), *Our Lady of Late* (mus. Monk, 1973), *Education of the Girlchild: An Opera* (complete version, 1973), *Chacon* (with Ping Chong; mus. Monk, 1974), *Roots* (with Donald Ashwander; mus. various, 1974), *Anthology and Small Scroll* (mus. Monk, 1975), *Quarry* (opera by Monk, 1976), *Venice/Milan* (with Ping Chong; mus. Monk, 1976), *Tablet: House of Stills* (mus. Monk, 1977), *The Plateau Series* (mus. Monk, 1978), *Recent Ruins: An Opera* (includes *Ellis Island*; mus. Monk, 1979), *Specimen Days: A Civil War Opera* (mus. Monk, 1981), *Turtle Dreams: Cabaret* (film; mus. Monk, 1983), *The Games* (with Ping Chong; mus. Monk, 1983), *The Ringing Place* (mus. Monk, 1987), *Book of Days* (mus. Monk, 1985; television version, 1988, film version, 1989), *Acts from Under and Above* (with Lanny Harrison; mus. Monk, 1986), *Facing North* (with Robert Een; mus. Monk, 1990), *Atlas: An Opera in Three Parts* (mus. Monk, 1991), *Three Heavens and Hells* (mus. Monk, 1992), *Street Corner Pierrot* and *Evanescence* (in *Particular People* by Donald Ashwander, 1993), *American Archaeology #1: Roosevelt Island* (mus. Monk, 1994), *Volcano Songs* (mus. Monk, 1994), *A Celebration Service* (mus Monk, 1996), *The Politics of Quiet* (mus. Monk, 1996).

Further reading

Interviews with Brooks McNamara, in '*Vessel*: The Scenography of Meredith Monk', *Drama Review*, March 1972; with Carole Koenig, in 'Meredith Monk: Performer-Creator', *Drama Review*, September 1976; with Connie Kreemer, in her *Further Steps: Fifteen Choreographers on Modern Dance*, New York, 1987; with Nicholas Zurbrugg, *Dance Theatre Journal*, Winter 1992/93.

Articles Constance H. Posner, 'Making It New: Meredith Monk and Kenneth King', *Ballet Review*, 1(6), 1967; Rob Baker, 'Landscapes and Telescopes: A Personal Response to the Choreography of Meredith Monk', *Dance Magazine*, April 1976; Sally Banes, 'Meredith Monk and the Making of *Chacon*', *Dance Chronicle*, 1(1), 1977; Sally Banes, 'The Art of Meredith Monk', *Performing Arts Journal*, Spring/Summer 1978; Kenneth Bernard, 'Some Observations on Meredith Monk's *Recent Ruins*', *Yale/Theater*, Spring 1980; Bonnie Marranca, 'Meredith Monk's *Recent Ruins*: Essaying Images', *Performing Arts Journal*, 4(3), 1980; Marianne Goldberg, 'Transformative Aspects of Meredith Monk's *Education of the Girlchild*',

MEREDITH MONK

Women and Performance, Spring/Summer 1983;
Allen Robertson, 'Renaissance Ms', *Ballet News*,
October 1984; Susan Foster, 'The Signifying Body:
Reaction and Resistance in Postmodern Dance',
Theatre Journal, March 1985; Meredith Monk,
'Some Thoughts about Art', *Dance Magazine*,
September 1990; Rob Baker, 'Material Worlds',
Parabola, Fall 1991; David Finkelstein, 'The
Films of Meredith Monk', *Ballet Review*, Summer
1991; Bonnie Marranca, 'Meredith Monk's *Atlas
of Sound*: New Opera and the American
Performance Tradition', *Performing Arts Journal*,
January 1992; Meredith Monk, 'Ages of the
Avant-Garde', *Performing Arts Journal*, 16(1),
1994.

Books Don McDonagh, *The Rise and Fall and
Rise of Modern Dance*, New York, 1970; Marcia
Siegel, *At the Vanishing Point*, New York, 1972;
Marcia Siegel, *Watching the Dance Go By*, Boston,
1977; Sally Banes, 'Meredith Monk: Homemade
Metaphors', in her *Terpsichore in Sneakers: Post-
modern Dance*, Boston, 1980; Deborah Jowitt,
Meredith Monk, New York, 1997.

MARK MORRIS

Mark Morris's historical importance is that
his work unites what were, before him, two
divergent trends. One is the traditional
modern dance, with its weightiness, its musicality, and its liberal humanism. The other
is the postmodern sensibility – with its insis-
tent irony, its self-conscious historicism, and
its political emphasis – that dominated
American art, including dance, in the 1980s.
When Morris began showing his work to
New York audiences, these two trends were
following widely separate paths. In traditional modern dance, there seemed to be
no young talent; in what the young were
doing, there seemed to be no dance, but
rather a sort of political theatre. Morris's
work bridged the divide. It was up-to-date,
full of 'styles' and mordancy and taboo-
breaching (particularly gender-violation:
unisex dances, women lifting men, and so
on). Yet it was dance, modern dance: plastic,
musical, fundamentally earnest. And the
combination seemed completely natural.

In view of Morris's education, it was
natural. Born in Seattle, Washington, in
1956, he grew up as the third and last child
of an ordinary middle-class family. (His
father taught at the high school down the
block; his mother stayed home with the children.) At the age of eight he received the
coup de foudre at a performance of José
Greco's flamenco troupe, and he soon began
lessons in Spanish dance. Thereafter – and
this is the crucial point about his dance background – most of his training was in folk
dance. He also began ballet training at the
age of ten, but his primary dance education
was in flamenco (which he also studied in
Madrid in 1974) and Balkan dance, which
he learned when, at the age of thirteen, he
joined the Koleda Folk Ensemble, a Seattle
troupe devoted to Balkan forms. In artistic
terms, the latter experience was the crucial
event of his youth. For three years, the
Koleda Folk Ensemble was the centre of his
life, social and artistic. From that troupe he
learned how he wanted a dance ensemble
to look – like regular people, full of human
variety – and how he wanted the dancing
body to look – sturdy, solid, with the weight
held low and the feet flat on the ground.
From the post-1960s spirit with which the
members of Koleda imbued their dances
he learned the utopianism that was to mark
his later work. Finally, Balkan dance and
also flamenco – both highly sophisticated
musically – taught him to see dance as
grounded in music. (He pursued music independently as well. His father showed him
how to read music as a child, and he taught
himself to play the piano.)

Morris had almost no training in modern
dance, with the result that he was never
affected by its generational disputes, never
saw himself as needing to throw off the past
– as well he might have done, for he had
grown up into a bad-boy type: long-haired,
loud-mouthed, provocative, forthrightly
homosexual. Yet from ethnic dance he was
learning all the values that would eventually
enable him to become an unselfconscious

practitioner of modern dance, and to place his new-style sensibility in the service of that old form.

Morris began choreographing at the age of 14 and went on making dances for school plays, recitals, and the like throughout his adolescence. In 1976, when he was 19, he moved to New York, where for the next seven years he danced with various troupes. In 1980, he founded his company, the Mark Morris Dance Group, and his fame, together with his skill and productivity, grew yearly. By 1986, the year he turned 30, he was being reviewed by national magazines, two major ballet companies had premiered dances by him, and he had been the subject of an hour-long Public Broadcasting Service television special. He was the foremost young choreographer in the United States.

In 1988 Morris moved his troupe to Brussels, to replace Maurice Béjart's Ballet of the 20th Century as the resident dance company of Belgium's national opera house, the Théâtre Royal de la Monnaie. The troupe spent three turbulent years in Brussels, receiving, for the most part, harsh reviews from a press unaccustomed to American modern dance. (Morris's third Brussels season was greeted by the front-page headline 'Mark Morris, go home!' in the city's leading paper, Le Soir.) Meanwhile, the company was undergoing painful internal changes. Essentially, the troupe's first generation began yielding to its second. Veteran dancers quit; new dancers arrived; the company became larger, younger, more technically skilled. Through all these disruptions, Morris went on working steadily. During the Belgian years he created – for his company and others (including Mikhail Baryshnikov's modern dance troupe, White Oak Dance Project, which he helped to found) – eleven dances, including two acknowledged masterpieces, L'Allegro, il penseroso ed il moderato (1988), to Handel's oratorio, and Dido and Aeneas (1989), a danced version of Purcell's opera. In recognition of this show of strength and courage,

he was awarded a MacArthur Fellowship in 1991. Shortly afterwards, the company returned to New York, becoming the fourth-largest modern dance troupe in the United States and probably the most discussed.

One of the first impressions to strike most spectators at a Mark Morris event is the seeming naturalness of his dances. His dancers are not glamorous and, by dance-company standards, not thin. They look like people one might meet on the street: tall and small, black and white. There is an informality in their bearing. They move with weight and effort. Morris seems to want to retain a certain measure of awkwardness in movement, as a mark of vulnerability, of human truth. The dancers squat and strain; one can see their buttocks, their tensed thighs. The result is an extreme physical immediacy, compounded by the fact that the dances are often performed to live vocal music (about half of Morris's works have been set to song), so that the music too reverberates with the force of the body. This is profoundly visceral choreography.

Yet unlike other naturalistic styles, Morris's makes no claim to be life rather than art. His work is artifice: largely abstract, a structure of open symbols. Though the dancers may be dragging themselves across the floor by their arms – which they do in Morris's popular Gloria (1981, rev. 1984) – they do so in a line of seven, in canon, in imitation of the structure of the music. Naturalism, for him, is an artistic strategy.

The basis of Morris's choreography is music. From adolescence he has been a passionate and erudite music-lover. He has set works to the music of nearly fifty different composers, together with many popular songs. He favours baroque music, by reason of its structural clarity, emotional directness, and danceability. (He has set four dances to Bach; his two most ambitious pieces, L'Allegro and Dido and Aeneas, were to Handel and Purcell, respectively.) And since his youth he has shown a fondness for choreographing to the West Coast experimental composers: Harry Partch, Henry Cowell, Lou Harrison. Still, his taste is very eclectic.

Whatever the music, he does not so much choose it; it chooses him. It is because that piece of music has given him choreographic ideas that he decides to set a dance to it, and the dance that he makes reflects the musical structure. (He ordinarily choreographs with the score in hand.) Musical ensembles become dance ensembles; musical solos, dance solos. Harmony, counterpoint, dynamics, key structures, not to mention rhythm, all become part of the dance. In consequence, Morris has occasionally been chided for 'music-visualizing', though the relationship between the musical structure and the dance structure in his work is usually quite elastic. Music may be his muse, but it is not the direct source of his choreography. The source is the imaginative process – a compound of thought and emotion, experienced as movement images – set off in his mind by the music. This process is something that an external pattern can only influence, never dictate. The pattern is necessary to him, however. Morris almost never commissions music. The music must be pre-existent; he must be able to hear it in order to want to make a dance to it.

Many of Morris's finest works are narrative. *One Charming Night* (1985) tells of a vampire seduction; *Lovey* (1985), of the murder of a child. *Dido and Aeneas* and *The Hard Nut* (1991), Morris's *Nutcracker*, tell the usual stories. Others of his dances, if they do not have stories, have clear subjects (in keeping, often, with their vocal text): love (*New Love Song Waltzes*, 1982; *I Don't Want to Love*, 1996), death (*The Vacant Chair*, 1984), terror (*Fugue and Fantasy*, 1988; *Behemoth*, 1990), dreaming (*Bedtime*, 1992), religious feeling (*Gloria*; *O Rangasayee*, 1984; *Stabat Mater*, 1986; *Strict Songs*, 1987; *Beautiful Day*, 1992; *Jesu, Meine Freude*, 1993), this last an important matter to him. Another persistent theme is community, group love. (Morris is not especially interested in romantic love. He tends to

choreograph solos and ensembles rather than duets.) But though he uses 'subject matter', he develops it not in a literary way – a linear way – but in a musical way, through the repetition and development of movement themes. The movements may begin as story, but they end as dance.

Morris's works tend to have double emotions. They present two opposing sides of an experience simultaneously: pathos and dryness (*Love Song Waltzes*), reverie and absurdity (*Ten Suggestions*, 1980), exultation and anguish (*Stabat Mater*), brassiness and horror (*Lucky Charms*, 1994). As an overarching opposition, they tend to use beautiful old music – which puts the audience into a worshipful mood – in combination with blunt, vernacular movement, which disrupts that mood. This persistent doubleness has caused Morris, at times, to be mistaken as simply an ironist. He is in fact quite earnest, but he is also witty and unsentimental, and there is a long streak of darkness in his vision of life. Hence the divided tone of his dances. Many of them have great pathos, but it is won from difficulty, from a criticism of pathos.

Morris is remarkably prolific. Since 1980, when he founded his company, he has created close to 100 works – nearly six per year. This includes ten classical ballets, for his own company and others (Joffrey Ballet, Boston Ballet, American Ballet Theatre, Paris Opéra Ballet, Les Grands Ballets Canadiens, San Francisco Ballet). He has also directed four opera productions (*Die Fledermaus*, Seattle, 1988; *The Marriage of Figaro*, Brussels, 1991; *Orfeo ed Euridice*, Iowa City, 1996; *Platée*, Edinburgh, 1997) and created dances for a number of operas, notably for productions directed by Peter Sellars (such as *Nixon in China*, 1987; *The Death of Klinghoffer*, 1991). His style has changed over the years. In 1985–86, when he began his immersion in baroque music, he became more interested in tight, complex dance structures – 'perfect systems', as he calls them – both as a reflection of that music and, it seems, as an organizer and container for themes of grief. Also in 1986 he broke his foot and had to stop dancing for five months. Morris has always been the star dancer of his company, but with that injury, which forced him to watch his work from the sidelines, he began to design his dances more in accordance to how it would be to look at them rather than how it would feel to dance them. And, it seems, he began more purposefully to design choreography for specific dancers rather than for a notional general dancer based on himself. Eventually, he took himself out of certain pieces, though he went on (and goes on today) creating superb roles for himself, most notably in *Dido and Aeneas*, where he played both Dido and the Sorceress, the greatest role of his career.

Another turning point was the period in Brussels. With the resources of the national opera house at his disposal, he was able to double the size of the company, and, for the first time in his career, to command sets, costumes, orchestras, and choruses. His work expanded in every way, not just in size (*L'Allegro* has a cast of twenty-four, *The Hard Nut*, thirty-three), but in clarity and boldness. In certain works of this period – *L'Allegro*, *Dido*, *Behemoth* (1990) – there are no soft parts, no fat; it is impossible to imagine this thing being said with greater imaginative force. At the same time, his style changed, as a result of several circumstances. He had many new dancers, and he had to train them. Furthermore, he now had a studio of his own (actually, several studios), so that he could train them. He began teaching a company class every morning, and it was a ballet class, for another influence of this period was ballet: he became more interested in it. (Since 1988 he has created nine classical ballets.) At the same time, he was caught up in a burst of creativity, with ideas newly clear to him, new things to say. Under all these pressures, his dances took on a new look. They shaded from the 'vernacular' style to something more formal, more

designed and legible, with the body more 'worked', the steps more complicated, the rhythms more difficult and exact. This change had been building for years, but in Brussels it became most noticeable, partly because one saw it on new dancers, who had not been trained in the older, shaggier style. Since the Brussels period, his style has not changed as much. The most notable development is his quest for larger genres: dance on video (*Falling Down Stairs*, 1994; *Dido and Aeneas*, 1995, both Rhombus Media); opera (*Orfeo ed Euridice*, *Platée*); musical comedy (*The Capeman*, 1998).

One thing has never changed in Morris's work, and that is its amalgamative nature. He himself is a combination of oddly assorted parts. In the words of David White, director of Dance Theater Workshop, where much of his early work was produced, 'Mark is a sort of car crash of personalities. There's this working-class guy and there's this music scholar guy, and there's this folk-dance guy and this gay guy, and they've all washed up into the same body' (quoted in Acocella, *Mark Morris*, p. 248). His work, likewise, is a great gathering-in. While Spanish and Balkan dance, together with ballet, have been his major influences, he has also been deeply affected by Asian dance, European court dance, and indeed major figures of American modern dance: Isadora Duncan, Ruth St Denis, Martha Graham, Merce Cunningham, Paul Taylor, Laura Dean, Lucinda Childs, Trisha Brown. Though music is the law of his mind, he is also passionately involved with stories, which work by an opposite logic. While his is a very modern mind – sophisticated, ironical, self-critical – he is also attached to old values, old music: Bach, Handel, and the things they felt were important. While he may be in one mood about something, he can see the other mood too. This is not to say that Morris 'can't be pigeonholed'. He can be. He has a specific style, specific concerns. But his habit has always been to join opposing things. This makes his work more difficult and more durable. It also produces a largeness of vision that has endeared him to the public.

Joan Acocella

Biographical details

Born in Seattle, Washington, United States, 29 August 1956. **Studied** flamenco dance from age nine, with Verla Flowers, and ballet with Perry Brunson in Seattle; later studied ballet with Maggie Black in New York, from 1976. **Career** danced with semi-professional Balkan dance troupe, the Koleda Folk Ensemble, from ages 13 to 16; later danced with numerous companies, including those of Eliot Feld, Lar Lubovitch, Twyla Tharp, and Laura Dean; began choreographing as a young student; founded Mark Morris Dance Group in 1980, bringing group to Europe to become the resident company of the Théâtre Royal de la Monnaie, Brussels, 1988–91. Co-founded, with Mikhail Baryshnikov, White Oak Dance Project, in 1990. Has choreographed for other companies, including Joffrey Ballet, Boston Ballet, American Ballet Theatre, Houston Grand Opera, Les Grands Ballets Canadiens, San Francisco Ballet, and Paris Opéra Ballet. Has also directed opera. **Awards** New York Dance and Performance Award ('Bessie'), 1984 and 1990; Guggenheim Fellowship, 1986; MacArthur Foundation Fellowship, 1991; *Dance Magazine* Award, 1991; Olivier Award, 1997; *Evening Standard* Award, 1997.

Works

Barstow (mus. Harry Partch, 1972), *Zenska* (mus. Bartók, Bulgarian folk music, 1974), *Brummagem* (mus. Beethoven, 1978), *Castor and Pollux* (mus. Harry Partch, 1980), *Dad's Charts* (mus. Milt Buckner, Illinois Jacquet, and Charles Thompson, 1980), *Ten Suggestions* (mus. Alexander Tcherepnin, 1980), *Etudes Modernes* (mus. Conlon Nancarrow, 1981), *I Love You Dearly* (mus. Romanian songs, 1981), *Gloria* (mus. Vivaldi, 1981), *Rattlesnake Song* (mus. Jimmy Driftwood, 1981), *Canonic 3/4 Studies* (mus. piano waltzes, 1982), *Junior High* (mus. Conlon Nancarrow, 1982), *New Love Song Waltzes* (mus. Brahms, 1982), *Not Goodbye* (mus. Tahitian traditional music, 1982), *Songs That Tell a Story* (mus. Louvin Brothers, 1982), *Bijoux* (mus. Satie, 1983), *Caryatids* (mus. Harold Budd, 1983), *Celestial Greetings* (mus. Thai popular music, 1983), *The Death of Socrates* (mus. Satie, 1983), *Deck of Cards* (mus. Jimmy Logsdon, George Jones, T.

Texas Tyler, 1983), *Dogtown* (mus. Yoko Ono, 1983), *Minuet and Allegro in G* (mus. Beethoven, 1983), *Ponchielliana* (mus. Ponchielli, 1983), *The 'Tamil Film Songs in Stereo' Pas de Deux* (mus. contemporary Tamil, 1983), *Come on Home* (mus. George P. Root, Oscar Robach, Carrie Jacobs Bond, 1984), *Forty Arms, Twenty Necks, One Wreathing* (mus. Herschel Garfein, 1984), *Love, You Have Won* (mus. Vivaldi, 1984), *My Party* (mus. Jean Françaix, 1984), *Mythology: Championship Wrestling* (mus. Herschel Garfein, 1984), *O Rangasayee* (mus. Sri Tyagaraja, 1984), *Prelude and Prelude* (mus. Henry Cowell, 1984), *She Came from There* (mus. Dohnanyi, 1984), *The Vacant Chair* (mus. various, 1984), *Vestige* (mus. Shostakovich, 1984), *Frisson* (mus. Stravinsky, 1985), *Handel Choruses* (mus. Handel, 1985), *Jealousy* (mus. Handel, 1985), *Lovey* (mus. Violent Femmes, 1985), *Marble Halls* (mus. J.S. Bach, 1985), *One Charming Night* (mus. Purcell, 1985), *Retreat from Madrid* (mus. Boccherini, 1985), *Aida* (mus. Verdi, 1986), *Ballabili* (mus. Verdi, 1986), *Esteemed Guests* (mus. C.P.E. Bach, 1986), *Mort Subite* (mus. Poulenc, 1986), *Soap Powders and Detergents* (mus. Herschel Garfein, 1986), *Striptease* (mus. Herschel Garfein, 1986), *Pièces en Concert* (mus. Couperin, 1986), dances in *Salomé* (opera by Richard Strauss, 1986), *The Shepherd on the Rock* (mus. Schubert, 1986), *Stabat Mater* (mus. Pergolesi, 1986), dances in *Nixon in China* (opera by John Adams, 1987), *Scarlatti Solos* (mus. Scarlatti, 1987), *Sonata for Clarinet and Piano* (mus. Poulenc, 1987), *Strict Songs* (mus. Lou Harrison, 1987), *Drink to Me Only with Thine Eyes* (mus. Virgil Thomson, 1988), dances in *Die Fledermaus* (opera by Richard Strauss, 1988), *Fugue and Fantasy* (mus. Mozart, 1988), *L'Allegro, il penseroso ed il moderato* (mus. Handel, 1988), dances in *Le Nozze de Figaro* (opera by Mozart, 1988), *Offertorium* (mus. Schubert, 1988), dances in *Orphée et Euridice* (opera by Gluck, 1988), *Dido and Aeneas* (mus. Purcell, 1989; television version, 1995), *Love Song Waltzes* (mus. Brahms, 1989), *Wonderland* (mus. Schoenberg, 1989), *Behemoth* (silent, 1990), *Ein Herz* (mus. J.S. Bach, 1990), *Going Away Party* (mus. Bob Mills and the Texas Playboys, 1990), *Motorcade* (mus. Saint-Saëns, 1990), *Pas de Poisson* (mus. Satie, 1990), dances in *The Death of Klinghoffer* (opera by John Adams, 1991), *The Hard Nut* (mus. Tchaikovsky, 1991), *A Lake* (mus. Haydn, 1991), *The Marriage of Figaro* (also dir., 1991), *Paukenschlag* (mus. Haydn, 1992), *Beautiful Day* (mus. attrib. J.S. Bach/Hoffman, 1992), *Polka* (mus. Lou Harrison, 1992), *Three Preludes* (mus. Gershwin, 1992), *Bedtime* (mus. Schubert, 1992), *Excursion to Grenada: A Calypso Ballet* (mus. Lionel Belasco and Orchestra, 1992), *Grand Duo* (includes *Polka*; mus. Lou Harrison, 1993), *Home* (mus. Michelle Shocked, Rob Wasserman, 1993), *Mosaic and United* (mus. Henry Cowell, 1993), *Jesu, Meine Freude* (mus. Beethoven, 1993), *A Spell* (mus. John Wilson, 1993), *Falling Down Stairs* (film; mus. J.S. Bach, 1994; stage version, 1997), *Maelstrom* (mus. Beethoven, 1994), *The Office* (mus. Dvořák, 1994), *Lucky Charms* (mus. Jacques Ibert, 1994), *Rondo* (mus. Mozart, 1994), *Quincunx* (mus. Donizetti, 1995), *Somebody's Coming to See Me Tonight* (mus. Stephen Foster, 1995), *Pacific* (mus. Lou Harrison, 1995), *World Power* (mus. Lou Harrison, 1995), *Three Russian Preludes* (mus. Shostakovich, 1995), *Orfeo ed Euridice* (opera by Gluck, 1996), *I Don't Want to Love* (mus. Monteverdi, 1996), *Rhymes with Silver* (mus. Lou Harrison, 1997), *Platée* (opera by Rameau, 1997), *The Capeman* (musical by Paul Simon, 1998).

Further reading

Interviews with David Vaughan, in 'A Conversation with Mark Morris', *Ballet Review*, Summer 1986; with Roslyn Sulcas, in 'Man on the Move', *Dance and Dancers*, January/February 1992; with Maura Keefe and Marc Woodworth, in 'An Interview with Mark Morris', *Salmagundi*, Fall/Winter 1994/95.

Articles Tobi Tobias, 'Mark Morris: Manchild in the Promised Land', *Dance Magazine*, December 1984; Laurie Lassiter, 'Mark Morris Dance Group', *Drama Review*, Summer 1985; John Gruen, 'Mark Morris: He's Here', *Dance Magazine*, September 1986; Clive Barnes, 'Mad about the Boy', *Dance and Dancers*, January 1987; Alastair Macaulay, 'Vivamus atque Amemus', *The New Yorker*, 20 June 1988; Lynn Garafola, 'Mark Morris and the Feminine Mystique', *Ballet Review*, Fall 1988; Don Daniels, 'Alone Together', *Ballet Review*, Winter 1988; Arlene Croce, 'Mark Morris Goes Abroad', *The New Yorker*, 16 January 1989; Christine Temin, 'The Triumph of Mark Morris', *Boston Globe Magazine*, 19 February 1989; Arlene Croce, 'Wise Guys', *The New Yorker*, 31 July 1989; Joan Acocella, '*L'Allegro, il Penseroso ed il Moderato*', *Ballet Review*, Summer 1989; Christine Temin, 'Mark Morris: Brussels and Boston', *Ballet Review*, Fall 1989; William James Lawson, 'In the Monnaie', *Ballet Review*, Summer 1989; Sophie Constanti, 'Mark Morris, Béjart Pulp, and Belgian Bores', *Dance Theatre Journal*, February 1990; David Vaughan, 'Two Leaders: Mark Morris and Garth Fagan', *Ballet Review*, Summer 1990; David Vaughan, 'Mark Morris Here and There', *Ballet Review*, Winter 1990/91; David Vaughan, 'Mark Morris: Here and There – II', *Ballet Review*, Spring 1991; Marcia Siegel, 'Decomposing Sugar Plums & Robot Mice', *Ballet Review*, Spring 1991; John Percival, 'The Mark Morris Dance Group', *Dance and Dancers*, November 1992; Arlene Croce, 'An American Ritual', *The New Yorker*, December 28 1992 and January 4 1993 (double issue); Joan Acocella, 'Mark Morris: The Body and What It Means', *Dance Now*, Summer 1994; Alastair Macaulay, 'The Last Great American Choreographer', *Dance Theatre Journal*, Summer 1995; John Gruen, 'Mark Morris: Breaking New Ground', *Dance Magazine*, July 1995; Roger Copeland, 'Mark Morris, Postmodernism, and History Recycled', *Dance Theatre Journal*, Summer 1997; Graeme Kay, 'Lost for Words' (on *L'Allegro*), *Dance Theatre Journal*, Summer 1997.

Books Arlene Croce, *Sight Lines*, New York, 1987; Tom Brazil, *Dances by Mark Morris* (photographs), New York, 1992; Joan Acocella, *Mark Morris* (biography), New York, 1993.

GRAEME MURPHY

In many ways, Graeme Murphy – choreographer, dancer, artistic director – can be regarded as the personification of Australian contemporary dance. Australian-born, he has a commitment to Australian dance and dancers that has been unrelenting, as has his commitment to other Australian artists – choreographers, composers, musicians, and designers among them. Through the auspices of the Sydney Dance Company, Murphy has also been instrumental in bringing Australian dance to the wider international stage. Thus few would challenge the claim that not only dance, but the performing arts as a whole in Australia owe much to this highly innovative and often iconoclastic artist.

If one were to pinpoint the characteristics of Murphy's dance, then 'eclectic' and 'theatrical' are perhaps the two most definitive terms: for whether in the choice of artistic medium, or in the choice of theme, movement style, and music, Murphy ranges over a wide field, drawing on whatever he considers necessary to realize his creative vision. That vision is firmly anchored in the belief that dance should be theatre that excites and stimulates its audience, not only in terms of its dance content, but also in terms of its overall production.

Murphy's movement style is a case in point. Classical ballet lies at the core;[1] however, at the same time, he freely calls on any number of movement sources – both dance and non-dance – if it suits his purpose to do so. The result is a rich tapestry of movement ideas that goes beyond any readily definable stylistic category. *Daphnis and Chloë* (1980), for example, moves freely across time periods and movement styles, distorting them while still working recognizably within them. Greek shepherds and shepherdesses dance an elegant stylized folk dance; Cupid zooms around on a skateboard while Daphnis and Dorcan vie for Chloë's favour with a ballroom-disco competition; and the dancing of the tough punk-rocker Bryaxis and his coarse sewer rats is peppered with gymnastic rolls and hand-stands.

Another dimension of Murphy's eclecticism is the frequent interplay between fact and fantasy, past and present, age and youth. While *Poppy* (1978), *After Venice* (1984), and *Beauty and the Beast* (1993), among others, show this thematic mix, it is the highly original version of Tchaikovsky's *Nutcracker* (created for The Australia Ballet in 1992) in which these dynamic shifts reach their peak. Here the essence of the original ballet is woven in and around a contemporary story-line that has a distinctively Australian orientation, but draws on Russian dance and political history at the same time. Clara is portrayed as an elderly Russian emigré looking back over her life as a famous ballerina who made her debut with the Imperial Ballet as the *Nutcracker*'s Sugar Plum Fairy. After fleeing the 1917 Revolution, she joins Diaghilev's Ballets Russes, arriving in Australia in 1940 with the De Basil company. Her career ends with the newly fledged

Borovansky Ballet (the precursor to the Australian Ballet).

This eclectic approach, together with Murphy's commitments to highly theatrical collaborative ventures with other leading artists (composers, set and lighting designers, choreographers and musicians) while retaining his commitment to breaking boundaries and challenging the *status quo*, suggests more than a mere hint of the Diaghilevian about Murphy and his work. Thus it is perhaps not all that surprising to find that a significant number of works in his extensive repertory relate in some way or another to Diaghilev or the Ballets Russes.

The full length *Poppy*, for example, takes the life and art of Jean Cocteau as its theme. Part biography, and part journey in the fantasy world of Cocteau's opium-heightened imagination, this critically acclaimed work includes not only a larger-than-life Diaghilev, but also refers choreographically to some of the Ballets Russes masterpieces (*Le Spectre de la Rose* and *Le Sacre du Printemps* among them). *Shéhérazade* (1979), *Daphnis and Chloë*, and *Late Afternoon of a Faun* (1987) further reinforce the Diaghilevian connection.

As the above works might also suggest, the reinterpretation of classics – whether dance, literary text, or film – is a common feature of Murphy's work. The high-tech *Beauty and the Beast* similarly identifies the choreographer's interest in taking a classic and interpreting it in a way that is both entertaining and thought-provoking. Elements from the familiar Gothic tale, and others from Cocteau's film version, are reworked into a contemporary moral fable that includes not only the Gothic Beast, but also his robotic Corporate Beast and drug-ravaged Rock Beast counterparts. Although serious messages are embedded in the work, they are off-set by a delightfully irreverent sense of humour – yet another Murphy trademark.

Central to Murphy's choreography is the belief that dance should surprise rather than lead an audience politely along a comfortably predictable path: Diaghilev's aphoristic 'astonish me!' could well be taken as one of Murphy's fundamental artistic credos. As many of his works reveal, he is an inveterate risk-taker who is prepared to challenge conventional practices in, and perceptions about, dance. To take his *Nutcracker* again, the work departs radically from the original (and courageously so, given the generally orthodox ballet audiences in Australia); but rather than being yet another reinterpretation of the rather improbable story, it is an entirely logical commentary and reflection both on the work itself and on the origins of Australia ballet, emphasizing its Russian roots.

The principle of surprise also underpins the music Murphy uses. Hence contemporary music dominates the repertory, with commissioned scores from leading Australia composers – Carl Vine and Graeme Koehne in particular – playing a major role. The diversity that marks Murphy's choreographic *modus operandi* similarly underlies his choice of music. The rock music of Iva Davies/Bob Kretschmer in *Boxes* (1985), the percussion scores used for *Synergy with Synergy* (1992), and the music of Iannis Xenakis (*Kraanberg*, 1988), or Karol Szymanowski (*King Roger*, 1990), give some indication of its extent.

Yet another aspect of Murphy's challenge to conventional norms and expectations is the fact that he does not shy away from nudity and sexuality in his works. While bare flesh undeniably abounds, there is rarely the sense that it is there merely for gratuitous display. Murphy simply revels in the body and its physicality, and as he points out, he has 'never looked at dance removed from sensuality and sexuality'.[2] The nudity ranges from the humorous (Cupid displays a wonderful pair of bare buttocks in *Daphnis and Chloë*), through the provocatively sensual (in the 1993 television work, *Sensing*), to the more overtly sexual (in *Beauty and the Beast*, for example).

Any commentary on Graeme Murphy would be incomplete without mention of the close relationship between him and his long-time partner (and acknowledged Muse), Janet Vernon, as well as with the Sydney Dance Company (SDC) itself.[3] The relationship is essentially symbiotic, one that has been of mutual benefit to those directly concerned, and so to Australian dance itself. Yet although Murphy and the SDC are regarded by many as one and the same, he has never been precious about demanding exclusive artistic ownership over 'his' company. Instead he has ensured that its dancers are consistently exposed to the influences of other choreographers and other companies. Louis Falco's feisty *Black and Blue* (1982),[4] Barry Moreland's *Daisy Bates* (1982) and *Mansions* (1982), Ohad Naharin's *Arbos* (1989), and Douglas Wright's *Gloria* (1991), for example, have either been set on, or created for, the company. Importantly, Murphy has also encouraged dancers from within the company to test their choreographic wings: Paul Mercurio,[5] Kim Walker, and Gideon Obarzanek[6] are among those to have taken up the challenge successfully.

Various co-company enterprises have been an important part of the SDC agenda. *Boxes*, for example, saw the collaboration between the company and the rock band Icehouse, with the band itself an integral part of the dance action. In the exciting *Synergy with Synergy*, the collage of scores for percussion was performed onstage by Australia's leading percussion ensemble Synergy, aided and abetted by the company dancers.[7] Perhaps one of the most ambitious – both artistically and logistically – of these collaborative ventures came about in 1988 with Australia's bicentenary celebrations: Murphy created the full-length *VAST* using seventy dancers from four widely dispersed companies – the Sydney Dance Company, the Australian Dance Theatre, the Western Australia Ballet, and the Queensland Ballet.[8] His 1997 *Free Radicals* continued the merging of dancers and musicians by having its three percussionists (playing on everything from drums to terracotta pots) weaving in and out of the dancers, while the dancers were themselves beating out rhythms.

A summary such as this can merely hint at the significance of Graeme Murphy's contribution, both quantitative and qualitative, to Australian dance and theatre arts. Given that he is still relatively young, there is little doubt that he will continue that contribution; but given his keen enthusiasm for finding new paths and byways, precisely what direction that contribution takes may be less easy to identify.

Anita Donaldson

Notes

1 Thus giving rise to the description – at times somewhat disparagingly used – of 'neo-classic'.
2 Quoted from the video documentary *Astonish Me!*.
3 As Murphy's words in *Astonish Me!* suggest, Vernon has played a pivotal role in his artistic life: 'When Janet Vernon first pointed her immaculate foot on stage, that was like a key opening a door that could not be closed for the next fifty minutes . . . or perhaps forever. In my mind, that door having been opened really has changed me.'
4 It was created for Falco's New York company in 1982, but set on the SDC in 1984.
5 Paul Mercurio achieved international recognition after he starred in the film *Strictly Ballroom*.
6 Gideon Obarzanek has also created works on Nederlands Dans Theater 2.
7 The dancers, musicians, and the percussion instruments themselves, become an interactive sound and movement ensemble.
8 Given the 'tyranny of distance' that pervades Australian life, to organize the logistics of getting these four companies together in the first instance, and then touring them around the country, was no small achievement. The work was 'vast' in more than name alone.

Biografhical details

Born in Melbourne, Australia, 2 November 1950. **Studied** with Kenneth Gillespie in Launceston, Tasmania, from 1961; at the Australian Ballet School 1966–68. **Career** Joined Australian Ballet as dancer, 1969, touring the United States in 1970; first choreography, 1971; spent six months with the Sadler's Wells Royal Ballet in London and on tour, 1972; danced with the Grenoble-based Ballets de Félix Blaska, touring Europe, 1972–74; returned to Australia via South-east Asian tour with Ballet Caravan, 1974–75; freelance choreographer in Australia, working for Tasmanian Ballet, Queensland Ballet, and Australian Ballet School; rejoined Australian Ballet, as dancer and resident choreographer, 1976, and toured the United States and the UK; appointed Artistic Director and Chief Choreographer, Dance Company New South Wales, November 1976; company renamed Sydney Dance Company, 1979. Has choreographed for the Nederlands Dans Theater, Australian Dance Theatre, West Australian Ballet, Australian Opera, Mikhail Baryshnikov's White Oak Dance Project, and the ice dancers Torvill and Dean; has also directed opera productions. **Awards and honours** *Canberra Times* Dance Competition award, 1976; Order of Australia medal, 1982; named Australian of the Year, 1987; Honorary Doctorate, University of Tasmania, 1990.

Works

Ecco (1971), *Off* (1974), *Sequenza V11* (mus. Luciano Berio, 1975), *Three Conversations* (includes *Third Conversation*; mus. Bartók, 1975), *Glimpses* (mus. Margaret Sutherland, 1976), *Volumnia* (mus. György Ligeti, 1977), *Tip* (mus. Carl Vine, 1977), *Fire Earth Air Water* (1977), *Poppy* (mus. Carl Vine, 1978), *Tekton* (mus. Tolia Nikiprowetzky, 1978), *Rumours I* (mus. Barry Conyngham, 1978), *Schéhérazade* (mus. Ravel, 1979), *Rumours II and III* (mus. Barry Conyngham, 1979), *Signatures* (mus. Scriabin, 1979), *Scintillation* (mus. Carlos Salzedo, 1979), *Viridian* (mus. Richard Meale, 1980), *Beyond Twelve* (mus. Ravel, 1980), *Daphnis and Chloë* (mus. Ravel, 1980), *An Evening* (mus. collage, 1981), *Hate* (mus. Carl Vine, 1982), *Homelands* (mus. Janáček, 1982), *Wilderness* (mus. Bartók, 1982), *The Selfish Giant* (mus. Graeme Koehne, 1983), *Some Rooms* (mus. various, 1983), *Meander* (1984), *Old Friends, New Friends* (mus. Graeme Koehne, 1984), *After Venice* (mus. Messiaen, Mahler, 1984), *Deadly Sins* (mus. collage, 1984), *Death in Venice* (opera by Britten, 1984), *Song of India* (ice dance, 1984), *Boxes* (mus. Iva Davies, Bob Kretschmer, Icehouse, 1985), *Sirens* (mus. collage, 1986), *Nearly Beloved* (mus. Graeme Koehne, 1986), *Shining* (mus. Karol Szymanowski, 1986), *Fire and Ice* (ice dances, 1986), *Late Afternoon of a Faun* (mus. Stravinsky, 1987), *Song of the Night* (mus. Karol Szymanowski, 1987), *Gallery* (mus. Graeme Koehne, 1987), *VAST* (mus. Barry Conyngham, 1988), *Kraanberg* (mus. Iannis Xenakis, 1988), *soft bruising* (mus. Gavin Bryars, 1990), *In the Company of Women* (with Paul Mercurio; mus. collage, 1990), *King Roger* (opera by Karol Szymanowski, 1990), *Bard Bits* (based on Shakespeare, 1991), *The Nutcracker* (mus. Tchaikovsky, 1992), *Piano Sonata* (mus. Carl Vine, 1992), *Synergy with Synergy* (mus. percussion, played by Synergy, 1992), *Salomé* (opera by Richard Strauss, 1993), *Beauty and the Beast* (mus. Carl Vine, 1993), *Sensing* (for television; mus. Ross Edwards, 1993), *The Protecting Veil* (mus. John Tavener, 1993), *Les Troyens* (opera by Berlioz, 1994), *Fornicon* (mus. Martin Armiger, 1995), *Berlin* (mus. Icehouse, 1995,), *Embodied* (mus. Alfred Schnittke, poetry by Joseph Brodsky, 1996), *Onomatopeaia* (mus. Nigel Westlake, 1996), *Free Radicals* (mus. Michael Askill, percussion, 1997).

Further reading

Interview with Hazel Berg, in 'Growing in Australian Soil', edited by Michelle Potter, *Brolga: An Australian Journal about Dance*, December 1994.

Articles Peter Rosenwald, 'The Other Australian Company', *Dance News*, December 1977; John Cargher, 'The Spice of Life: The Sydney Dance Company', *Ballet News*, May 1981; Jill Sykes, 'The Sydney Dance Company', *Dance Magazine*, May 1981; Jill Sykes, 'Vigour and Variety', *Dance and Dancers*, June 1982; John Byrne, 'Hurried Creation', *Dance Australia*, September/November 1984; Patricia Laughlin, 'A Murphy Showcase', *Dance Australia*, December/January 1987/88; Andrea Borsay, 'Graeme Murphy: Kraanberg and the Rest', *Dance Australia*, December/January 1988/89; Karen Van Ulzen, 'Murphy's Back on Deck', *Dance Australia*, April/May 1990; Andrea Borsay, 'Another Murphy Success', *Dance Australia*, June/July 1990; Karen Van Ulzen, 'Tasteless and Silly', *Dance Australia*, October/November 1990; Karen Van Ulzen, 'The Past Revisited', *Dance Australia*, June/July 1991; Karen Van Ulzen, 'A Return to Integrity', *Dance Australia*, August/September 1991; Karen Van Ulzen, 'Dance Greats: The Choreographer: The Making of Murphy', *Dance Australia*, April/May, 1996.

Books Edward H. Pask, *Ballet in Australia: the Second Act, 1940–1980*; V. Craig, *Dance: 'Café' and 'Boxes': Contextual Notes for the Study of Two Works from Sydney Dance Company*, Sydney, 1993.

LLOYD NEWSON

As a choreographer who has made a dramatic impact on the contemporary dance scene in Britain and Europe by challenging it and defining a new language, Lloyd Newson, with his company DV8 Physical Theatre, has pushed dance-theatre into areas previously unexplored by dance. He has also been influential in the rise of issue-based work across the arts. Having originally trained and practised as a psychologist in Melbourne before becoming a dancer, Newson has created works like a psychologist's playground, exposing human emotions and feelings, and investigating questions of sex, identity, and relationships. Together with his insight into human behaviour, Newson's skill at evoking images, structuring movement, and creating theatre makes for gripping, disturbing, and thought-provoking performances. The raw 'in-your-face' portrayal of extreme human behaviour, particularly among homosexual men, is intended to question assumptions that society makes and to communicate with, rather than to shock, audiences, while the honesty and vulnerability with which the dancers perform reveals a deep self-questioning on the part of both themselves and Newson.

Newson began his career dancing with the New Zealand Ballet. After spending one year at London Contemporary Dance School on a scholarship, he went on to work with the repertory company Extemporary Dance Theatre, as both a dancer and choreographer, from 1981. His frustration with the general direction of contemporary dance and the lack of meaning for the sake of technique prompted him in 1986 to form his own company, DV8 (which refers to the 'deviant' homosexual identity Newson declares in his work) along with the independent dancers Nigel Charnock, Michelle Richecoeur, and Liz Rankin. Newson's first hit was *My Sex, Our Dance* (1986), a charged duet for himself and Charnock in which the physical risks evoked the emotional risks of two men in love, struggling with their sexuality, and with masculinity and the restrictions it imposes. Newson's choice to call his performance style 'physical theatre' indicated a departure from the accepted contemporary dance styles in that it did not rely on a traditional dance vocabulary, but demanded athletic physicality and stamina from his dancers, as well as the ability to improvise. The use of weight exchange, lifts, and holds in Newson's work is rooted in contact improvisation but is usually performed with a faster, more violent dynamic, and is mixed with pedestrian movement and body language, while the repetitions and heightened stylization can be traced back through to Pina Bausch's expressionistic dance theatre. Hurling the body onto another at speed, climbing up a body, falling or being thrown, often repeated until a state of real exhaustion and desperation is reached to evoke the nihilistic aspect of relationships in an unsympathetic society, recall the movement and themes often apparent in a Bausch performance. Another similarity with Bausch is the importance of the individuality of each performer, and the way that this is projected onto the audience.

Newson works closely and collaboratively with his performers, sharing the artistic process, channelling ideas, and improvising to uncover material that is always drawn from the performers' characters or their personal experiences. Each performance is so physically and mentally demanding for the dancers, who have to maintain authenticity and honesty throughout, that the works only have a limited performance life. Newson does not believe in churning things out on demand, stating, 'I only create when I have something to say ... The work is always about issues; things that concern or affect my life at this given time' (*Dance Now*, Summer 1993), and dancers are chosen according to their appropriateness to the given subject-matter for each new project.

From the stark, non-narrative, almost workshop-like qualities of the earlier works, such as *My Sex, Our Dance, Deep End* (1987) – a gruelling quartet which explored female-male partnerships – and *My Body, Your Body* (1987) – which exposed traps and rituals in such relationships with its cast of eight men and eight women playing out sexual stereotypes in tortured movements – Newson's subsequent work has incorporated the raw energy and themes, layering them with more theatrical devices, such as text, sets, sound-scores, and even linear narratives, as in *Strange Fish* (1992). In *Dead Dreams of Monochrome Men* (1988), based on the life of the London serial killer Dennis Nilson, traces of a 'pick-up' night-club environment and a flat where the killer took his victims were suggested by minimal set designs; and action poses, surreal images, and body language carried a deeper probing of homoeroticism, with its dark, sadomasochistic message powerfully evoked by the four male performers. *Never Again* (1989), which was filmed in a derelict warehouse, developed the nightmarish surrealism hinted at in *Dead Dreams*, showing a room filled with naked bodies hanging upside down and a public lavatory in which frozen poses of bizarre people standing in the cubicles included two ballet dancers wearing tutus. Shots of the performers running down endless corridors and entering dark empty rooms suggested the psychological fear of not belonging anywhere and of being ostracized by society.

Strange Fish marked another departure, as it merged dance with a more sophisticated use of theatre and conceptual art. Newson also here avoided exploiting physical risk as he had done so much in previous work, and instead focused more on subtleties and teasing out not only the pain of not belonging or of being alone, but also the humour of people playing the fool to attract attention. Elaborate images of religion were offered, including a dominating crucifix, with a naked female Christ, and a singer who sang in Latin

and was part of the cast. A subterranean
water tank suggested the subconscious or
death, while a cascade of rocks evoked chaos
and confusion. *MSM* (1993) was a piece of
text-based theatre for seven actor-dancers
based on 'cottaging', the activity of men
picking up other men for sex in public lava-
tories. The text was extracted from interviews with fifty homosexual and bisexual
men, and was accompanied by a sound score
by Jocelyn Pooks (with whom Newson has
collaborated on several works) and by a revolving set of washbasins, cubicles, and stalls.
Receiving rave reviews from theatre critics,
it expanded Newson's reputation as a choreographer into that of a theatre director.

Enter Achilles (1995) took straight male
bonding as its theme, and was a physical
manifestation of the 'new lad' imagery that
was being promoted in the media at the time.
This work was both nationally and internationally an enormous success, and was
made into a film. It was a striking piece of
popular culture, which exposed the crisis
of masculinity through movement, sound,
and design. *Bound to Please* (1997) also
focused on popular media themes, and was
partly inspired by Elizabeth Wurtsel's pop
psychology book, *Prozac Nation*. Newson
was interested in how our Western consumer
culture rejects bodies that are not econom-
ically or sociably viable, such as the old, the
fat, and the disabled. Newson's point – that
the dance world is particularly to blame
for this – was conveyed through a send-up
of the dance profession. *Bound to Please* was
full of technical dance steps, a parody of how
beauty-obsessed dancers behave. 'Beautiful'
dance images were constantly juxtaposed
with seamier events – the realities, according
to Newson, of a dysfunctional society. The
climax of this work was a steamy naked duo
between an elderly woman and a young man,
which boldly questioned society's attitude to
the older woman, especially in a sexual
context. With this work, Newson had tackled
yet another taboo.

Josephine Leask

Biographical details

Born in Albury, New South Wales (date not
publicly known). **Studied** dance when at college;
gained degree in psychology at the University
of Melbourne (before 1979); attended London
Contemporary Dance School (scholarship), 1980–
81. **Career** Dancer with New Zealand Ballet, 1979;
came to United Kingdom, 1980; after LCDS, company member and sometime choreographer,
Extemporary Dance Theatre, 1981–85; has danced
with Karole Armitage, Michael Clark, David Gordon, Daniel Larrieu, and Dan Wagoner; freelance
music-video choreographer by mid-1980s; co-
founder, as dancer and principal choreographer,
DV8 Physical Theatre, 1986, along with Nigel
Charnock, Michelle Richecoeur, and Liz Rankin;
DV8 Films formed in 1991. Has also choreo-
graphed for opera, and taught in Australia and
South America as well as in the United Kingdom.
Awards *Manchester Evening News* Theatre
Award, 1987; Digital Dance Award, 1987, 1988,
1990; London Dance and Performance Award for
Choreography, 1988, 1990, 1991; *Time Out* Award,
1989; *Evening Standard* Ballet Award, 1989; IMZ
Dance Screen Award, 1990, 1993, 1996; Golden
Pegasus Award (Australia), 1990; Prudential
Award, 1991, 1992; SADAC Award (France),
1992; Festival International du Film sur l'Art
award (France), 1992; Grand Prix International
Video-Danse (Pierre Cardin Award), 1993; TZ
Rose (Germany), 1993; Prix Italia, 1994, 1996;
Festival International Danse Visions Award, 1994.

Works

Breaking Images (1982), *Beauty, Art and the
Kitchen Sink* (1984), *Bein' a Part, Lonely Art*
(1985), *My Sex, Our Dance* (duet, 1986), *Elemen
Three Sex* (1987), *Deep End* (1987), *My Body,
Your Body* (mus. Sally Herbert, 1987), *Dead
Dreams of Monochrome Men* (mus. Jocelyn
Pook, Sally Herbert, 1988; film version, dir. David
Hinton, 1989), *Never Again* (for television, 1989),
'if only . . .' (mus. Sally Herbert, 1990), *Strange
Fish* (mus. Jocelyn Pook, Adrian Johnston, 1992;
television version the same year, dir. David
Hinton), *MSM* (mus. Jocelyn Pook, 1993),
Ariodante (opera by Mozart, 1993), *Enter Achilles*
(mus. Adrian Johnston, 1995; television version,
dir. Clara van Gool, 1995), *Bound to Please* (mus.
Adrian Johnston, 1997).

Further reading

Interviews with Andy Solway, in 'Lloyd Newson
Interview', *New Dance*, Autumn 1985; with Nadine
Meisner, in 'Strange Fish', *Dance and Dancers*,

Summer 1992; with Louise Levene, in 'Fish out of Water', *The Independent*, 11 July 1992; with Ellen Cranith, in 'Quest for an Unholy Grail', *Sunday Times*, 26 July 1992; in Jo Butterworth and Gill Clarke (eds.), *Dancemakers' Portfolio: Conversations with Choreographers*, Bretton Hall, 1998.

Articles Sophie Constanti, 'Spring Loaded: The Opening Shots', *Dancing Times*, March 1988; Sophie Constanti, 'Giving Birth to *Dead Dreams*', *Dance Theatre Journal*, Spring 1989; Christopher Winter, 'Love and Language, or Only Connect the Prose and the Passion', *Dance Theatre Journal*, Spring 1989; 'DV8 Physical Theatre in Rouen', *Dance Theatre Journal*, Summer 1990; Nadine Meisner, 'You Must Go On', *Dance and Dancers*, October 1990; Sophie Constanti, 'Dance Scene: DV8', *Dancing Times*, October 1990; Allen Robertson, 'Letter from Europe', *Dance Ink*, December 1990; Alex Mallems, 'DV8 Refusing to Compromise', *Parachute* (Montreal), July-September 1993; Lloyd Newson, 'Lloyd Newson on ... Dance', *Dance Now*, Summer 1993; Ian Somerville, 'Black and White Dance on Brown Tape' (on *Never Again* video), *Dance Now*, Autumn 1994; Josephine Leask, 'The Silence of the Man: An Essay on Lloyd Newson's Physical Theatre', *Ballett International*, August/September, 1995; Paul Jackson, 'Becoming Lloyd', *Dance Now*, Autumn 1995; Allen Robertson, 'DV8 × 2' (on videos of *Dead Dreams* and *Strange Fish*), *Dance Now*, Winter 1995; Keith Watson, '*Enter Achilles*', *Dance Theatre Journal*, Winter 1995/96; Lloyd Newson, 'Talkback' (response to review of *Enter Achilles*), *Dance Europe*, February/March 1996; Rupert Christiansen, 'Weakness in the Heel', *Dance Theatre Journal*, Summer 1996; Josephine Leask, 'Not the Body Beautiful', *The Independent on Sunday*, 27 July 1997; Beth Cinamon, 'Newson and Bacon', *Dance Now*, Autumn 1997.

Books Allen Robertson and Donald Hutera, *The Dance Handbook*, Harlow, Essex, 1988.

ROBERT NORTH

Robert North is an eclectic choreographer whose work sits happily in the repertory of both classical and contemporary companies. He is not a choreographer of great individuality, but one whose work appeals to a wide audience. In his shorter works, whether they have a narrative or not, the focus is on the choreography as a response to the music used – but in his 1990's role as choreographer of full-evening works, North has placed a greater emphasis on production ideas.

As a choreographer North developed slowly. His early workshop pieces, choreographed soon after graduating, were disastrous. In the early 1970s, however, he revealed his skill with the all-male *Troy Game* (1974), with *Still Life* (in which film was successfully incorporated as an integral part of the work), and with *Running Figures* (also 1975; variations on running movements to Geoffrey Burgeon's *Goldberg's Dream*). He quickly rebelled against gimmicks in dance for their own sake, and derived little pleasure from postmodern dance. He became recognized as a creator of well-crafted works and, as a showman himself, he appreciated the benefits of sharing the stage with star dancers. Thus in 1975 he joined forces with Wayne Sleep to create *David and Goliath*, a joke on their contrasting statures, and he collaborated with the ballerina Lynn Seymour on *Gladly, Badly, Madly, Sadly*. Seymour then invited North to create the role of the Bandit in *Rashomon* for Sadler's Well Royal Ballet.

American by birth but educated in Britain, North claimed to have become a victim of the 'dancing bug' in the 1960s, an exciting era for London dance, with performances by Nureyev and Fonteyn attracting enormous publicity and with contemporary American dance making a terrific impact with visits by Martha Graham, Merce Cunningham, Paul Taylor, and Alvin Ailey to London's theatres. North was nineteen years old and studying architecture at the Central School of Art when he began to study dance, training for a year with Kathleen Crofton and for two years at the Royal Ballet Upper School. At the graduating performances he appeared as Rothbart, and later, as Prince Siegfried in *Swan Lake*. At the end of his course at the Royal Ballet School, North also studied contemporary dance at the newly formed

London Contemporary Dance School, and he appeared in London Contemporary Dance's first London season in 1967. By the late 1960s and early 1970s, North was commuting across the Atlantic to appear with, and create roles for, the Martha Graham Company. As a dancer North was a significant performer, particularly during his twelve years with London Contemporary Dance Theatre (he was one of the most skilled of the first generation of LCDT dancers) and during his four years with Ballet Rambert. Tall, strikingly good-looking, and with dramatic presence, North was also a strong and sympathetic partner. His performing career was summarized by the critic Cormac Rigby in 1982:

> He is a dark, handsome man, who made a natural hero in many of LCDT's works. In Robert Cohan's *Cell*, his king-size gentleness was both vulnerable and strong. In Richard Alston's *Tiger Balm*, he was a tense intruder erupting naked into a world of tranquillity and gradually soothed to become himself serene and calm. That multi-faceted extravaganza, *Stages*, he held together with great skill and assurance, as the ultimate mythical Hero. He was a stunning partner – particularly with Linda Gibbs and Siobhan Davies.[1]

Although catagorized as a contemporary choreographer, North has worked with several classical ballet companies, creating works for Scottish Ballet, New London Ballet, Stuttgart Ballet, and English National Ballet as well as for 'cross-over', hybrid companies such as Geneva Ballet and Göteborg Ballet (of which he was director from 1991 to 1996). In 1997 North became artistic director of the Verona Ballet, supervising the opera ballets performed in the Arena each summer as well as developing the company's own repertoire. In his works for these companies, North's early classical training is clear. He was attracted to work with Ballet Rambert, where he was artistic director from 1981 to 1986, because

of the dancers' strong classical training and because of the company's rich musical resources. North's choreography draws on a range of styles, notably jazz and flamenco. His *Lonely Town, Lonely Street* (1980), once described as 'slick and fast and eminently watchable', is dedicated to his jazz-dance teacher Matt Mattox. Jazz and flamenco combine in *Entre dos Aguas* (1984), a show-stopping work. Its creation began with the energetic, final Rumba section as a show-piece for the students of the Rambert Academy in 1982, and the complete ballet coincided with the release in Britain of Carlos Saura's film of *Carmen* and the consequent wide interest in Spanish dance. In Turin, where North was artistic director of the ballet company (1990–91), he created a musical to tangos, *In the Little Hours*, and for Paris he created *Light Fandango* (1997), variations to Irish and Scottish folk music.

North's first major success was *Troy Game*, a work that has secured its place in numerous repertories for companies as diverse as the Batsheva Dance Company, the Royal Ballet, the Dance Theater of Harlem, San Francisco Ballet, Stuttgart Ballet, and the National Ballet of Canada. Originally it was created for six men of tremendous stamina from London Contemporary Dance Theatre, but the cast is usually increased, and may range from between eight and seventeen dancers. *Troy Game* is a lighthearted work which 'takes the mickey out of the macho spirit'. As North commented:

> ... we decided it should be about what young men get up to – practical jokes, undergraduate humour – that sort of thing. So the first part of the dance has some funny things in it but in a sense it's concerned with different styles of fighting, and warming up for a fight, and then towards the end it slips into a bit of under-graduate slapstick.[2]

Troy Game was choreographed as a response to London Contemporary Dance

Theatre's tour of Brazil in 1973. North and other members of the company were fascinated by the rhythms of Batucada folk music and the Capoeira style of dance – which complemented the Japanese martial art, Aikido, that they were already studying. The work further drew on *The Troy Game* by Lincoln Kirstein, which discussed ancient Roman dances and their Greek origins. From the book North discovered the 'stork dance' for young men, which involves hopping on one leg while trying to push over a rival, and the Spartan Pyhrric, which North has described as 'a warm-up for battle, done to music'.

North has a particular passion for the Romantic music of Schubert, to whose scores he has created a number of works. These follow romantic ideas and iconography, suggesting a journey through life and symbolically portraying the constant presence of fate or death. This allegorical figure (usually dressed in black) is as much a companion as a foe; in *Death and the Maiden* (1980), he is presented as a gradually accepted and welcomed friend, not an object of terror. In *Songs and Dances*, also created for London Contemporary Dance Theatre in 1981, there is a sense of warmth to the carefree community with its meetings and partings in the first 'Out of doors' section. This is replaced by a bleaker atmosphere, for the soirée 'Indoors', and the mood of the songs, notably, is interpreted dramatically North returned to Schubert's music, drawing on the Winterreise songs and similar thematic material for 1985's *Einsame Reise* (Lonely Journey) for Stuttgart Ballet and *A Stranger I Came* (1992) for English National Ballet.

Andrew Storer is the designer with whom North has most frequently and successfully worked. Storer understands well the requirements of dancers, and his own clear designs enhance but do not intrude on the choreography. In particular he has collaborated with North to animate and evoke the work of major artists. In 1982 North created

Pribaoutki (1982) (his first original work as artistic director for Rambert) to songs by Igor Stravinsky, with designs in homage to Pablo Picasso. This marked the centenaries of the births of Stravinsky and Picasso, and was originally performed at the Brighton Festival, which focused on 'Picasso and the Theatre'. *Pribaoutki* took a succession of well-known images and brought them to life. North explained,

> I have taken some pictures and some characters from Picasso, and sometimes I've just danced out of the pictures – like I've done with *The Three Musicians* and *The Acrobats* and with the Minotaur and the Young Girl. The face of the woman screaming from the painting *Guernica* I have used on a long piece of material which Lucy Burge wears . . . In my dances Picasso characters like centaurs and fawns cavort about as they do in the pictures.[3]

Two years later Henri Matisse was given similar treatment in *Miniatures* for Janet Smith's Company. *Miniatures* was enlarged and the two works were performed at Göteborg as a double bill, *Picasso and Matisse* (1990), at the outset of North's period there. More recently North created a third work in this genre, *Animation*, which took Renoir's painting as its stimulus.

Other artists have provided design ideas. *Elvira Madigan* (1987) for the Royal Danish Ballet had designs based on pictures by the Norwegian Edvard Munch, but the most interesting animation of paintings in his career has come with North's collaboration with Bridget Riley on *Colour Moves*, the optical illusions for which Riley is noted in her use of colour and geometry were enhanced by the interaction and juxtaposition of five cloths (predominantly green, yellow, blue, salmon, and finally a rainbow of vertical stripes), with dancers in costumes of similar colours.

In the 1990s North has increasingly focused on full-evening works. His own first long ballet was *Elvira Madigan* in 1987. This was based on a true episode in 1880s Sweden, in which a tight-rope walker from a circus eloped with a lieutenant, eventually to commit suicide. The romantic narrative had been popularized in 1967 by Bo Widerberg's film, but the ballet had nothing of the film's impact. In Eric Aschengreen's review of the ballet he suggested that North was undecided as to whether this should be a drama about fate, or a study of *fin-de-siècle* society, and at any rate the focus of the work was on production elements rather than the dance itself.

North had much greater success with his *Romeo and Juliet* (1990) for Geneva Ballet. For this he used Serge Prokofiev's famous score but included narrative detail not used by either Shakespeare in his original play or other choreographers of the ballet. For example, he included brief scenes showing the protagonist's childhood – Juliet as a baby with her nurse, mischievous young Romeo at lessons with Friar Lawrence. North's *Romeo and Juliet* was of necessity a chamber production, and the focus was on how all the characters influence the ultimate tragedy. It was danced with the women on *demi-pointe*, and North's admirers found much to praise in the variety of the production. For the critic Nicholas Dromgoole, North's balcony scene 'challenged comparison with the finest'.

North has not depended on well-known stories for his full-evening ballets. In 1991 he choreographed *Living in America* to music mostly taken from Aaron Copland's scores. The work had three acts devoted successively to the 'Wild West', 'Prohibition', and 'Contemporary Society'. For this production North drew on a variety of dance styles including jazz and Hispanic; only the role for the Secretary was created on *pointe*, and here the noise of her toe-shoes suggested the tapping of the typewriter keys. North also probably drew on his own heritage of earlier works such as *Whip it to a Jelly* (1987), a blues-inspired work for Janet Smith and Dancers which evoked 1930s American city life, and *Lonely Town, Lonely Street*.

Other full-evening works include *Life, Love and Death* (1993), *The Russian Story* (1993), and, in 1996, *Eva* (about an imaginary author, her artistic heritage and her life story). He has also created family ballets with an obvious appeal to young children, and with both *Prince Rama and the Demons* (1992) to music by Christopher Benstead, and *The Snowman* (1993; based on the story by Raymond Briggs, originally for Göteborg, then revised for Birmingham) to a score by Howard Blake, North worked again with regular collaborators.

Jane Pritchard

Notes

1 Cormac Rigby, 'Robert North', *Set to Music*, November/December 1982, p. 18.
2 Penelope Easton, 'North Comes to the North-West', *Arts Alive Merseyside*, April 1981 p.4.
3 Richard Davies, 'Double Century Dances', *Classical Music*, 22 May 1982, p. 24.

Biographical details

Born Robert Dodson in Charleston, South Carolina, United States, 1 June 1945. **Studied** architecture at the Central School of Art, London, 1963; studied ballet with Kathleen Crofton, and at the Royal Ballet School, London, 1965–67, also attending the London Contemporary Dance School, from 1966; later studied with Martha Graham and Merce Cunningham in the United States. **Career** Danced with London Contemporary Dance Group, 1967, Martha Graham Company, 1968–69, and London Contemporary Dance Theatre, 1969; associate choreographer, London Contemporary Dance Theatre, 1975; guest choreographer for Ballet Rambert, Janet Smith and Dancers, and other companies, including Stuttgart Ballet, Balletto di Toscana, Zurich Ballet, Zurich Dance Theatre, Hong Kong Ballet, Royal Danish Ballet, Geneva Ballet, Ballet Jazzart (Paris), and Compagnia Fabula Saltica (Italy); also choreographer for film, opera, and theatre; contemporary dance teacher at Royal Ballet School, 1979–81, and international guest teacher; co-artistic director, London Contemporary Dance Theatre, 1981; artistic director, Ballet Rambert, 1981–86; ballet director, Teatro Regio, Turin, 1990–91; artistic director, Göteborg Ballet,

Sweden, 1991–96; artistic director, Verona Arena Ballet, Italy, from 1997. **Awards** include Prague Gold Award, 1983.

Works

Death by Dimensions (mus. Michael Parsons, 1967), *Out of Doors* (mus. Bartók, 1967), *Pavane for a Dead Infanta* (mus. Ravel, 1967), *Conversation Piece* (mus. Michael Parsons, 1970), *One Was the Other* (mus. Michael Finnissy, 1970), *Brian* (mus. Michael Finnissy, John Dodson, 1970), *Troy Game* (mus. Batacuda, Bob Downes, 1974), *Dressed to Kill* (mus. Henry Miller, Dennis Smith, 1974), *Gladly, Badly, Madly, Sadly* (with Lynn Seymour; mus. Davis, 1975), *Running Figures* (mus. Geoffrey Burgon, 1975), *David and Goliath* (with Wayne Sleep; mus. Davis, 1975), *Still Life* (mus. Bob Downes, 1975), *Just a Moment* (mus. Bob Downes, Kool and the Gang, 1976), *Reflections* (mus. Howard Blake, 1976), *Meeting and Parting* (mus. Howard Blake, 1977), *Nightwatch* (with Micha Bergese, Robert Cohan, and Siobhan Davies, mus. Bob Downes, 1977), *Scriabin Preludes and Studies* (mus. Scriabin, 1978), *Dreams with Silences* (mus. Brahms, 1978), *Reflections* (revised version; mus. Howard Blake, 1979; revised version, 1979), *Annunciation* (mus Howard Blake, 1979), *The Water's Edge* (mus. Anderson, Palmer, Barre, 1979), *January to June* (1979), *Death and the Maiden* (mus. Schubert, 1980), *Lonely Town, Lonely Street* (mus. Bill Withers, 1980), *Songs and Dances* (mus. Schubert, 1981), *Pribaoutki* (mus. Stravinsky, 1982), *Electra* (mus. Britten, 1982), *For My Daughter* (mus. Janáček, 1983), *Colour Moves* (mus. Christopher Benstead, 1983), *Entre dos Aguas* (mus. Paco de Lucia, 1984), *Miniatures* (mus. Stravinsky, 1984), *Light and Shade* (mus. Stravinsky, 1985), *Changing Shape* (mus. Talking Heads, 1985), *Dances to Copland* (mus. Copland, 1985), *Einsame Reise* (mus. Schubert, 1985), *Fool's Day* (mus. Renaissance songs, 1986), *Der Schlaf der Vernunft* (mus. Shostakovitch, 1986), *Whip It to a Jelly* (mus. popular, 1987), *Elvira Madigan* (mus. various, 1987), *Sebastian* (mus. Menotti, 1988), *Romeo and Juliet* (mus. Prokofiev, 1990), *Carmina Burana* (mus. Orff, 1990), *Picasso and Matisse* (revised versions of *Pribaoutki* and *Miniatures*; mus. Stravinsky, 1990), *In the Little Hours* (mus. tangos, 1991), *Living in America* (mus. various, 1991), *A Stranger I Came* (mus. Schubert, 1992), *The Heat* (mus. Peter Gabriel, 1992), *Prince Rama and the Demons* (mus. Chris Benstead, 1992), *The Russian Story* (mus. Tchaikovsky, Shostakovich, 1993), *The Snowman* (mus. Howard Blake, 1993), *Life, Love and Death* (mus. various, 1993), *The Cradle Will Rock* (mus. Christopher Benstead, 1995), *Eva* (mus. Howard Blake, 1996), *Light*

Fandango (mus. Scottish and Irish Folk, 1997), *Ragazzi selvaggi* [Wild Boys] (mus. Enrico Rava, arr. Paolo Silvestri, 1997), *Hamlet, Prince of Denmark* (mus. Shostakovich, 1997).

Further reading

Interviews with Penelope Easton, in 'North Comes to the North-West', *Arts Alive Merseyside*, April 1981; in 'Trends in British Ballet: Discussion with Robert Cohan, Norman Morrice and Robert North', *Ballett International*, October 1983.

Articles Noël Goodwin and Peter Williams, 'Rambert at the Roundhouse', *Dance and Dancers*, June 1975; Richard Davies, 'Double Century Dances', *Classical Music*, 22 May 1982; John Cowan, 'Rambert Rediscovered', *Dance and Dancers*, July 1982; Mary Whitney, 'Proud Export', *Ballet News*, October 1982; Cormac Rigby, 'Robert North', *Set to Music*, November/December 1982; Mary Clarke, 'Rambert at the Wells', *Dancing Times*, May 1984; Alastair Macaulay, 'The Rambertians', *Dancing Times*, May 1985; Sophie Constanti, 'Ballet Rambert', *Dance Theatre Journal*, Summer 1985; Fiona Malcolm, 'Such Stuff as Dreams Are Made On', *Sunday Times Magazine*, 28 June 1987; Nicholas Dromgoole, 'The Banished Star of British Dance', *The Sunday Telegraph*, 25 February 1991; Nicholas Dromgoole, 'Praising North and His Heavenly Host', *The Sunday Telegraph*, 31 March 1996.

Books Peter Brinson and Clement Crisp, *The Pan Book of Ballet and Dance*, London, 1980; Mary Clarke and Clement Crisp, *London Contemporary Dance Theatre: The First 21 Years*, London, 1989; Jane Pritchard, *Rambert: A Celebration*, London, 1996.

KAZUO OHNO

Kazuo Ohno is the grandfather of the controversial Japanese avant-garde dance form Butoh. Known for its shocking, contorted body gestures and dedication to breaking taboo, Butoh rose out of postwar Japan as a renegade performance form. Ohno, with his partner, the late Tatsumi Hijikata, fostered the early experimental development of Butoh in the 1960s, and was instrumental in making it an influence on many twentieth-century modern dancers.

Even at his advanced age, Ohno in the 1990s has been teaching twice a week in his Yokohama studio, choreographing a new work annually, appearing worldwide in dance and theatre festivals, lecturing, and taking part in a variety of symposia.

Ohno is choreographer, solo dancer, writer, and teacher, and a truly charismatic figure, who has charmed audiences and critics from Paris to São Paolo. His dance, which primarily focuses on death, birth, and re-birth, personifies universal emotions. His choreographic aesthetic travels from the darkest subconscious memory to the quirkiest sense of humour. The major influences that have marked his work over the years are his mother, his collaborator Tatsumi Hijikata, his religious beliefs, and German Expressionist dance.

Ohno was born in rural northern Japan in 1906, the eldest of twelve siblings. His obsessive love for his mother prompted his solo work, *My Mother* (1981). Kneeling on a small Japanese lacquer table in a tight spotlight, he transforms into both his mother's ghost and himself as a child. He crawls under the table, wears it like a turtle shell (or a womb?), caresses and embraces it. The table, a relic from his childhood, is the likely personification of his mother, and in his own works, 'his first source of nourishment'. His mother's umbilical cord (symbolically represented by a heavy rope) was his first food; later the table replaced her. In the work, Ohno offers reverence to his mother, and mourns her loss, as he slowly bows his head to the ground, then, even slower, lifts his chin to the sky. *My Mother* draws on a profound part of Ohno's life: it is his emotional response to love, devotion, and grief. The dance has elements of mime and theatricality that are based on reality: a nursing baby, a child reaching up, and the silent scream of mourning. Ohno seamlessly ties the images together in a complete abstract dance, with only glimpses of the realistic gestures. Watching him, one would not easily perceive each image independently, but the intensity with which Ohno performs is readily conveyed and is the riveting element of his dance.

Ohno taught physical education at a Yokohama secondary school for forty-six years until his retirement in 1980. In the mid-1930s, in order to bring dance into his gym curriculum, he began to study modern dance with the Japanese pioneers Baku Ishii and Takaya Eguchi, who had studied with the German Expressionists Mary Wigman and Harald Kreutzberg. German Expressionism became a foundation for all Ohno's dances; eventually he was able to see Kreutzberg dance in Japan. The emotional passion of the works of Wigman and Kreutzberg gave Ohno the impulse to expand the limits of his own choreography. Often, in lectures and interviews, he refers to Mary Wigman's landmark *Witch Dance*, which impressed him so much that he has viewed the film countless times.

Ohno converted to Christianity while he was a young teacher, and his religious beliefs have some bearing on his sense of beauty, love, and benevolence, and are apparent in works such as *My Mother*, and *Water Lilies* (1987), which, like most of Ohno's works, was created as a tribute to a personal hero. *Water Lilies* was choreographed as a dedication to the impressionist painter, Monet. In the work, Ohno greets the invisible 'ghost' of Monet on a bridge (also invisible) over Monet's famous water lily pond, then dances a duet with his imaginary companion, offering his admiration in a silent ritual. For Ohno, the dance is both a memorial to a great artist, and a celebration of Nature's perfection. Ohno claims to be dancing in a garden, although there is no set, and by the waterside, although there is no water on stage; most of the 'dancing' takes place inside his head, within the landscape of his vast imagination, while convincing viewers that they have seen an actual set on stage.

In 1956, Ohno began to work with Tatsumi Hijikata (1926–86), a prominent

figure in the experimental theatre movement of the 1950s and 1960s, and together
they are credited with founding Butoh.
Early experiments in the 'Ankoku Butoh'
('Dance of Darkness') genre were fired by
the passions of Antonin Artaud, Marquis de
Sade, and Georges Bataille, whose works
were translated into Japanese at the time.
Taking the darkest imagery from these
works, the collaborators staged wild happenings: they painted their bodies with thick
white paste, often included live animals in
performances, and used every kind of music
from the Beatles to Japanese traditional
samisen. Ohno featured as a soloist in most
of the Butoh performances and films of the
1960s and 1970s.

Ohno continued working with Hijikata
until 1968, at which point they went their
separate ways, forming two tracks of Butoh.
Hijikata continued to explore the dark
side of Butoh, and led a company that eventually spawned many Butoh artists such
as Sankai Juku's artistic director, Usio
Amagatsu, Muteki-sha's director, Natsu
Nakajima, and other internationally known
Butoh figures. Ohno took a 'lighter', more
individual path, and was more reticent as a
teacher, although he continued to strengthen
as a solo performer. Hijikata made dance
with others – watching them, directing them,
pushing them. In contrast, Ohno has always
created dance from and for himself. That is
why it is rare for Ohno to dance with others.
It is as if the stage were already filled with
his ghosts, leaving no room for a living
partner. The only person he has danced with
over the years since Hijikata is his son,
Yoshito Ohno, who was a young member of
Hijikata's early group. When son and father
dance together, it is a kind of parallel
motion, rather than a duet, as if their souls
are existing on a similar plane, with little
physical relationship.

When not touring, Ohno has taught in his
hilltop Yokohama studio. Ohno's teaching
directly reflects the manner in which he
creates dance. In the class there is no set

routine or warm-up, no specific 'Butoh' technique. Class begins with Ohno lecturing on
his latest fixation (he has many) – familial
love, a painting he saw in Europe, a church
he visited in Israel, or a story from his volu-
minous daily journal. (His autobiography,
published in Japanese in 1990, is the formidable size of a New York City phone book.)
The lecture is meant to stimulate movement
ideas. Later, the students improvise to all
kinds of music, from Pink Floyd to Wagner
opera, keeping in mind the theme of Ohno's
talk. Ohno's philosophy is summed up in
his essay, 'Lessons': 'I think you dance only
because you want to seriously and consciously deal with the fact that you are
living.' The long-time member of the Butoh
movement, Tomiko Takai, describes a 1960
Ohno class:

> He would offer us a theme and we would
> dance, with him beating on a drum. His
> teaching was not really about movement
> style, but more about words and language.
> He would recite a series of images and we
> would respond with our bodies. I remem-
> ber once he told me to walk as though a
> bird was resting on my shoulder, without
> upsetting the bird. If I moved too quickly,
> the bird would fly away. So I had to con-
> centrate and move very very slowly . . .

This combination of daily philosophical
speculation and structured improvisation
found in his class informs all of his stage
work. A finished Ohno dance is a series of
vignettes, each scene set to a different piece
of music. Ohno often rearranges the order,
exchanging the scenes until he finds the right
rhythm to the whole work.

Speaking of improvisation he writes:

> . . . the empty stage, the bare stage you
> appear on without any preparation, does
> not mean that it contains nothing . . . The
> vacant space is gradually being filled and
> in the end, something is realized there . . .
> It may be the kind of thing that takes a
> lifetime to learn, in my case I instanta-
> neously knew that the empty space was

actually very full. I merely danced in joy and excitement.

Ohno's trademark work, *Admiring La Argentina*, a dance dedicated to the great flamenco dancer, was choreographed in the 1970s, although Ohno was inspired by a 1929 theatre experience, when he saw the real Argentina dance in Tokyo. He harboured the memory for nearly fifty years, then brought the dance to the stage. Musically, the work features flamenco music, Bach, and a recording of Argentina's own castanets which Ohno obtained from her family. There is melodrama and sentimentality in his selections, beginning with Bach's *Tocata and Fugue in D minor*, which brings Ohno from audience to the stage; and later a live pianist is rolled onto the stage, pushing Ohno (dressed only in his underwear) in a mock struggle. His elaborate notation for *Argentina* is full of historical and philosophical references: a few lines, curves, and arrows indicate direction, with words covering the page. Ohno embodies the Argentina; she is inside him, prodding him, urging him to manifest her memory. Like a persistent muse, Argentina's ghost leads Ohno across the stage, to a scene in which he stands with his mouth open upwards, a beam of light piercing his body. His vocabulary, a deceptively simple series of gestures, has become condensed and distilled over the years. Each step, each stride is complete, unpredictable, and exudes great emotion. 'The best thing someone can say to me,' Ohno relates, 'is that while watching my performance they began to cry. It is not important to understand what I am doing, in fact perhaps it is better if they don't understand, but just respond to the dance.'

As Argentina, Ohno dances in a wardrobe of antique women's dresses and an elegant, French-cut tuxedo, which he wears for an encore. With whitened face, a smudge of rouge on his lips and blue eye-shadow, he would appear to a backstage visitor more like an aged wreck of a Pierrot or an over-dressed transvestite than a modern dancer. But the male and female fuse in his portrayal of Argentina, and although he embodies his heroine, he is not imitating her in a vaudeville sense. Rather, his dance elevates and personifies the spirit of flamenco.

Ohno does everything contrary to what is expected from a man of his age. In true Butoh fashion, he has seemed to defy death itself. Dance is his life, and he appears to be dancing at the edge of death. But for Ohno there is no separation between life and dance, or between death and life. Every dance is a natural continuation of existence, and he dances to confirm the cycle of life. In the words of Yoshito Ohno, his son, 'My father is a person who could die for dance; he will dance until the very end.' And in the words of Kazuo Ohno, 'By the grace of those who have gone before we are able to grow to exist. We must cherish the souls of the dead. If you took them out of my dance, there would be nothing left'. This is the essence of Butoh – the power to bring memories to the surface, and to give breath to ghosts.

Bonnie Sue Stein

Biographical details

Born in Hakodate, island of Hokkaido, Japan, in 1906. **Studied** at the Japan Athletic School (later renamed Japan Athletic College), 1926–29 (with interruption for military service), taking classes in, for example, Denmark exercises and Rudolf Bode exercises; attended the Baku Ishii Dance School, 1933–34; trained with Takaya Eguchi, learning Mary Wigman's techniques, 1936–38. **Career** Teacher of physical education at a Catholic High School in Yokohama from 1929; called up for military service in 1938, and spent the next seven years in northern China and New Guinea, rising to rank of captain; returned to Tokyo, and resumed classes with Takaya Eguchi, 1946; began choreographing and performing in 1949; met dancer/choreographer Tatsumi Hijikata (1926–1986) in 1954, and began intensive collaboration with him from 1960, developing a new dance style through the Ankoku Butoh group (1961–66) and staging happenings; independent performer and choreographer from 1967, often as guest choreographer/performer with other groups and artists, including

Hijikata, Mitsutaka Ishii, Tomiko Takai; danced and acted in three films about 'Mr O.', directed by Chiaki Nagano, 1969–73; founded Kazuo Ohno Dance School, 1977; retired from schoolteaching, 1980; gave first performances in Europe and North America, 1980, and performed and taught throughout the world during the 1980s and early 1990s, sometimes in collaboration with his son Yoshito; in recent years has written an autobiography, while continuing to teach at his studio in Yokahama and perform occasionally. **Awards and honours** include Dance Critics Award, 1977; created 'Illustrious Citizen' of Japan, 1992.

Works

Modern Dance Concert 1 (1949), *Cry of the Devil* (1949), *Tango* (1949), *Modern Dance Concert 2* (1950), *Sea of Spring* (1951), *Urban Dance* (1951), *The Reclining Stone Figure* (1953), *Forgotten Thoughts* (1953), *No Results* (1953), *Kazuo Ohno Dance Concert* (includes *The Old Man and the Sea*, based on the novel by Ernest Hemingway, 1959), *Old and Divine Prostitute* (with Hijikata, 1960), *Our Lady of the Flowers* (with Hijikata, based on the novel by Jean Genet, 1960), *Spot Testament* (based on *The Lay of Maldoror* by Lautréamont, 1960), *The Hermaphrodite's Secret Ceremony* (with Hijikata, 1961), *Sugar Lump* (1961), *Dance of the Furies* (1961), *Sacrificial Ceremony* (1963), *Rose-Coloured Dance* (with others, 1965), *Hall* (1966), *Genet* (with Tatsumi Hijikata, 1968), *Mandala Mansion* (with Hijikata, based on poems by Kuniya Kato, 1968), *The Revolution of the Body* (with Hijikata and others, 1969), *Japanese Military Spirit* (1972), *Admiring La Argentina* (solo; 1977), *Divine* (1977), *A Little Girl* (1977), *Jesus Christ* (1977), *Dark Priest* (1977), *Epilogue* (1977), *Modern Dance Performance* (based on poems by Kazuko Schiraichi, 1979), *The Dream of the Foetus* (1980), *Dream of the Sea* (1981), *Desire* (1981), *Last* (1981), *My Mother* (1981), *Dead Sea* (1985), *Water Lilies* (inspired by Monet's paintings, 1987), *Ka Cho Fu Getsu* (with Yoshito Ohno, 1990), *The Wolf* (1994).

Further reading

Interviews with Ulrike Döpfer and Alex Tangerding, in 'Dance on the Borderlands of Life and Death', *Ballett International*, August/September 1994; with Richard Schechner, in 'Kazuo Ohno Doesn't Commute', *Drama Review*, Summer 1986.

Articles Peter Ryan, 'Kazuo Ohno: North American Premiere', *Vandance* (Vancouver),

September 1980; Mindy Aloff, 'Classical Performing Arts Friendship Mission of Japan ... Admiring La Argentina performed by Kazuo Ohno', *Dance Magazine*, January 1982; Daniel Dobbels, 'Kazuo Ohno: Hommage à la Argentina', *Empreintes* (Paris), March 1983; Bonnie Sue Stein, 'Twenty Years Ago We Were Crazy, Dirty, and Mad', Kazuko Kuniyoshi, 'Butoh Chronology: 1959–1984', Kazuo Ohno, 'Selections from the Prose of Kazuo Ohno' and 'Performance Text: *The Dead Sea*', all in Butoh section of *Drama Review*, Summer 1986; Richard Schechner; 'Out of Darkness: Butoh', *Dance Magazine*, April 1986; Lizzie Slater, 'Kazuo Ohno and Butoh Dance', *Dance Theatre Journal*, Winter 1986; Bonnie Sue Stein, 'Celebrating Hijikata: A Bow to the Butoh Master', *Dance Magazine*, May 1988; Kazuo Ohno, 'Through Time in a Horse-Drawn Carriage', *Ballett International*, September 1989; Miyabi Ichikawa, 'Butoh: The Denial of the Body', *Ballett International*, September 1989; Judith Hamera, 'Derevo, Butoh, and Imagining the Real', *High Performace* (Santa Monica, California), Spring 1990; Lise Brunel, 'Simplicité, generosité, humanité', *Les Saisons de la Danse*, January 1991; Sibylle Janzen, 'Intuitionen und Körpererinnerungen: Ein Workshop mit Kazuo und Yoshito Ohno', *Tanz Aktuell* (Berlin), February 1991.

Books Gustavo Collini Sartor, *Kazuo Ohno: El último emperador de la danza* (Spanish text), Buenos Aires, 1996.

STEVE PAXTON

To watch Steve Paxton dance is to witness an insatiable curiosity about the movement potential of the human body. As the lights come up and the music begins, Paxton nonchalantly plunges into a series of skips, spins, twists, and tilts, taking his body (and his audience) on an adventure across the last four decades of American contemporary dance. The corporeal is clearly his medium, the raw material which he forms and reforms depending upon his particular focus. His recent physical obsession has been the spiralling and unspiralling of the spine and the various ways the arms and legs can complete or disrupt that core movement direction. While his work may be motivated primarily by an investigation of muscle and bone, Paxton's dancing is never simply a matter of physical actions. For Paxton, the physical is never a simple matter. It is, rather, 'a complexity of social, physical, geometric, glandular, political, intimate and personal information which is not easily renderable'.[1] Despite his protestations to the contrary, Paxton, in fact, has spent a lifetime attempting to render just that.

In a 1993 solo work, Paxton weaves his way back and forth across the performing space to the quick, classically complex beats of *Some English Suites* (J.S. Bach, played by Glenn Gould), pirouetting at one moment, and then crawling across the floor at the next. Clearly enjoying himself, he seems to be revelling in the legacy of his long dancing career which bridges the historical shift from modern to postmodern dance. His early training in the dance styles of Martha Graham and then Merce Cunningham has infused his body with a proud, almost classical deportment that the relaxed pedestrian demeanour he has cultivated since the 1970s cannot completely dislodge. In his dancing there are breathtaking moments of a crystal-clear motion – such as a spin that turns fiercely, yet elegantly, to stop on a dime – which exude the quiet groundedness of a Zen master. Yet these moments may immediately give way to clowning with a highly exaggerated and slightly awkward drop to the floor, executed with a slight smile which seems to acknowledge the restrictions of his ageing body and, at the same time, to remind the audience not to take him or themselves too seriously.

Although he has been a major catalyst for many of the significant innovations in American dance over the past four decades, Steve Paxton is less well known to the general public than are some of his contemporaries. Rather than building a company to showcase his own choreography, Paxton has chosen to focus his intellectual and physical energies on improvisational dance.

Because he is committed to the flexible, open, often anti-hierarchical structure of much contemporary improvisation, Paxton has eluded a more public recognition for the less marketable, but nonetheless influential, work of teaching and performing improvisation. Among contemporary dancers, he is best known as the man who pioneered the earliest form of contact improvisation. Yet his influence spans beyond the genre of contact improvisation to include almost all dancers studying a form of contemporary dance technique.

Arriving as a young dancer in New York City at the beginning of the 1960s, Paxton quickly became a key figure in the development of postmodern dance. He danced with Merce Cunningham's company, and participated in Robert Dunn's legendary composition course, which was taught at the Cunningham studio and included a number of important dancers, choreographers, artists, and composers. This class and Paxton's friendships with the likes of Yvonne Rainer and Robert Rauschenberg paved the way for the extraordinary collaborations of the Judson Dance Theater. By all accounts, Paxton played a seminal role in forming the Judson aesthetic.

Judson Dance Theater was formed in 1962, and although it officially lasted only two years, it set the stage for the evolution of American postmodern dance. Throughout all the wacky experimentations with a variety of compositional forms and contents (including story-telling and musical theatre, as well as minimalist assemblage), much of the work that came out of Judson Dance Theater's collaborations with dancers, artists, and musicians highlighted the performer's body as a physical body, emphasizing the raw materiality and potent concreteness of that dancing body. This desire to unmask the physical body – which is often euphemistically referred to in modern dance as the dancer's 'instrument' – as a culturally determined body plugged the Judson experiments directly into the

1960s' burgeoning ethos of radicalism and freedom.

If we look as several of Paxton's dances from that time, we can see a number of typical Judson stylistic innovations at work. Like his peers, Paxton became increasingly interested in working with movement repetition, uninflected dynamics, the use of props, and alternative performance sites (including a wood in *Afternoon* (1963)), as well as working with pedestrian and found movement. *Proxy* (1961), for instance, was a dance piece based on a visual score made up of sports photographs and other media images.[2] Paxton asked the dancers to copy the poses as directly as possible, making their own choices about how to achieve the necessary transitions from one pose to another. *Proxy* also included staged actions culled from everyday living such as eating, drinking, and walking.[3]

In her extensive research on Judson Dance Theater, Sally Banes identifies the preoccupation with walking in Judson as a significant break from the traditional modern dance aesthetic. Walking refuted the elitism of dance training and suggested that a dancer could be an ordinary person who was interested in looking at and experiencing some of the simplest kinds of everyday actions as dance movements. Similarly, this belief opened the door for 'average' bodies to participate in the new crop of Judson dances. Paxton was particularly attracted to this new openness to what could constitute dance movement, and to who could be identified as a dancer. As Banes comments in her discussion of the development of Paxton's work, walking was crucial:

It opened up a range of nondance movement, a variety of nonhierarchical structures, a performance presence that could be simultaneously relaxed and authoritative. It became the currency of Paxton's populist stance. Walking is something that everyone does, even dancers when they are not 'on'. Walking is a

sympathetic link between performers and spectators, a shared experience that allows for personal idiosyncracies and individual styles. There is no single correct way of walking.[4]

Paxton made quite a few dances in the late 1960s which incorporated large groups of people walking. *Satisfying Lover* (1967) and *State* (1968) both used thirty or more performers who walked and stood at different intervals according to a predetermined score.[5] Jill Johnston's description of *Satisfying Lover* in her 14 April 1968 *Village Voice* column gives us a good sense of the dance's priorities:

The fat, the skinny, the medium, the slouched and slumped, the straight and tall, the bowlegged and knock-kneed, the awkward, the elegant, the coarse, the delicate, the pregnant, the virginal, the you name it, by implication every postural possibility in the postural spectrum, that's you and me in all our ordinary everyday who cares splendor.[6]

It was this sort of egalitarian ideology, combined with a growing curiosity about the possible physics of human bodies, that brought Paxton to the form of duet partnering called contact improvisation.

Contact improvisation began as a communal experiment. During the summer of 1972, Paxton was joined by a group of dancers, mostly students, from Oberlin, Bennington, and Rochester – places where he had taught workshops the previous winter and spring. Working and living together in a loft space in New York City, the group spent two weeks investigating different states of dancing, including standing still (and feeling the small adjustments that one's body makes to keep standing – what Paxton calls the 'small dance'), falling, and hurling one's body at another person. What developed in that time were the seeds of a dance form based on the exchange of energy, weight, and momentum between two (or more) people. Influenced by Asian martial arts such as Tai Chi and Aikido, as well as the release work being taught by Mary Fulkerson, contact improvisation literally embodied many of the cultural values being championed in the early 1970s.[7]

It is telling that when Paxton and some of the group that worked together that summer later went on an *ad hoc* tour of the West Coast, they entitled their performances *You come, we'll show you what we do*. As it developed under Paxton's guidance, contact improvisation became a relatively unpretentious, democratic dance form. Dance events called jams integrated people from all walks of life and of all different dance abilities. The casual, spontaneous nature of the dancing allowed many people (especially men) who could not (or would not) think of themselves as dancers to participate in this movement form. Contact improvisation also incorporated into its movement training many of the Eastern philosophical principles that Paxton was absorbing at the time. Contact dancers try to cultivate a full yet easy awareness in their minds and a readiness in their bodies in order to prepare them for the unexpected. This ability to observe and react, rather than to manipulate and direct the dancing, is one of the core principles in contact improvisation.

Although Paxton is considered the founder of contact improvisation, and although he still teaches workshops in the form throughout the world, contact improvisation has grown beyond his influence into a complex, multi-dimensional dance genre, complete with its own journal (*Contact Quarterly*) and multinational network. One of the most recent developments in this hybrid genre is the inclusion of dancers with different abilities. In his work with Anne Kilcoyne at Touchdown Dance in England and his presence at the yearly Dance Ability workshops in Eugene, Oregon, Paxton has played a key role in furthering this work.[8]

Given Paxton's devotion to improvisation, and his belief that dancing should be an experience available to everyone, it is not surprising that he should enjoy the challenges of teaching and dancing with people whose movement styles are determined by physical disabilities.[9] Yet it is important to note that Paxton is not limiting his involvement with this work to that of altruism. The experience of dancing with a blind person or a dancer with cerebral palsy informs his own physicality in myriad ways, becoming a part of the movement material that he relies on for his solo improvisational performances. Knowing about his movement history makes watching Paxton's solo performances especially delightful, as one can pick out the physical movements and theatrical images which seem to point to key moments in his long and multifaceted dancing career.

Ann Cooper Albright

Notes

1 Steve Paxton, 'Drafting Interior Techniques', *Contact Quarterly*, Spring/Winter 1993, 18(1), pp. 61–6.
2 Banes, Sally, *Terpsichore in Sneakers*, Boston: Houghton Mifflin, 1980, p. 59.
3 Ibid.
4 Ibid, p. 60.
5 After the chapter on Steve Paxton in *Terpsichore in Sneakers*, there is a published score of this dance, pp. 71–4.
6 Reprinted in Jill Johnston, *Marmalade Me*, New York: E.P. Dutton & Co., 1971, p. 137.
7 For a detailed discussion of the development of contact improvisation see Cynthia Novack, *Sharing the Dance: Contact Improvisation and American Culture*, University of Wisconsin Press, 1990.
8 For more information see the 'Dancing with Different Populations' issue of *Contact Quarterly*, Winter 1992.
9 Steve Paxton, '3 Days', printed in *Contact Quarterly*, Winter 1992, p. 13.

Biographical details

Born in Tucson, Arizona, United States, 21 January 1939. **Studied** at the American Dance Festival, Connecticut College, New London, 1958–59; with Merce Cunningham and Robert Dunn, from 1958; also studied with José Limón, 1959. **Career** Danced with José Limón Company in 1959; member of the Merce Cunningham Dance Company, 1961–64; also danced with Trisha Brown, Lucinda Childs, Yvonne Rainer, and Simone Forti; founder member of Judson Dance Theater, 1962; founding member, the Grand Union, 1970–76. Has also worked extensively in Europe and North America as a teacher of his contact improvisation methods since 1972, particularly for Workcentrum in Amsterdam, Bennington College (Vermont, 1973–76), Dartington College of Arts (Devon, England; full-time teaching, 1978–80), and on courses at Oberlin College (Ohio), Rochester (New York), and Eugene (Oregon). Member of the improvisational ensemble Free Lance Dance, 1977–79. In the 1990s has contined performing and teaching, including at the American Dance Festival (Durham, North Carolina), Touchdown Dance (Dartington College, 1987–93), DanceAbility (Eugene, Oregon; annually), and Diverse Dance (Vachon Island, Seattle; annually). Has also been a contributing editor to *Contact Quarterly* and *Dance Magazine*.

Works

Proxy (1961), *Transit* (1962), *Music for Word Words* (1963), *English* (mus. Philip Corner, 1963), *Afternoon* (1963), *Left Hand* (1963), *Flat* (1964), *Rialto* (1964), *Jag ville görna telefonera* (1964), *title lost tokyo* (1964), *Section of a New Unfinished Work* (1965), *Augmented* (1966), *The Deposits* (1966), *Physical Things* (1966), *A.A.* (1966), *Earth Interiors* (1966), *Somebody Else* (1967), *Love Songs* (1967), *Satisfying Lover* (1967), *The Sizes* (1967), *The Atlantic* (with spoken text, 1968), *Lecture on a Performance* (1968), *Walking There* (1967; later retitled *Audience Performance #1*), *Audience Performance #2* (with texts read by the audience, 1968), *Salt Lake City Deaths* (1968), *State* (1968), *Beautiful Lecture* (mus. Tchaikovsky, 1968), *Intravenous Lecture on Sponsors and Products* (1969), *Lie Down* (1969), *Smiling* (1969), *Collaboration with Winter Soldier* (mus. soundtrack to film *Winter Soldier*, 1971), *Benn Mutual* (with Nita Little; mus. David Moss and sound collage, 1972), *Air* (mus. Tchaikovsky, with soundtrack and speech by Richard Nixon, 1973), *With David Moss* (mus. David Moss, 1974 and later versions), *You come, we'll show you what we do* (1975), *Backwater: Twosome* (mus. David Moss, 1977 and later versions), *Pa ... rt* (with Lisa Nelson; mus. Robert Ashley, 1978), *Ave Nue* (1981), *Audible Scenery* (1986), *Suspect Terrain* (with Laurie Booth, Dana Reitz, and Polly Motley; mus. Hans-Peter Kuhn, 1989), *Flyside* (1993), *Some English Suites* (mus. J.S. Bach, 1993), *Long and Dream* (with Trisha Brown, 1994).

Further reading

Interviews in Jane McDermott, 'An Interview with Steve Paxton', *New Dance*, Autumn 1977; in 'Trance Script: Judson Project Interview with Steve Paxton', *Contact Quarterly*, Winter 1989.

Articles Steve Paxton, 'The Grand Union', *Drama Review*, September 1972; Rob Baker, 'Grand Union: Taking a Chance on Dance', *Dance Magazine*, October 1973; Elizabeth Kendall, 'The Grand Union: Our Gang', *Ballet Review*, 5(4), 1975/76; Eleanor Rachel Luger, 'A Contact Improvisation Primer', *Dance Scope*, Fall/Winter 1977/78; Sally Banes, 'Steve Paxton: Physical Things', *Dance Scope*, Winter/Spring 1979/80; Yvonne Rainer, '*Backwater: Twosome*', Paxton and Moss', *Dance Scope*, Winter/Spring 1979/80; Allen Robertson, 'Newer than New: The Post-Modern Choreographers', *Ballet News*, October 1981; 'Performing Improvising Performing Improvising', *Contact Quarterly*, Spring/Summer 1981; Barry Laine, 'In Search of Judson', *Dance Magazine*, September 1982; Marcia B. Siegel, 'The Death of Some Alternatives', *Ballet Review*, Fall 1982; Sarah Rubidge, 'Steve Paxton', *Dance Theatre Journal*, Winter 1986; Barbara Newman, 'Steve Paxton', *Dancing Times*, November 1986; Robert Ellis Dunn, 'Judson Days', *Contact Quarterly*, Winter 1989; 'Dancing with Different Populations', *Contact Quarterly*, Winter 1992; Steve Paxton, 'Surfing with Steve Paxton' (e-mail dialogue), *Dance Theatre Journal*, 14/1, 1998.

Books Don McDonagh, *The Rise and Fall of Modern Dance*, New York, 1970; Jill Johnston, *Marmalade Me*, New York, 1971; Don McDonagh, *The Complete Guide to Modern Dance*, Garden City, New York, 1977; Peter Wynne (ed.), *Judson Dance: An Annotated Bibliography of the Judson Dance Theater and of Five Major Choreographers*, Englewood Cliffs, New Jersey, 1978; Sally Banes, *Terpsichore in Sneakers: Post-Modern Dance*, Boston, 1980; Sally Banes, *Democracy's Body: Judson Dance Theater 1962–1964*, Ann Arbor, Michigan, 1983 (reprinted, Durham, North Carolina, 1993); Deborah Jowitt, *The Dance in Mind*, Boston, 1985; Cynthia Novak, *Sharing the Dance: Contact Improvisation and American Culture*, Madison, Wisconsin, 1990; Margaret Hipp Ramsay, *The Grand Union: 1970–1976*, New York, 1991.

STEPHEN PETRONIO

Stephen Petronio makes dances that are aggressive, stylish, athletic, and highly sexed. His choreography surges with urban speed and power, but the individual movements are often both quirky and oddly juxtaposed. Unexpected tics and pauses texture and gnarl the rhythms of his hard-driving works. The distinctiveness of Petronio's choreography owes a great deal to his own idiosyncratic movement style, a connection that is immediately apparent when the tall, muscular choreographer dances. He has a loose-limbed ease in awkward step combinations, an unusual fluidity that the *Village Voice* critic Deborah Jowitt calls a 'slippery grace'.[1] He is a prodigiously talented performer, as are the nine dancers of the Stephen Petronio Company, who plunge headlong into his vernacular with the abandon of native speakers.

Petronio carefully calculates step sequences that do not flow naturally or easily, that go against the grain of his dancers' co-ordination. Perverse directional changes yank the dancers from the course of their momentum, while ungainly, but interesting, positions misshape their bodies in the weirdest configurations imaginable, as when the torso arches back while the legs turn way, way in. In his choreography, says Petronio, 'a verb follows straight after a verb'.[2] This description evokes well his action-packed dances, dense with an explosive accumulation of unlikely actions.

Petronio prizes movement that is difficult and odd, and he packs a particular wallop in steps that parcel out activities to every part of the body, so that arms, hands, legs, head, and torso each get their own thing to do. These steps give a rippling, double-jointed look to the dancing that is fascinating. Jowitt describes a typical sequence: 'Up will fly a leg, but at the same time a shoulder will curl in, one portion of the rib cage will shake down.'[3] This 'busyness in the joints' derives, as Jowitt and others have noted, from Trisha Brown, the seminal post-modern choreographer, with whom Petronio performed for seven years. Like Brown, Petronio initiates his movements from any part of the body, in any direction – a whip of the head may initiate a turn, a hinging elbow may lead the way for the next change of direction.

But though one can trace Brown's influence on his work, Petronio has significantly altered the accents and phrasing of Brown's choreographic language. Whereas Brown's trade-mark rhythm, for example, is a swingy purr of hushed, introspective, looping movement, Petronio could be said to have grabbed hold of one end of this terpsichorean rope and given it a great injection of anger and speed: in his hands, dance rhythm is no longer a looping cable but a cracking whip. He has forsaken Brown's cooler fluidity in favour of aggressive coils of movement that drive as hard and relentlessly as the loud, pounding electronic scores that he prefers. (David Linton has composed several scores.) Because Petronio allies a slamming force to the busyness of his choreography, his dancers are frequently described as seeming on the verge of ripping apart from their centres.

As their titles indicate, early works such as *Walk-In* (1986) and *Simulacrum Reels* (1987) were mostly concerned with movement invention, another Brown legacy. In these pieces Petronio announced that his was a fierce new voice characterized by quirky punctuation and illogical interjections. The words themselves – the steps – were also wonderfully imaginative and strange: his striking, hybrid movements deformed the body while at the same time glorifying it in dizzying bouts of virtuosity.

Petronio's works took a new direction as the 1980s turned into the 1990s and he began collaborating with the English choreographer Michael Clark, a self-styled 'bad boy of British ballet'. Until 1991 the two performed in each other's dances – Clark is a mesmerizing dancer, mercurial and feline – and they also jointly choreographed, though always under one name.[4]

During this period Petronio, like Clark, carefully cultivated an outrageous public image. Media coverage from these years tended to dwell on the *outré* costumes he commissioned from hip fashion designers, as though wearing a women's corset upside down and backwards were reason enough to be considered a maverick. Among the first prominent dancers to sport a shaved head, Petronio was quickly dubbed a 'punk choreographer' by the press. In fact, he is a postmodern choreographer, one whose work not only fits into a clearly discernible tradition but shares characteristics with other choreography from his generation; in both the United States and Europe, for instance, aggression and speed are the predominant themes in 1990s choreography.

Most notorious among Petronio's so-called punk dances is *MiddleSex Gorge* (1990), the piece featuring the corsets (designed by H. Petal; G-strings complete the outfit). A signature work, *MiddleSex Gorge* reveals the dancemaker no longer trusting dance alone to draw an audience. This is choreography burdened with hype and subtext; some steps seem created precisely to show off the men's near-nakedness. In one motif, a dancer repeatedly weaves in and out of the action exposing his bare buttocks in knifelike *arabesques* that aim directly for the spectators.

Petronio calls this piece more politically engaged than his previous works. In a profile written when the work had its premiere, he stated, 'The body is the last bastion of freedom. . . . My politics is the action of my body.'[5] In other words, the personal had become political, and never more so than in 1990, the year that the United States Congress passed a law requiring the National Endowment for the Arts to consider standards of decency when awarding grants. The so-called decency test – upheld as Constitutional by the Supreme Court in 1998 –

threw down a kind of gauntlet for artists, even those not previously concerned with such issues.[6] Petronio was not the only dancemaker to create more provocative work in response to this notorious ruling: the increasing influence of the so-called 'religious right' in national politics, and the group's hostile attacks on the arts and on artists, especially those concerned with explicitly gay or lesbian subjects, mobilized many choreographers to forsake formalism for activism.

Petronio continued to test the decency test in 1992's *Full Half Wrong*, a savage and sensual dance set mainly to Igor Stravinsky's epoch-defining *Sacre du Printemps*, a ballet score that, alongside Vaslav Nijinsky's raw, explosive choreography, created a *succès de scandale* when it was first performed in 1913's Paris. *Full Half Wrong* aptly mirrors the violence and brutal beauty of the score, but Petronio undercuts his achievement by projecting ponderous epigrams onto the back wall of the stage. Inspired by the aphorism-based installation art of Jenny Holzer, a key figure in the United States art scene of the late 1980s, these deadpan observations on sex and sexual truisms – 'women don't have penis envy/men have Venus envy' is one – seem sophomoric next to Stravinsky's colossal music.

Petronio's concepts work best when they surface as choreography, not as written commentary or titillating costume design. In an interview with Suzanne Scott in 1992, he noted interestingly that one way he translates sexuality into movement is by initiating a step from the pubic bone. 'It doesn't look like sex,' he observed, 'but you get a very visceral feeling.'[7]

In the same article, Petronio asserted, 'I am trying to make movement that speaks of the time I am living in.' He has unquestionably succeeded at this. His fast, tough, cynical dances speak of a culture defined by speed, impersonality, and violence. Fractured and dangerous, his choreography takes place in a world that can be exciting or pleasurable but never perfect. Even his fascination with sex and violence should be viewed in the context of broader cultural currents in the 1980s and 1990s: at the same time that these subjects were being attacked by politicians waging a 'family values' crusade, they were acquiring a new legitimacy as topics for serious academic study. In recent years studies of eroticism and 'histories' of the body have proliferated, heavily influenced by such philosophers as Georges Bataille and Michel Foucault.

Petronio's best work has a Baudelairean quality in which the beautiful and the noisome inseparably intertwine. His dances are not quite flowers of evil, but they are often flowers with menace. The critic William Harris has aptly described the simultaneous discomfort and fascination provoked in watching Petronio's creations: 'His dances are not easy to watch, and also not easy to forget,' he writes.[8]

In his more recent pieces, such as *Drawn That Way* (1996), *ReBourne* (1997), and a solo for himself, *I Kneel Down Before You* (1997), Petronio has returned to his initial interest in pure-dance experimentalism. The anger has subsided, though aggression remains; the pace is still furious, the dancers as tough as ever – they all look as though they lift weights – but the music has become less of an assault, and so has the dancing. A cynic might note that Petronio's self-conscious softening, the new theme of his interviews, reflects the late 1990s zeitgeist as much as much as his earlier persona did that at the decade's start. But his renewed commitment to choreography without hype indicates a positive direction: this is Petronio at his best. His work is most interesting for its imaginative, seemingly inexhaustible arsenal of new, unusual steps, hybrids in which modern dance and even ballet technique look as though they've taken a trip through an insane asylum. His vocabulary is as unique as any among his generation of choreographers. Set in motion by his splendid dancers, it's a feast of *fin de siècle*

virtuosity characterized by defiant energy, depraved pyrotechnics, and a marvellous appetite for risk.

Nicole Dekle Collins

Notes

1 Deborah Jowitt, 'Conversation Pieces', *The Village Voice* (New York), 2 June 1992.
2 Quoted in Sarah Woodward, 'Naked Truth', *Mirabella* (New York), October 1990.
3 Jowitt, op. cit.
4 Gia Kourlas, 'A Star is Re Bourne', *Time Out New York*, 11–18 September 1997.
5 Ellen Cranitch, 'Moving Over', *City Limits* (London), 11–18 October 1990.
6 For an account of the US Supreme Court decision and a brief legal history of the decency test, see Linda Greenhouse, 'Justices Uphold Decency Test', *The New York Times*, 26 June 1998, p. A17.
7 Suzanne Scott, 'In Step with the Times', *Sunday Times* (London), 25 October 1992.
8 William Harris, 'Dancing Out of Control', *The Village Voice* (New York), 31 January 1995.

Biographical details

Born in Nutley, New Jersey, United States, 20 March 1956. **Studied** pre-medicine before taking up dance; studied contact improvisation with Steve Paxton. **Career** Danced with Trisha Brown Company, 1979–86; began choreographing in 1979; founder, artistic director and choreographer, Stephen Petronio Company, from 1984; has also choreographed for Frankfurt Ballet, Rotterdam Dance Company, German Opera Ballet (Berlin), Charleroi Dance Company (Belgium), and Lyon Opéra Ballet. **Awards** include a Guggenheim Fellowship and a New York Foundation for the Arts Award; National Endowment for the Arts Fellowships, 1985–88 and Advancement Program Grant, 1994; New York Dance and Performance Award ('Bessie'), 1986; American Choreographers Award, 1987.

Works

Adrift (with Clifford Arnell, 1984), *The Sixth Heaven* (mus. Pat Irwin, 1984), *#3* (mus. Lenny Pickett, 1985), *Walk-In* (mus. David Linton, 1986; revised version, 1992), *Simulacrum Reels* (mus. David Linton, 1987), *AnAmnesia* (mus. Peter Gordon, 1988), *Surrender II* (mus. David Linton,

1988), *MiddleSex Gorge* (mus. Wire, 1990), *Close Your Eyes and Think of England* (1990), *Full Half Wrong* (mus. Stravinsky, Mitchell Lager, 1992), *She Says* (mus. Yoko Ono, 1993), *The King is Dead, Part 1* (mus. Elvis Presley, Ravel, 1993), *Extravenous* (1994), *Lareigne* (mus. David Linton, 1995), *#4* (mus. Diamanda Galás, 1996), *Drawn That Way* (mus. Andy Teirstein, 1996), *ReBourne* (mus. Beastie Boys, Sheila Chandra, 1997), *I Kneel Down Before You* (solo; 1997), *Not Garden* (based on Dante, 1997).

Further reading

Interviews with Sarah Woodward, 'Naked Truth', *Mirabella*, October 1990; with Suzanne Scott, 'In Step with the Times', *The Sunday Times*, 25 October 1992.

Articles Tobi Tobias, 'Stephen Petronio', *Dance Magazine*, April 1985; Stephen Petronio, with David Allan Harris, 'The Stephen Petronio File', *Drama Review*, Summer 1985; Amanda Smith, 'Stephen Petronio and Dancers', *Dance Magazine*, July 1986; William Harris, 'Petronio's Mind-body Splits', *Connoisseur* (February 1987); Perry Bialor, 'Man-Made', *Attitude*, Spring 1990; Sally R. Sommer, 'A Duet is More Than Two People Dancing', *Dance Ink*, May/June 1990; Louise Levene, 'From Corsets to Cassocks', *Dance and Dancers*, December 1990; Catherine Brownell, 'Petronio and His Political Body', *Dance Theatre Journal*, Spring 1991; Tobi Tobias, 'Déjà Vu', *New York Magazine*, February 4, 1991; Deborah Jowitt, 'Conversation Pieces', *The Village Voice*, June 2, 1992; John Gruen, 'Stephen Petronio: Mixing It Up', *Dance Magazine*, June 1994; William Harris, 'Dancing Out of Control', *The Village Voice* (New York), 31 January 1995; Tobi Tobias, 'Second Sight', *New York Magazine*, February 20, 1995.

Books Allen Robertson and Donald Hutera, *The Dance Handbook*, Harlow, Essex, 1998.

PILOBOLUS

Pilobolus, sometimes called Pilobolus Dance Theater, and once upon a time known as Vermont Natural Theater, has been as pervasive an influence on American dance theatre in the latter part of our century as was Denishawn during the earlier part.

In impact, this small ensemble – more or less consistently limited to a core company of four men and two women – recalls the popularity held by the St Denis and Shawn enterprise during the 1920s. In kind, the mixed bills put on by Pilobolus are similar to the 'high-art' vaudeville fare of the Denishawn troupe. In tone, Pilobolus are more artfully outrageous, somewhere between naughty and nice, where the Denishawners were lofty and decoratively exotic. Both aesthetics, however, can be said to centre on the sensual projection resulting from the direct display of the dancer's body.

Indeed, with over 25 years already to its credit, Pilobolus has proven itself to have even greater staying-power than Denishawn. Since its very modest beginnings in 1971, when the burgeoning group was little more than one three-man work entitled *Pilobolus*, this innovative and hard-to-categorize entity has remained popular over its public and influential over its fellow practitioners in dance theatre. The influence of Pilobolus on various kinds of choreography in the 1980s and 1990s may be hard to name – Pilobolusian? Pilobuluslike? – but it is not hard to recognize: intriguingly massed clusters of bodies and/or gymnastically levered processes of partnering or grouping. A few other distinguishing Pilobolus characteristics, such as artful nudity, and a taste for surreal twists of visual logic, also tend to be emulated, though to a lesser extent.

The most common misinformation regarding the troupe is that its founders were gymnasts. In fact, the original trio grew out of Alison Chase's dance composition class at New England's Dartmouth College, an all-male institution where dance was not a major subject and where the future Pilobolus founders were athletic collegians, not college athletes. Moses Pendleton was an English literature major and a cross-country skier; Jonathan Wolken was a philosophy and science major who fenced, did folk dancing, and played the banjo; and Steve Johnson was a pre-medical student who pole-vaulted.

(Lee Harris and Robert Barnett joined up when Johnson left to continue his medical studies. The former, who also left shortly afterwards, was a computer science major; the latter, who stayed on and served as an artistic director once he stopped performing, was an art major.)

The individuals who brought Pilobolus to its first flowering made up the group's first sextet unit. Half were founding (or nearly-founding) members: Pendleton, Wolken and Barnett. The other half were Michael Tracy, who replaced Harris; Chase, who joined her former students as an equal; and Martha Clarke, a Juilliard Dance School graduate and former performer with the Anna Sokolow Dance Company, who had been working with Chase on experimental choreography. Chase and Clarke were the first female Pilobolus members. These six, who were in place by 1974 for the reworking of *Ciona* (a 1973 sextet and the first Pilobolus piece integrating women into its work), formed the company that put the Pilobolus aesthetic indelibly in the minds of the dance-eager audiences of the United States' so-called 'dance boom'. In one sense, both the audience for Pilobolus and the troupe itself developed along similarly fresh and unpredictable lines. In the 1960s, with its freewheeling, flower-power, youth cult aspects, dance and dancers caught media attention as the 'hot' art form. The growing audience for dance and the dancelike theatre of Pilobolus were encumbered by few preconceptions regarding dance's historical traditions or expectations.

Central to the post-1960s pedigree of Pilobolus was its very way of working. Instead of following the pervasive single-dancer/choreographer scheme that had dominated American modern dance companies since the birth of the artform in the earlier part of the century, Pilobolus chose a communal angle. Every performer was also directly involved in the creation of choreography. Any work they appeared in they had in some way helped to develop.

The fashion for communal living situations during this age was mirrored in the artistic process promoted by Pilobolus. Longstanding Pilobolus repertory staples such as the sextets *Monkshood's Farewell* (1974) and *Untitled* (1975), *Pseudopodia* (a 1974 solo), and *Shizen* (a 1978 duet) all date from this period. By 1978, Clarke had left to do her own work, which, sometimes classified as 'theatre of images', she continues to do. (She was replaced by Elisa Monte, who is now a choreographer and director of her own echt-Pilobolus troupe.) Understandably, the one-big-family-of-artists way of working was not easy to keep in order. Those who could cope with the ever-present battle of artistic egos stayed on and thrived amid the commotion, while those who couldn't left, usually for the more traditional route of the single boss/choreographer dance troupe. Chase once likened the Pilobolus experience to 'six radios, all on different stations at the same time'.

The early 1980s included ambitious and eagerly attended seasons, especially in New York City, which involved expanded companies of performers, in some cases appearing as guest artists. A 1981 season at Broadway's ANTA Theater included five additional performers besides the five 'original' members, as well as one soloist, Kammy Brooks, officially designated 'guest artist'. The youthful-looking Tracy stayed on stage the longest, but by 1989 even he had retired to the artistic ranks, joining Pendleton, Wolken, Barnett and Chase above the line-up of new-generation Pilobolus members, Jack Arnold, Jim Blanc, Austin Hartel, Carol Parker, Peter Pucci, and Jude Woodcock. (Arnold and Blanc stayed the shortest time; the others went on to Pilobolus or Pilobolus-related careers of some note.) By 1992, Pendleton was no longer an artistic director though his work, notably the lush, sensual, and playful *Debut C* (a 1988 sextet), continued to be a staple of the Pilobolus repertory. This well-known and, arguably, most talented member from the founding trinity was by this time concentrating on directing and creating works for Momix, the Pilobolus offshoot Pendleton founded in 1979.

One of the most enthusiastic and powerful champions of Pilobolus has been Charles Reinhart, director since 1969 of the American Dance Festival (ADF), an institution devoted to the development and promotion of modern dance. An outgrowth of the Bennington College festivals that supported early modern dance artists such as Martha Graham and Doris Humphrey, ADF frequently commissioned Pilobolus work, starting in 1973. Sometimes when expressing his enthusiasm for the work of Pilobolus, Reinhart would recall the controversy surrounding the group and remember its work being described as 'interesting, but not dance'.

Both those admiring and those leery of Pilobolus have tussled with the 'not dance' question. '"Dance" is not what I would say Pilobolus does, and it is not what I would want it to do. Its art, which is based on gymnastics, is already complete', noted dance critic Arlene Croce, a champion of classicism, especially Balanchine's, in her first major review of the troupe in 1976. 'Gymnastics', Croce further observed, 'present the body in complicated feats of coordination without reference to what dancers call dynamics'. This lack of 'dynamics' proved to be a more serious problem for other critics, often those grounded in Rudolf von Laban's effort/shape theory of dancing. In 1977, the dancer/choreographer/writer Deborah Jowitt countered Croce, reporting on the 'seductive designs' of Pilobolus that tended to 'bewitch' audiences, with a focus on other audience members – 'quite a few at the ADF' (in the case of this report), 'who're appalled by the heartless beauty of the company's jointly made dances'.

Pilobolus did not dance, *per se*, partly because the group came into being out of a non-dance environment. A hybrid at best, the Pilobolus product remained a kind of visual poetry shaped from movement theatrics, though not necessarily danced moves. Leveraged, counter-balanced weight, acrobatic emphases, anthropomorphic shape modulations and often surreal, pictorial groupings all inter-related to give life and force to Pilobolus creations. The group's somewhat frequent use of unashamed nudity or semi-nudity consistently reinforced art critic Kenneth Clark-like theories that distinguished the 'nude' from the 'naked'. Anna Kisselgoff, chief dance critic of *The New York Times*, identified the nudity of Pilobolus as consistently being 'on the skinny-dipping level: fun and intended to make a splash with the audience'. She elaborated her observation by adding that the company's dancers 'have always had a healthy uninhibitedness'. Such perceptions are not, however, shared far and wide; the troupe has met up with producers around the United States who ask the performers to exclude nude-dancer works from their local repertory, or to add 'figleaf' costuming to soften the 'shock'. When the troupe recorded *Untitled* for television in 1977, it costumed the normally nude men in skin-tone dance belts, which some observers thought made almost obscene what was merely innocently natural.

By the late 1980s, when the first generation had all graduated to positions of artistic authority, the troupe was made up of individuals with more traditional dance backgrounds. Though the repertory in this period included some Pilobolus 'classics', it continued to include new works made by the 'artistic directors' in collaboration with the newer Pilobolus members. Longtime company-watchers sometimes found the newer pieces inferior in impact to the older works. Some of this was no doubt the result of audience nostalgia as well as of the fact that more and more 'cooks' were involved in these Pilobolus brews. *I'm Left, You're Right, and She's Gone*, a short-lived dance suite to Elvis Presley's music created in 1987, is a prime example of such complexity.

This work for six dancers was performed by none of the original Pilobolus six, it bore a 'directed by' credit to four Pilobolus artistic directors and a 'choreographer by' credit to a separate set of ten names.

Robert Greskovic

Biographical details

Dance company founded by dancer-choreographers Moses Pendleton, Jonathan Wolken and Steve Johnson (all students of dance composition teacher Alison Chase) at Dartmouth College, Hanover, New Hampshire, in 1971; joined by Lee Harris and Robert Barnett (on departure of Johnson, 1971); made New York debut in December 1971; joined by Michael Tracy (on departure of Harris, 1974), and by Alison Chase (1973) and Martha Clarke (1973–78, and then guest performances); has retained original name and stylistic identity throughout various subsequent changes of personnel, including Pendleton's departure (1979) to form Momix. In 1997 the artistic directors of Pilobolus were Barnett, Chase, Tracy, and Wolken. Pilobolus has also choreographed for Hartford Ballet, the Juilliard School, and the National Theater for the Deaf. Pilobolus Too (dancers Rebecca Stenn and Adam Battelstein) was created during 1997 to perform duets and solos from the Pilobolus repertoire.

Works

(choreographers in parentheses)

Geode (Barnett, 1971), *Pilobolus* (Johnson, Pendleton, Wolken, 1971), *Walklyndon* (Barnett, Harris, Pendleton, Wolken, 1971), *Anaendrom* (Barnett, Harris, Pendleton, Wolken, 1972), *Aubade* (Barnett, Clarke, 1972), *Cameo* (Chase, Clark, 1972), *Ocellus* (Barnett, Harris, Pendleton, Wolken, 1972), *Spyrogyra* (Barnett, Harris, Pendleton, Wolken, 1972), *Terra Cotta* (Barnett, Clarke, 1973), *Ciona* (Barnett, Chase, Clarke, Pendleton, Tracy, Wolken, 1974), *Monkshood's Farewell* (Barnett, Chase, Clarke, Pendleton, Tracy, Wolken, 1974), *Pseudopodia* (solo; Wolken, 1974), *Alraune* (Chase, Pendleton, 1975), *Untitled* (Barnett, Chase, Clarke, Pendleton, Tracy, Wolken, 1975), *Pagliaccio* (solo; Clarke, 1975), *Vagabond* (solo; Clarke, 1975), *Lost in Fauna* (solo; Chase, Pendleton, 1976), *Bone* (solo; Barnett, 1977), *The Garden Gate* (solo; Clarke, 1977), *The Eve of Samhain* (Barnett, Chase, Pendleton, Tracy, Wolken, 1977), *Renelagh on the*

Randan (solo; Wolken, 1977), *Molly's Not Dead* (Barnett, Chase, Pendleton, Tracy, Wolken, 1978), *Moonblind* (solo; Chase, 1978), *Shizen* (Chase, Pendleton, 1978), *The Detail of Phoebe Strickland* (Kammy Brooks, Chase, Pendleton, 1979), *Tendril* (Tracy, 1979), *Day Two* (Pendleton, Tracy, 1980), *The Empty Suitor* (Jamey Hampton, Tracy, Wolken, 1980), *A Miniature* (Chase, 1980), *Momix* (Pendleton, 1980), *Tarleton's Resurrection* (Barnett, Félix Blaska, 1981), *Elegy for the Moment* (Chase, 1982), *What Grows in Huygen's Window* (Wolken, 1982), *Stabat Mater* (Pendleton, 1982), *Mirage* (Tracy, 1983), *Hot Pursuit* (Wolken, 1984), *Return to Maria La Baja* (Barnett, Chase, 1984), *Carmina Burana, Side II* (Pendleton, Tracy, 1985), *Televisitation* (Barnett, Chase, 1985), *Land's Edge* (Barnett, Chase, Wolken, 1986), *I'm Left, You're Right, She's Gone* (Barnett, Chase, Tracy, Wolken, 1987), *The Golden Bowl* (Barnett, Chase, 1987), *Debut C* (Pendleton, 1988), *The Particle Zoo* (Barnett, Tracy, Wolken, 1989), *Coming of Age in the Milky Way* (Barnett, Tracy, Wolken, 1989), *Axons* (Chase, 1990), *Cedar Island* (Chase, 1990), *Clandestiny* (Tracy, 1990), *Ophelia* (Barnett, 1990), *Sweet Purgatory* (Barnett, Chase, Tracy, Wolken, 1991), *Duet* (Barnett, Chase, Tracy, 1992), *Solus* (Wolken, 1992), *Slippery Hearts* (Barnett, Félix Blaska, 1992), *Bedtime Stories* (Wolken, 1993), *A Portrait* (Chase, 1993), *Rejoyce* (Barnett, Tracy, Wolken, 1993), *Animundi* (Chase, Tracy, 1994), *Collideoscope* (Chase, Tracy, 1994), *Quatrejeux* (Barnett, Wolken, 1994), *Vestidigitations* (Barnett, Wolken, 1994), *The Doubling Cube* (Barnett, Chase, Tracy, Wolken, 1995), *Pyramid of the Moon* (Chase, Tracy, 1995), *Masters of Ceremony* (Barnett, Chase, Wolken, 1995), *Aeros* (Barnett, Chase, Tracy, Wolken, 1996), *Elysian Fields* (Chase, Tracy, 1997), *Peer Gynt* (play by Henrik Ibsen; with the National Theater for the Deaf, 1997), *Gnomen* (Barnett, Wolken, 1997), *Solo* (Chase, 1997).

Further reading

Interview with Elvi Moore, in 'Talking with Pilobolus', in *The Vision of Modern Dance*, edited by Jean Morrison Brown, Princeton, New Jersey, 1979, London, 1980.

Articles Iris Fanger, 'Pilobolus', *Dance Magazine*, July 1974; J. Bulaitis, 'Pilobolus', *Dancing Times*, May 1978; John Gruen, 'Dance Vision', *Dance Magazine*, July 1985; Patricia Barnes, 'Welcome Variety', *Dance and Dancers*, February 1986; Susan Reiter, 'Dance Watch', *Ballet News*, February 1986; Clive Barnes, 'Turning to the

Light', *Dance and Dancers*, March/April 1987; Larry Stevens, 'A Fabulous Company with a Fabulous Name', *Dance Pages*, Summer 1993.

Books Arlene Croce, *Afterimages*, New York, 1977; Tim Matson, *Pilobolus*, New York, 1978; Arlene Croce, *Going to the Dance*, New York, 1982; Deborah Jowitt, *The Dance in Mind*, Boston, 1985; Arlene Croce, *Sight Lines*, New York, 1987; Deborah Jowitt, *Time and the Dancing Image*, New York, 1988; Allen Robertson and Donald Hutera, *The Dance Handbook*, Harlow, Essex, 1988.

IAN SPINK

Ian Spink's dance background was initially in classical ballet, and later influences have been, variously, Jaap Flier, Merce Cunningham, Yvonne Rainer, Trisha Brown, and Mary Fulkerson. He has developed his choreographic work and style very much through the collaborative process, whether with dancers themselves in the rehearsal studio, or with designers, composers, and playwrights in the overall conception of a work. Spink is clearly a choreographer who likes to work with other artists and to develop ideas through these interchanges. Indeed, he has said that he considers himself 'a general manipulator of people'[1] rather than a choreographer, and one who may move into the territory of movement, or, equally into the territory of text or music. Spink has also worked alongside other choreographers, for example Ashley Page in *Escape at Sea* (1993). His role, then, is often as much to do with the organization of material as with its generation, and his interest in forms and structures is reflected in this. The extent to which he successfully manipulates structures frequently determines the success of the work in question.

The designer Craig Givens was one of Spink's early collaborators, and had a significant influence on Spink's interest in and development of theatrical elements. More recently Antony McDonald and Orlando Gough have been regular collaborators. The playwright Caryl Churchill has worked with Spink in the making of several works. Spink's interest in opera and theatre is evident in both the range of his work and the character of individual pieces. The classical derivation of his movement vocabulary, alongside the contrasting postmodern use of weight and contact work, is also clear. The use of space and spaciousness, fragmentation, repetition, and image-making characterizes his work, and reflects both roots and influences, but individual inflections separate his work from, for example, Siobhan Davies and Richard Alston, even when all three choreographers were producing quite similarly styled work for the dance troupe Second Stride in the early 1980s. Spink's divergence from the others is apparent even in *There is No Other Woman* (1982), a very 'dancey' piece because of both the costumes, which set up expectations of something with a dramatic thread, and Spink's particular way of structuring movement and deploying groups and partnerships throughout the work.

In *De Gas* (1981), the use of economical everyday movements to translate into 'dance' movement, along with the even dynamic flow, and the use of unison and canon, are characteristic Spink features. Also evident is his typical use of disjunctive images, here in the casting of three men in male attire, but in the context of the familiar Degas image of a woman washing her hair. The spacious nature of the structure allows for leisured contemplation of the images and their transformation through time.

There is No Other Woman, made for Second Stride, shows evidence of a 'house style' when compared to works of the same period by Davies and Alston, and Spink here exploits the particular strengths of the dancers in their movement style – fluid, soft, weighty, and technically accomplished. Dance technique is evident, but controlled in a manner which appears relaxed, comfortable, even spontaneous. Although the choreography is quite dense, in terms of the amount of material and the variety of structure in groups, solo material, and partnering, Spink's characteristic clarity shines through in the spacious effect produced by the unhurried pace of the movement and by the disposition of dancers in the space – two partnerships working in diagonally opposite corners of the performance area, for example, allowing for a relationship between them to be discerned. His manipulation of unison movement, which emerges and then dissolves, is also in evidence in this work. The outward focus and use of turn-out reflect the balletic roots, with clearly recognizable references such as *cabrioles*, *piqués*, and so on appearing in the choreography, especially in the *adagio* male duet.

Although the overall style of Spink's choreography may be seen as directly comparable to that of Alston and Davies in this period of their creativity, there are important differences. In some of Spink's work the movement seems to be shot through with a controlled energy, one which is more buoyant, though perhaps less subtle, than that of Davies and Alston. Spink's use of stillness and pauses suggests both contemplation and the gathering of forces for continued action – this is somewhat akin to part of Davies's work, but markedly different from Alston's.

Further and Further into Night (1984), based on ideas from Alfred Hitchcock's film *Notorious*, emanated from a collaboration between Spink, Gough, and McDonald. Judith Mackrell describes is as 'stunningly innovative'.[2] In it, Spink employs spoken text, both from the film itself and from the dancers' comments in rehearsal. Images from the film are repeated and then developed upon – with different gender relationships, echoing *De Gas* – to produce a layered effect that encourages an active engagement on the part of the spectator to make sense of the event and allow visual and aural effects to resonate. Mackrell writes of the centrality of dance in this work, and the fact

that this is a key factor in the work's success because the dance, although clearly not virtuoso movement, is an underlying structuring feature. She speaks of 'the rhythm and pacing of formalised variations', and later describes *Further and Further into Night* as 'a study of the aggression that lies beneath the surface of social conventions'.[3]

Sophie Constanti, similarly, has noted that 'this is a work where formality acts as a perfect structure in which human conflict and passion are exposed from beneath the protective layers of velvet, satin and diamanté and studied mannerisms'.[4] Images are repeated in a way that highlights the clarity of structure, and they are varied – for example by moving between sexes, by having a phrase echoed by several additional dancers – so that meaning is constantly changeable. Again, there is an expansive quality to the choreography that allows time for images to evolve and disperse and reform. The apparent simplicity of structure reveals choreographic devices of repetition and variation, and Spink employs these as means of layering and constructing meanings.

L.-A. Davies, however, has a different view of the balance of form and content in *Further*, stating that 'the dramatic content of each scene was virtually concealed beneath a baroque weight of embellishment and elaboration'.[5] This suggests that too great an emphasis on formality can result in a cold and empty effect overall. These contrasting views illustrate the problems presented by border-crossing work. The extent to which images may resonate with significance is very much dependent on the particular range of experience and the individual disposition of each audience member. Formality as a theatrical device may not always be entirely successful.

Bösendorfer Waltzes (1986) was a collaboration between Spink, Gough, and McDonald again, but with dancers also contributing, and Peter Mumford's lighting design playing a significant part. Whether this work was perceived as full of richness, or as incomprehensible, varied from critic to critic, again because of the characteristic interweaving of elements and the manipulation of images, ideas, and text in tapestry-fashion to create a multi-faceted whole. The need for active engagement with the work on the part of the spectator is particularly highlighted in such a piece. With or without background knowledge of Spink's allusions, however, images, ideas, fragments of text may equally well resonate in the individual in unforeseeable ways. Angela Kane recognizes this and suggests that it is an intentional approach: 'As the Surrealist artists intended in their work, a first viewing of *Bösendorfer* confuses the mind and baffles the eye'.[6] Kane also points out that Spink in this work 'transmutes previous innovations into a new form'.

In *Weighing the Heart* (1987), the music provides a propelling force in its rhythmic insistence, contributing to the wider accessibility of the work as a whole, and lessening the effect of fragmentary and changing images. The central position of myth and ritual reflects recurrent concerns in Spink's work, highlighting his interest in the potential for myths, legends and fairy-stories to provide the source material for theatrical ideas. Again, the sometimes deceptively simple movement vocabulary provides a clear point of access and, in conjunction with evocative costume and lively music, creates dance theatre of a kind immediately attractive to many. The movement, while simple, has an amplitude about it which suggests the happy cross-fertilization of dance influences in Spink's background: the apparently leisurely action reflects the disguised control of ballet as well as the pedestrian flow of Trisha Brown, for example. The sense of spaciousness apparent in *De Gas* and *Heaven Ablaze in His Breast* (1989) is also evident in *Weighing the Heart*, although the increased layering of theatrical devices and effects makes this element less obvious. The dance vocabulary, however, does frequently show a breadth of movement, an openness of aspect, which implies a sense of space, whether inward or outward.

Spink's wide-ranging dance experience is apparent in *Heaven Ablaze*, where much of the movement has the sustained precision and outward focus of ballet, in addition to more specific features such as strong leg extensions, leaps and *pirouettes*, and a frequent drawing upon the *demi-caractère* vocabulary of nineteenth-century ballet. One is reminded especially of *Coppélia*, both in the movement and in Judith Weir's music, which manipulates familiar themes rhythmically and harmonically to create a prismatic, time-stalling effect. The dance and music in conjunction here allow for layers of possible meaning to evolve, as the music's fragmented aspect is reflected in the dance's manipulation of movement ideas and relationships.

Spink speaks of 'pulling threads out of the fabric and looking at them in a new light'.[7] He also refers to the Gothic aspect of Hoffmann's story (*Coppélia*'s source), and its links with Expressionism. The process of moving from stage to film was, for Spink, another part of the process and development of the work, further illuminating the choreographer's approach to the making of work as an ongoing, collaborative process. He comments on the suggestions of madness recurring in the story, and of its being many years ahead of Freud in apparently looking as issues such as family relationships, delusions, dreams, and nightmare fears. Notions of the 'real' and the constructed run through the piece, as they do in many of Spink's choreographies, not only in the obvious role of the doll, Olimpia, but also in the appearance of photographs, and the central theme of sight and blindness, implying tensions between appearance and reality, and the fear and experience of pain as part of this network of experience.

In *Lives of the Great Poisoners* (1991) the balance of component parts is markedly different from *Heaven Ablaze*, although operating in the same border-shifting genre of dance, opera, and theatre. In this work, dance recedes more often, and text is more extensively used, sometimes to comic effect (for example in Jason's self-justification tactics to Medea). Again, however, the dance movement shows its roots in classical ballet quite often – perhaps suggesting the presence of cultural and social strictures by referring to these culture-bound traditions. At other times, the free, loose, and weighty swing of arms, legs, and body, and of contact and weight-bearing between dancers reflect other influences. However, the different balance of elements in this work, where text is arguably of foremost importance, opera and theatre secondary, with dance some way down the list, could be seen as uneasy and ultimately incoherent. The contrast between the more static theatrical elements and the 'dance' movement is more marked, and could be deemed a less felicitous union than in some of Spink's work in which the dance is more abstracted from its roots and more successfully interwoven with other components.

Critics again differed in their response to this work. Alastair Macaulay, discerning the layered effect and its potential for constructing meaning on different levels, described the work thus: 'It has moral force, impish wit and disturbing ambiguity; its episodes lodge in the mind' and 'numberless repetitions build up suggestions of vulnerability, need, trust and secrecy'.[8] For other critics, however, the use of repetition dulled rather than intensified the effect of the whole.

While critics respond in various ways to Spink's work, sometimes identifying the very same features as worthy of either praise or detraction, it is clear that his exploration of creative work operating within and among the genres of dance, theatre, and music-theatre offers sometimes exciting, sometimes tedious, but often stimulating experiences. The extent to which Spink successfully manipulates structures and balances disparate elements in a single work

determines the work's overall coherence and effectiveness. In recent years his activities have tended to move even more decisively towards opera and music-theatre, and further away from dance, although they always include dancers. His 1996 work, *Hotel*, is a good example of his movement into music-theatre. A collaboration with playwright Caryl Churchill and composer Orlando Gough, the piece utilizes many more singers than dancers (only two of the latter), and reflects the broader perspective of Spink's theatrical vision.

Rachel Chamberlain Duerden

Notes

1 Spink, quoted by R. Cave, 'Interview with Ian Spink', in *Border Tensions: Dance and Discourse* (5th study dance conference), University of Surrey, 1995.
2 Mackrell, Judith, 'The Dance Umbrella Festival: Three Views: Words, Words, Words', *Dance Theatre Journal*, 3(1), 1985.
3 Mackrell, Judith, *Out of Line: The Story of British New Dance*, London, 1992.
4 Constanti, Sophie, 'The Dance Umbrella Festival: Three Views: Passion in Parts', *Dance Theatre Journal*, 3(1), 1985.
5 Davis, Lesley-Anne, 'The Dance Umbrella Festival: Three Views: Collaborations', *Dance Theatre Journal*, 3(1), 1985.
6 Kane, Angela, 'Forward to the Past: *Bösendorfer Waltzes*', *Dance Theatre Journal*, 4(2), 1986.
7 Spink speaking in *Dance Makers*, BBC television broadcast, 18 May 1991.
8 Macaulay, Alastair, 'Second Stride: Riverside Studios', *Financial Times*, 14 March 1991.

Biographical details

Born in Melbourne, Australia, 8 October 1947. **Studied** at Australian Ballet School, 1967–68, and briefly with Merce Cunningham; later studied Graham technique in Sydney with various instructors. **Career** Danced with Australian Ballet, 1969–74, and Dance Company of New South Wales (now Sydney Dance Company), 1975–77; choreographed first works for Australian Ballet Workshop, 1971, thereafter staging works for Australian Dance Theatre, Queensland Ballet, and Dance Company of New South Wales; came

IAN SPINK

to England to attend International Course for
Choreographers and Composers, University of
Surrey, 1977; founded Ian Spink Group, 1978;
merged company with Siobhan Davies's company
to form Second Stride, 1982, becoming its sole
artistic director in 1988. Has choreographed for
theatre and opera, including for Royal
Shakespeare Theatre, English National Opera,
Royal Opera, Opera North, Scottish Opera, Welsh
National Opera, and in collaboration with play-
wright Caryl Churchill. Has also directed
productions for Glasgow Citizens Theatre,
Scottish Opera, and at the Battignano Festival.
Awards Barclays Bank New Stages Award, 1996.

Works

Starship (mus. MC5, 1971), *Waltzes* (mus. Brahms,
1972), *Four Explorations* (mus. Prokofiev, 1973),
Landscape (mus. Peter Sculthorpe, 1973), *Game*
(mus. Stravinsky, 1974), *Aspects* (mus. Hans
Werner Henze, 1974), *Couple* (mus. Hans Werner
Henze, 1974), *Players* (mus. Romano Crevicki,
1976), *New Work I* (mus. Elhay, 1976), *New Work
II* (mus. Iannis Xenakis, 1976), *Cut Lunge* (mus.
Vine, Fontana, 1976), *Slow Turn* (mus. Cameron
Allan, 1977), *Two Numbers* (mus. Allan,
McMahon, 1977), *Work in Progress* (1977), *Low
Budget Dances* (mus. Tim Lamford, Keith Wilson,
1977), *Conspectus I* (mus. Stephen Strawley,
1978), *Duet* (1978), *Trio* (mus. Beethoven, 1978),
Elly's Arm (1978), *Goanna* (mus. Julian Spink,
1978), *26 Solos* (1978), *Autumn Walk* (sound
effects tape, 1978), *Nude Banana* (text improvised,
1979), *Low Budget Dances II* (1979), *Standing
Swing* (1979), *Tropical Flashes* (mus. Carl Vine,
1979), *Three Dances* (mus. John Cage, 1979),
Cloud Cover (mus. Brian Eno, 1979), *Elly's Arm
II* (1980), *Death in Venice* (opera by Britten, 1980;
film version, 1981; revised version 1992), *Return*
(mus. Carl Vine, 1980), *Solo* (mus. Bernd
Zimmerman, 1980), *Solo with Sheep* (mus. Yuji
Takahashi, 1980), *Scene Shift* (mus. Carl Vine,
1980), *Three Poems* (mus. Yuji Takahashi, 1980),
When Soft Voices Die (mus. Alan Holley, 1980),
Dead Flight (mus. Brian Eno, 1980), *Ice Cube*
(mus. Carl Vine, 1980), *Kondalilla* (mus. Carl
Vine, Simone de Haan, 1980), *Madrigal for Donna*
(mus. Carl Vine, 1981), *Some Fugues* (mus. J.S.
Bach, 1981), *Blue Table* (mus. Jane Wells, 1981),
Being British (mus. various, 1981), *Coolhaven*
(mus. J.S. Bach, 1981), *De Gas* (mus. Jane Wells,
1981), *Canta* (mus. David Cunningham, 1981),
Canta II (mus. David Cunningham, 1981), *War
Crimes* (theatre adaptation of Peter Carey novel,
1981), *Vesalii Icones* (mus. Peter Maxwell Davies,
1982), *There is No Other Woman* (mus. Stravinsky,

1982), *Secret Gardens* (theatre adaptation of
Frances Hodgson Burnett's novel, 1983),
Threeway (mus. Jane Wells, text Michael Birch,
1983), *New Tactics* (mus. Orlando Gough, 1983),
Under Western Eyes (theatre adaptation of Joseph
Conrad's novel, 1983), *Lean, Don't Lean, Jasper*
(mus. David Owen, 1984), *Work in Progress* (text
improvised, 1984), *Coco Loco* (mus. David Owen,
1984), *The Winter's Tale* (play by Shakespeare,
1984), *The Crucible* (play by Arthur Miller, 1984),
Further and Further into Night (mus. Orlando
Gough, 1984), *Mazeppa* (opera by Tchaikovsky,
1984), *Slow Down* (mus. Man Jumping, 1985),
Orlando (opera by Handel, 1985; revised version,
1992), *Solo* (1985), *The Midsummer Marriage*
(opera by Tippett, 1985), *Bösendorfer Waltzes*
(mus. Orlando Gough, 1986), *The Marriage of
Figaro* (opera by Mozart, 1986), *Mercure* (mus.
Satie, arr. Harrison Birtwistle, 1986), *The Trojans*
(opera by Berlioz, 1986), *A Mouthful of Birds*
(play by Caryl Churchill and David Lan, 1986),
Weighing the Heart (mus. Orlando Gough, 1987),
The Winter's Tale (play by Shakespeare, 1987),
Tannhäuser (opera by Wagner, 1987), *Carmen*
(opera by Bizet, 1987), *Left-Handed Woman* (mus.
John Thorne, 1988), *Dancing and Shouting* (mus.
Evelyn Ficarra, 1988), *The Love of a Nightingale*
(play by Timberlake Wertenbaker, 1988), *Some
Fugues* (with Caryl Churchill, for television, 1988),
Heaven Ablaze in His Breast (mus. Judith Weir,
1989; television version, 1991), *Macbeth* (opera by
Verdi, 1990), *Clarissa* (opera by Robin Holloway,
1990), *Vanishing Bridegroom* (opera by Judith
Weir, 1990), *Lives of the Great Poisoners* (mus.
Orlando Gough, text Caryl Churchill, 1991),
Heaven Ablaze in His Breast (for television; mus.
Judith Weir, 1991), *4 Marys* (mus. Peter Salemi,
1992), *Death in Venice* (opera by Britten, revised
version, 1992), *Why Things Happen* (mus. J.S.
Bach, Judith Weir, 1992), *5 Dances/5 Floors* (mus.
Hans-Peter Kuhn, 1992), *Antony and Cleopatra*
(play by Shakespeare, 1992), *Escape at Sea* (mus.
Orlando Gough, with text, 1993), *Inquest of Love*
(opera by Jonathan Harvey, 1993), *The Skriker*
(play by Caryl Churchill, 1994), *Fast and Dirty II:
Fragments* (1994), *Badenheim 1939* (mus. Orlando
Gough, 1995), *Weird Actions* (mus. Moritz Eggert,
1996), *Hotel* (mus. Orlando Gough, text Caryl
Churchill, 1996).

Further reading

Articles David Vaughan, 'Hitting Their Stride',
Dance Magazine, July 1982; Nadine Meisner,
'Striding On', *Dance and Dancers*, August 1982;
Jann Parry, 'Striding Sideways?', *Dance and
Dancers*, September 1983; Alastair Macaulay,

'Secret Gardens of Dance Theatre', *Dancing Times*, April 1983; Judith Mackrell, 'Words Words Words', *Dance Theatre Journal*, Spring 1985; Lesley-Anne Davis, 'Collaborations', *Dance Theatre Journal*, Spring 1985; Sophie Constanti, 'Passion in Parts', *Dance Theatre Journal*, Spring 1985; Sarah Rubidge, 'Ian Spink', *Dance Theatre Journal*, Autumn 1985; Alastair Macaulay, 'Second Striders Past and Present: Alston, Clayden, Spink', *Dance Theatre Journal*, Summer 1986; Sarah Rubidge, 'Weighing Spink's Heart', *Dance Theatre Journal*, Summer 1987; Julia Pascal, 'The Spink School of Dance', *Illustrated London News*, October 1988; Stephanie Jordan, 'Second Stride: The First Six Years', *Dance Theatre Journal*, Winter 1988; Sarah Rubidge, 'The Spink-Gough Collaboration', *Choreography and Dance*, 1(4), 1992.

Books Allen Robertson and Donald Hutera, *The Dance Handbook*, Harlow, Essex, 1988; Stephanie Jordan, *Striding Out: Aspects of Contemporary and New Dance in Britain* (includes chapter on Spink), London, 1992.

ELIZABETH STREB

Elizabeth Streb's choreography does not look much like other current dance. While compellingly physical, it is not at all 'dancerly'; its technical vocabulary – created anew, depending on the task the dancers are to perform – seems to have more in common with that of the gymnast, the circus aerialist, or the astronaut than with conventional dance. But it is also firmly rooted in the ideology of American postmodern dance.

Streb's pieces owe much of their conceptual basis to Merce Cunningham's ideas about choreography, but they give that tradition a unique and specialized interpretation. Like Cunningham, with whom she studied for several years, and whom she reveres, Streb pursues movement that is insistently present in time, and in particular places. Like Cunningham, she is also interested in expanding possible perceptions of space and time. But whereas Cunningham has used chance structures, indeterminacy, and computer simulation to reconfigure the predictable line and habitual kinaesthetics of a balletic style of movement, Streb choreographs the performance of tasks in restricted, risky settings to generate high-intensity movement that keeps her dancers constantly off balance and hyper-aware – and points out the natural laws with which the dancer is always engaging. She calls this movement 'honest', in that it cannot be marked or faked, and must be performed with full commitment, for otherwise the dancer could get hurt.

In some of her earliest dances, Streb manipulated poles or rings, tossing them in the air, catching them, sliding them around her body, jumping over them. The issue was not simply discovering all the things that could be done with a particular piece of apparatus, but also sensing the effects of gravity on the object, learning how to engage with momentum and, in constructing a dance, figuring out how lift, weight, and rebound define choices about the sequencing of tasks. In most of her dances since, Streb has constructed special equipment to place her entire body within the apparatus's field. As Streb herself described it in a press release for *Space Object* in 1984, 'With these objects, I confront space to create movement that becomes functional and integral to that object.'

So in *Fall Line* (1981), Streb and the late Michael Schwartz scrambled, rolled, leap-frogged, and slid up and down a platform angled at 35 degrees; and in *Add* (1983), Streb's movements were defined and restricted by a cross taped to the floor, onto which she dived, fell, folded herself, and flipped like a fish, seeking new sources of impetus. In her signature piece *Little Ease* (1985) she performed in a box a little bigger than a coffin, turned on its side, dramatically framing her inability to initiate any movement from an upright position. Not only did these characteristic dances force the body into new relationships with the natural laws that govern movement; the very calculated spaces in which they occurred framed and condensed the energy of her effort so that what was dramatized was the supremacy of natural laws as well as the heroic effort of the dancer, to become a sort of theatre of the physics of pure movement.

Since 1985, when Streb formed her own company, Ringside, she has been making dances for larger groups of three to seven, or more, dancers, thereby multiplying the energy and momentum of her dances, as well as the risk (of collisions, for example) and the need for attentiveness, collaboration, and precise organization. At the same time she has ventured into more sophisticated encounters with space, relentlessly mapping out the placements of her dances with walls (fixed or movable), colour, and lighting that precisely mark the multiplicities of movement at any given time.

Since the late 1980s, Streb's choreography has moved increasingly off the ground and further out of conventional relationships to gravity. One might say that Streb has taken Merce Cunningham's ideas about a field of infinite points in space and expanded it into three – or more – dimensions. 'Dancing in the air', Streb has said, 'is like being in the center of space. I want to be in places seemingly too unnameable to mention ... on every point between two points, onward and into infinity' (Streb, talking during rehearsals in New York, July–August 1993). In one version of *Impact* (1991), the dancers dived against the walls of a plexiglass cube suspended above the audience, their bodies mostly horizontal, hurtling and ricocheting like bullets shot from guns. The walls that reorientated their momentum were transparent, so that what both started and stopped the movement was nearly invisible, leaving only the movement itself. In one of Streb's many aerial dances, *Lookup* (1993), four dancers wearing omni-directional harnesses walked, spun, dived, and swooped against a forty-foot high wall (which was also a floor) as they were slowly lowered down the wall. At any given moment in the dance

the performers might be head down, face down, back down, or side down as they did everything from forward somersaults to *chaîné* turns. In the different environments in which this dance has been shown, Streb has tried to manipulate the entire theatrical space so that not only the dancers but also the audience experience the maximum disorientation by being as close as possible – even directly beneath – the dancers.

Like many post-Cunningham choreographers, Streb honours the injunction that a movement take as much – and only as much – effort and time as the movement itself dictates (a rejection of either expressive or musical phrasing). But Streb goes further: the apparatus she uses, and the momentum required for much of her choreography, tend to mobilize the whole body as a unit, and necessitate timings that are often at the edge of human comfort and control. In *Up* (1995), the dancers rebound, often at high speed, off an Olympic-quality trampoline whose extremely live surface can be touched by only one dancer in any given instant, lest the dancers ricochet in unexpected and dangerous directions. Streb's dances deliberately 'push' both dancers' and audiences' perceptions of time by taking the body outside the kinaesthetic parameters that conventionally determine timing, making palpable the warping of conventions of time and space that come with brutally immediate movement. At the same time, performing – and watching – Streb's work not only sharpens one's sense of timing; it also increases the actual speed at which one can perceive movement, allowing one to see dazzling images that seem to defy natural law.

In its uncompromising functionalism, and in its almost scientific emphasis on pure movement, Streb's work resonates with allusions to first-generation postmodern choreography of the 1960s and 1970s. Some of Streb's pieces seem like direct descendants of early postmodern dances: *Lookup*, for example, seems to be an elaboration of Trisha Brown's walking-on-the-walls dances;

and Streb's preoccupation with risk and planned chaos seem to hark back to Brown's and Yvonne Rainer's dances in which, for example, participants took turns falling and catching one another.[1] While most of Streb's generation of postmodern choreographers – those who began working in the late 1970s and early 1980s – turned to experimentation with narrative structures and performance art, Streb has remained a functionalist. However, in many other ways her work has become more characteristic of 1980s and post-1980s choreography. For example, her dances, always based on skills associated with sports, have become even more athletic, more high-energy, speedy, and demanding, in keeping with the pumped-up, power dynamics of the 1980s. And like second-generation postmoderns who have drawn on an eclectic variety of techniques – including ballet, modern dance, contact improvisation, gymnastics, martial arts, and body therapies – to create a new standard of dance virtuosity, so Streb and her dancers (particularly Paula Gifford and Mark Robison) have welded gymnastics, ballet, weight training, yoga, and release work into a specialized strength, endurance, and focus that is as virtuosic in performance as any ballet technique.

Perhaps most importantly, Streb, like many choreographers of the time, has increasingly embraced both reflexivity and theatricality. Always witty, her work has played more and more with visual puns on the natural laws she so relentlessly pursues. Lighting and sound have become sophisticated partners in this theatricality, sculpting space and flattening the dancers' bodies into streaks of movement. In *Line* (1994), a dancer assumes different positions while clinging to the narrow yellow horizontal ledge that runs beside her, across the middle of an otherwise black wall. The lighting makes it appear that she is floating in space, even while the effort of her muscles tells us something very different is happening. A related kind of sensory confusion is often at work in the use of microphones on the

surfaces with which the dancers interact. Most recently, the sounds from the microphones have become less naturalistic, or even merely hyperbolic, and instead seem brittle and hollow, evoking vast spaces and visceral unease. It almost seems as though Streb is using sound as a Brechtian alienation effect, disrupting the audience's easy pleasure in the dances' athleticism, and shocking viewers into seeing movement in a fresh way. Streb has also carried this cognitive dissonance into some dances made specifically for video in collaboration with the videographers Michael Schwartz and Mary Lucier, especially Schwartz's and Streb's *Airdance* (1987).

All of this is a far cry from Streb's earliest dances, in which her engagement with natural forces seemed literal and unadorned. Yet Streb's growing theatricality merely expands into new sensory realms her ever-restless concern with exploring and communicating the intensity and immediacy of movement. As Streb put it in a 1990 *Dance Magazine* interview, 'I've tried to examine a "real move" for a long time now. Not to fabricate movement but to get at the inside gut of it . . . this wild, untamed animal.'

Judy Burns

Note

1 See Marianne Goldberg, *Reconstructing Trisha Brown: Dances and Performance Pieces 1960–75*. Ph.D. dissertation, New York University, 1990.

Biographical details

Born in Rochester, New York, United States, 23 February 1950. **Studied** at the State University of New York, Brockport, 1968–72, obtaining a B.S. in Modern Dance (Cum Laude): taught by Susannah Payton, Daniel Nagrin, Irma Plyshenko, Mary Edwards; also received tuition under Diana Byer, Janet Panetta, Viola Farber, Merce Cunningham, Jocelyn Lorenz, and June Finch. **Career** Dancer with Margaret Jenkins, San Francisco, 1972–74; since 1974 based in New York; founder, Streb/Ringside company, 1985. **Awards** Creative Artists Public Service Program Award,

1981; National Endowment for the Arts Choreography Award, 1984, and Fellowships, 1985–88, 1989–92, 1992–94, 1994–96; Foundation for Contemporary Performance Arts Fellowships, 1985, 1988; Art Matters Fellowship, 1985, 1987, 1992; New York Foundation for the Arts Fellowship, 1987, 1990, 1994; Corporation for Art and Television Award, 1987; New York Dance and Performance Award ('Bessie'), 1988, 1989, 1990; Guggenheim Fellowship, 1989; Brandeis University Creative Arts Award, 1991.

Works

Earlier works had no music; later works included amplified movement sounds, and since 1994 Streb has worked with composer Matthew Ostrowksi.

Springboard (1979), *Pole Vaults* (1980), *Fall Line* (1981), *Fall Line Inside Out* (video; dir. Michael Schwartz, 1982), *Space Object* (1983), *P.S. 1* (1983), *Whiplash 1* (1983), *Add* (1983), *Runway* (1983), *Ringside* (1982), *Marathon Dance* (1983), *Blackboard 1* (1984), *Target* (1984), *Whiplash 4* (1985), *Blackboard 4* (1985), *Little Ease* (1985), *Roller Board* (1985), *Amphibian* (video; dir. Mary Lucier, 1985), *Airlines* (1987), *Midair* (1987), *Freeflight* (1987), *Airwaves* (1987), *Airdance* (video; dir Michael Schwartz, 1987), *If I Could Fly I Would Fly* (video; dir. Mary Lucier, 1987), *Massfloat* (1988), *Massdance* (1988), *Spacehold* (1989), *Log* (1989), *Rebound* (1990), *Soaring* (1990), *Mass* (video; dir Mary Lucier, 1990), *Impact* (1991), *Groundlevel* (1991), *Wall Drive* (1991), *Link* (1992), *Surface* (1993), *Lookup* (1993), *Bounce* (1994), *Line* (1994), *Up* (1995), *Rise* (1995), *Breakthru* (1995), *Pop Action* (1996).

Further reading

Interviews with Michael Sapir, *Dance Theatre Journal*, Autumn 1994.

Articles Judy Burns, 'Wild Bodies, Wilder Minds: Streb, Ringside and Spectacle', *Women and Performance*, 7(1), 1994; Robert Greskovic, 'Elizabeth Streb', *Dance Magazine*, October 1994.

KEI TAKEI

Kei Takei's lifetime work is a series of related theatre pieces under the designation *Light*. Takei is not generally named among the pantheon of 'postmodern' dancers, although *Light* was initiated at a period when the definitions of dance and dancing were being questioned by the avant-garde.

Takei shared many of the beliefs and working methods of the downtown New York dance community, but she was always hard to classify. She studied with the approved modern and ballet teachers, but her works in New York were not preoccupied with dancing. Divested of the technical virtuosity and the lyrical plastique that the postmoderns despised, Takei's work was nevertheless too theatrical for the minimalist downtown taste. Drawing from her native culture, Takei played unselfconsciously with Japanese folklore and ignored the exotic but better known Noh and Kabuki. With bizarre actions and designs woven into monotonous periods of treading, bending, or squatting, she anticipated for American audiences Butoh dance, which wasn't seen in the United States until the 1980s.

Takei arrived in New York in 1967, and soon embarked on *Light*. She had almost no spoken English, but her work immediately attracted dancers, actors, designers, and musicians, who helped her establish the ensemble, Moving Earth. With an elastic membership that could embrace whole groups of university students or shrink to a few close colleagues, Moving Earth became a collaborative workshop that eventually produced more than thirty parts of *Light*.

From the first, *Light* made an impact as the strange and harshly beautiful work of an authoritative talent. Over three decades, the work accumulated a repertory of objects, actions and characters. These elements were extremely concrete and integral to each new instalment, but they often carried over, with slight mutations, to later parts. In the process, they gained the resonance of metaphor without being limited by any specific narrative. *Light* thus became an unfolding myth.

Some of this mythic power came from the overlapping of reality and representation, which was one of the great subjects for investigation among performance artists in the 1960s. *Light* was performed by a real community, which enacted a community. Not only was each part created jointly and often improvisationally by the performers, the action of the piece frequently required them to work together. Paired in little folk dances where they knocked stones together in rhythm, or piling up sticks, or planting balloons in precise rows like rice seedlings, they needed each other's cooperation to construct images and so to perform the piece.

The community was not always amicable, but even when it broke into warring camps, each side might demand a reciprocal action from the other. A pair of men squared off and wrestled; the winner stayed on to fight the next man. Couples ran together to embrace; a blob of material came off one partner and stuck to the other. The sharing of energies, of work, of hostility was necessary for the survival of the group as a whole. In the most memorable of these images (*Part 5*), three people of greatly differing physical types clung together until one began to buckle. With the first failure in their mutual support system, the whole structure collapsed and they all fell, only to scramble up into another interlocking but temporary monolith.

Pedestrian movement was the idiom, yet the performers seemed removed from everyday life. Their walking, carrying, putting objects in place – all seemed reduced, almost regressive, taken back to utterly functional levels. Their fixed, frequently sightless stares, their exaggeratedly slow or dangerously forceful energies, and especially their apparent alienation from one another made them seem precivilized, driven by biological programming. They seemed unable to use the normal channels of comfort or empathy in the concentrated, repetitive tasks they had to do, yet they were drawn together as if by some primal necessity.

New people arrived, new tasks were introduced, but some of the work had to be done over and over again. There were cycles of planting, land-clearing, building, wrapping and carrying things, creating designs, and defining pathways. Objects, slightly changed, took on new meanings. Actions previously completed could be symbolically recollected. Actions that had no visible usefulness were compulsively, ritualistically repeated. For example, in one section (*Part 8*), partners threw beans at each other while reciting 'Good – In', 'Bad – Out'. In another section (*Part 10*) two men threw stones at Takei's feet. Her eyes covered with a painted 'X', she blindly tried to avoid stumbling but wouldn't be deterred from continuing her own dance. In a later part (*12*), the same stones were swept into piles and became the material for mandala-like designs that a group of people shaped around themselves.

Individual character could emerge from this communal striving. There were tyrannical leaders (sometimes played by Takei) and crafty caretakers. People made mistakes and recovered. They went to extremes and continued implacably. They envied each other and showed off and fought for something they would have to give up. They were afraid of the dark but they charged into places they couldn't see. They were determined to survive, and they struggled just as hard if they knew their adversary might destroy them.

Light also had overtones of Eastern meditative practice, which was of great interest to Americans beginning in the 1960s. Each part unfolded slowly, with sequences of repetitive activity that went on long after the viewer could foresee the outcome. A character would continue methodically placing pieces of board down on the floor until the whole floor was covered, instead of ending the scene at a point where the audience could be expected to understand the whole project from a partial indication. Sometimes these ritualistic behaviours might not end as expected, but the audience would only gradually notice that the pattern was shifting into another direction.

Takei seemed convinced that meaning can be revealed only through contemplation. In one early part of *Light*, she squatted and stared into a spotlit area of the floor while the sound of rain was heard. In another, she danced and pulled items of clothing out of a huge pile, dressing and wrapping herself in one garment at a time until she became nothing but a round soft ball, dancing and waving its foetal arms and legs. Fatalistic and resourceful, the various parts of *Light* constitute an affirmation of a life-force and a life-process that is portrayed as constantly threatened by extinction.

Marcia B. Siegel

Biographical details

Born Keiko Takei in Tokyo, Japan, 30 December 1946. **Studied** at the Sakaki Bara Children's Dance School, Kaitani Ballet School, both in Tokyo, and trained in creative dance (Kenji Hinoki) and Japanese Classical Dance (Fujima Kiyoe), 1965–67; awarded Fulbright Fellowship to study dance at the Juilliard School, New York, 1967–69; in New York studied with Alfred Corvino (ballet), the Merce Cunningham Studio, the Alwin Nikolais School, Trisha Brown, and Anna Halprin. **Career** Began to choreograph while still a student in Japan; after moving to New York, founded own company, Moving Earth, in 1969, for which she has subsequently choreographed the various parts of *Light*: the company, renamed Moving Earth Orient Sphere, is now based in Tokyo. Has also choreographed for Nederlands Dans Theater, Inbal Dance Theatre (Israel), Concert Dance Company (Boston), Shaliko Theater Company (New York), Reinhild Hoffmann Tanztheater/Schauspielhaus Bochum (Germany), Shinjinkai Theatre Company (Japan), and Ju San Ko No Tsuki [Work Media Theatre Company] (Japan). **Awards** National Endowment for the Arts Choreography Award, U.S.A., 1974–75, 1977, 1980, 1983–92, and Fellowship, 1980–81; Guggenheim Fellowship, 1978, 1988; Japanese Dance Critics Award, 1979; New York Foundation for the Arts Fellowship, 1986.

Ritter, 1970), *Light, Part 5* (mus. Marcus Parsons III, 1971), *Light, Part 6* (mus. Jacques Coursil, Marcus Parsons III, 1971), *Playing this Everyday Life* (with Ben Dolphin, 1971), *Talking Desert Blues* (1972), *Light, Part 7 (Diary of the Field)* (mus. Maldwyn Pate, Lloyd Ritter, Spanish folk music, 1973), *Light, Part 8* (mus. Buddhist chanting, 1974), *Light, Part 9* (1975), *After Lunch* (1975), *Light, Part 10 (The Stone Field I)* (1976), *Light, Part 11 (The Stone Field II)* (1976), *Light, Part 12 (The Stone Field)* (mus. traditional Japanese, 1976), *Light, Part 13 (The Stone Field III)* (1977), *Windfield* (1978), *Light, Part 14 (Pine Cone Field)* (mus. Welsh folk song, dancers' voices, 1979), *Light, Part 15 (The Second Windfield)* (mus. Japanese traditional song, 1980), *The Dreamcatchers* (1982), *Light, Part 16 (Vegetable Fields)* (mus. live Buddhist chanting, 1982), *Daikon Field Solo I* (mus. chanting, 1982), *Light, Part 17 (Dreamcatcher's Diary I)* (mus. Norma Dalby, 1982), *Whirlwind Field* (1982), *Light, Part 18 (Wheat Fields)* (mus. David Moss, 1983), *Daikon Field Solo II* (1983), *Light, Part 19 (Dreamcatcher's Diary II)* (mus. Suzanne Northrop, 1984), *Light, Part 20 (Dreamcatcher's Diary III)* (mus. David Moss, 1985), *Light, Part 21 (The Diary of the Dream)* (mus. David Moss, 1985), *Light, Part 22* (mus. Japanese folk song, 1986), *Flower Field* (1986), *Light, Part 23 (Pilgrimage, section I)* (mus. Michael de Roo, 1986), *Light, Part 23 (Pilgrimage, section II)* (mus. Yukio Tsuji, 1986), *Light, Part 23 (Pilgrimage, section III)* (mus. Japanese drums, 1986), *Light, Part 23 (Pilgrimage, sections IV-V)* (1986), *Light, Part 24 (Chanting Hills)* (mus. Norma Dalby, 1987), *Light, Part 25 (One Woman's Pilgrimage)* (silent, 1988), *Light, Part 26 (One Woman's Death)* (mus. Yukio Tsuji, 1988), *Light, Part 27 (The Last Rice Field)* (mus. Yukio Tsuji, 1989), *Wild Grass River Festival* (mus Yukio Tsuji, 1989), *Light, Part 28 (Okome O Arau Onna: The Rice Washer)* (mus. Yukio Tsuji, 1991), *Light, Part 29 (Hof)* (mus Elena Chernin, 1991; revised version, mus. David Moss, 1992), *24 Hours of Light* (mus. Yukio Tsuji, David Moss, 1991), *Light, Part 30 (One Man's Pilgrimage)* (mus. Yukio Tsuji, David Moss, 1991), *Time Diary (Nakaniwa)* (mus Yukio Tsuji, 1994), *Zenryoku Shiso (The Never-ending Path)* (mus. Yujio Tsuji, 1995), *Light, Part 31 (Empyrean Passage)* (mus. Yukio Tsuji, 1996).

Works

Voix/Ko-E (mus. John. W. Wilson, 1968), *Light, Part I* (silent, 1969), *Lunch* (mus. John W. Wilson, 1970), *Light, Part 2* (mus. Geki Koyama, 1970), *Light, Part 3* (1970), *Light, Part 4* (mus. Lloyd

Further reading

Interviews in *Dancers on Dancing*, edited by Cynthia Lyle, New York, 1977; in *Further Steps: Fifteen Choreographers on Modern Dance*, edited by Connie Kreemer, New York, 1987.

Articles Rob Baker, 'Liberated Dance: Out of the Concert Hall and into the Streets', *Dance Magazine*, August 1972; Rob Baker, 'New Dance', *Dance Magazine*, December 1972; Katharine Cunningham, 'Choreographers in Concert', *Dance and Dancers*, January 1974; Rob Baker, 'Dancing Ladies: Two Years After', *Dance Magazine*, March 1974; Marcia B. Siegel, 'New Dance: Individuality, Image and the Demise of the Coterie', *Dance Magazine*, April 1974; Robert J. Pierce, 'Viene la primavera .... Kei Takei's Moving Earth', *Dance Scope*, Spring/Summer 1975; Carol Egan, 'Choreographer in Search of Truth: Kei Takei', *Dance Magazine*, March 1978; Tullia Bohen, 'Making Television Dance', *Ballet News*, May 1980; Pamela Sommers, 'Kei Takei's Moving Earth Orient Sphere', *Drama Review*, Summer 1981; Marcia B. Siegel, 'Tales of Love and Saki (section on *Light*, parts 16 and 17), *Hudson Review*, Winter 1982/83; Dan Cox, 'Moving More than Earth with Kei Takei', *Dance Magazine*, March 1984; Joan Acocella, 'Kei Takei's Moving Earth: *Light*', *Dance Magazine*, October 1985; Lynn Garafola, 'Variations on a Theme of Butoh', *Dance Magazine*, April 1989.

Books Don McDonagh, *The Complete Guide to Modern Dance*, Garden City, New York, 1976; Deborah Jowitt, *Dance Beat: Selected Views and Reviews, 1967–1976*, New York, 1977; Deborah Jowitt, *The Dance in Mind*, Boston, 1985; Allen Robertson and Donald Hutera, *The Dance Handbook*, Harlow, Essex, 1988; Marcia B. Siegel, *Tail of the Dragon: New Dance 1976–1982*, Durham, North Carolina, 1991.

PAUL TAYLOR

Paul Taylor has described himself as an 'American mongrel'. It is an apt assessment, given the range of ideas and influences that permeate his choreography, and it is also indicative of his resistance to being pigeon-holed. Critics have referred to the 'dark' and 'light' sides of Taylor's choreography; his dance vocabulary is an ingenious mix of pedestrian movements alongside the most rhythmic and sweeping of steps (sometimes within the same work); his musical choices are wide-ranging and his collaborations with visual artists have been equally eclectic.

Taylor's early career provides several clues to the rich diversity that characterizes his choreography. He created his first work, *Hobo Ballet* (1952), while still a student at Syracuse University, where he divided his time between courses in painting and the training demands of a swimming scholarship. During the 1950s, he worked with a variety of teachers and choreographers, and he came into contact with many of New York's most avant-garde artists. Taylor's first work for the experimental New York group Dance Associates, *Jack and the Beanstalk* (1954), was designed by Robert Rauschenberg. They collaborated on ten subsequent productions, including *Three Epitaphs* (1956)[1] and *Seven New Dances* (1957), and it was through Rauschenberg that Taylor met Gene Moore, the designer of later works such as *Images* (1977), *Airs* (1978), *Arden Court* (1981), and *Musical Offering* (1986).

During this period, Taylor's choreographic musings seemed at odds with his parallel development as a performer. As a member of the Martha Graham Dance Company in the late 1950s, he was soon dancing in increasingly prominent roles. A pinnacle of success was his starring role in George Balanchine's choreography for *Episodes* in 1959, which helped to establish Taylor as one of New York's leading dancers. Taylor's choreography, however, received less support at first, mainly because some critics regarded it as an apparent rejection of the dramatic, all-dancing, 'grand' modern tradition.

Much has been written about the iconoclastic nature of Taylor's early choreography, and particularly of *Seven New Dances*, a concert which critics claimed had notoriously little dancing in it. Ironically, it was Louis Horst's non-review of the concert (a blank column with only the place and date printed),[2] rather than the seemingly non-dance content of the programme itself that caused the greater furore – and, indirectly, it also brought Taylor his first taste of fame.

Taylor had, in fact, spent several months evolving the programme through a series of choreographic discoveries; his intention had been to find an 'alphabet' from which he could form steps, phrases, and, ultimately, dances. It was a turning-point in Taylor's career. As he confirms, 'after that my dances began to move, a lot of movement, very wild, flung, I call it "scribbly".' These 'scribbles' evolved into large, legible phrases – phrases in which each movement was defined spatially, but with such fluency that body shapes registered without ever being fixed in a position. Certain contours and steps soon became Taylor hallmarks. Recurrent features are the spiralling, open-chested torso; extended 'V' or curved 'C' arms; and skimming *sissonnes* and successive jumps in first position (both performed with the legs in parallel and rarely fully stretched).

Seven New Dances also taught Taylor much about stillness. In many of his works, he illuminates the dance 'moment' – and its dramatic intent – through such theatrical means as posture and timing. (A more recent 'still life' collage, *Lost, Found and Lost* (1982) actually draws upon many of the poses and postural changes in *Seven New Dances*.)

Taylor's theatrical manipulation of dance time is matched by an instinctive (and sometimes irreverent) response to music. When he first choreographed to Baroque music – *Junction* to Bach in 1961 and *Aureole* to Handel the following year – many of his avant-garde colleagues felt that he had abandoned experiment in favour of more mainstream, and popular, aims. But in creating *Junction*, Taylor's intention was 'to find what musicality meant'. By matching the mellow rhythms of Bach's cello music to the quirky, grounded movements of his choreography, he began to forge complex, contrapuntal dance–music relationships. Importantly, *Junction* initiated a particular familiarity with, and mastery of, music by Bach – an interest that led, ultimately, to *Musical Offering*. Most remarkable of all was the speed and competence with which Taylor developed this new musical sensibility – one which was evident in the lyricism and detail of *Aureole* and, by 1966, in his

sophisticated handling of Beethoven's last quartets for the hour-long work *Orbs*.

It was the success of *Aureole* that persuaded Taylor to commit himself full-time to his own choreography and company. The international appeal of this work – and its complementary role in Taylor's rapidly evolving repertory – also meant that the Paul Taylor Dance Company became one of the busiest touring groups of the time. Even today, *Aureole* remains one of his most popular works.

Another pivotal work was *Esplanade* (1975), not only because of its sheer physicality and exuberance, but also because it confirmed that Taylor's company could be equally successful after he retired from performing. By this time, he had evolved a repertory of very different types of dances, and in all of these the central male presence of Taylor himself had dominated the work. From 1975 onwards, Taylor became one step removed from the realization of his ideas and, working in this new way, he became open to new possibilities, both in his own selection and structuring of material and in the particular talents of each of his dancers.

During the next decade, Taylor assembled a company of outstanding performers while, simultaneously, creating a series of great works. *Runes* (1975), a work that celebrates Taylor's interest in symbolic gesture, ritual practices, and transformation, was created only months after *Esplanade*. Its subtitle – 'Secret Writings for Use in Casting a Spell' – hints at the exhaustive attempts made by Taylor and his dancers to find appropriate material for the series of danced incantations that feature in the work. As with *Musical Offering*, it is the originality and unprecedented stylization – particularly for the two female soloists – that makes *Runes* a truly distinctive work.

Originality of a different kind prompted *Le Sacre du Printemps (The Rehearsal)* in 1980. The latter part of the title alludes to the context within which Taylor set his version of Stravinsky's well-known scenario.

Instead of the primitivism of most previous productions, his *Le Sacre* is set very much in the postmodern present, with its downtown locations (a dance studio and gangland Chinatown) and its pastiches of 1920s movie stereotypes. Taylor mixes his narratives: the daily rituals of a dance company are enacted while a detective story about a kidnapped baby unfolds. (Taylor has described it as 'a sort of Runyonesque gumshoe story'.) Curiously, despite this duality, *Le Sacre* is Taylor's most linear storyline. With the death of the baby and the mother's frenzied solo, the detective story reaches a clear dénouement and, as if to reaffirm the Taylor company's perpetual round of rehearsal–performance, *Le Sacre* ends where all its dances begin – back in the studio.

Le Sacre du Printemps (The Rehearsal) was Taylor's last collaboration with the designer John Rawlings, who died later the same year. Rawlings had first worked with Taylor on *Piece Period* in 1962 and, subsequently, had created designs for several key works, including the Americana epic *From Sea to Shining Sea* (1965) and *Esplanade*. Taylor later claimed that Rawlings was 'one of the few people I've ever really collaborated with', and this is borne out by accounts of Rawlings's ongoing discussions with Taylor and his involvement during rehearsals of a new work. At the opposite extreme is Taylor's association with Alex Katz, whose designs have sometimes been produced prior to Taylor beginning a work. These 'obstacle courses' as Taylor has referred to them – such as the stand-up metal dogs in *Diggity* (1978) and the mirrored prisms in the apocalyptic *Last Look* (1985) – thus became an organizing principle of the choreography.

Katz's association with Taylor is the longest-surviving, from *Meridian* in 1960 to *Ab Ovo Usque Ad Mala (From Soup to Nuts)* in 1986. Another designer, George Tacet, has featured in programmes since 1960 as well. Tacet is, in fact, Taylor himself, and although financial constraints have been the main reason for 'in-house' designs at various times, they have prompted such important works as *Aureole*, *American Genesis* (1973), and *Runes*.

The intermittent pattern of the design contributions of Katz, Rawlings and also of Gene Moore, is typical of Taylor's tendency to work with a small, select group of designers while staggering the sequence of their involvement. (Other designers have included Rouben Ter-Arutunian, Alec Sutherland, and William Ivey Long.) An exception to this pattern is Taylor's association with Santo Loquasto who, from *Speaking in Tongues* (1988) onwards, has designed the vast majority of Taylor's work. (Also, since the mid-1960s, Jennifer Tipton has lit almost all of Taylor's dances.)

Another important long-term associate of Taylor's is Donald York, who has composed music for several works, including *Diggity*, *Last Look*, and the evening-length *Of Bright and Blue Birds and the Gala Sun* (1990). Especially crucial has been York's contribution as music director and conductor of Taylor's company. Since first working with the company in 1976 – a time when Taylor's creativity was reaching new heights – York has guided Taylor's musical choices. Taylor's use of 'difficult' scores, such as those by Scriabin (*Nightshade*, 1979), Radzynski (*Profiles*, 1979), Milhaud (*House of Cards*, 1981), Varèse (*Byzantium*, 1984), and Ligeti (*Counterswarm*, 1988), has increased noticeably under York's musical direction.

Most telling of all, in terms of Taylor's musical development, is his glorious command of Bach's *Musical Offering*. Significantly, the score was a product of many years of musical experimentation and development by the composer; similarly, Taylor's *Musical Offering* is a consummate synthesis of several previously explored elements in his choreography. It is Taylor's greatest rite and his greatest work to date. Once again, a subtitle – 'a requiem for gentle primitives' (added after the work's premiere) – helps to contextualize both the subject-matter and movement style. A single female protagonist is the chief celebrant, who begins and ends the dance. She introduces all the main themes of the work and, as the fugal and canonic accumulations of Bach's music become more densely textured, other dancers become part of the requiem. Although Taylor cannot read music in the conventional sense, the parallels between the choreography and score of *Musical Offering*, particularly in terms of their structural and sectioning correspondences, are unequivocal.

Some time after the premiere of *Musical Offering*, Taylor revealed why he had interpreted the score – one of Bach's last compositions – as a requiem. 'I see this old man saying goodbye,' he said, 'and to a degree, this farewell can also be seen as autobiographical. Taylor has created, on average, two works per year since 1986, so his *Musical Offering* was certainly not a 'last' work. However, it did represent the end of one phase of his career and a farewell to many influential colleagues. Since then, his music and design interests have changed direction and he has successfully overcome an almost complete turnover of dancers.

More than twenty years on from *Esplanade*, Taylor has created a new generation of dancers and, inevitably, his choreographic concerns have been shaped differently by this younger group. Age distinctions are now more pronounced in his work and a new historicity, especially related to Taylor's own past, has emerged as subject-matter. In *Kith and Kin* (1987), contrasting dances for three generations of a familial group are the main focus; in *Speaking in Tongues* (1988), generational stereotypes of a small-town community are the social fabric around with Taylor weaves his themes of wrong-doing and redemption; in *Company B* (1991), the war-time milieu of Taylor's youth is recalled in the ten dances set to songs by the Andrews Sisters; and in *Spindrift* (1993), a single male figure bids farewell to his friends, and possibly to this world.

A wealth of past experiences inform Taylor's work, the focus of which continues to be the creation of new choreography. Forever the 'mongrel', Taylor will undoubtedly continue to create dances that are typically and excitingly unpredictable.

Angela Kane

Notes

1 Taylor's first version of the work was in 1956. It was briefly performed later the same year as *Four Epitaphs*, but was revised again and staged as *Three Epitaphs* in 1960. In 1991, Taylor created new choreography and costumes for *Fact and Fancy*, a work which begins with a complete performance of *Three Epitaphs* in Rauschenberg's original costumes.
2 In 'Reviews of the Month' in *Dance Observer*, 24(9), November 1957, p. 139.

Biographical details

Born in Allegheny County, Pennsylvania, United States, 29 July 1930. **Studied** fine arts at Syracuse University, New York, 1950–53; studied modern dance with Martha Graham, Doris Humphrey, José Limón, and Merce Cunningham; also studied ballet with Antony Tudor and Margaret Craske. Danced with various modern companies, including those of Merce Cunningham, 1953–54, Pearl Lang, 1955, and Martha Graham, 1955–62; made first choreography in 1952, and founded Paul Taylor Dance Company in 1954. Has also worked widely as a guest choreographer. Retired from performing in 1974, but has continued to choreograph. **Awards** Théâtre des Nations Dance Festival Best Choreographer Award (Paris), 1962; Premio de la Crítica (Chile), 1965; Capezio Dance Award (USA), 1967; Chevalier de l'Ordre des Arts et des Lettres (France), 1969; *Dance Magazine* Award, 1980; Officier de l'Ordre des Arts et des Lettres (France), 1984; Commandeur de l'Ordre des Arts et des Lettres (France), 1990; Emmy Award (for television production of *Speaking in Tongues*), 1991; Kennedy Center Award, Washington, DC, 1992; National Medal of Arts (US), 1993; Algur H. Meadows Award for Excellence in the Arts (US), 1995.

Works

Hobo Ballet (1952), *Jack and the Beanstalk* (mus. Hy Gubernick, 1954), *Circus Polka* (revised as

Little Circus, mus. Stravinsky, 1955), *The Least Flycatcher* (mus. Robert Rauschenberg, 1956), *Three Epitaphs* (mus. jazz, 1956; briefly performed as *Four Epitaphs* later the same year), *Untitled Duet* (1956), *Tropes* (mus. Robert Rauschenberg, 1956), *The Tower* (mus. John Cooper, 1957), *Seven New Dances: Epic, Events I, Resemblance, Panorama, Duet, Events II, Opportunity* (mus. John Cage, sound effects, 1957), *Rebus* (mus. David Hollister, 1958), *Images and Reflections* (mus. Morton Feldman, 1958), *Option* (mus. Richard Maxfield, 1960), *Meridian* (mus. Pierre Boulez, Morton Feldman, 1960), *Tablet* (mus. David Hollister, 1960), *Three Epitaphs* (revised version; mus. jazz, 1960), *The White Salamander* (Joop Stockermans, 1960), *Fibers* (mus. Schoenberg, 1960), *Insects and Heroes* (mus. John Herbert McDowell, 1961), *Junction* (mus. J.S. Bach, 1961), *Tracer* (mus. James Tenny, 1962), *Aureole* (mus. Handel, 1962), *Piece Period* (mus. various classical, 1962), *Poetry in Motion* (mus. Leopold Mozart, 1963), *La Negra* (mus. Mexican folk music, 1963), *Scudorama* (mus. Clarence Jackson, 1963), *Party Mix* (mus. Alexeii Haieff, 1963), *The Red Room* (mus. Gunther Schuller, 1963), *Duet* (mus. Haydn, 1964), *Nine Dances with Music by Corelli* (mus. Corelli, 1964), *Post Meridian* (revised version of *The Red Room*, mus. Evelyn Lohoeffer DeBoeck, 1965), *From Sea to Shining Sea* (mus. Charles Ives, later changed to John Herbert McDowell, 1965), *Orbs* (mus. Beethoven, 1966), *Agathe's Tale* (mus. Carlos Surinach, 1967), *Lento* (mus. Haydn, 1967), *Public Domain* (mus. John Herbert McDowell, 1968), *Private Domain* (mus. Iannis Xenakis, 1969), *Duets* (mus. medieval, 1969), *Churchyard* (mus. Cosmos Savage, 1969), *Foreign Exchange* (mus. Morton Subotnick, 1970), *Big Bertha* (mus. band machines, arr. John Herbert McDowell, 1970), *Book of Beasts* (mus. various, 1971), *Fêtes* (mus. Debussy, 1971), *Guests of May* (mus. Debussy, 1972), *So Long Eden* (mus. John Fahey, 1972), *West of Eden* (mus. Martinu, 1972), *American Genesis: Before Eden, So Long Eden, West of Eden, Noah's Minstrels* (mus. Handel, J.S. Bach, Haydn, John Fahey, Martinu, Louis Moreau Gottschalk, 1973), *Sports and Follies* (mus. Satie, 1974), *Untitled Quartet* (mus. Stravinsky, 1974), *Esplanade* (mus. J.S. Bach, 1975), *Runes* (mus. Gerald Busby, 1975), *Cloven Kingdom* (mus. Corelli, Henry Cowell, 1976), *Polaris* (mus. Donald York, 1976), *Images* (mus. Debussy, 1977), *Dust* (mus. Poulenc, 1977), *Aphrodisiamania* (mus. various, 1977), *Airs* (mus. Handel, 1978), *Diggity* (mus. Donald York, 1978), *Nightshade* (mus. Scriabin, 1979), *Profiles* (mus. Radzynski, 1979), *Le Sacre du Printemps (The Rehearsal)* (mus. Stravinsky, 1980), *Arden Court* (mus. William Boyce, 1981), *House of Cards* (mus. Milhaud, 1981), *Lost, Found and Lost* (mus. various popular, 1982), *Mercuric Tidings* (mus. Schubert, 1982), *Musette* (mus. Handel, 1983), *Sunset* (mus. Elgar, 1983), *Snow White* (mus. Donald York, 1983), *Equinox* (mus. Brahms, 1983), *Byzantium* (Varèse, 1984), *Last Look* (mus. Donald York, 1985), *Roses* (mus. Wagner, Heinrich Baerman, 1985), *Musical Offering* (mus. J.S. Bach, 1986), *Ab Ovo Usque ad Mala* (mus. P.D.Q. Bach, 1986), *Kith and Kin* (mus. Mozart, 1987), *Syzygy* (mus. Donald York, 1987; revised version 1989), *Brandenburgs* (mus. J.S. Bach, 1988), *Counterswarm* (mus. György Ligeti, 1988), *Danbury Mix* (mus. Charles Ives, 1988), *Speaking in Tongues* (mus. Matthew Patton, 1988), *Minikin Fair* (mus. David Koblitz, Douglas Weiselman, Thaddeus Spae, 1989), *The Sorcerer's Sofa* (mus. Paul Dukas, 1990), *Of Bright and Blue Birds and the Gala Sun* (mus. Donald York, 1990), *Fact and Fancy* (mus. jazz, reggae, 1991), *Company B* (mus. Andrews Sisters, 1991), *Oz* (mus. Wayne Horvitz, 1992), *A Field of Grass* (mus. Harry Nilsson, 1993), *Spindrift* (mus. Schoenberg, 1993), *Moonbine* (mus. Debussy, 1994), *Funny Papers* (with other company members, mus. popular, 1994), *Offenbach Overtures* (mus. Offenbach, 1995), *Prime Numbers* (mus. David Israel, 1996), *Eventide* (mus. Vaughan Williams, 1996), *Piazzolla Caldera* (mus. Astor Piazzolla, 1997), *The Word* (mus. David Israel, 1998).

Further reading

Interviews in 'Down with Choreography', *Modern Dance*, Middletown, Conn., 1965; with Cynthia Lyle, in *Dancers on Dancing*, New York, 1977; with Lillie F. Rosen, in 'Talking with Paul Taylor', *Dance Scope*, Winter 1979; with Jack Anderson, in 'Choreographic Fox: Paul Taylor', *Dance Magazine*, April 1980; with Tobi Tobias, in 'In Conversation with Paul Taylor and George Tacit', *Dance Magazine*, April 1985.

Articles Selma Jeanne Cohen, 'Avant-Garde Choreography', *Dance Magazine*, 3 parts: June, July, and August 1962; Don McDonagh, 'Paul Taylor in Orbit', *Dance Scope*, Fall 1966; Clive Barnes, 'Paul Taylor', *Ballet Review*, 2(1), 1967; Elena Bivona, 'Paul Taylor: Two Works', *Ballet Review*, 2(5), 1969; L.E. Stern, 'Paul Taylor, Gentle Giant of Modern Dance', *Dance Magazine*, February 1976; Jack Anderson, 'Paul Taylor: Surface and Substance', *Ballet Review*, 6(1), 1977/78; Elizabeth Kendall, 'American Mongrel', *Ballet News*, April 1980; Ron Daniels, 'Paul Taylor and the Post-Moderns', *Ballet*

Review, Summer 1981; C. Adams, 'The Paul Taylor Mystique', *Dance Theatre Journal*, 1(1), 1983; Joel Lobenthal, 'Christopher Gillis: Dancing for Paul Taylor', *Ballet Review*, Spring 1985; Marcia Siegel, 'Thirty Years in Eden's Dustbin', *Hudson Review*, Autumn 1985; Carolyn Adams, 'Lifeline to Taylor', *Ballet Review*, Winter 1986; Ina Sorens, 'Taylor Reconstructs Balanchine', *Ballet Review*, Summer 1986; Susan Reiter, 'Baroque and Beyond with Paul Taylor', *Ballet Review*, Fall 1986; Alastair Macaulay, 'The Paul Taylor Dance Company', *Dance Theatre Journal*, Summer 1987; Alastair Macaulay, 'The Music Man', *The New Yorker*, 2 May 1988; Daniel Jacobson, 'Private Domains in Public Spaces', *Ballet Review*, Spring 1989; Laura Jacobs, 'Light and Dark', *Ballet Review*, Fall 1990; Nancy Dalva, 'Paul Taylor: A Very Appealing Genius', *Dance Magazine*, October 1991; Joseph Mazo, 'Paul's Women: Motivator, Matriarch, Muse', *Dance Magazine*, October 1991; Christopher Bowen, 'Paul Taylor Dance Company at the Edinburgh Festival', *Dance Theatre Journal*, Winter 1995/96.

Books Don McDonagh, *The Rise and Fall of Modern Dance*, New York, 1970; Moira Hodgson, *Quintet: Five American Dance Companies*, New York, 1976; Arlene Croce, *After Images*, New York, 1977; Joseph H. Mazo, *Prime Movers: The Makers of Modern Dance in America*, New York, 1977; Marcia Siegel, *The Shapes of Change: Images of American Dance*, Boston, 1979; Arlene Croce, *Going to the Dance*, New York, 1982; Robert Coe, *Dance in America*, New York, 1985; Edwin Denby, *Dance Writings*, edited by Robert Cornfield and William Mackay, New York, 1986; Paul Taylor, *Private Domain* (autobiography), New York, 1987; Jack Anderson, *Choreography Observed*, Iowa City, 1987; Arlene Croce, *Sightlines*, New York, 1987.

GLEN TETLEY

Glen Tetley is an enigma. His success is as natural to some as it is controversial or even outrageous to others. His work produces annoyance and tedium in a surprisingly wide range of critics in North America, where he is repeatedly charged with pointlessness and gratuitous sensuality. Here, for instance, is Graham Jackson writing in 1994 on one of Tetley's recent works: '*Oracle* features five men and five women copulating in that fero-

ciously aggressive ballet-moderne manner ... [it] is soft core show-and-tell which uses the magnificent bodies of the National's dancers ... as a tease'.[1] Nor does this represent a new criticism or even a new phase; compare Arlene Croce writing in 1978 on Tetley's famous *Voluntaries* (of 1973):

I guess people think Tetley makes dancers look sexy. Dancers in his ballets ... always seem to be writhing and stretching in a steam bath ... [but] there's never any meaning in his sequences; the continuity seems designed to keep dancers narcissistically happy ... *Voluntaries* is his tribute to John Cranko ... let Heaven defend Cranko from his friends.[2]

But after the tragic death of Cranko in 1973, it was to Tetley that the Stuttgart Ballet turned for a new director; in Europe Tetley has had, from the earliest days of his choreographic career, a tremendous impact. Having trained with Hanya Holm, Martha Graham, Antony Tudor, and Jerome Robbins, all before striking out on his own as a choreographer, Tetley was seen by European companies like the Nederlands Dans Theater and the Ballet Rambert as the man who could revivify classical companies in the 1960s with a judicious injection of modern dance.

Why this difference in perception between the two continents? And if narcissism is an inadequate explanation (as it surely is) for Tetley's popularity with dancers, what is the explanation for Tetley's enigmatic and controversial appeal?

Bridging the treacherous gap between classical and contemporary dance is difficult, and one of the keys to Tetley's success in the classical dance world is the cleanness and precision of his technique. He began as a medical student, and was attracted initially to Hanya Holm's methods because of their anatomical purity: Mary Wigman, he said, had been 'brilliant, erratic – and a genius', but her chief assistant, Holm, 'was cooler, more theoretical, and a great teacher'. He had been fascinated by the German attempts to 'find a language of dance that would underlie all forms of dance ... The beauty of Hanya's technique was its absolutely sound basis, anatomically, physiologically, and every way'.[3] By the time he worked with Martha Graham, he had become, in his own words, 'quite a strong technician', but it was Graham who taught him to 'open up, and let the emotional quality take control of the movement'.[4] The result is a powerful mix: in his own choreography he demands a wider range of expressiveness, especially physically, than many classical artists expect. As the ballerina Karen Kain says, 'his style demands a fluid, expressive torso, which poses a great challenge to classically trained dancers'[5] – this is Croce's 'writhing and stretching in a steam bath' seen from the other side, and it is a more attractive view. Moreover, it is nearly always classically trained dancers he choreographs for, and even though he himself is quite unaware of the synthesis of traditions ('which, consciously, I have never tried to do'[6]), it has become the signature of his style, and his dancers are emphatically aware of the challenge and, apparently, mesmerized not just by the gorgeousness of it, but by the soundness of the technique, and the organic way in which the choreography develops. Here is Tetley commenting on his own process:

> When I work with dancers, I work in a very physical way, and I've learned not to prejudice myself – not to prepare myself in movement ... I begin through my own body, but immediately I want to see how the dancer will transform that ... When I choreographed *Field Notes* ... I said, 'I know you're all waiting. But let me tell you something: There's no story, and there are no steps. We're going to have to make them together.'[7]

And here is how it looks, again, from the dancer's perspective; this is Karen Kain, speaking of *Alice* (1986):

> Glen always arrived fully prepared for rehearsals, but ... with Glen, we were co-creators; he'd sketch the movement and then ask us to expand it, flesh it out, and adapt his idea as closely as possible to our own bodies ... Every day with Glen was a joy; [he] was never threatened by our contributions: he suggested, we experimented, and he edited. This was the best rehearsal period I'd ever experienced.[8]

Tetley's pieces seem to work well for his dancers for precisely these reasons: his democracy; his technical soundness; his wide range of movement vocabulary ('to survive I had to learn everything, from Broadway musicals to television to concert dance to Martha Graham to classical ballet ... For me there was never any difference between these things'[9]); his tendency to create luxurious, sensual movement which, in combination with frankly voluptuous costume designs like those of Nadine Baylis (*Oracle*, 1994), John MacFarlane (*La Ronde*, 1987), and Rouben Ter-Arutunian (*Voluntaries*), serves to showcase dancer's bodies and allow new scope for movement. Tetley's dancers are never encumbered by costume – his heavy, symbolic effects are displaced into the set design (in 1977's *Sphinx*, for instance, the Sphinx's wings are attached to the set, *not* the dancer) – an area in which, like Graham, he is liable to be imposing and innovative.

With all these strengths (and these are mostly strengths), why is the result so often a type of dance that seems to challenge and interest the performers more than the audience? ('There's lots of lush sensuous movement in Tetley's trademark style of streamlined, modern classicism ... but at the end of it all it was hard to suppress a yawn', wrote Michael Crabb of *Oracle*.[10]) One problem in his choreography is definitely pacing – there is too much sleek, fast-paced movement, too much climax, not enough variation of tone and depth. Related to this is the simple problem of finding the landmarks in a Tetley ballet. Perhaps for this

GLEN TETLEY

reason Tetley seems to be at his best when working with a familiar storyline (the great success of *Alice* comes to mind here, as does his *Tempest* of 1979). It may be significant that *The Tempest* remains his only full-length ballet, and this is surprising in such a prolific and established choreographer. But narrative ballet is apparently not natural to him, as it is to, for instance, James Kudelka, or indeed as it was to Tetley's own mentor, Antony Tudor. Even where there is a pre-existing story, Tetley's tendency has often been to submerge it under a stream of undifferentiated movement, as he did, for instance, in *La Ronde*, a good example of Tetley at his most glib. This was a seemingly endless series of interlocking *pas de deux* segments, all more or less (usually more) explicitly miming sexual encounter, all giving dancer after dancer a chance for a slightly more arched back, a slightly more voluptuous stretch, a slightly more risqué lift than the previous moment (and there are hundreds upon hundreds of such moments). Based on Schnitzler's provocative play about the facades covering social corruption of *fin-de-siècle* Vienna, the ballet moves from an encounter between the Soldier and Parlour Maid, to the Parlour Maid and Young Man, to Young Man and Young Wife, and so on, to, finally, the Count and the Prostitute – thus making the 'round' complete. Since all the characters were to be, in Tetley's words, 'concerned with showing greed – the possession of one person by another',[11] there was no principle for tonal variation. Tetley here was not able to separate thematic boredom from choreographic boredom.

By contrast, *Sphinx* has all of Tetley's characteristic qualities, but here they are used to advantage. Based on a mythologically inspired theme such as Martha Graham herself might have chosen, the piece's impact owes much to designer Rouben Ter-Arutunian's regal, silken-winged throne (and ramp) for the Sphinx, which he conceived as 'a sculptural form suggesting mystery, desire and the air of the unattainable'.[12] This

startling, carefully crafted chamber ballet bridges the modern and classical traditions effortlessly in its balanced use of vocabulary from both. It requires only three dancers, a female lead *en pointe*, and two males; all three dancers are required to shift quickly between idioms. (The Sphinx moves, for instance, from a pirouette *en pointe* to full-body rolls on the floor.) The Sphinx is accompanied by Anubis, the jackal-headed Egyptian God of the Dead, and Oedipus, who comes to solve the Sphinx's riddle and gain the throne of Thebes by overpowering her. Tetley's choreography is based on Jean Cocteau's 1934 play, *La Machine infernale*, which used the story to make a biting commentary on the growth of fascism in Europe. *Sphinx* is set to another anti-fascist work, the *Double Concerto* of Czech composer Bohuslav Martinu, which was written in a state of helpless fury in 1938 as the Nazis invaded his homeland, and he searched, as Martinu said, for 'encouragement and hope that did not come'.[13] Both the music and the play grapple with European interwar horror at the menace of a large, impersonal force of evil; and the play is more explicitly about heartlessness, about love and humanity rejected and mechanically ground underfoot. Tetley's use of these themes, however, is emphatically late twentieth century and American in its stress on individuality and heroism. Critics often say that Tetley's ballets are plotless, that they reject the mime and gesture of the classical vocabulary and other narrative devices; but *Sphinx* actually follows Cocteau surprisingly closely.[14] It uses deft, quick mime at key moments, such as the gesture the Sphinx makes to awaken Anubis (a stylized turning away of the head and reach of the hand), or the symbolic blow Anubis gives Oedipus. Tetley also makes stunning use of 'still' moments, opening with the Sphinx lying majestically in a cobra position on the long, silver metallic ramp, or the vertical leaning pause she repeats to indicate yearning or indecision. Tetley has retained Cocteau's characterization of

Oedipus as conceited, hot-headed, and vapid; his Anubis is vigilant and protective of the Sphinx, but unimaginative and unmoved by the possibility of becoming human. The hero, then, must be Sphinx herself – the only character capable of comprehending the possibility of human love. Her initial desire to become human is portrayed by a painfully slow mime walk, which looks as if she were moving underwater or through a medium not natural to her, in imitation of Oedipus's over-important, straight-legged gait. In their *pas de deux*, the lifts allow her only to struggle like a trapped animal; the turns begin as perfect classical pirouettes, but the angle of her backbend rapidly becomes so steep that by the third turn in a sequence both her arms and legs are in an open, cruciform position, and she is bent precariously back from the waist – a motif that will be repeated when she dances her dying *pas de deux* with Anubis. Her death throes begin with a series of Graham contractions, followed by sudden, dramatic 'falls' not from, but within, Anubis's grasp and with desperate last attempts to take those large 'human' steps like Oedipus's again. Although in the storyline Anubis's intervention does not prevent her death, it does allow her to die in dignity – in Tetley's version Oedipus is not allowed to carry her body off (jackal-headed to hide her ugliness, as in Cocteau) in triumph, but, rather, at the sound of the three rising chords, chillingly repeated four times at the end of Martinu's *Concerto*, Sphinx runs back up her winged ramp to die in a final slow agonizing backbend.

Compared to many of Tetley's works, the narrative of *Sphinx* is tight; the scope, economical; the characterization, sharply defined; the sensuality, carefully husbanded for maximum effect; the blending of contemporary and classical tradition, seamless. Like the great spectacle (or 'opera house') choreographers of Europe (Macmillan, Cranko, Béjart), Tetley knows how to manipulate great classical themes on stage; like Martha Graham, he knows how to evoke the power

of myth; but he may be best at doing it over a short stretch of music.

Kathryn Kerby-Fulton

Notes

1 Graham Jackson, 'And No One Invited Eros', *Dance International*, 22(2) (1994), p. 13; see also Michael Crabb's 'The Toronto Scene' in the same issue, p. 25, for a similar opinion.
2 Arlene Croce, *Going to the Dance* (New York: Knopf, 1982) pp. 81–2.
3 Tetley in interview with John Gruen, transcribed in Gruen's *The Private World of Dance* (Harmondsworth, UK: Penguin, 1975), p. 427.
4 Gruen, p. 429.
5 Karen Kain, with Stephen Godfrey and Penelope Reed Doob, *Movement Never Lies* (Toronto: McClelland & Stewart, 1994), p. 202.
6 Gruen, p. 431.
7 Gruen, p. 432.
8 Kain, p. 203.
9 Gruen, p. 431.
10 Crabb, p. 25.
11 Cited in 'The Ballet', *Ballet Notes: La Ronde*, compiled by A. Carreiro (Toronto: National Ballet of Canada, n.d.), [p. 2]. (*Ballet Notes* are information packs put together by the Education Director and Archivist for the NBC, sponsored by IMB Canada, and available upon request from the NBC, 157 King St East, Toronto, Canada, M5C 1G9; I have supplied page numbers.)
12 Ter-Arutunian, quoted 'The Design', *Ballet Notes: Sphinx*, compiled by A. Carreiro (Toronto: National Ballet of Canada, n.d.), [p. 22].
13 'The Music', *Ballet Notes: Sphinx*, [p. 20].
14 Act II of Cocteau's play is conveniently reproduced in *Ballet Notes: Sphinx*.

Biographical details

Born in Cleveland, Ohio, United States, 3 February 1926. **Studied** at Franklin and Marshall College, Lancaster, Pennsylvania, 1944–46, and at New York University 1946–48; studied modern dance with Hanya Holm and Martha Graham in New York; studied ballet with Margaret Craske, Antony Tudor, and at the School of American Ballet, New York. **Career** Danced with Hanya Holm's company, 1946–51, New York City Opera, 1952–54, John Butler company, from 1953, Joffrey Ballet, 1956–57, Martha Graham Dance Company, 1958, American Ballet Theatre,

1960–61, and on tour with Jerome Robbins's Ballets: USA, 1961; founded Glen Tetley Dance Company in New York, acting as its director, 1962–69; joined Nederlands Dans Theater in The Hague in 1969, becoming co-director, 1969–71; appointed director (succeeding John Cranko), Stuttgart Ballet, Germany, 1974–76; choreographer and artistic associate for National Ballet of Canada, Toronto, 1987–89. Has acted as guest choreographer for many companies including Ballet Rambert, Hamburg Ballet, Bavarian State Opera Ballet (Munich), Royal Danish Ballet, American Ballet Theatre, and Royal Ballet (London). **Awards** include German Critics Award, 1969; Queen Elizabeth II Coronation Award, Royal Academy of Dancing, 1981; RAI Prize (Italy), 1982; Edinburgh Festival Tennant-Caledonian Award, 1983; Ohioana Career Medal, 1986; New York University Alumni Achievement Award, 1988.

Works

Richard Cory (text Edward Arlington Robinson, 1946), *The Canary* (mus. Berg, 1948), *Triptych* (mus. Joseph Wilson, 1948), *Daylight's Dauphin* (mus. Debussy, 1951), *Hootin' Blues* (mus. Sonny Reilly, 1951), *Western Wall* (mus. Ravel, 1951), *Mountain Way Chant* (mus.Carlos Chavez, 1959), *Ballet Ballads: The Eccentricities of Davy Crockett* (mus. David Moss, 1961), *Birds of Sorrow* (mus. Peter Hartman, 1962), *Gleams in the Bone House* (mus. Harold Shapero, 1962), *How Many Miles to Babylon?* (mus. Carlos Surinach, 1962), *Pierrot Lunaire* (mus. Schoenberg, 1962), *Harpsichord Concerto* (mus. Manuel de Falla, 1963), *The Anatomy Lesson* (mus. Marcel Landowski, 1964), *Sargasso* (mus. Ernst Krenek, 1964), *Fieldmass* (mus. Martinů, 1965), *The Game of Noah* (mus. Stravinsky, 1965), *Mythical Hunters* (mus. Partos Hezionot, 1965), *Chronochromie* (mus. Messiaen, 1966), *Lovers* (mus. Ned Rorem, 1966), *Psalms* (mus. Partos-Tehilim, 1966), *Ricercare* (mus. Mordecai Seter, 1966), *Dithyramb* (mus. Hans Werner Henze, 1967), *Freefall* (mus. Schubell, 1967), *The Seven Deadly Sins* (mus. Weill, 1967), *Ziggurat* (mus. Stockhausen, 1967), *Circles* (mus. Luciano Berio, 1968), *Embrace Tiger and Return to Mountain* (mus. Morton Subotnick, 1968), *Arena* (mus. Morton Subotnick, 1969), *Field Figures* (mus. Stockhausen, 1970), *Imaginary Film* (mus. Schoenberg, 1970), *Mutations* (mus. Stockhausen, 1970), *Rag Dances* (mus. Antony Hymas, 1971), *Laborintus* (mus. Luciano Berio, 1972), *Small Parades* (mus. Varèse, 1972), *Strophe-Antistrophe* (mus. Sylvano Bussotti, 1972), *Threshold* (mus. Berg, 1972), *Gemini* (mus.

Hans Werner Henze, 1973), *Moveable Garden* (mus. Lukas Foss, 1973), *Rite of Spring* (mus. Stravinsky, 1973), *Stationary Flying* (mus. George Crumb, 1973), *Voluntaries* (mus. Poulenc, 1973), *Alegrías* (mus. Carlos Chavez, 1975), *Daphnis and Chloe* (mus. Ravel, 1975), *Greening* (mus. Arne Nordheim, 1975), *Strender* (mus. Arne Nordheim, 1975), *Tristan* (mus. Hans Werner Henze, 1975), *Poème Nocturne* (mus. Scriabin, 1977), *Sphinx* (mus. Martinů, 1977), *Praeludium* (mus. Webern, 1978), *Contredances* (mus. Webern, 1979), *The Tempest* (mus. Arne Nordheim, 1979), *Dances of Albion* (mus. Britten, 1980), *Summer's End* (mus. Henri Dutilleux, 1980), *The Firebird* (mus. Stravinsky, 1981), *Murderer Hope of Women* (mus. percussion, 1983), *Odalisque* (mus. Satie, 1983), *Pulcinella* (mus. Stravinsky, 1984), *Revelation and Fall* (mus. Richard Maxwell, 1984), *Dream Walk of the Shaman* (mus. Ernst Krenek, 1985), *Alice* (mus. David del Tredici, 1986), *Orpheus* (mus. Stravinsky, 1987), *La Ronde* (mus. Erich Korngold, 1987), *Tagore* (mus. Alexander Zemlinksy, 1989), *Dialogues* (with Scott Douglas; mus. Ginastera, 1993), *Oracle* (mus. Carl Vine, 1994), *Amores* (mus. Michael Torke, 1997).

Further reading

Interviews in 'American Dancer', *Dance Magazine*, February 1963; in 'Pierrot in Two Worlds', *Dance and Dancers*, December 1967; in 'Tai-chi and the Dance', *Dance and Dancers*, November 1968; in 'Dutch Mutations', *Dance Magazine*, February 1971; with Allen Robertson, in 'Talking with Tetley', *Dance Magazine*, October 1971; with John Gruen, in his *The Private World of Ballet*, New York, 1975; in 'Prospero's Island', *Dance and Dancers*, May 1979; with Elinor Rogosin, in her *The Dance Makers: Conversations*, New York, 1980.

Articles Donald Duncan, 'One Dancer, Many Faces', *Dance Magazine*, October 1960; Jack Anderson, 'A Gallery of American Ballet Theatre Choreographers', *Dance Magazine*, January 1966; John Percival, 'Tetley All the Way', *Dance and Dancers*, September 1969; John Percival, 'Glen Tetley', *Experimental Dance*, London, 1971; 'Glen Tetley', in *Current Biography Yearbook 1973*; 'Glen Tetley', *Tanzblätter*, March 1980; Noël Goodwin, 'Alchemist', *Ballet News*, October 1982; Michael Crabb, 'Uncovering Alice', *Dance Magazine*, July 1986; Michael Crabb, 'Tetley Makes *La Ronde* go 'round', *Dance Magazine*, July 1988; Graham Jackson, 'And No One Invited Eros', *Dance International*, 22(2), 1994; Michael Crabb, 'The Toronto Scene', *Dance International*, 22(2), 1994.

Books Don McDonagh, *Complete Guide to Modern Dance*, New York, 1976; Arlene Croce, *Going to the Dance*, New York, 1982; Allen Robertson and Donald Hutera, *The Dance Handbook*, Harlow, Essex, 1988; Karen Kain (with Stephen Godfrey and Penelope Doob), *Movement Never Lies*, Toronto, 1994; Harro Eisele, *Glen Tetley: Tänzer, Poet, Pioneer/Dancer, Poet, Pioneer* (in English and German), no place indicated, 1996.

TWYLA THARP

Twyla Tharp began her career in 1965, at the age of nearly 23, with *Tank Dive*, a work in three movements, choreographed for herself and four non-dancers. It was performed partly to the accompaniment of Petula Clark's recording of 'Downtown', in Room 1604 – a small, Bauhaus-style auditorium – of Hunter College in New York City. *Tank Dive* lasted for seven minutes. Tharp began the first section wearing high-heeled bedroom slippers. She then changed into wooden shoes with rigid, flipper-like extensions in front. These confined her to one spot, but allowed her to move her upper body freely. Soon, she discarded the shoes, performing the rest of the work barefoot. At the end, she threw herself to the floor, face downwards, and then made her exit. She took no bows, declining to acknowledge the presence of the small group of people who had been watching her, though the fact that the performance was given in public, and that she had mailed out notices for it, implied her desire to make contact with an audience.

Though Tharp had also invited the press, there were no reviews. This critical silence disconcerted her. From the start, she was filled with ambition, a drive to succeed beyond the ordinary. Success took eight years to arrive, and once it came there was no stopping her – for a while, at any rate. By the end of 1973, she was big news, not simply in the newspapers, but also in weeklies,

monthlies, and glossy magazines. The watershed in her career was *Deuce Coupe* (1973), which Robert Joffrey commissioned for his ballet company. Set to a montage of recordings by the Beach Boys, the piece brought together, for the first time in a major dance piece, the techniques and attitudes of both classical ballet and postmodernism, the latter enriched by movements taken from teenage dancing: limply held hands, raised shoulders, undulating hips, snapping fingers, eyes lowered in an ecstatic-seeming withdrawal from reality. The juxtaposition of styles – the work was performed simultaneously by the Joffrey company and by Tharp's own dancers – was not only enjoyable to watch, it was resonant with meaning, a metaphor for the coexistence of tradition and youth. Though essentially conceptual – and though, as Tharp's autobiography has since revealed, its audience-pleasing effects were all carefully calculated – the piece was also emotionally reverberant. The references to love in the Beach Boy's songs were bodied forth with warmth and conviction.

Deuce Coupe, first presented at New York's City Center Theater, was an instant hit, bringing Tharp for the first time to the attention of the public at large. Over the years, the Joffrey Ballet had cultivated with great success an audience responsive more to the thrills of cultural modishness than to the niceties of classical ballet. To these Joffrey fans, *Deuce Coupe* made an instant appeal, if only on account of its novelty. In 1973, ballet companies had hardly yet begun to use pre-recorded pop music. Nor, apart from Balanchine, had they started to mix high art and low; and they had only rarely invited non-ballet dancers to join them on stage, though, again, Balanchine had anticipated Tharp in this respect. Intriguing though these features were, it soon became clear that what lifted the ballet out of the ordinary and made it worth seeing more than once was the visceral excitement it communicated, the energy and passionate commitment to dance that Tharp drew from her cast. However titillating the ballet's references to contemporary social attitudes were, its ultimate worth lay in its dynamism, inventiveness, and grace.

The courage shown by Robert Joffrey in asking a choreographer without any experience of working with classically trained performers to make a piece for his company paid off handsomely, both at the box office and in terms of prestige. Joffrey was praised for having sponsored a significant development in American dance: because of him, at the beginning of the 1970s, a choreographer had succeeded in expressing the attitudes of the younger generation in a work that linked the iconoclasm of the previous, revolutionary decade with a centuries-old, traditional art. But though Tharp was praised for having made a major populist statement, some people remained seemingly unaware that *Deuce Coupe* was also fastidiously constructed, and, despite its flippant and trendy tone (augmented by the presence on stage of a bunch of kids who, during the performance, created graffiti with spray cans at the back of the stage), was a serious work of art.

Success brought not only the fame Tharp had yearned for, but also for the first time a certain amount of carping: *Deuce Coupe* offended those guardians of aesthetic purity who felt that the use of elements from rock-and-roll constituted a threat to the artistic integrity of ballet, apparently unaware that ballet over the centuries had been enriched by absorbing elements from social dancing and popular theatre. Criticism of this kind, however, tended to disappear after 1976, the year in which Tharp created *Push Comes to Shove* for American Ballet Theatre (ABT). By the mid-1970s, the juxtaposition of pop dancing and ballet no longer produced much of a shock. However, there was now criticism from the standard-bearers of avant-garde dance. Because *Push Comes to Shove* was an even greater hit than *Deuce Coupe* – indeed, it proved to be the most successful American dance work since

Jerome Robbins's *Fancy Free* of 1944 – many felt that Tharp had sold out, that her extraordinary ability to reach big, popular audiences had necessarily entailed the loss of artistic integrity. For these critics, the accessibility of *Push Comes to Shove*, which made use of the same blend of styles as in *Deuce Coupe*, but with a new, comic component derived from Old-Time vaudeville, was proof of Tharp's self-betrayal. For everyone else, *Push Comes to Shove* was a revelation, a brilliant comic gloss on classical ballet that demonstrated the latter's infinite adaptiveness.

Push Comes to Shove, set to Haydn's *Symphony No. 82*, and preceded by a rag by Joseph Lamb, also provided Mikhail Baryshnikov, the ballet's star and the most gifted male dancer of his day, with the finest new role he had found since his defection from the Soviet Union – indeed, with what remains the only starring role of real artistic distinction to have been made for him by a Western choreographer. Tharp had long since demonstrated that she could enhance and refine the natural qualities of dancers as different as the tall Rose Marie Wright and the dark, intensely lyrical Sara Rudner, two of the pillars of her company. She proceeded to extend the range of Baryshnikov.

In *Push Comes to Shove*, she created a new personality for him: a blend of the sly, the unpredictable, the wryly self-mocking, the witty, and the prodigiously virtuosic – though in *Push Comes to Shove* he displayed his virtuosity so insouciantly that his brilliance seemed almost inadvertent. Technically, Tharp's demands on Baryshnikov were nearly superhuman. From him, she wanted speed, not merely in performing specific movements, but in making transitions from one to the next. She also wanted him to dance in a manner that minimized the decorum inherent in the *danse d'école*. Thus, he had to perform multiple *pirouettes* with great velocity, but at the same time keep his body off-centre. In addition, she offered him the chance to reveal a hitherto unsuspected stage persona: that of the cool cat/wise guy/prankster/lady-killer. With this ballet, Baryshnikov received, so to speak, his naturalization papers as an American dancer.

Tharp's progression from *Tank Dive* to *Push Comes to Shove*, from avant-garde iconoclasm to mainstream populism, took her just over a decade. On the way, she created a variety of avant-garde, often non-theatrical works, some austere in mood and dauntingly rigorous in structure. In *The Fugue* (1970), three dancers performed twenty variations on a twenty-count theme. At the climax of *The One Hundreds* (1970), a hundred people (for the most part non-dancers) executed a hundred different eleven-second movement phrases. Other works from this period were frankly rebarbative: in the final section of *Re-Moves* (1966), the dancers performed inside a large plywood box and were thus invisible to the audience. Some works were geographically diffuse, like *Sunrise*, *Midday March*, and *Evening Raga* (1971), which took place in different locations of New York, beginning before dawn in Fort Tryon Park and ending at dusk in City Hall.

During these years, Tharp and her dancers took no curtain calls. At the end of each piece, they simply left the stage or performing space. Until almost the end of 1971, the company was entirely female. Tharp's decision to take in Kenneth Rinker opened up new creative possibilities for her, at once technical and expressive. In 1971, moreover, she created her first piece to music: *Eight Jelly Rolls*. (The Petula Clark record she had used in *Tank Dive* was an incidental feature of the piece.) Before then, she and her dancers had performed, if not to silence, then without music – the sound of footfalls in *The Fugue* was a constituent expressive element of the piece, and one she made more important in due course by amplifying the stage on which *The Fugue* was danced.

From *Eight Jelly Rolls* on, music, to which Tharp is remarkably responsive, became central to her work, supplying the dances in which she used it with rhythmic impetus, structural guidelines and an overall mood. In *Eight Jelly Rolls*, first seen at Oberlin College, Ohio, then revised for the New York Shakespeare Dance Festival in Central Park, she used jazz recordings from the 1920s by Jelly Roll Morton and his Red Hot Peppers. The first performance of the revised version elicited so enthusiastic a response that Tharp decided her dancers would henceforth acknowledge the audience's applause. Two months after this, she created *The Bix Pieces*, set to recordings by jazzman Bix Beiderbecke, and, a year later, *The Raggedy Dances* to music by Scott Joplin. These works, all clearly designed to appeal to the taste of general audiences, confirmed the change in her outlook. No longer did she feel that she had to be so aggressively earnest and uncompromisingly ascetic to win respect. These three works foreshadowed the more complex *Deuce Coupe*.

After *Push Comes to Shove*, Tharp found herself sought out as a choreographer. As a result she began to ask for substantial financial recompense; today, she is in all likelihood the most well-paid choreographer of her time. She also received invitations to collaborate on movies, a medium to which she felt a strong attraction – as, indeed, she did to any performing art that would extend her expertise as a performer and a creator. In 1982, she appeared in New York in an experimental play, *Bone Songs*, opposite its author, André Gregory, but she proved to have no skills as an actress. Unfortunately, none of the films on which she worked (*Hair*, *Ragtime*, *Amadeus*, and *White Nights*, with Baryshnikov and the great tap dancer Gregory Hines) offered her opportunities worthy of her gifts. In *Hair*, she made an appearance as a dancer. For *Amadeus*, she not only provided the choreography, she also staged and directed the operatic scenes.

Both *Amadeus* and *Ragtime* required period dances, the former from the eighteenth century, the latter from the early twentieth century. Though *Ragtime* did not do her career much good, it taught her a great deal about ballroom dancing, knowledge she put to use two years later in *Nine Sinatra Songs* (1982), one of her finest achievements.

Tharp's eagerness to work in films – like her forays into ice skating (she created two pieces for the Olympic Champion, John Curry), theatre, and television (over the years, she has made a series of triumphant excursions into the latter medium) is evidence of a deep-seated urge to diversify, and thus more certainly to conquer. In 1984, she teamed up with Jerome Robbins to create a work for New York City Ballet, *Brahms/Handel*. In 1985, she directed as well as choreographed a stage version of the classic Gene Kelly musical, *Singin' in the Rain*, an ambitious venture but inevitably (she was allowed to make no changes to the film when she translated it to the stage) an artistic failure as well as an expensive, uninteresting commercial flop.

Some of Tharp's ambitiousness can no doubt be traced to the choreographer's relationship with her powerful mother, who saw to it that her eldest child took lessons in ballet, flamenco, acrobatics, tap, violin, viola, and baton twirling, as well as various languages. The memory of her childhood, revealed in Tharp's 1992 autobiography *Push Comes to Shove* to have been very unhappy, has clearly haunted her for many years. In 1980, she created a quasi-autobiographical full-length work, *When We Were Very Young*, which incorporated a framing text by the playwright Thomas Babe. It is characteristic of the desperate need she has to master her past that she should have accepted a script as sophomoric as Babe's.

Though it dispensed with words, *The Catherine Wheel*, which followed a year later, was another confused act of psychic exorcism, a convoluted and cloudy family psychodrama to music commissioned from the talented David Byrne. What saved *The Catherine Wheel*, which, like *When We Were Very Young*, was aimed at general audiences and performed in a regular Broadway house, was its final abstract sequence, which Tharp called *The Golden Section*. This, unlike everything that had preceded it, was daring, thrilling and clear, a succession of brilliant, demanding, non-stop dances that showed very clearly where Tharp's talent lay. But, as she has shown increasingly over the years, she herself still has an uncertain conception of this talent. The persistent need to confront her early experiences and to deal in some creative way with the pain of her childhood and family life has led her to deliver some very confused choreographic messages to the world.

Most of her failures since *When We Were Very Young* have either implied or presented a narrative, like *Short Stories* (1980), *Bad Smells* (1982), *Bum's Rush* (1989), and *Everlast* (1989). Her greatest success, artistic and commercial alike, since *Push Comes to Shove* has been *Nine Sinatra Songs*, and it expresses its insights about men and women through a love of dance rarely visible in the works with stories or literary themes. Both *Bum's Rush* and *Everlast* were given their premieres by ABT, of which company she became an artistic associate for a while. For ABT she made a variety of interesting works in modes other than the narrative, such as *Once Upon a Time* (later called *The Little Ballet*, 1983), *Bach Partita* (1983), *Quartet* (1989). Before her association with the company was ended by a new management at ABT, who found her too expensive, she created a joyous piece for the company's young virtuoso, Julio Bocca, called *Brief Fling* (1990), the only new ballet of his career to make him look like a star.

Since then, Tharp has begun to choreograph again for the troupe. In May 1995, she was accorded the honour of providing all the works that made up the programme of ABT's annual fund-raising gala at the Metropolitan Opera House. It was an evening, though, to sadden her admirers. All three premiers lacked coherence, and, more surprisingly, originality. Indeed, the vapid *Americans We*, set to nineteenth-century American music, invoked memories of other choreographers' works, principally Antony Tudor's *The Leaves are Fading* and Jerome Robbins's *Ives Songs*, the first Tharp ballet ever to do so. *Jump Start*, danced to live contemporary jazz, was a new and exhausted version of her early youth-dance ballets. *How Near Heaven*, to Britten's *Variations on a Theme of Frank Bridge*, was simply unfocused.

Tharp no longer has a permanent company. Over the years, she has occasionally worked for troupes other than her own. After *Deuce Coupe*, she made a couple of ballets for the Joffrey dancers, one of them, *As Time Goes By* (1973), being superb. More recently, she has made a fine work, to klezmer music, for the Martha Graham dancers (*Demeter and Persephone* of 1993). And in 1996 she choreographed her first work for London's Royal Ballet, *Mr Worldly Wise*. Some of her older pieces she has given to the modest and youthfully talented Hubbard Street Dance Company of Chicago, a move that reveals her desire to preserve at least some of her compositions. The powerful and aggressive *In the Upper Room* (1986), which always wins an ovation, is part of ABT's basic repertoire. But now, whenever she has something new to say she brings together a group of fresh young dancers, not to perform repertory but to present what are essentially lecture-demonstrations. On these occasions, she often dances with them, though the difference in generations is now sadly evident. Nevertheless, more than thirty years after her first choreographed piece, she is still creating new works, most recently *Roy's Joys* for the 1997 tour of her new company of twelve dancers, 'Tharp!'. It is still too soon to say that she has lost her way.

Dale Harris (updated by the editor)

Biographical details

Born in Portland, Indiana, United States, 1 July 1941. **Studied** at Pomona College, California, transferring to Barnard College, New York, obtaining a BA degree (majoring in art history), 1963; while at college, studied ballet with Igor Schwezoff, American Ballet Theatre School, and with Richard Thomas and Margaret Craske in New York; studied modern dance with Martha Graham, Merce Cunningham, and Alwin Nikolais, and jazz dance with Eugene 'Luigi' Lewis and Matt Mattox. **Career** Made debut as a dancer with Paul Taylor Dance Company, 1963; founder, dancer, and choreographer of own company, 1965, which became the Twyla Tharp Dance Foundation in 1973; company reformed as the 12-member Tharp! in 1996. Has also choreographed for Joffrey Ballet, American Ballet Theatre (artistic associate, 1988–90), John Curry (Olympic ice skater), Paris Opéra Ballet, the Martha Graham Company, the Royal Ballet (London), as well as for feature films, including *Hair* (dir. Forman, 1979), *Ragtime* (dir. Forman, 1981), and *White Nights* (dir. Hackford, 1985). **Awards** include Brandeis University Citation, 1972; *Dance Magazine* Award, 1981.

Works

Tank Dive (mus. Petula Clark, 1965), *Stage Show* (1965), *Cede Blue Lake* (1965), *Unprocessed* (1965), *Re-Moves* (1966), *Yancey Dance* (1966), *One Two Three* (1967), *Jam* (1967), *Disperse* (1967), *Three Page Sonata for Four* (1967), *Forevermore* (1967), *Generation* (1968), *One Way* (1968), *Excess, Idle, Surplus* (1968), *After 'Suite'* (1969), *Group Activities* (1969), *Medley* (1969), *Dancing in the Streets of London and Paris, Continued in Stockholm and Sometimes Madrid* (1969), *Pymffyppmfynm Ypf* (1970), *The Fugue* (1970), *Rose's Cross Country* (1970), *The One Hundreds* (1970), *The History of Up and Down, I and II* (1971), *Eight Jelly Rolls* (mus. Jelly Roll Morton and the Red Hot Peppers, 1971), *The Willie Smith Series* (video, 1971), *Mozart Sonata, K.545* (mus. Mozart, 1971), *Sunrise, Midday March, Evening Raga* (1971), *Torelli* (mus. Torelli, 1971), *The Bix Pieces* (mus. Bix Beiderbecke, Thelonius Monk, 1971), *The Raggedy Dances* (mus. Scott Joplin, Mozart, 1972), *Deuce Coupe* (mus. the Beach Boys, 1973), *As Time Goes By* (mus. Haydn, 1973), *In the Beginnings* (mus. David Moss, 1974), *All about Eggs* (mus. Bach, 1974), *The Bach Duet* (mus. Bach, 1974), *Deuce Coupe II* (revised version of *Deuce Coupe*; mus. the Beach Boys, 1975), *Sue's Leg* (mus. Fats

Waller, 1975), *The Double Cross* (mus. various, 1975), *Ocean's Motion* (mus. Chuck Berry, 1975), *Push Comes to Shove* (mus. Joseph Lamb, Haydn, 1976), *Remembering the Thirties* (for television, 1976), *Give and Take* (mus. various, 1976), *Once More, Frank* (mus. Frank Sinatra, 1976), *Country Dances* (mus. country, arr. Richard Peaslee, 1976), *Happily Ever After* (mus. country, arr. Richard Peaslee, 1976), *After All* (mus. Albinoni, 1976), *Mud* (mus. Mozart, 1977), *Simon Medley* (mus. Paul Simon, 1977), *Cacklin' Hen* (mus. country, arr. Richard Peaslee, 1977), *1903* (mus. Randy Newman, 1979), *Chapters & Verses* (mus. various, 1979), *Baker's Dozen* (mus. Willie Smith, 1979), *Hair* (film, dir. Milos Forman, 1979), *Three Fanfares* (for closing of the Winter Olympic Games, 1980), *Brahms' Paganini* (mus. Brahms, 1980), *When We Were Very Young* (mus. John Simon, 1980), *Dance is a Man's Sport Too* (for TV, 1980), *Assorted Quartets* (mus. traditional, 1980), *Short Stories* (mus. Supertramp, Bruce Springsteen, 1980), *Third Suite* (mus. J.S. Bach, 1980), dances in *Ragtime* (film, dir. Milos Forman, 1980), *Uncle Edgar Dyed His Hair Red* (mus. Dick Sebouh, 1981), *The Catherine Wheel* (mus. David Byrne, 1981), *Nine Sinatra Songs* (mus. Frank Sinatra, 1982), *Bad Smells* (mus. Glenn Branca, 1982), *Once Upon a Time* (later retitled *The Little Ballet*; mus. Glazunov, 1983), *Bach Partita* (mus. J.S. Bach, 1983), *Fait Accompli* (mus. David Van Tieghem, 1983), *Telemann* (mus. Telemann, 1983), *Amadeus* (film, dir. Milos Forman, 1984), *Brahms/Handel* (with Jerome Robbins; mus. Brahms, 1984), *Sorrow Floats* (mus. Bizet, 1985), *Sinatra Suite* (mus. Frank Sinatra, 1985), *Singin' in the Rain* (musical by Comden and Green, 1985), *White Nights* (film, dir. Taylor Hackford, 1985), *In the Upper Room* (mus. Philip Glass, 1986), *Ballare* (mus. Mozart, 1986), *Quartet* (mus. Terry Riley, 1989), *Bum's Rush* (mus. Dick Hyman, 1989), *Rules of the Game* (mus. J.S. Bach, 1989), *Everlast* (mus. Jerome Kern, 1989), *Brief Fling* (mus. Percy Grainger, 1990), *Grand Pas: Rhythm of the Saints* (mus. Paul Simon, 1991), *The Men's Piece* (text Tharp, 1991), *Octet* (mus. Edgar Meyer, 1991), *Sextet* (mus. Bob Telson, 1992), *Let's forget domani* (mus. 1993), *Brahms' Paganini (Book Two)* (mus. Brahms, 1993), *Demeter and Persephone* (mus. klezmer music, 1993), *Red, White & Blues* (mus. various, 1994), *Americans We* (mus. Henry Fillmore, Stephen Foster, 1995), *How Near Heaven* (mus. Britten, 1995), *Jump Start* (mus. Wynton Marsalis, 1995), *Mr Worldly Wise* (mus. Rossini, 1996), *The Elements* (mus. Jean-Féry Rebel, 1996), *Heroes* (mus. Philip Glass, 1996), *66* (mus. 1950s and 1960s popular, 1996), *Sweet Fields* (mus. Shaker songs, sacred, 1996), *Roy's Joys* (mus. Roy Eldridge, 1997).

Further reading

Interviews in 'Space, Jazz, Pop ... ', *Dance and Dancers*, May 1974; with Suzanne Well, in her *Contemporary Dance*, New York, 1978; with Elinor Rogosin, in her *The Dance Makers: Conversations with American Choreographers*, New York, 1980; with Deborah Jowitt, in 'The Choreographer and the World', *Ballett International*, June/July 1984; with Emma Manning, in 'Twyla Tharp', *Dance Europe*, October/November 1997.

Articles Twyla Tharp, 'Group Activities', *Ballet Review*, 2(5), 1969; Tobi Tobias, 'Twyla Tharp', *Dance Scope*, Spring 1970; Susan Buirge, Marcia Siegel, and Bill Kosmas, 'Twyla Tharp: Questions and Answers' *Ballet Review*, 4(1), 1971; Deborah Jowitt, 'Twyla Tharp's New Kick', *New York Times Magazine*, 4 January 1976; Allen Robertson, 'Tharp Comes to Shove', *Ballet News*, March 1980; Michael Robertson, 'Fifteen Years: Twyla Tharp and the Logical Outcome of Abundance', *Dance Magazine*, March 1980; Marcia Siegel, 'Success Without Labels', *Hudson Review*, Spring 1983; Marcia Siegel, 'Couples', *Hudson Review*, Summer 1984; Alastair Macaulay, 'Twyla Tharp Dance', *Dancing Times*, August 1984; David Vaughan, 'Twyla Tharp: Launching a New Classicism', *Dance Magazine*, May 1984; Matthew Gurewitsch, 'Kinetic Force', *Ballet News*, October 1984; Steven Albert, 'Utopia Lost – and Found?', *Ballet Review*, Spring 1986; Clive Barnes, 'Twyla Tharp and the Modern Classicism', *Dance and Dancers*, September 1987; Clive Barnes, 'Daring, Newness and Occasion', *Dance and Dancers*, September 1989; Marcia Siegel, 'Strangers in the Palace', *Hudson Review*, Autumn 1989; Joan Acocella, 'Balancing Act', *Dance Magazine*, October 1990; Barbara Zuck, 'Tharp Moves', *Dance Magazine*, January 1992; Joan Acocella, 'Twyla Tharp: Divided Loyalties', *Art in America*, May 1992; Marcia Siegel, 'Both Doors Open', *Hudson Review*, Summer 1992; Clive Barnes, 'Attitudes: Cunningham and Tharp – Originals', *Dance Magazine*, March 1993; Barbara Zuck, 'Together Again: Tharp and Baryshnikov in Ohio', *Dance Magazine*, March 1993; Marcia Siegel, 'Twyla's Tour', *Ballet Review*, Spring 1993; Ann Nugent, '*Till* and Twyla: A Myth and a Legend', *Dance Now*, Spring 1994; Mary Clarke, '*Mr Worldly Wise*', *Dancing Times*, January 1996; Susan Manning, 'Cultural Theft – or Love?', *Dance Theatre Journal*, 13(4) [Summer] 1997; Nadine Meisner, 'Conquering Hero?', *Dance Theatre Journal*, 14(1), 1998.

Books Moira Hodgson, *Quintet: Five American*

Dance Companies, New York, 1976; Don McDonagh, *Complete Guide to Modern Dance*, New York, 1976; Arlene Croce, *Afterimages*, New York, 1977; Cynthia Lyle (ed.), *Dancers on Dancing*, New York and London, 1977; Joseph H. Mazo, *Prime Movers: The Makers of Modern Dance in America*, New York, 1977; Anne Livet (ed.), *Contemporary Dance*, New York, 1978; Marcia Siegel, *The Shapes of Change*, Boston, 1979; Arlene Croce, *Going to the Dance*, New York, 1982; Robert Coe, *Dance in America*, New York, 1985; Deborah Jowitt, *The Dance in Mind*, New York, 1985; Arlene Croce, *Sight Lines*, New York, 1987; Twyla Tharp, *Push Comes to Shove* (autobiography), New York, 1992.